Maintaining Sanity in the Classroom

Maintaining Sanity in the Classroom

Classroom Management Techniques

Second Edition

The Late Rudolf Dreikurs, M.D.
Chicago Medical School
Director of Alfred Adler Institute of Chicago
Bernice Bronia Grunwald
Floy Childers Pepper

HarperCollins*Publishers*, **New York**
Cambridge, Philadelphia, San Francisco,
London, Mexico City, São Paulo, Sydney

Sponsoring Editor: George A. Middendorf
Designer: Michel Craig
Production Manager: Willie Lane
Compositor: Maryland Linotype Composition Co., Inc.

Art Studio: J&R Technical Services

MAINTAINING SANITY IN THE CLASSROOM
Classroom Management Techniques
Second Edition

Library of Congress Cataloging in Publication Data

Dreikurs, Rudolf, 1897–1972.
  Maintaining sanity in the classroom.

  Includes bibliographies and index.
  1. Educational psychology.   2. Motivation in educa-
tion.   3. Group work in education.   4. Learning disabil-
ities.   5. Problem children—Education.   6. Home and
School.   I. Grunwald, Bernice Bronia.   II. Pepper,
Floy C.   III. Title.
LB1065.D72   1982   371.1'02   81-6400
ISBN 0-06-041761-7   AACR2

Contents

PART 3   Coping with Special Academic Problems   193

PART 4   Coping with Special Behavior Problems   229

PART 5   Parental Involvement   301

Foreword

In the Foreword of the first edition of *Maintaining Sanity in the Classroom,* the authors stated that "The purpose of this book is to encourage teachers, who in these troubled times, are beginning to doubt their own ability to motivate children in school, and who are either accepting defeat and are leaving the teaching profession, or who are resigned to a fate of failure and misery until such time as they can retire."

The encouraging spirit of the book is evidenced by a new glimmer of optimism that is becoming visible within the teaching profession. Classroom teachers, often in isolation, have found a new spirit of survival and a new challenge in teaching from the philosophy and understanding generated by the late Dr. Dreikurs. In other situations entire school faculties have adopted the tactics and attitudes presented by the authors of this book. Some teacher training institutions do not train teachers to understand the psychological dynamics of why children do not learn or refuse to learn. However, teachers are well trained to teach subject matter. These institutions are now offering courses to teachers that teach the skills necessary for creating a classroom atmosphere that permits learning to take place.

This book focuses on the process of encouragement, which is the most essential aspect in motivating children to learn. The seemingly insurmountable obstacles created by social conditions, as well as the impossible and contradictory demands placed upon educators by the public, lead to feelings of helplessness and dismay on the part of teachers who are faced with the day-to-day responsibilities in the classroom. Although they do not minimize the disadvantaged backgrounds of many children, the methods described in this book offer teachers a variety of practical suggestions for what can be done in spite of these conditions.

Some basic solutions to adult-child conflicts are presented in a most understandable manner, pointing to the bankruptcy of the authoritarian tradition of adult supremacy. The advancement of a working model for a new tradition in adult-child relationships is effectively presented without violating the ultimate responsibility of the adult and of the teacher.

This book is the principal reason that I have never written one. Everything I would want to say has been said most effectively in the many books authored or coauthored by Dr. Dreikurs.

I have used this book since 1971 when it was first published and have found the ideas presented in it to be profound in their simplicity. It is for these reasons that it is extremely unusual to find a used copy of *Maintaining Sanity in the Classroom* in a campus bookstore, which attests to the fact that teachers rarely give up ownership of this book because it is a very valuable text.

I am delighted that the coauthors, Bronia Grunwald and Floy C. Pepper, have enhanced the optimistic and encouraging characteristics of the original text in this revised edition.

Oscar C. Christensen, Professor
The University of Arizona

Preface

We witness a peculiar dilemma with regard to our schools. Teachers, more than any other professional group, are sincerely concerned with establishing and maintaining democratic procedures. This is the result of Dewey's teaching. He established the notion that autocratic methods infringe on children's rights and diminish their cooperation. Unfortunately, Dewey's ideas were misunderstood and, consequently, many school systems that followed his leadership in progressive education became overpermissive and thereby failed to stimulate optimal achievement and to maintain order and discipline among students. As a result, this type of education fell into disrepute, and the pendulum began to swing in the opposite direction. The trend toward strictness and the resumption of autocratic methods culminated in the demand for physical punishment. It met with little success, however, because children no longer were willing to be subdued and to submit to punitive action. Now a tragic vicious circle began. The more the schools became determined to impose their will on the students, the more the students rebelled openly and defiantly. This in turn provoked the schools to apply stricter measures. At the present time, the war between the generations is in full force. This is the so-called generation gap. The flames of this rebellion were further kindled by the intrusion of the fight for racial equality.

Until now educational policies have been mostly concerned with two alternatives in dealing with children: permissiveness or strictness. But permissiveness leads to anarchy, and strictness leads to rebellion. Thus, it was assumed that a happy mixture of both or a way of avoiding either extreme could be the answer. This is a wrong assumption. Unless teachers learn to stimulate and to influence children from within instead of applying pressure from without, they are in no position to overcome whatever resistance they may encounter in the classroom. Most of the corrective suggestions that teachers receive today are not only ineffective but often harmful. Despite reward and punishment, despite criticism and humiliation, children continue their disturbing or defiant behavior. Consequently, in our school systems we are raising an increasing number of illiterates— children who do not learn to read or to write properly.

Many children develop a distaste for and an opposition to the institutions of learning. We have the underachievers, who flatly refuse to learn, and the dropouts, who see no purpose in attending school, because often they are ashamed to be placed at the scholastic level with children who are much younger. Dropping out from an institution that they have learned to hate seems to be the best solution for them. There are few indications that give us hope of averting a steadily worsening relationship between teachers and students. Unless future teachers learn how to understand children and influence them, they will start with a great deal of idealism and hope that will give way to despair when they find that their best efforts and most sincere intentions are thwarted.

At present, teachers are not prepared to understand children, but without an understanding of children's motivation, teachers are hardly in a position to change it. As long as a child wants to study and to behave, the teacher finds little difficulty in teaching, but if a child decides not to study, the teacher is at a loss and does not know what to do. For this reason, teachers need guidelines that can be applied in the classroom, which would enable them to help the child who is deficient academically or socially.

Maintaining Sanity in the Classroom directs itself to these issues. The goal of this book is to aid teachers who teach normal children who have the ability to learn but who resist learning and cooperating because they have misleading concepts. Although the book can be of great aid to school counselors and social workers, and can be used as a supplementary text in educational psychology, its primary purpose is to provide teachers with an understanding of behavior problems and with techniques in how to deal with them. This book focuses on a humanistic Adlerian approach dealing with behavior management in the classroom.

The text is divided into five parts. Part 1 deals with a psychological model of human beings—a theory of human behavior that every teacher can learn—that will be helpful in the teacher's efforts to understand motivation. The theory and practice were developed by the Viennese psychiatrist Alfred Adler and his associates.

We see the child as a social being who wants to find his place at home, in school, and in the world. If he misbehaves, he has developed erroneous ideas about how to belong. The behavior of children can be understood only when we know its purpose. All behavior is goal-directed; it indicates the ways and means in which each child has discovered his expression to gain status and significance. The child decides what he intends to do, although he is usually not aware that he has made a decision and that he can change his decision.

Part 2 deals with group dynamics and democratic practices. The child can function fully only if he feels accepted by the group as a worthwhile member. His ability and willingness to function depend on what we call his "social interest."

Part 3 deals with learning deficits. Part 4 is concerned with behavior problems. The main problem is motivation. Disturbances and deficiencies indicate a lack of social interest and of concern with the welfare of others. The restriction of social interest is usually due to feelings of inferiority and doubt that he can find a place through useful means. It is the task of the teacher to help the child to overcome his mistaken self-evaluation and, thereby, increase his social interest. For this reason, the art of encouragement is one of the most crucial tools that can be used to correct and to improve the adjustment that each child makes.

Part 5 focuses on parent involvement, on child-parent-teacher conferences, on the family council, and on parent education.

Many of the suggestions made throughout this book are based on common sense; others, however, offset present concepts about children and require considerable relearning on the part of the teacher. One of the first steps that a teacher has to take is to give up punitive retaliation. This alone would revolutionize almost any school system that heretofore used punishment, grades, and other forms of patronizing superiority. A new relationship of equality between adults and children is incomprehensible for teachers who were never exposed to such a concept. They may find it difficult to share their responsibility with the children and let them participate in decision making.

An end to the present warfare between adults and children can only come about when our schools become truly democratic, governed by representatives of all segments of the school population. Administrators, teachers, counselors, and maintenance personnel must get together with the students to find a common ground of procedure. We can no longer run schools for children; we must let them participate in the process of education. In order to do so, a new relationship between adults and children is needed—one that reflects mutual trust and respect. Without this, the war can go on indefinitely.

Most of the group discussions presented in this book were transcribed from tapes.

The authors are aware of the equal treatment of the sexes in textbooks, but we feel that the use of "he or she" or of alternating between masculine and feminine pronouns interrupts the flow of our written communication. Therefore, our decision is to use "she" and "her" when referring to the teacher and to use "he" and "him" when referring to the child.

Bernice Bronia Grunwald
Floy Childers Pepper

Part 1
Theoretical Premises

Chapter 1

Development of a Child's Potential

The development of a child's potential depends on the ability of the teacher to perceive the child's possibilities, to stimulate the child to learn, and, thereby, to make the child's latent potentiality a reality. The educator is constantly confronted with the problem of developing methods and techniques aimed at reaching the child and helping him develop his intellectual capacities.

The ability of the teacher to develop successful methods depends on the general assumptions that she has made regarding the nature and capacity of children to learn and to achieve. She may assume that many children could do more than they do, or she may equate what the child is doing with what the child can do. It is our belief and contention that, for the most part, teachers are unaware of the tremendous potential within each child.

A consideration of a child's potential must first include what children are innately capable of. Adults usually do not give credit to a child's abilities. Although we cannot base our estimate of the child's potential on any proof, we do find some agreement among people with vision (Otto, 1966) that we are all operating at about 15 percent of our potential ability. If anything close to this estimate is correct, then we can attribute part of this generalization to our educational practices, which actually impede the development of children. It should make us reflect when we see how much children learn before they go to school, and what little progress they make thereafter. The artistic ability and creativity of young children are obvious, yet often, very little remains as they grow older and set higher expectations and become more critical of their performance.

We need a new concept of children that takes into account the tremendous power, planning, and persistence with which they become able to manipulate their environment. Such a concept would be in stark contrast to a prevalent notion that children are victims of the world around them and that they have little or no sense of identity or direction.

Effective methods of stimulating growth and making use of the child's potential can be put into practice when new techniques that stimulate growth and learning are known. The greatest progress may come through new learning theories. The discovery of how very young children learn will lead to totally new approaches in teaching.

The way in which children derive lessons from their environment that they then use to control their environment can be seen very early in their lives. Babies can learn how to dominate the family within the first four weeks of their lives. The child is unaware of what he is doing, but conscious awareness is by no means a requirement for well-designed activities. The infant is not just a bundle of uncoordinated drives and needs; he is a social being, concerned not only with physical needs that require satisfaction but with the social atmosphere around him. The infant relates himself to his surroundings to satisfy his social needs.

The infant operates through trial and error. When he discovers—long before he can think consciously—that he likes to be picked up and to be fondled, and if he encounters a receptive environment that responds to his crying demands, then he will have learned this first lesson, that is, the benefit of crying. It does not take the infant long to find out when crying will be beneficial and when it will not be beneficial. Therefore, soon the child will learn to modify his behavior according to the responses that he gets. This holds true for a wide variety of behaviors and situations. A child's behavior pattern is well-designed, and he will not continue any behavior pattern if it does not achieve the desired results. It is difficult to understand a child's purposes and goals unless we accept the basic concept that all behavior (of both children and adults) is goal oriented.

Personality Development

This concept extends to the development of the child's personality. The development of personality, of a life-style, is based on the opinions that the child forms about himself and others and on the goals that he sets for himself (see Chapter 4). He probably begins with random decisions, perceiving and evaluating the reactions. After having established a frame of reference within which he operates based on these perceptions and evaluations, the child is free to choose ways to achieve his life-style goals from a variety of alternatives. Some examples of these alternatives are listed below.

1. He may overestimate the importance of winning his parents' approval.
2. He may find difficulty in accepting criticism.
3. He may be overly sensitive and try to let others make decisions for him, thus avoiding responsibility for his actions.
4. He may try to control and manipulate everything.
5. He may want to be right all the time.
6. He may feel that he cannot trust or depend on others.
7. He may think that being good is the only way to have status. He may be a perfectionist, like to sit in judgment of others, feel morally superior, or overreact to any mistake others make.
8. He may rebel in one form or other, convinced that he is entitled to have his own way.

Each child can and does decide what he is going to do. The realization of the child's real ability to determine whether he wants to change, to learn, and to decide what and when he wants to learn opens new vistas for the understanding and teaching of children.

There is a profound difference in whether one regards the past as the cause of this deficiency or difficulty or as an explanation of how and why he developed his ideas and concepts. But the basis for his behavior is what he thinks, believes, and intends to do. We do not regard the child as the victim of forces that converge on him: hereditary, talent, or environmental influences, traumatic experiences, psychosexual development, and so on. What he is when he is born is less important than what he does with it afterwards. The living conditions in which he finds himself are less important than what he does with himself in those conditions. This view opens the way for change through new and more appropriate concepts and goals. It is the basis for a more optimistic outlook.

Decisions Are Based on Choices

In order to understand a child, we have to keep in mind that whatever the child is doing depends on his decisions. Thus, inappropriate behavior may result not from deficiencies but from wrong decisions. The present psychological investigations that try to establish certain qualities and deficiencies of the child, as well as his abilities and inabilities are based on a psychology of possession and of inventory, while our approach based on Adlerian psychology is one of use. We are not interested in what a child is or what he has, but only what he does with what he is or what he has.

Before we can help children to fulfill their potential, we have to change the practices presently used in raising and in teaching children. Parents often are not familiar with alternative ways of raising children and, therefore, raise children in methods based on tradition. However, the traditional form of raising children, handed down from an autocratic past, no longer brings desired results. Similarly, current teaching methods are also limited by autocratic traditions. So long as children behave and want to learn, our teachers are effective, but many teachers do not know what to do in moments of conflict or defiance when a child has decided not to behave or to study. In reviewing many such cases, disciplinary pressure of various sorts from without brings no satisfactory results. Discipline through reward and punishment was and is only possible in an autocratic setting. In a democratic setting it has to be replaced with methods that stimulate the child from within. With such stimulation, most educational influences actually undermine rather than enhance the development of the child.

Parents and teachers unconsciously and unintentionally can have considerable negative effects on a child. For them the child is never good enough as he is. It is as if they are afraid that he will not grow and develop unless they instill him with fear. The child cannot use his potential of creativity if he is afraid.

Development of Social Interest

In the presence of discouragement the strongest motivation to grow and to fulfill himself in a broad way retreats. This motivation is what Alfred Adler called "social interest," a feeling of belonging in society. It alone stimulates a person to contribute to the welfare of all and to increase his function and his abilities, not for his own sake, but as a member of the group. The child's interest in belonging exists from the outset. It may take a positive or a negative turn, depending on the nature of social feeling that comes about through activity and communication between the adult and the child. For this reason, the adult's approaches to teaching and to the child are important and must serve to promote social interest in the best way possible.

The child's potential for learning is greatly enhanced when the child is viewed with mutual respect and when he is given a sense of equality and of equal responsibility along with an acknowledged role in decision making. In such a democratic atmosphere, children can learn skills far more advanced than those they are now learning. Unusual feats of memory can be achieved. For instance, today very young children can learn to compose music. Shinichi Suzuki in Japan teaches groups of children aged 3 to 5 to play violin concertos. Many other skills and abilities, such as time perception, space orientation, an understanding of people, and the perception of new patterns of various kinds of achievements far beyond the reach of our contemporaries, can be acquired. Any new ability would increase the child's mastery of life.

We may stand on the threshold of a new culture, if we can remove the obstacles to intellectual growth and to social and moral development. It seems that we are on the verge of achieving this. If so, we may, in a relatively short period of a few generations, acquire such a high degree of knowledge, skill, performance, and morality that humanity will be as different from us then as we are now from people during the Dark Ages.

REFERENCE

Otto, H. A., *Exploration in Human Potentialities*. Springfield, Ill.: Charles C. Thomas, 1966.

Chapter 2
Goal-Directed Behavior

Every educator's approach to the educational process is based on a certain concept of human nature. The concept helps provide the educator with reasons for the behavior of children and the means by which she responds to them. However, today there is confusion about how we should deal with children since we do not have a universally accepted concept of human nature. Little or no agreement has been reached about the way in which children should be taught and raised.

There is still strong adherence to causative-deterministic explanations of personality development as believed by seventeenth-century science, which says that all events can only be explained by their causes. We suggest that this kind of thinking poses an obstacle to the understanding of people, particularly children, and must be replaced.

Behavior Is Goal-Directed

The model of humanity that we propose was developed by Alfred Adler and provides new concepts with which to approach the understanding of children. Some of these concepts postulated by Adler are:

1. Behavior is purposive or goal-directed. Only if we can accept this premise and then recognize the purpose of a child's behavior, can the methods that we recommend make any sense. To correct goals is different from correcting deficiencies. Viewing a child through labels such as learning disabled, dyslexic, mentally retarded, and hyperactive, is of little or no use in helping him discover better alternatives. However, if the child's goal is recognized, we can help him change or obtain his goal through useful and acceptable means.

2. The teleological model (goal-directed behavior), as developed by Adler, found much opposition in the psychoscientific oriented people. The strongest opposition came from scientists who rejected teleology as unscientific. Since the doctrine of causality permeates our entire society, it is very difficult for people to grasp and understand that it is not the cause but the purpose of the goal that explains behavior. Behavior makes sense only when we understand its purpose. The goal of the behavior itself, is the cause.

3. The force behind every human action is its goal. To a certain extent, everybody knows what he wants and acts accordingly. The consequences of his actions, however, reveal his intentions, whether he is aware of them or not. In general, only a small portion of a person's intentions reach the conscious level. We do what we feel like doing without knowing why we felt so inclined.

4. Humans are social beings with the overriding goal of belonging or finding a place in society. This is in opposition to the view of humans as biological beings with drives and physically related motivations as the guiding force. The child's behavior indicates the ways and means by which he tries to be significant. If these ways and means are antisocial and disturbing, then the child did not develop the right idea about how to find his place. The antisocial ways or "mistaken goals," which we will discuss in the next chapter, reflect an error in the child's judgment and in his comprehension of life and the necessities of social living. To understand a child, we must understand the child's purpose of behavior, a purpose of which the child may be unaware.

5. We further assume that the individual has the power to move in any self-determined direction: He is not driven through life by the past but moves of his accord. All the individual's actions, qualities, and characteristics, as well as emotions, can be understood by his efforts to find a place for himself in society. However, a child's actions, and the choices he makes, may be based on faulty assumptions about life and about himself. Although the behavior may appear inappropriate, it reflects the conviction that this is the only possible way for him to be significant. Through his own private logic his behavior becomes appropriate to him.

6. In order to understand how a child can develop faulty assumptions, we have to realize that human beings are biased in their perception of the world around them. They cannot experience reality as it is but only as they perceive it. We cannot be fully objective in our evaluation of any given situation because we have a biased perception—a private logic. Asking a child why he does something wrong is useless, because he does not know why he does it. How the child looks at life, at others, and at himself, and what he decides to do about it, depends on his private logic, for it alone is used to develop courses of action. The trained educator has to help the child understand himself, his way of thinking, and his goals.

7. The child is sensitive to the social atmosphere around him and very

early experiments with it to get what he wants. Through the growth process he integrates his experiences into concepts and accordingly sets his goals. These take on significance with respect to his actions and development and become his "life-style." Without proper, effective guidance in dealing with the social intricacies of finding a productive, cooperative place in society, a child can form a faulty self-evaluation leading to a mistaken or a fictitious goal for the organization of his life, which is the basis of his life-style. We call the goal "fictitious" because the child assumes that only under certain conditions can he really be sure of his place. Let us illustrate this through the following example.

At the dinner table the parents were telling each other the events of the day.

Marlene who was sitting next to her mother broke into the conversation: "I learned how to pedge legence in school today." She waited for a reaction from her parents, but they ignored her remarks and continued with their conversation.

Marlene tried once more but with no more success than before. Suddenly she stood up on her chair, put her right hand over her heart, and in a loud voice began to recite, "I pedge legence to United States of America." At this, the parents looked at each other and then Marlene, and they started laughing because they were so happy. Marlene started all over again, this time even louder than before.

"So you can recite 'The Pledge of Allegiance.' Did you hear that, Mother? Our little girl can say 'The Pledge of Allegiance.' Say it again, darling." Marlene became the center of attention.

When Eddie, who was 3 years old, came into the kitchen, he noticed that his mother was sewing, his father was fixing a kitchen cabinet, and his older sister was making a cake. Eddie wanted very much to do something too— something that would make his mother happy. He took some shoe polish and a shoe brush and started polishing his shoes. His father said, "That's great, son. Make sure that they shine." His mother smiled at him.

Some time later, Eddie was found polishing the bedspread on his mother's bed. Unfortunately, his mother was not as happy this time as she was before, for he had used dark shoe polish on her satin spread. He received a shaking and a scolding for being a naughty boy.

Herbert, 11 years old, is the oldest of three children. He is a very shy boy, speaks inaudibly, has no friends, and avoids people outside his family. He stays in the house except during those times when he is in school or when his parents send him to the store. At home he keeps busy either cleaning his room, straightening up the basement, or helping his mother with whatever she is doing.

His sister, Melanie, is two years younger. She is a very outgoing, happy, rather aggressive child. She is popular with the children. At home the parents have to force her to take care of her room and to do whatever chores they assign to her. Usually, Herbert does her work before Melanie has a chance to do it (at times when she wants to do the work). It is not unusual for her to come into her room and find that Herbert has already made her bed, hung up her clothes, and put away whatever she has left lying around.

Although Melanie enjoys this service, she is constantly complaining about her brother to her parents. "Why is he such a ninnie? Why does he walk so slowly?" She never misses an opportunity to call him names, such as "sissie" or "stupid."

The child's deductions from his experiences and the resulting behavior can be understood only if we know how the parents reacted to it. All three examples help us understand how the child derives his conclusions and how he perceives his place in his social milieu. This perception becomes the basis for his life-style.

Life-style Goals

These basic guidelines or life-style goals permit the child to establish a certain stability and consistency in his movement through life. His life-style also sets certain restrictions and leads to the possibility of frustration under certain situations. A crisis situation develops when his life-style clashes with the needs of the situation. At this point, his ability and willingness to participate and to contribute end, and antisocial movements of a neurotic or even psychotic pattern may ensue. Even then, the most antisocial form of existence has a purpose; its recognition is an important factor in therapy and reorientation with children and adults alike.

Within the framework of the life-style, based on long-range goals in life, there are immediate movements, or short-range goals, as they may be called. Although the concept of his life is unique for each person and may distinguish one person from the other, the immediate responses related to short-range goals and used in dealing with concrete life situations are peculiarly similar across individuals.

We find that there are four possible goals of disturbing behavior in children. These must be considered before we can understand their behavior. The four goals are:

1. to gain attention
2. to seek power
3. to seek revenge
4. to display inadequacy (real or imagined).

It may seem unrealistic to expect psychological insights from a teacher who is supposed just to teach and to impart knowledge. However, any teacher—and for that matter, any adult—can acquire this skill in a relatively short period of time. As long as teachers were supposed to teach and children were supposed to learn, it was not necessary to understand children and to change their motivation. Today, when the pressure from without has lost its effectiveness and has to be replaced by stimulation from within, such skills and abilities are a prerequisite for every teacher.

Chapter 3
The Four Mistaken Goals

Teachers often question the reason for a child's misbehavior. "What makes him act like this?," they wonder. They may attribute the misbehavior to meanness, stupidity, laziness, lack of motivation or ambition, lack of "proper" upbringing, and so on, all of which indicate speculation without any real basis.

Each person is unique in his method of approaching social situations and of seeking a place for himself. Viewed from this perspective, all disturbing behavior indicates a mistaken concept of the child about himself within the group and thereby a mistaken approach to others.

Our descriptions of the four mistaken goals of behavior offer the teacher an opportunity to understand the psychological motivation of the child rather than to grope in the dark as to why the child behaves as he does. It permits the teacher to develop diagnostic skills and psychological sensitivity.

Most adults have no idea why a child misbehaves and are unaware of the purposes of the child's actions. Children are not born with a conscience or with good manners. These have to be developed, but acquiring them is a slow, painful process. As a child struggles to learn the ways of the adult world, he is bound to make mistakes. Learning what society in general and parents and teachers in particular expect is a difficult job.

Every action of the child has a purpose, and the child never wastes energy unless it pays off. The child's basic aim is to belong and to find his place in the family or in the group in which he functions.

Useful and Useless Behavior

There are two ways of movement in the social scene: the useful and the useless. Useful behavior is behavior that is turned toward cooperative action for the common good. The person moves toward others with concern and tends to bring about happiness and satisfaction for others as well as for himself, useless behavior is turned toward promoting the self. The person moves away from others and is concerned only with his own elevation and achievement. There is a tendency to criticize others and degrade himself. The well-adjusted child finds his way toward social acceptance through his concern for the welfare of the group, family, or school and through his useful contributions. The child who misbehaves has lost his belief that he can find the belonging and recognition that he desires and erroneously believes that he will find acceptance through provocative behavior by pursuing the mistaken goals of behavior.

In order to achieve his ends, a child may adopt four mistaken goals without being aware of them (Dreikurs, 1948). They are:

1. to gain undue attention
2. to seek power
3. to seek revenge or to get even
4. to display inadequacy (real or assumed).

Regardless of which of these four goals the child adopts, his misbehavior results from his conviction that it will secure his place in the family or group in which he functions. The child is usually not aware of the purpose of his behavior. It is useless to ask a child "Why did you do this?" He does not know. He recognizes his goal, however, when it is disclosed to him.

It may be difficult for many to accept the fact that children who misbehave and fail to cooperate, to study, and to apply themselves are motivated by one or the other of the four mistaken goals. We are often asked on what grounds we can make such generalizations, which attempt to pigeonhole the great variety of children's misbehavior into one of the four goals. Dreikurs studied children's behavior for many years, and concluded that in their misbehavior, children pursue one or more than one of the four goals. We would be more than willing to include other goals for children's misbehavior if they could be suggested and proven. In each case we can find one or several of these goals existing. They explain the child's misbehavior and can be recognized by the child if he is properly confronted with them.

The four mistaken goals of behavior can be observed in young children up to the age of ten. It is difficult for parents and teachers to recognize that the child's disturbing behavior is directed against them. In early childhood, the status of the child depends on the impression he makes on adults. Later, he may develop different goals to gain social significance in his peer group and later still, in adult society. But these original four goals can still be observed in people of every age, except that in adulthood they are not all-inclusive. One must keep in mind that status and prestige can be achieved, frequently more easily, through useless and destructive means as well as through useful and constructive ones.

Table 3–1 gives a complete account of the four mistaken goals of misbehavior with a description of the child's behavior when pursuing any of these goals. It also helps the teacher to understand the goals by recognizing the feeling as described in the table.

Goals May Change

The child's behavior may vary with circumstances; he may act to attract attention at one moment and assert his powers to seek revenge at another.

Table 3–1   The Four Mistaken Goals and Teacher's Reactions to the Child's Behavior

Goal	Child's Action and Attitudes	Teacher's Reaction
1. Attention	Is a nuisance in class	Gives undue service
	May show off	Reminds often
	May be lazy	Coaxes
	Puts others in his service	Feels annoyed
	Keeps teacher busy	Shows pity
	Thinks: "I have a place only when people pay attention to me."	May think: "Child occupies too much of my time."
	May cry	May feel resentment
	May use charm	
	May be overly eager to please	
	May be overly sensitive	
2. Power	May be stubborn	May feel defeated
	Often argues	Feels threatened in her leadership
	Must win	
	Must be the boss	Concerned with what the others will think of her
	Often lies	
	Is disobedient	Feels she must force the child to obey
	Does the opposite of what is asked of him	Gets angry
	May refuse to do any work	Must show the child that she is running the class
	May think "I count only if others do what I want."	
	Must be in control of every situation	May be determined not to let him get away with his behavior

Table 3–1 Continued

Goal	Child's Action and Attitudes	Teacher's Reaction
3. Revenge	May steal Is vicious Hurts children and animals Is destructive May lie Often pouts and accuses others of their unfairness May believe that nobody likes him May want to get even for the hurts he believes others have inflicted upon him	Feels hurt Gets mad Wants to hurt back May dislike child Considers child ungrateful Wants to teach the child a lesson for his mean behavior May ask the other children to avoid this child May report the child to his parents in the hope that they will punish him
4. Inadequacy	Feels helpless May feel stupid in comparison to others Gives up and does not participate in any activities Feels best when left alone and when no demands are made on him May set too high goals for himself and not touch anything that does not measure up to his high self-expectations	May try various approaches to reach the child and become discouraged if she meets with failure. She may then give up trying

The child can also use a variety of techniques to obtain his goal, or, conversely, the same behavior can serve all four goals.

The following example illustrates how a child changes from one goal to another within the same situation and within seconds.

Jason, age 9, was the first to complete the math assignment correctly. The standard procedure in this classroom was to be able to assist others who were having difficulty with their lessons. Jason wandered around the room trying to get the teacher and the aide to pay attention to him. When he was unsuccessful he sat down at his desk and asked if he could assist Danny, who needed help. After awhile he asked to mark the grade on Danny's record sheet. Recording had previously been discussed and the class had agreed that this was the teacher's responsibility. When the teacher pointed this out to him he said he did not care and that he was going to record the grade. This was a direct challenge of the teacher's authority. The teacher did not take the bait and fall into Jason's play for power. She continued to work with other students. Jason became upset, screamed, and yelled about the unfairness of the teacher. Jason left the classroom, but after a few minutes he returned and spent the rest of the afternoon doing nothing.

The same behavior can be used for more than one goal, as the following example illustrates.

Leroy, age 14, did not work at his writing assignment and frittered away his time by looking out the window or doodling on his paper. The teacher kept reminding Leroy that he would not finish in time if he did not get busy. Every few minutes she would check to see how much work he had completed, thereby paying attention to Leroy's behavior. No amount of coaxing or threatening by the teacher could budge him. The teacher accused him of being lazy. In reality he was determined to show her that "she couldn't make him." (*power*)

When the teacher kept Leroy after school so that he could finish the assignment, he passed the time by drawing nasty pictures on his paper. This reinforced the teacher's conviction that Leroy was lazy. She did not realize that Leroy intended to upset her and to get even with her. (*revenge*)

Goal 1, Attention, is the only goal that often confuses adults because the same behavior could also fall under power and revenge. We found that a child may seek attention through the following four behavior patterns. See Table 3–2.

1. active-constructive
2. active-destructive
3. passive-constructive
4. passive-destructive.

The choice of method (constructive or destructive) that the child will employ depends upon his feelings and his perception of his position in the group in which he finds himself. If he interprets his position as inferior, he is bound to become antagonistic and to express this in destructive acts.

The amount of courage the child possesses is indicated by his use of active or passive behavior. Passivity is always based on personal discouragement. If his antagonism is successfully beaten down, he may be discouraged to such an extent that he loses hope for any significance and will not engage in open warfare.

Attention Getting Mechanism (AGM)

The attention getting mechanism (AGM) operates in most young children. It is characteristic of our culture that we provide our children with few opportunities to establish their social position through useful contribution. Whatever has to be done in the family is done by parents or older siblings.

Table 3–2 The Four Mistaken Goals of Misbehavior

Useful Behavior		Useless Behavior		Direction of Maladjustment
Active-Constructive	Passive-Constructive	Active-Destructive	Passive-Destructive	Goals
Success The model child The teacher's pet Is very industrious Exaggerated conscientiousness Is very reliable Often tattles Performs for praise and recognition	*Charm* The clinging vine Vain Cute Flatters Sensitive	*Nuisance* Show-off Obtrusiveness Mischief maker Acts tough Tattles Teases The "walking question mark" Instability "Enfant terrible" Fresh	*Lazy* Bashful, shy Dependent Anxious Reading & speech difficulties Cries Pokey Untidy Frivolous Fearful Lacks concentration May have eating problems	(AGM) Attention-Getting Mechanism (1)
		Rebel Argues, bickers Contradicts Temper tantrums Lies Spiteful Provocative Loiters Bull-headed	*Stubborn* Forgetful Daydreams Dawdles Indolence Loafing & idling	Power Seeking (2)
		Vicious Contemptuous Steals Insolent Violent Brutal	*Violent Passivity* Sullen Unmerciful Enjoys watching violence Malicious	Revenge Seeking (3)
			Hopeless Pseudo-retarded Listless Sluggish Lackadaisical	Display of Inadequacy (4)

The most frequent deteriorating sequence is from active-constructive AGM to active-destructive power to active-destructive revenge (line a). Another frequent sequence goes from passive-constructive AGM to passive-destructive AGM to display of inability (line b). In most cases this development goes through a passive demonstration of power. Sometimes passive-constructive behavior can turn directly to the open display of inadequacy (goal 4) (line c). Improvement does not follow the same lines. Even a revengeful child, who generally presents the most disturbed behavior patterns, can become adequately adjusted if he can be convinced that he is liked and can be useful.

Seeing no chance to gain status through constructive contributions, the child may seek proof of his acceptance through charm and affection or at least through *undue* attention. Since none of these increase the child's self-reliance and belief in his own strength, he constantly seeks new proof. He may first try to get his satisfaction through socially acceptable and pleasant means. When these methods no longer prove effective, he may try any other conceivable method to put others in his service and to get attention. Humiliation or punishment do not matter as long as he achieves his purpose; they are preferable to being ignored. (We should like to point out that attention getting is the only goal that can be achieved by all four subdivisions of behavior patterns. Power and revenge can be achieved through active-destructive behavior. Power, revenge, and display of inadequacy can be achieved through passive-destructive behavior.)

Active-Constructive

The active-constructive AGM resembles a very cooperative and conforming behavior. This child is extremely ambitious and wants to be the first or the best in his activities. His goal orientation is toward success. This child usually has a poor social relationship with his own age group: if he cannot shine, he feels lost. The child's desire to be perfect, to be correct, to be superior is often stimulated by overambitious and perfectionistic parents who encourage such traits. They often play the child against other siblings. Competition with others leads to the development of striving for applause. In order to maintain his superiority over others or to match and possibly exceed over everyone else, the child tries to become good, reliable, considerate, cooperative, and industrious, seeking and accepting any possible responsibility. This competitive behavior is confirmed by our experience that when the "bad" child improves, the "good" child gives up and often becomes a behavior or a learning problem.

> Dorrie, age 8, was an especially "good" girl. She always did the work assigned to her by the teacher. She usually finished her work and then constantly asked the teacher, "What can I do to help you?" or "See, I finished all my work."
>
> During lunchtime, Dorrie came into the classroom and busied herself with extra projects or reports. She always called her teacher's attention to the projects. Her teacher was very pleased with Dorrie and often said, "If only the rest of the class were as good as Dorrie!"

In the above example, most adults would not look at Dorrie's behavior as an act of misbehavior. However, let us look more closely at her actions. She always called the teacher's attention to her "good" behavior: "See how good I am." She was doing the work purely for the teacher's approval and *not* because she really wanted to learn. She was doing the right things for the wrong reasons. This teacher was not aware of Dorrie's mistaken goal and unwittingly reinforced her.

This type of child is usually spoken of in glowing terms as "such a lovely child," or "such a nice girl" and is usually labeled as the "teacher's pet" or the "model child."

> Dorrie suddenly lost interest in her work. She looked depressed and withdrawn. Since no incident occurred, the teacher could not account for the change. After probing and examining the situation from all angles, the teacher learned that Dorrie had given up when another child caught up with her and performed just as well.

Dorrie had to be the best or she put forth no effort. Her discouragement and withdrawal also indicated the degree to which this child competed.

Active-Destructive

The active-destructive child is one who may be impertinent, defiant, clownish, or bullying. This type of behavior may resemble that used to achieve the second goal (power) or the third goal (revenge) but distinguishes itself from these goals only by the lack of violence and antagonism. The childe who seeks attention will stop his provocation when his goal is achieved. In contrast, the child who wants to demonstrate power is not satisfied with mere attention; he wants his way. The active-destructive child annoys his parents and teachers with his "nuisance" behavior, such as showing off, tattling, asking unnecessary questions, and others.

> The teacher helped Mike, who was in the sixth grade, with his Social Studies assignment. As she started to walk away, Mike mumbled, "Aw, f__ you Mrs. __." The teacher replied, "Not just now, thank you." Mike cracked up with laughter, and thereafter he decreased his mouthings of verbal garbage. (Had the teacher made an issue of Mike's provocation, she would have fallen into his trap.)

Passive-Constructive

Some children are passive in their actions. The passive-constructive child achieves his goals through charm and thus manipulates people to serve him. He uses his facade of helplessness to put others into his service. These children never disturb or destroy, because then they might lose their charm and their power. They are very self-centered, while on the surface they appear to be interested in others. Other children tend to be of the clinging vine type. Some are very vain.

Shirley, age 6, was a very attractive child who was very conscious of her looks. She had several little tricks with which she got people to admire her. She would stand and tug slightly on her long blonde curls and people would say, "Doesn't Shirley have beautiful hair," as they patted her on the head. At other times she would look shyly down her cheeks and then up at the adult who would comment on her gorgeous long eyelashes. When asked to do something, Shirley would sigh deeply, bat her eyes, and the adults would fall all over themselves to help *her*.

Passive-Destructive

The passive-destructive child is characterized as "lazy." He may manifest his laziness in actions ranging from ineffectual responses to total inaction. Through his behavior he forces other people to be concerned with him and to help him. These are the "help me; it's too hard; I can't do it; I don't understand" children. Other behaviors usually shown by these children include bashfulness, dependency, untidiness, lack of concentration, and self-indulgence.

Sonja, age 8, was given an assignment to study her reading cards and prepare for her reading lesson. The other students were busy with their work. Sonja picked up the cards and started to cry. A couple of the boys became concerned and asked Sonja what was wrong. She shook her head and said, "Nothing, the words are too hard for me." The boys called the teacher's attention to Sonja. At this point, Sonja started to cry a little louder. Sonja aimed for attention.

When teachers are asked which of the four types of attention getting they consider to be least disturbing, they usually name the active-constructive. Such a child cannot easily be distinguished from a child who does not seek any special attention or who enjoys doing his job without the need for approval.

As far as attention getting devices go, these children are most easily influenced, since they usually respond to the application of logical consequences. However, the opinions vary as to which is the most difficult child. Teachers not familiar with the motive behind the child's behavior may be inclined to consider the active-destructive as the worst of the four, because such children cause the most disturbance. Most teachers name the passive-constructive behavior of a child as the second best. These children use charm and appeal to get recognition. Thus, we find many teachers inclined to regard the active-constructive behavior as the best, the passive-constructive as the next, the active-destructive as the worst, and the passive-destructive in between. From a point of tractability and adjustment they are not entirely correct.

The most desirable behavior pattern is understandably active-constructive AGM. The next desirable is not the passive-constructive but the active-destructive, provided the child seeks only attention and not power. Both passive types are actually more discouraged. It is easier to help an active-destructive child to find useful means of achieving significance than it is to move a passive child to active participation. Therefore, in this light, the active-destructive child, difficult as he may be, is less disturbed and can be motivated to the useful side. The passive-destructive child is most maladjusted, although he may not cause too much trouble. It is this child who can move directly toward giving up completely.

Power Seeking

Children who drive for power or superiority should not be exposed to pressure because it leads to a power contest. In such a contest the adult rarely wins. Today society does not let the adult abuse the child, nor does the child in his sense of his own equality let an adult impose her will on and control him.

Efforts to control the child lead to a struggle for power. Trying to pull this type of child down from his "high horse" only increases his underlying sense of inferiority and futility. No final victory by the adult is possible. In most cases the child will win, since he is not restricted in his fighting methods by any sense of responsibility or moral obligations. The child's conscience does not redirect him. He knows where to hit and he hits hard. He will argue, cry, contradict, have temper tantrums, lie, become stubborn, or become disobedient in order to prove that he is the boss, that he can do what he wants to do, that he is the stronger, and that he has a right to be "top dog."

> Bernd, age 11, was talking to his neighbor while the teacher was explaining a new step in mathematics. The teacher stopped several times to remind him that he would not know what to do if he did not listen. After each reminder, Bernd would stop for a few seconds and then return to talking with his neighbor.

We may have the impression that all Bernd wanted was attention, which the teacher gave him. The fact that Bernd continued his behavior indicates that although he enjoyed the attention it was not enough. No one was going to stop him from what he wanted to do.

> After several reminders, the teacher became angry. She demanded that Bernd leave his seat and wait in the back of the room until she finished the lesson.

Bernd refused to go. The teacher waited for a minute. When Bernd did not budge from his seat but stared at her with angry eyes, she tried to force him out of his seat. A tug of war proceeded, she pulling one way and he the other.

Both are determined to have their way. The teacher's reaction and Bernd's response to it reconfirms our guess that both entered a power contest. If the teacher had refused to "fight" with Bernd she could have removed "the sail from his wind" and refused to become emotionally involved.

The first obstacle toward an application of a conflict solving technique is the widespread assumption that the adult has to subdue the defiant child—to show him who is boss and make him respect law and order. The second stumbling block is the adult's personal involvement in a power conflict. The teacher cannot avoid the conflict unless she is free from the feeling of inadequacy and concern with her own prestige. No conflict can be resolved as long as she is afraid of being humiliated, taken advantage of, and personally defeated.

After a teacher has decided to avoid both fighting and giving in, which is the first step in conflict solving, she then can concern herself with the issue at hand. What makes a child strive for power? A power drunk child is always ambitious, but his ambition is directed almost exclusively toward defeating those who try to suppress him. His success in defeating adults often brings him considerable status among his peers. This realization helps the teacher to focus on changing the values not only of the child in question but of the entire class. This can be dealt with only in group discussion.

Once a power conflict ensues, the relationship between the child and the adult can only further deteriorate and the child may move to the next goal, which is seeking revenge.

Revenge Seeking

Children who feel that people are unfair to them, disregard their feelings, and hurt them are determined to get even. They take their revenge on anyone, not just on those they think have hurt them. These children may deliberately knock things off other children's desks, trip them as they walk through the aisle, scribble on their papers, hit, kick, scratch, or strike out at others, destroy property, insult and use obscenities, and even soil themselves. They reason: "If others have the right to hurt me, I have the right to hurt back." These children are very difficult to help. It takes a complete change of group atmosphere (see Chapter 14).

These children are convinced that nobody likes them, and since their goal is always to be right, they provoke others to a point where the others retaliate. In this way they have the proof that they were right from the beginning and they cannot be liked.

> Earl told the school counselor that he had "a mean teacher who punished him for no reason." When the counselor asked him for an example of such a situation, Earl told him that the other day he had dropped a thumbtack on the teacher's chair while the teacher was out of the room. When the teacher hurt herself, she demanded to know the name of the culprit. Someone in class told her that it was Earl, whereupon she punished him. When the counselor asked Earl why he had not picked up the thumbtack before the teacher sat down, he replied, "How could I? When the teacher returned to the room, she told us to take our seats and that is what I did!"

Earl, like other children who seek revenge, saw no connection between his actions and those of the teacher. The children usually do not see their behavior as faulty; the fault lies always with what the other person is doing. We will cite another example of a child hurting someone in class as an outlet for anger against his parents.

> One day Jessie, a seventh-grader, came to Home Economics class and cut a big hole from the center of another's girl's fabric. In discussing this incident with Jessie, it became apparent that she was angry with her mother and quite regularly did destructive acts for which her mother had to pay.

Revenge seeking is one of the most difficult behaviors to change and usually involves a considerable length of time. First, the teacher must keep in mind what she should not do. She should not retaliate or become emotionally upset. She will need to make a special effort to show respect to the child. She cannot help a revengeful child unless she realizes how much the child suffers. It is exactly the hurt that the child has felt that prompts him to hurt others. For this reason, the teacher has to generate an attitude of understanding and assistance. It may be difficult to evoke it, but it is essential not only for the sake of the child but for the morale of the entire class. Instead of pitching one against the other, we have to teach children to be their brothers' keeper.

Display of Inadequacy

There are children who after unsuccessful attempts to find significance through using goals of attention, power, or revenge, become so discouraged that they give up and move toward the goal of inadequacy. However, there are children who at a very early age draw conclusions from their environment that they are not as capable as others and have no chance to find a place. These children then move toward goal four. These children want nothing more than to be left alone, and as long as nothing is asked of them, they can still appear as members of the group. If not left alone, they hide behind a display of real or imagined inadequacy, which justifies their resignation. By avoiding participation and contribution, they think they can avoid more humiliating and embarrassing situations. This behavior may characterize all actions of a child or it may only appear in those situations in which he is avoiding an activity in which he feels deficient.

Overcoming a child's discouragement is the most common and urgent task for the teacher. Many times a teacher gives up easily when her first attempts in trying a new technique end in failure. So it is with children who are having difficulty socially and academically.

Recognizing the Child's Goals

There are two reliable indications of recognizing the four goals of misbehavior.

1. The most reliable is the observation of our immediate reaction to the child's provocation. What is our "gut reaction"?
   a. When we feel annoyed because the child does not respond to our reminding, pointing out, coaxing, or nagging, we usually deal with the child who wants attention.
   b. When we feel threatened or challenged in our position because the child does not cooperate and feel compelled to force him to cooperate, we are dealing with a child who seeks power.
   c. When we feel defeated and hurt by the child and are no longer concerned with what is good for the child but instead are ready to "kill him," we are dealing with a child who wants revenge.
   d. When we have tried everything without success and we throw up our arms in despair and say, "I give up," we are dealing with a child who is displaying inadequacy.

2. The second indication of the child's goal will show itself in the manner in which the child responds to our reprimand.
   a. If the child responds to our reprimand and stops his behavior, then we know he wanted attention. He may, however, start again, hoping for additional attention.
   b. When the child continues his behavior, in spite of being reprimanded, he is usually seeking power. He may even intensify his behavior.
   c. If a child becomes angry and abusive when reprimanded, he feels unjustly accused and wants to get revenge.
   d. When a child does nothing and just sits after being reprimanded, he is usually operating out of a real or imagined inadequacy goal.

Since the passive-destructive child who is seeking attention and the child who is displaying inadequacy may show almost the same type of behavior, we think it is necessary to make a distinction in recognizing the difference between the two goals. The passive-destructive child who is seeking attention demands service and may be saying, "Help me, I can't do this," whereas the child who displays inadequacy is not asking for help.

There are no definite rules with regard to the child's choice of a goal or of the means by which he can obtain it. By and large, each disturbing child has made a subconscious decision that guides all his actions.

We should like to point out that the four mistaken goals of behavior apply only to children who create problems for themselves and for us. It does not refer to children who are cooperative, enjoy learning, live up to their potential, and have healthy social relationships. There are many such children. Because they constitute no problem for the teacher, we will not discuss these children in this book, except to make teachers aware that these children can be a great asset to her in dealing with those who provoke and worry her. Table 3–2 should help teachers to understand how a child may move from one goal to another and the specific behavior that a child may use.

REFERENCE

Dreikurs, Rudolf. *The Challenge of Parenthood.* New York: Duell, Sloan and Pearce, 1948.

Chapter 4

Private Logic:
A Diagnostic Technique for Understanding Behavior

In this chapter we will attempt to help teachers develop psychological sensitivity to and understanding of children's behavior. Because we are frequently referring to goal-directed behavior, we believe it is necessary to discuss this area in more depth. Our suggestion that teachers develop a psychological understanding of a child's behavior has often been interpreted to mean that they should become psychologists. This is a misleading concept. We do not intend to make psychotherapists or group therapists out of teachers, but we do know that some of the principles developed in the following material can be effectively and responsibly applied.

We begin by presenting the concepts needed to understand the child's motives and acts. These are followed by several specific diagnostic techniques that are used in diagnosing the child's motivation. Together they provide an operational framework through which the teacher can view and work with the psychology of children in the classroom.

Private Logic

Private logic or private intelligence is a "mistaken reason" in which an individual solves his problems in a "private sense" that is not understandable to others.

An individual's private logic consists of what he *really* believes and intends. It includes the long-range goals of the life-style, the short-range goals of the immediate situation, and the rationalizations he gives himself for what he is doing. This rationale is referred to as "the hidden reason."

Private logic involves a process, beginning in childhood, by which a person explains his experiences to himself with varying degrees of insight and by which he produces and justifies his behavior. In this light, an individual's private logic may be seen to reflect a person's degree of social interest and adjustment or maladjustment.

We are mainly concerned with the child's short-term goals. These are immediate goals that we must deal with and respond to on the spot. Understanding a person's life-style or long-term goals would certainly be helpful to the teacher of older children. However, we do not recommend using long-term or life-style goals in dealing with children's misbehavior unless the teacher is well trained in this field.

The child is not aware of his goals. However, the child recognizes the purpose of his behavior when we disclose his goals to him. Younger children betray themselves through an obvious "recognition reflex."

The Recognition Reflex

Younger children will either admit that they do the misbehavior for the reason we have suggested or they give themselves away through some facial or bodily mannerism that we term the *recognition reflex*. This recognition reflex usually expresses itself through a smile, a grin, an embarrassed laughter, or a twinkle in the eye.

Older children are too sophisticated to admit that they want attention or to show their power, since they consider this childish behavior, and so they either say "no" to our disclosure or they have deadpan expressions on their faces. But they betray themselves through their body language. Their lips may twitch, their eyes may blink or bat more frequently, they may readjust their seating positions, swing a leg, tap with their fingers, or even wiggle their toes. It takes careful observation of their body language in order for us to know if we have made the right guess.

We recommend a specific procedure for the disclosure of the child's goal. It is very important that this procedure be followed as closely as possible, because from our experience only then do we get a reliable recognition reflex.

Disclosing the Goal to the Child

In the process of confronting the child with his goal we suggest the following procedure:

1. "Do you know why you — — — —?" We know that the child does not know the reason why he misbehaves. However, we ask this question because it is necessary as a preparation for the next step.
2. "I would like to tell you what I think."

In the confrontation we use one or more of the following suggested questions for each goal. Questions should be asked in sequence from each goal, even though the youngster may give himself away, as he may be operating on more than one goal. For example, we may get a recognition reflex when we pose an attention question and stop there. Later we find that the child is really operating on borderline attention but more on power seeking.

The goal is presented as a guess in the form of "could it be that ——?" followed by a reference to the specific goal.

Attention—Could It Be That
You want to keep me busy with you?
You want me to do more for you?
You want me to notice you more?
You want me to help you more?
You want me to come and be with you?
You want me to do something special for you?
You want to keep the group busy with you?
You want to be special to the group?

Power—Could It Be That
You want to be the boss, be in charge?
You want to show me that you can do what you want
   —that I cannot stop you?
   —that I cannot make you?
You want to do
   —what you want to do?
   —when you want to do it?
   —when you want and no one can stop you?

Revenge—Could It Be That
You want to punish me?
You want to get even? get back at ——?
You want to hurt me (or him, her, them)?
You want to make me feel bad?
You want to show me how it feels?
You want to make me suffer?
You want to show me how much you hated what I did?
You want to show me that I cannot get away with that?
You want to hurt me and the pupils in the class?

Display of Inadequacy (Withdrawal)—Could It Be That
You want to be left alone because
   —you cannot do anything?
   —you are afraid to fail?
   —you can't be on top? first? the winner?
You want me to stop asking you to do it?

You feel like you do not know the answer and do not want people to
    know?
You just do not want to do it, no matter what?

We must be careful not to confront the child with an accusation such
as "You do it to get attention," because the child will resent this and deny
it. "Could it be" is not an accusation; it is only a guess that may be correct
or incorrect. If it is incorrect, we should guess again.

One method of reaching a resistant child is through the "hidden reason"
technique. When a child says or does something that is out of the ordinary,
you can guess at what is in his mind, that is, his reason for what he is doing.
This is not the psychological reason but rather the one in his mind formed
in his own words. This technique is not easy to learn, but it can be very
effective and is highly reliable. If the child says "no" to your guess, then
you are wrong. If he says "maybe," you are getting close. When you guess
correctly, he compulsively says "Yes." There is no harm in guessing, since
if you guess incorrectly, it is merely shrugged off. In the moment that you
guess correctly, the child feels understood and changes from being hostile
and resistant to being cooperative. This again forms the beginning of a
working relationship in which the child can receive help in changing some
of his mistaken ideas. It is also important to recognize that the individual
is not usually aware of his hidden reason, but in the moment during which
you have guessed correctly, suddenly he becomes clearly aware of the
validity of the guess. It is a joyful experience for the person who has been
pushed around and feels he has no place in society to feel understood.
This is the beginning of trust and confidence (Dreikurs, 1971).

The hidden reason may be disclosed to him in a manner similar to dis-
closing the four goals but with the use of different questions, which are
presented below.

1. Could it be that you feel insignificant unless you are the best in
   whatever you do?
2. Could it be that you feel rejected unless everybody likes you?
3. Could it be that you feel that you must never make a mistake?
4. Could it be that you feel that you are trying your best and people show
   no appreciation?
5. Could it be that you want to be better than —?
6. Could it be that you want to make me feel guilty and sorry for what
   I did to you?
7. Could it be that you do not care about the price you will have to pay
   for making me (him, her) feel this way?
8. Could it be that you want to show me how much smarter you are
   than me?
9. Could it be that you feel superior to me when you put me in a position
   in which I do not know what to do with you and I feel helpless?

10. Could it be that you are not talking in order to frustrate me (and others) and make me feel helpless and defeated?
11. Could it be that you are willing to do anything in order to feel like a big-shot?
12. Could it be that you want people to feel sorry for you and give in to you?
13. Could it be that you use sickness in order to have a legitimate excuse for not living up to your responsibilities?
14. Could it be that you believe that as a minor you cannot be punished for stealing or destroying other people's property?
15. Could it be that you are very pleased with yourself when you make other people suffer or feel foolish?

We may also illustrate this with the following example:

Ona, a freshman, was an excellent student; however, she had to put forth great effort and time to maintain a straight A average. The teacher confronted Ona with a possible reason for her overcompensation.

TEACHER: "Ona, could it be that you want to be the best in the class?"

ONA: "Well, not exactly."

TEACHER: "Could it be that you want to be first or always right?"

ONA: "No—that's not right."

TEACHER: "Ona, how many children are in your family and how old are they?"

ONA: "I have two older brothers—ages 16 and 18."

TEACHER: "Could it be that you want to be better than your brothers?"

(At this point, Ona beamed and said, "Right on."

These are a few suggestions, and the teacher would have to know the child, his problem, and his behavior pattern in order to know which questions to ask. In each case, the child needs to be helped to realize his overdependency on having these needs met and to realize that he has other choices and alternatives in order to feel significant.

Disclosure and identification of the child's private logic utilizes techniques that are more difficult and involved in their application. Exploration of the family constellation (see Chapter 7) and the individual's family atmosphere (see Chapter 6) provide information that allows us to sort out the uniqueness of the child and how he views and responds to life.

In conclusion, we would say that the recognition reflex and the teacher's own reaction to the child's misbehavior are the best guides to an understanding of the child's goal.

Finally, having identified and disclosed a child's goals, a teacher should never blame the child for his goals or refer to them during regular activities. Goals should be discussed only at the proper time, either in a personal talk or during a weekly group discussion.

REFERENCE

Dreikurs, Rudolf. In a television series, "Counseling the Adolescent," Neysa A. Peterson, ed. Burlington: University of Vermont, 1971.

SELECTED READINGS

Adler, Alfred. *Understanding Human Behavior.* New York: Fawcett, 1957.
Dreikurs, Rudolf. *Psychology in the Classroom.* New York: Harper & Row, 1968.
Dreikurs, Rudolf. "Private Logic" in Harold Mosak, ed., *Alfred Adler: His Influence on Psychology Today.* Parkridge, N.J.: Noyes Press, 1973.

Chapter 5

Changing the Child's Goals

In this chapter we will focus on the immediate corrective steps possible in a classroom situation. One must keep in mind that the response to the child's disturbance in the moment it occurs is only one aspect of corrective efforts. However, teachers need to develop skills of responding to the *immediate* problem in a constructive way. Most teachers, even the most experienced, feel at a loss when a child disturbs the class, defies her, refuses to cooperate, and so forth. Often what she does may do more harm than good, for if she is not familiar with the child's goal, she may unwittingly reinforce his erroneous behavior.

Because teachers often do not know what to do when a child provokes them, they either overlook the disturbance or scold or threaten the child. This may take care of the problem temporarily, but it rarely solves the problem.

An interesting study was conducted in Germany (Tausch, 1967). Forty-four teachers were observed in 51 periods, during which time the frequency of disturbances requiring the teacher's intervention and the kinds of interventions were studied.

It was found that on the average each teacher had to interrupt classroom procedures every 2½ minutes in order to take some corrective step and that 94 percent of all interventions were autocratic and ineffective. Only 6 percent of the interventions improved the situations. We would probably find a similar situation in the United States if such a study were to be conducted. From this study we can see how ineffective corrective methods are if we do not understand the purpose of the child's misbehavior.

The desire to belong is one of the basic needs of children. It is most painful and difficult to tolerate when any person, especially a child, assumes that he is worthless, inadequate, and unloved. As long as the child does not doubt his value and his place in the social group in which he lives and in which he moves, the child is bound to cooperate and to do whatever the situation demands, even when he does not like the task. However, if, for whatever reasons, the child feels that he is not valued, that others are preferred to him, or that he is not as capable as others or as adults expect him to be, the child becomes discouraged and often feels that he does not belong. Through the child's mistaken evaluation of the situation, he tries to find his place through behavior which often sets him in conflict with adults. The child may defy orders, resist learning, provoke the teacher to a point where teaching becomes impossible.

Attention Getting Devices

The teacher who is confronted with a child's provocation will, through her reaction, either reinforce or thwart it if she ignores the behavior. However, the question of ignoring the disturbing behavior poses a dilemma: will it be effective? Here is a typical example of how ignoring the child's disturbing behavior was sufficient for the child to discontinue it:

> After a workshop with the faculty, a teacher reported the perplexing effects of ignoring a child's behavior.
>
> In her kindergarten class she had one boy and one girl who always demanded special attention when the group sat in a circle for storytelling. The boy always flopped down on his belly, and she had to tell him to sit up, which he did, but not for long, and the girl always interrupted with silly questions.
>
> During the workshop she found out how children manipulate teachers with their demands for attention, and she got angry when she realized how the two children had manipulated her. She decided then and there that she would pay no more attention to the boy's antics and the girl's questions. And this is what she did. To her amazement, after a few unsuccessful attempts to annoy the teacher, the children stopped.

Ignoring the child's behavior may bring the desired result; however, in some cases the child continues his efforts. At this point, continuing to disregard the child's behavior may be inadvisable, since it disturbs the class atmosphere or the learning procedure and gives the child the green light to continue his behavior. We are not opposed to giving children attention. On the contrary, what we find harmful is giving children attention for negative behavior. The teacher needs to become sensitive to the child and to the situation in order to know when and what kind of attention she should give to the child in question. Each teacher should experiment and, depending on her own resourcefulness and temperament, establish her own technique. Often it suffices to call a child by name without further comment and just look at him (make eye contact). Humor helps. If a child whispers something to his neighbor in a disturbing way, the teacher can express her curiosity. This must be done without anger or annoyance, which is contrary to what the child expects of her. If a child disrupts the class through inattentiveness, it is a passive way of demanding attention. The teacher can ask the child's opinion about what has been said. In this way she draws the child's attention to the class procedure without scolding him about his inattentiveness. If a child clowns around, the teacher can stop and invite the class to watch him perform. This does not mean that the teacher is encouraging clowning; rather, it deprives him of his success in annoying the teacher. However, the purpose of clowning should be discussed with the entire class during a group discussion. The following are illustrations of how children seek attention.

When the class returned from recess, April remained in the hall. When the children brought this fact to the teacher's attention, she told them that this was April's choice and that the class should not spoil it for her.

After waiting a few minutes, April walked into the room, stood at the door long enough for all to see her, and then walked out again into the hall. She repeated this procedure several times. During all this time, the teacher went about her work, paying no attention to her.

April made a few entrances and exits and then returned to her seat and proceeded with her work. When the teacher passed her desk, she merely complimented her on her neat writing.

Adeline, a fourth-grade student, surprised and shocked the children in class because of the long, dangling earrings she was wearing. At first, the teacher decided to ignore this, hoping that the children would soon ignore it also. However, the children's subdued but excited noise continued. Everyone wanted to see and touch the earrings. The teacher then invited Adeline to come up to the front of the class, so that everyone could see her. She inquired where Adeline got the earrings and learned that they belonged to her older sister and that she had borrowed them without her sister's knowledge. The teacher suggested that after wearing the earrings for a while, and if Adeline wanted to, she would be glad to put them away for her in a safe place and return them when it was time to go home. After an hour, Adeline handed the earrings to the teacher.

Both of these incidents might have developed into major problems, taking up much of the teacher's time. These children's erroneous concepts of how they could receive attention would only have been fortified had the teacher made an issue out of them.

There is a principle that can be followed. A disturbing form of demanding attention can be turned into a constructive one, passive into active, until the child no longer feels the need to receive special attention in order to secure a place in the group. He can receive recognition for useful efforts and accomplishments, but until they are actually accomplished the teacher must be careful not to fall for his provocations. Any scolding, reprimanding, or threatening violates the principle of mutual respect and prevents problem solving, since it expresses warfare. It prevents the teacher from helping the child to overcome his feeling of inadequacy and to gain self-confidence about his place in the group, which is a prerequisite to his enjoyment in participating without concern for status.

Here is an important point of which few teachers are aware. A special bid for attention does not have to be made through disturbing behavior. Many children succeed in getting attention through constructive means. But there are others who study, not for the enjoyment of it, but for the recognition they receive. In many cases they are the teacher's pets. We caution the teacher not to fall for the child who makes no real contribution but who uses passive means such as charm and cuteness to get attention.

Ways to Handle Attention Getting Behavior

There are various techniques that the teacher can use effectively to handle attention getting behavior. What she uses will depend on the type of child she is dealing with and on the situation. What may work with one child may not work with another. What may be comfortable techniques for one teacher may be uncomfortable for another. We do not come with a bag of tricks but with suggestions that have been tested by the authors for more than 25 years. Our recommendations will provide the teacher with a frame of reference. Each teacher has to find her own approach within this frame of reference.

1. The teacher should discuss the goal with the child.
2. We suggest that the teacher reinforce positive behavior and ignore negative behavior. If she is consistent, the child after several unsuccessful attempts will start to associate attention with socially acceptable behavior. Teachers who complain that they use the technique of ignoring without success make the following mistake. They stand with their hands on their hips, look intensely at the child, tighten their mouths, narrow their eyes, or address themselves to the class group with statements such as, "Class we will be quiet until —— is ready and we can continue our lesson." In this way the child becomes the center of attention and he achieves his goal, even if the attention is of a negative nature. We suggest that the teacher should stop, remain calm and relaxed, and not look at the child. When he stops his misbehavior, the teacher may nod, thank him, and continue the lesson.
3. The teacher may address herself to the child and say, "——, could we work out a plan that would be satisfactory to you and to us? How many times do you wish to be noticed during this period or day?" (Coming to an agreement with the child.)
4. A child cannot possibly always disturb the class. The teacher will have to be alert and watch for opportunities conducive to giving the child

attention for positive behavior at such times. She may walk over to the child, pat him on the shoulder, and thank him for helping her to make the lesson enjoyable. It is advisable not to remind him of his usual behavior.

5. It may happen that a child may raise his hand but when the teacher attends to him his question may not pertain to the lesson or he may attempt to engage her in conversation. We suggest that the teacher merely walk away.

    Should the child and the teacher have an agreement and should he break the agreement, then we may be certain that this child is seeking not only attention but also power, and the teacher would have to respond to the child as she would to a child who is seeking power.

6. Sometimes the teacher can use logical consequences as explained in Chapter 12.

7. Although all these techniques may be effective at the moment, they do not help the child understand why it is so important for him to exhibit this disruptive behavior, and they do not allow for time to show him alternatives to being noticed and appreciated. This is handled through *group discussions* (see Chapter 14), where the teacher may not necessarily discuss the child's behavior but the purpose of such behavior in general. The topic of such a discussion might center around, "Why is it so important for some people to interrupt a lesson and disturb?" Although the child is not discussed personally, he learns vicariously.

Seeking Power

If it is difficult to resist the child's provocation when he seeks attention, it is even more difficult for the teacher to restrain herself when he strives for power. An ever growing number of children defy the teacher, both in their behavior and in their refusal to learn, and very few teachers are able to cope with them. Many teachers are not prepared personally or emotionally to stay out of a power struggle with a child who threatens their authority and prestige. They are too deeply steeped in an autocratic educational tradition that prescribes that teachers must show the children that their behavior will not be tolerated.

Teachers may be surprised to read that a teacher does not have to fight with a child, but neither does she have to give in to a child. Not yielding to the child's demands does not preclude fighting. The teacher may say, "I'm sorry you feel unhappy, but we cannot allow you to continue with this behavior, or, "Yes, life is tough but you force me to. . . ." There are times when it is advisable to admit to a power seeking child: "You are right, I cannot make you." Teachers do not lose in status if they openly make such an admission.

It can be seen that to resist a child who wants to force us into a power struggle is not easy. It is obvious that some teachers will have greater difficulty with such children. One teacher accepts the challenge, fights back, and is defeated again and again; another remains calm and composed and eventually wins the child's cooperation.

We cannot demand changes from the child as long as we are determined to fight it out, which, in a sense, is a subconscious agreement to fight.

The degree of a child's rebellion is usually in direct proportion to the degree of autocratic imposition: both parties are alike and equal in their destructive endeavors. It is almost comical when one compares the complaints of teachers about their students and the complaints of students about their teachers. Each one sees what the other one is doing wrong, and neither one has any idea of what to do about it, as shown in the following examples.

A teacher kept a child after school so that he could finish his assignment. While he was doing his work, she was working at her own desk. The child worked very diligently. The following exchange took place.

TEACHER: I can't understand why you are so mean to me during class hours and so nice when everyone has gone.

CHILD: Funny that you should say that. I was just thinking the same thing of you.

During a music lesson, while the teacher was trying to demonstrate the rhythm of a song, Joel took out two pencils and proceeded to drum with them on a book. The teacher stopped playing and demanded to know who was drumming. No reply came forth, so she resumed her playing. At that very instant, the drumming started again. The teacher, who had been on the alert, caught Joel in the act. She scolded him and asked him to put his pencils in his desk. Joel made no move to obey her order. She asked once more. This time Joel put his elbows on his desk, grinned, and held up the pencils for all to see. In a rage, the teacher snatched the pencils, threw them on his desk, and demanded that he wipe the grin off his face. Everyone watched the spectacle with tenseness and expectation. Joel continued to grin. Once more the teacher ordered him to stop grinning. She threatened to take him to the principal if he continued to be disobedient. Since he showed no inclination to change his behavior, she took a firm hold of his arm and tried to pull him out of his seat, demanding that he come with her to the principal. Joel stiffened and resisted. A tug-of-war began between the teacher and the boy.

In this incident the situation might have been handled as one of minor significance, but it turned into a major episode because of the teacher's inability to understand Joel's behavior and because of her incompetence in handling him. The skillful teacher would have had very little trouble with Joel. She would have handled this episode successfully using any of the following techniques.

1. The teacher might have asked Joel if he would demonstrate the rhythm by using his pencils as drumsticks. And she could have suggested that he use the real drum that she kept in a closet.
2. She might have suggested that he beat the rhythm right along with her— she on the piano and he on the drum or with his pencils.
3. She could have suggested that they alternate—he on the drum and she with the pencils.

An unexpected and friendly reaction might have taken all the enjoyment out of the satisfaction Joel derived from defying the teacher. He might have been quite satisfied with the attention of the teacher and the class.

What else could the teacher have done? She might have reminded Joel of a previous conversation in which he had agreed to the idea that everyone should have the same rights and privileges in class and asked, "Are you changing your mind about this? You see, by disturbing the class you are infringing on our rights—mine to teach and the students to learn. You are welcome to join us whenever you are ready to be part of the group." The teacher could stop the lesson and tell the class, "It will depend on Joel what we will do. I will not continue with the lesson as long as he disturbs this class." The teacher should then wait, remaining calm, and continue her lesson when everyone quiets down. She should nod to Joel and give him some sign of appreciation when he complies. In most cases, children who challenge the teacher, as Joel did, give up the provocation when the teacher does not get into a power contest with them. It may happen that a power seeking child will continue the disturbance throughout the lesson, but rarely does such a child resume this kind of behavior during the next lesson.

The teacher may use another approach and appeal to the entire class. She may say:

"Boys and girls, I'm powerless. I'd like to continue with my lesson but I can't. You may be more successful in handling this situation than I. I'm going to leave it to you. I'll be waiting while you discuss this problem. I will wait at my desk until the class has decided to continue with the lesson. You may discuss this amongst yourselves, if you wish, and when you decide to go on with the lesson, let me know about it."

If the class is trained in handling their own problems, it rarely happens that bedlam breaks loose if the teacher allows the class to handle problems and the teacher withdraws.

By withdrawing from the provocation, the teacher automatically takes all the fun out of Joel's play. By handing the problem over to the class, she makes the children aware that this is everybody's problem and that all share in the responsibility of solving it.

Some teachers will argue that this procedure might give Joel a sense of victory. Such an argument only confirms the theory that often teachers are more concerned with their prestige than with the need to train children to understand the cause and effect of behavior as well as the power that a group has over the individual. The more the teacher is concerned with her own need to show the child who is in command, the more the child will resist. In the end, the teacher is usually the loser.

The power struggle between the teacher and the student can take many forms. Very often children look down at the teacher, for whatever reason, in order to show their superiority. This is difficult for the teacher to tolerate, since she is supposed to be superior. Here is an interesting example.

Chip, a senior in high school, tries to outsmart every adult with whom he comes in contact. His need to feel superior is so strong that he spends hours plotting how he can achieve this goal. He goes to the library to look up definitions and trivial information and then confronts the teacher with questions such as, "What kind of dress did Josephine wear when she married Napoleon?" The teacher probably cannot answer this question, so Chip proceeds with his information and proves his superiority to the whole class. He shows his power also by refusing to spell correctly because he feels that no one has the right to tell him that a word must be spelled in just one way. He argues that somebody made up the spelling once upon a time and has no right to impose it on others. He, Chip, has just as much right to make up his own spelling of words.

Here the rejection of rules and order is preposterous; even more ludicrous is his way of demonstrating his superiority to the teacher. Any effort to reason with him is hopeless, as he will outsmart anybody intellectually. The only way of dealing with him is by making him aware of his exaggerated need to be superior and to acknowledge his success. There would be little pleasure left for him in trying so hard to prove a superiority that is not contested. More important, however, is his form of justification for not accepting order, that is, the rules of spelling. This is a more serious problem because many children and adults alike assume that democracy means everybody can do what he wants. This is not democracy but anarchy, and out of such a perspective comes the anarchy found in many classrooms. This is a test of the teacher's ability to withstand powerful pressure, be it in action or words. She has to acknowledge the right of her students to participate in setting rules, as far as the situation permits, but she also has to lead them to recognize the limitations of reality. Such discussions can have a considerable effect in shaping the value system on which the children operate. This can be done only when the teacher refuses to be drawn into a power struggle.

Other Ways to Handle the Power Seeking Child

We suggest the following:

1. Disclose the goal (see Chapter 4).

2. The cardinal rule is to avoid a power struggle. The teacher can admit her defeat openly by saying, "Could it be that you want to show me that I can't make you do your assignment? If so, you are right. I can't make you." This kind of reaction is not desired or expected by the child. While he may continue in his stubbornness, the teacher's reaction takes all the pleasure out of his attempt "to force her." There is no sense in challenging an authority who does not feel challenged!

3. Should the child persist in his provocation, the teacher may remind him of a previous discussion in which he agreed that everyone in the class should have the same rights (see Chapter 14) and may say, "Let us find a way in which each of us can have his own rights. You want to hum; I want to teach; the rest of us want to work. I have no right to force you to work, nor do you have the right to force us not to work. You have a choice to remain in your seat without disturbing the class or to go to the back of the room (or any other designated place) where we will not disturb you. You may return to your seat whenever you decide to respect our rights."

4. As with the child who seeks attention, the teacher should watch for opportunities that will encourage this child to be more cooperative. Anytime the child participates in class activity without challenging the teacher into a power conflict the teacher may show pleasure and pride in the child's progress. She may say, "You should be pleased with yourself and proud that you were a part of the group and participated in the class activities. I know what a hard decision this was for you, but you did it!" This is positive reinforcement.

5. Doing the unexpected is often extremely effective, because it takes the "teachers sail out of the child's wind." In other words, the child can blow as much as he wants to, but with no sail, he can go nowhere.

The teacher must consider her immediate emotional reaction to the child's provocation and then do the exact opposite of what she feels or wants (see Chapter 3). This puts the child off balance because the teacher's behavior is not what the child expected.

6. We experienced that the application of logical consequences is not always effective with children who are in an intense power conflict and who are rebellious. With such children, the teacher must change the relationship before she can apply logical consequences effectively (see Chapter 12).

7. We should like to make the reader aware that these suggestions serve only for the moment. Ultimate help comes through group discussions.

Seeking Revenge

Desire for power and for revenge can easily overlap. If a child is convinced that he has the right to do whatever he pleases and that anyone who tries to stop him is his enemy, he may decide on revenge. This is more probable if the teacher has responded to his bid for power by punishment, for then the child will use punitive retaliation. Such a child is almost inaccessible to reasoning with him. Convinced that he is hopelessly disliked and has no chance within the group, he responds with deep distrust to any effort to convince him otherwise. The teacher is exposed to all kinds of well-designed provocations, which make it difficult for her to convince the child that he is worthwhile and can be liked.

In such a situation, the class as a group can be a great help, but it also can be a dangerous accomplice. Some pupils will eagerly identify with the teacher in a consolidated front against the troublemaker. Too often, the teacher accepts this alliance because of her own sense of failure in dealing with such provocations. In this way, the attitudes of the good students aggravate the problem instead of solving it, for they add to the child's feelings of isolation and to his desire to retaliate or to get even.

Can the teacher treat the revengeful child with respect? Teachers have great difficulty showing respect for a child who challenges their authority in an insulting way. However, if the teacher accepts the premise that problems should be solved on the basis of mutual respect, she is bound to get better results. Readers may question the idea of mutual respect and understandably so, but the chances of winning the child and gaining his respect are much greater when the teacher refrains from retaliation. The following example will illustrate this point.

> Eleven-year-old Daryl handed his assignment to the teacher. The paper was dirty and greasy. The teacher told him that she would gladly check his paper if he were to rewrite it on a clean sheet of paper. Daryl became very angry and said that he would not do it. The teacher told him that she would leave this up to him. At this, he called her "a mean old witch," and ran out of the room. All the children's eyes were glued on the teacher, wondering what she would do. She continued with her lesson. Every few minutes Daryl would stick his head in the door and call out some provocative remarks. The teacher ignored them. During lunchtime, when all the children had left and the teacher sat at her desk correcting papers, she noticed someone standing at her side. It was Daryl. She greeted him with, "Hi, Daryl. Can I do something for you? Have you had your lunch already?" Daryl literally threw himself on her chest, sobbing, "I'm sorry, I'm sorry." The teacher told him to forget what happened, that she was glad that they were friends, and that she hoped to see him in class in the afternoon. Daryl rewrote his paper the moment he returned to class, and handed it to the teacher.

From this example, we can see how a child may react if we ignore his provocation. In the case of Daryl, he was won over by this teacher. How differently this incident and the relationship between student and teacher might have turned out if the teacher had been overly concerned with her prestige, had made a case out of the incident, and had seen to it that Daryl was punished for what he did.

One pitfall for the well-meaning teacher is to treat the revengeful child with preference in order to show him that he can be liked and appreciated. In this way, she may exert a good influence on him but at tremendous expense. She intensifies the rift with the rest of the children, who resent such preferential treatment, and she makes it impossible for any other teacher to be acceptable to him unless she too gives him special attention.

The teacher can solicit the help of a pupil, preferably one who is highly esteemed by the class, to take special interest in the outcast, drawing him into the group and demonstrating appreciation. In this way, it is often possible to build a bridge across the hateful and fearful barrier that the child has erected between himself and society. A sociogram may often help to produce better relationships (see Chapter 13). Teachers and children need to give each other moral support in this endeavor so that they will not become discouraged. The antagonism a revengeful child shows in the face of friendliness and kindness is understandable, but it is difficult to withstand. To convince a child that you want to be his friend when he is convinced that he cannot trust anyone requires fortitude and persistence. Often, in the moment when the teacher believes she has gained the child's confidence he puts her to a test in the most outrageous manner, as Chip did (and as shown in the following example).

Jacque, age 10, was probably the most selfish and meanest child the teacher had ever encountered. He did not physically abuse other children. He was too much of a coward for that. But he played nasty tricks on children—tricks that hurt them physically. For instance, he would offer a child a piece of candy that was filled with hot chili pepper and then laugh hysterically when the child bit into it and gasped. He would double up with laughter when a child would open a box that Jacque had given him and would be scared to death when a mouse jumped out. He called the children nasty names and often insulted their parents. The children did not like him, and they made no bones about it.

Jacque was born out of wedlock, and his grandparents brought him up. Jacque was aware of this, and he was very bitter about it. He was also aware that the children did not like him, and he often expressed his feelings about this. His usual way of dealing with this problem was by saying, "Nobody likes me, but wait and see. I will make the kids like me even if I have to kill them first."

In order for Jacque to feel better about himself, it was important that he should experience acceptance by the group, considering the kind of boy he was. This was slowly achieved through group discussions, and when the students began to understand Jacque and his behavior, they started to show concern.

When Jacque had to go to the hospital for an operation, the students felt that they had a chance to show him that he was important to them. They arranged that each day two students would go visit him. They also called him on the telephone. When he returned to the class they gave him a big welcome, with a party and a present. When they called on him to make a speech, he was all choked up. He said, "I know that I have not been very nice to you. I always thought that you hated me. But now I see how wrong I was. I never had any friends, but now I do. I know that I do. Wait until my grandma hears about this. She won't believe it." This was the start of a change in Jacque.

Children who pursue goals of attention or power are usually not aware of the purpose for their behavior, whereas children who feel hurt and disliked are often very much aware of their aims. They do not know, however, that they view almost every situation with suspicion and the conviction that they will, again, be the victims. They always feel unfairly treated. They disregard experiences pointing to the contrary, and they do not know that they provoke the experiences to which they respond with hostility. In provoking others to abuse them, they display a kind of moral superiority, looking down on those who are wrong and who, by their actions, are responsible for their own misbehavior. Then they become firmly convinced that they are right in their convictions and justified in their retaliation. These are psychological factors that the teacher can and should discuss with her class.

Ways to Help a Revengeful Child

We make the following suggestions to the teacher:

1. She must confront him with his goal (see Chapter 4).
2. She must also discuss with him a number of situations in which he provoked others to test their acceptance of him and point out that he has many good qualities that he ignores and that he rarely uses to make himself likeable.
3. She may appeal to him to experiment and to agree not to provoke anyone for a determined length of time in order to find out if others can like him or not.
4. She may also assure him that she empathizes with his feelings, that she is sincerely concerned about him, and that she will help him wherever possible.
5. Although we empathize with a teacher in a difficult situation, especially when she feels defeated by the child, we cannot emphasize enough the danger of retaliation.
6. As in other situations, we can help this child best through group discussions, encouragement, and group acceptance.

Displaying Inadequacy

Overcoming a child's discouragement is the most common and urgent task for the teacher. In almost all poor performances, be they academic or social, the child expresses discouragement.

An assumed or real disability or inadequacy is used by the child to protect himself against the demands of life. The child employs a cloak of inadequacy in order to be left alone. This behavior may characterize all actions of the child or it may only appear in situations in which he feels deficient and wants to avoid certain activities.

Many times a teacher gives up easily when her first few attempts in trying a new technique ends in failure. So it is with children who are having difficulty socially and academically.

Children who are extremely discouraged, defeated, and have assumed the role of "a blob" usually operate from four premises:

1. overambition—cannot do as well as he wants to
2. competition—cannot do as well as others
3. pressure—does not do as well as he ought to
4. failure—is convinced that he will fail.

Overambition

Overambition is perhaps the most frequent cause for giving up. The desire to be superior may bring about despair, so that the child sees no chance to be as good as he wants to be. The feeling of personal superiority sooner or later gives way to lack of courage. If he cannot be first, have the best grades, be his mother's favorite child, be the leader of the group, or be the homecoming queen or the football hero, he will reach the point of giving up and will refuse to put forth any effort.

> Joe, a junior in high school, did not work. When the counselor discussed this with him, Joe said, "I am never going to make the honor roll, so what's the use? You've either got it, or you don't. Well, I guess, I don't."

The child who assumes disability because of his overambition will not participate in an activity that does not provide him with the opportunity to prove his superiority. For this reason, many teachers find it difficult to accept a psychological interpretation of overambition in a child who does not try at all. The only way to help such a child is by making him aware of how he defeats himself, specifically labeling his actions.

Competition

The *competitive child* is convinced that he has no chance to do as well as others. This child has always been impressed with the fact that he is not good enough and has always been pushed to do better. Teachers and parents, in trying to motivate the competitive child, constantly say defeating things such as, "When I had your sister in my room, she was an A student" and "Why don't you get higher marks, like Mary?"

Some children may respond by withdrawing because they are actually unable to keep up with others. The sense of being inferior to others and the conviction of not being good enough bears no relation to the child's actual ability.

Pressure

The *pressured child* who is constantly criticized by parents and teachers feels that whatever he does is not as good as others think it should be. Passing a course or making a B is not enough for some teachers and parents. They often make defeating and discouraging remarks. Some teachers also discourage the pressured child at a nonverbal level. Their facial expressions and shrugs are as defeating as their remarks.

Teachers need to convey to the child that he is good enough just as he is. They need to remove the pressure by being less critical, less fault-finding, and less picky. They need to give the child time to solve problems and to perform at his own speed. They need to allow time for the child to learn a skill so that he can improve his rate of performance.

Our present educational system, which emphasizes mistakes and tries to motivate children through criticism and competition, makes it difficult to encourage the children who need it the most. The technique of encouragement that the teacher has to learn is discussed in Chapter 11. It may be difficult for the teacher, but it is essential to her corrective ability that she watch for every critical, condemning, disapproving, and impatient sign in her reactions. The difficulty lies in the fact that the discouraged child is prone to impart a conviction of inadequacy to the teacher. This conviction of inadequacy must be met with methods that will not perpetuate or increase it. To avoid this, the teacher must be aware of her contribution to the deterioration of the child's ability. Recent studies have shown the tremendous influence exerted by the expectations of the teachers about a given child.

Failure

Failure is probably the most discouraging experience for any person. In most cases the child perceives the true meaning of failure only after the end of kindergarten, when all the other children are promoted to first grade and he is retained. Prior to that time, a child may be aware that he can't do things as well as other children, but he does not connect this with failure. Once the child fails, he almost always begins to doubt his ability. Furthermore, students who fail instill in their teacher the expectation that they will fail again, which in turn confirms the student's doubt in his ability and hinders his progress.

Other Ways to Correct Feelings of Inadequacy

We make the following suggestions:

1. Disclose the child's goal (see Chapter 4).
2. Help the child realize that he will never know his true capacity without trying.
3. Tell him that if he tries to do the work and indeed cannot, then the teacher and the students will show him the areas in which he needs help and they will help him.
4. Find activities in which he will succeed. Never give this child the kind of work that is bound to result in failure.
5. Since this child is usually ignored or forgotten by the others, the teacher needs the assistance of the group to help her in the process of encouragement.
6. Through group discussions the children will develop understanding, empathy, and a sense of responsibility to these children.

Teachers have to learn to recognize these goals, first by mere observation and later by discovering the child's movements toward one of the four goals. See Table 5–1.

Table 5–1   Child's Reaction to Reprimand and Some Corrective Measures

Goal	Child's Reaction to Reprimand	Corrective Measures from Teacher
Attention	Stops disturbing behavior for a while but then starts all over again	Disclose the goal to the child Stop and wait until the child realizes that he will get no other attention and give up his behavior
	May feel satisfied and stop disturbing	
	May realize the absurdity of his behavior and give it up	Ask child how often he would like to disturb during this session and come to an agreement Watch for a moment when child does not disturb and show appreciation

Table 5–1 Continued

Goal	Child's Reaction to Reprimand	Corrective Measures from Teacher
		Consider what you would like to do and do the opposite
		Discuss the purpose of disturbing a class during group discussions
		Give child positive attention
Power	May resent it and intensify his disturbing behavior	Do not get involved in a power struggle
	Is determined to show that he is the boss and will do what he wants	Disclose the goal to the child
		Agree that you cannot "make" him behave
	May overtly or covertly demand of the teacher "What can you do about it?"	Appeal to the child for his help
		Refer to his agreement that all have equal rights, and that you want and must teach, while he may continue his behavior in the back of the room or any other place
		(Find discussion on Equal Rights in Chapter 14)
		Discuss this with the group
Revenge	Child wants to get even for the hurt he experienced from others.	Disclose goal
	May become worse	Avoid retaliation
	May accuse teacher that she doesn't like him	Help child see that his conviction that nobody likes him prompts him to test people in an obnoxious way
	May threaten to do horrible things	He can then feel justified in his feelings because the others will not respond kindly to his provocations
	May run out of the classroom and disappear	
	May use foul language and become abusive	Discuss this with the group. Elicit from the students statements of any positive qualities in this child
Inadequacy	There may be no reaction from the child	Disclose goal
	Child may insist that he can't do what the teacher requires of him	Confront the child with his convictions that he is incapable of doing anything right without having given himself a chance to find out if he is right or wrong
	The child may withdraw even more	
		Assure the child that he is wanted and needed and that you are there to help him. Do not give up on the child

REFERENCE

Tausch, Anne-Marie. Besonere Erziehungssituationen des praktischen Schulun-
terrichtes, Haufickeit, Veranlassung und Art ihrer Losunger Durch Lehrer,
Zt. f. Exper. und angew. *Psychologie*. Band V/ 4, Verlag F. Psychologie
Goettingen, 1967.

Chapter 6
The Family Atmosphere

The concept of the family atmosphere originated with the work of Alfred Adler. It was Dreikurs, however, who specifically formulated it into a workable framework for use by parents, teachers, and counselors. Dreikurs noted that if the family atmosphere is strongly opposed to the general demands of society, children may experience difficulties in school and in life.

In the family the child learns the interactional patterns that operate among family members—the hardships, the conflicts, the frictions, the competition, and the alliances. It is in this atmosphere that the child is exposed to the competencies or the lack of them to solve these conflicts.

The relationships of the parents is like an umbrella over other members of the family. The family atmosphere is created mainly by them. It is usually established before the birth of their first child. The atmosphere they create becomes the testing ground for the child's interactions and transactions. The attitudes of the parents, their character traits, and the general quality of their marital relationship have a great impact on the family atmosphere.

The Role of the Parents

The parents are the first and major sex identity models for their children. They influence their children's attitudes toward social living, race, color, religion, politics, and material values. We suggest that the family is the intermediary between the culture and their children. They provide the medium for the establishment of a value system that influences each member of the household. If the parents compete with each other, the child is bound to become competitive himself in every situation. Children who compete are basically not sure of their places and are worried that someone may overtake them and push them out of their favorite position. They live in constant dread.

When parents openly show preference for one of their children and if they convey to another child that he is a disappointment to them, it may leave permanent scars on this child. There is nothing as painful to a child as the conviction that a sibling is preferred and more loved than he is.

Today's parents need guidance to understand why they often have difficulties with their children. They need direction in how to be effective in winning and influencing their children. Without this help few parents realize that the kind of relationship they have with their children and the kind of home atmosphere they create strongly influence the child's personality development. Without this guidance parents are bound to remain unaware of how they, unwittingly, and with their best intentions, have made it possible for the child to become what he is.

We must also take into account not only what the parents are doing but also what the child is doing in order to understand the interaction between the two and their relationship. Because of erroneous conclusions, the child often induces the parents to react as they do, convinced that this kind of behavior will help him realize his goal. Whatever the child and his parents do is based on perfect communication. This is illustrated by the following example.

> George was jabbing his fork into the tablecloth as he was eating his dinner. His mother asked him to stop, and she threatened him with punishment. He paid no heed to her. Finally, she took the fork out of his hand and then slapped his hand.
>
> When this incident was discussed with George he was asked if he knew what his mother might do to him. He replied with glee in his eyes, "This is her best tablecloth. She never uses it unless we have company." Although he gave no direct answer of "yes" or "no," it was obvious from his reply that he knew exactly how his mother felt and what might happen. There was perfect communication between the two, for each one sent out a very direct message.

Love

Many parents believe that giving in to a child is an expression of love and that feeling loved will make the child secure in life. No one will argue with the importance of giving love to a child, but we may argue about what constitutes real love. When we truly love someone, we must be ready to make emotional sacrifices if they are for the good of the other person. If we love the child, we may have to let the child cry if he demands unjustified service or unnecessary things, or we may have to forego a visit with friends and return home when the child acts up in the car.

Children sense their parents' dependency on their love and they exploit this mercilessly. They often demand over and over again, "Do you love me?" or, if they cannot get what they want, they threaten with, "I don't love you." If parents have to spend so much time reassuring their child that they love him, and if they are so afraid that the child may feel unloved unless they give in to his demands, then we question their love. These parents contribute to the child's use of emotional blackmail in order to get what he wants.

In homes where there is mutual respect and consideration, children are bound to feel secure in their parents' love and rarely resort to threats and emotional blackmail.

Pampering and Spoiling

Pampered and spoiled children are the least prepared to meet life's demands. Pampering and spoiling takes on a number of forms, and each of these has a very definite impact on the child.

There are four definite kinds of pampering and spoiling:

1. overindulgence
2. overpermissiveness
3. overdomination
4. overprotection.

Whereas they may resemble one another and overlap in their application, they each send out very special messages to the child.

Overindulgence

In this category belongs the child to whom everything is given. All the child has to do is demand or, if the parents deny his wishes, throw a tantrum and then he gets what he wants. This child demands to be the center of attention in the family.

Giving children too many things has many pitfalls and dangers. The child may start measuring his worth by the number of things that he gets; he may associate getting with being loved and being important. Once the child has been brought up to feel entitled to get whatever he wants, he may feel threatened in the relationship when the parents do not let him have what he wants. But more devastating is the child's "gimmee" attitude and his expectations that adults always have to bring him something without having to give anything in return. From our experiences, we have found that the overindulged child often displays symptoms of anger, discontent, disorderliness, unwillingness to go to school, and in some cases even enuresis.

Overpermissiveness

The child who is brought up in an overpermissive home is given the right to do as he pleases with complete disregard of how it affects others. This is the result of a psychology that advocates the importance of letting children express themselves and of not exposing them to frustration. These children show no concern for other people's time or discomfort; they put their parents, their teachers, and often their older siblings into their services. They leave their things all over, expecting somebody to pick them up. Someone usually does, perhaps with a fight, but the adults comply.

We have found that many children who grew up in a permissive home have learned how to get out of unpleasant situations and how to protect themselves by setting up excuses in advance: "My teacher doesn't like me; that's the reason I got a bad grade." "I couldn't help it, I could not hear what mother said. I was in another room." "I was absent on the day the teacher explained this lesson." What happens to them is never their fault but always someone else's fault. Often these are tyrannical children. They tyrannize through charm or intimidation. These children are mostly interested in "right now" and are not concerned with consequences.

Overdomination

These parents do not give the child an opportunity to make mistakes and to learn from them because they make all decisions for the child on the assumption that they are for his own good: "Read your Social Studies book instead of wasting time on that stupid comic strip." "Don't play with Susan. I would rather you would play with Helen. She is more your type." They tell their children what to do with their allowances; how much to spend and on what, and how much to save and for what. These children cannot take a step without an adult's directions.

These children do not develop confidence in their own judgment, and when they have to depend on themselves, they can never make up their mind what to do. Even when they take an examination they often do poorly because they are afraid to make a decision; often they leave many questions unanswered. Children who come from overdomineering homes also may become rebels and defy their parents openly or covertly.

Overprotection

Overprotection and overdomination are somewhat related, but on closer examination we can observe quite different patterns of pampering. While the overdomineering parent instills in the child a fear of using his own judgment, the overprotective parent instills in the child a fear of life. The overprotective parent overestimates possible dangers and, therefore, constantly points them out to the child: "Do not run or you may fall; do not venture away from home for more than a block, because you may get lost; chew your food or you may choke; don't play with the big kids because they are tough and may hurt you." They often do not allow their children to participate in school excursions because they fear that the bus may have an accident. They keep the child home at the slightest sniffle or when the weather is mildly bad. Some parents manage to get their children excused from gymnastics (especially the girls) because the exercises are too strenuous. These children often do not have normal social contact with other children. They are often lonely and become overly dependent on the company of their parents.

We have children who are brought up in homes where they are not pampered and spoiled but dictated to. They grow up with "the boss."

Authoritarian Atmosphere

In an authoritarian home atmosphere the parents resort to pressure and to autocratic means to bring up their children. These parents demand, "Do as I say or else." If the child questions the reasons for their parents' demands, the parents usually reply, "Because I say so."

Some people argue that children who are brought up in an authoritarian atmosphere do what the parents expect of them. This is often true, but such obedience is due to fear and not to cooperation. Adults mistake this kind of obedience with cooperation. Others do not care why the children obey as long as they do.

Overdomineering upbringing is often confused with autocratic unbringing. On closer examination we see that the two are not synonymous. The overdomineering parent takes over for the child because of overambition for him, while the autocratic parent instills fear into the child because he refuses to relinquish power. Such a parent is more concerned with the control he exercises over the child than with the consequences it may have on the child. If the child resents this control, the parent argues that the child will outgrow this stage. Often they actually admit that they are not concerned with how the child feels and that the children's feelings must not be taken seriously.

The autocratic upbringing does not prepare children to function well in a democratic society. These children rarely develop a sense of self-reliance; they have to be controlled and watched all the time. If they are left to their own devices, they go wild. Although some children obey on the surface, there are others who resent the parents' or teachers' efforts to control them and they refuse to obey their commands. They rebel and often become serious delinquents. This is their way of getting even with controlling adults. They quite often lack creativity, spontaneity, and resourcefulness.

Our contention is that children function better if they are brought up in an atmosphere of mutual respect and consideration. Children need leadership, yes, but good leadership, which guides and influences them to be concerned with others and to do whatever a situation demands. Proper behavior must be stimulated. It must be won; it can never be forced.

Other family influences, which have been described by Dewey (1971) include: perfectionism, pity, a punitive atmosphere, inconsistency, and suppression of feelings.

Perfectionism and High Standards

There are parents who have such high standards that they withhold acceptance of anything that is not at the highest level. Children of such parents feel discouraged when they have failed to live up to their parents' expectations regardless of their accomplishment. They may feel a constant need for *total* success.

Pity

Pity is most discouraging because it conveys to the child that he is hopeless. The child may then feel sorry for himself, perceive life as unfair, and expect privileges. This gives him the excuse for inactivity and nonparticipation. He may view himself as a victim of people and of circumstances.

Punitive Atmosphere

The child who lives in a punitive atmosphere may develop a revengeful attitude toward his parents and others. The child also may develop a punitive attitude toward those who are smaller or younger.

Inconsistency

When parents vacillate from one decision to another, discipline becomes erratic or nonexistent. The child, not knowing what is expected of him or what to expect from others, may become unstable and lacking in self-control or motivation.

Suppression of Feelings

Parents who do not express their feelings or do not allow the child to express honest thoughts or feelings may force the child to either lie to them or to "put up a front" in order to avoid frequent reprimands. This child often puts distance between himself and others, avoids close relationships, has difficulty with intimate relationships, and often escapes into daydreaming.

Family Atmosphere and the Child's Attitude Toward School

The school is the second group in which the child has to function. In a sense, it is an extension of his home in terms of social living; it stands between home and society. The school provides the opportunity to change many of the influences made by the parents, assuming that the teachers are trained to motivate both parents and their children to change. Many teachers make the same mistakes that the parents are making and only reinforce the child's erroneous conception of how he must behave in order to secure a place in the group.

Parents who have helped the child develop self-reliance and social interest will rarely have difficulties when the child is of school age. There is a direct correlation between the family atmosphere and how children are treated at home and the problems they encounter in school.

REFERENCE

Dewey, Edith. "The Family Atmosphere" in Arthur Nikelly, *Techniques for Behavior Change*. Springfield, Ill.: Charles E. Thomas, 1971.

Chapter 7

The Family Constellation

A different approach to understanding a child's behavior in the classroom is through a study of the characteristics of the family constellation. The relationships that the child forms within the family contribute greatly to his personality development and to his transactions in the world outside the family. In the family each child develops his frame of reference through which he perceives, interprets, and evaluates the world. The knowledge, habits, and skills that he acquires in the home determine his capacity for dealing successfully with all life situations. We shall concern ourselves here with what happens to the child in the family—the opportunities and the barriers, and the challenges and the expectations that are influenced by his position of birth and by his individual relationships with all other members of the family. These insights can aid the parent or teacher in understanding the child's goals and convictions.

Personality and character traits are expressions of movement within the family group; they indicate the means by which a child tries to find his place within the family. They cannot be fully explained by either heredity, psychosexual development, past traumatic experiences, or other environmental stimulations. The concept of the family constellation as a dynamic force affecting the child's development must be understood as the result, not so much of factors that converge on the child, but of his own interactions. He influences other members of the family as much as he is influenced by them and in many respects even more, because his own concept forces them to treat him the way he expects to be treated. Each child in his early relationships with other members of the family establishes his own approach to others in his effort to gain a place in the group. All his strivings are directed towards achieving or maintaining a feeling of security, a sense of belonging, and a certainty that the difficulties of life will be overcome and that he will emerge safely and victoriously. He cultivates those qualities by which he hopes to achieve significance or even a degree of power and superiority in the family constellation.

Human beings often react differently in the same situation. No two children born into the same family grow up in the same atmosphere. The family environment that surrounds each individual child varies. The environment of each child within the same family may be different for several reasons.

With the birth of each child the situation changes. The parents may become older and more experienced or more discouraged if they have had difficulties with their first child. During each child's formative years the financial situation of the family may have changed, the parents may have moved to another neighborhood or city or even country, or their marital status may have changed. These and other possibilities may affect one or the other. A sickly or crippled child, a child born just before or after the death of another, an only boy among girls, an only girl among boys, an obvious physical characteristic, an older person living in the home, or the favoritism of the parents toward a child—all these may have a profound effect on the child's environment.

Although there are children who are happy in their ordinal position, there are others who are not. How they feel will depend on the conclusions they draw from their experiences and their interpretation of them.

In the life pattern of every child there is the imprint of his position in the family, which has definite characteristics. It is upon this one fact—the child's subjective impression of his place within the family constellation—that much of his future attitude toward life depends.

The Only Child

The only child has a decidedly difficult start in life, since he spends his entire childhood among persons who are more proficient. He may try to develop skills that will gain approval of the adult world, or he may solicit their sympathy by being shy, timid, or helpless. He usually measures himself by adult standards and often has high aspirations. (A majority of the astronauts were either only children or firstborn sons.)

Parents who wanted more than one child but could not have more may create a close, overprotective, constricting relationship with their child. On the other hand, if the parents did not want their child, they may be cold, unemotional, or they may feel guilty and act overly concerned in order to hide their true feelings. An only child may have trouble relating to his peers and may have problems later in life. The following characteristics are sometimes found in an only child.

1. The child is often pampered and enjoys his position as the center of interest.
2. The child may become self-centered.
3. If the child has a relationship that is too close with the parent of the opposite sex, it may create discord in the family relationship.
4. The child may feel insecure because of the anxiety of his parents who often remind him that "you're all we have."
5. If his parents are overindulgent he may feel unfairly treated and refuse to cooperate if his requests are not granted.
6. The child may be too adult centered and, therefore, may have difficulty in relating to his peers.
7. The child usually accepts the values of his parents.
8. The child is often conservative and serious.
9. The child is often highly ambitious and achievement oriented.

The Firstborn Child

The first child has a precarious position in life. Being the oldest should entitle him to the favored spot and frequently does. The firstborn is quite often the parents' most wanted child. He represents their dreams and ambitions. He may become discouraged upon the birth of the second child and refuse to accept responsibility, but in general he tends to be responsible It has been noted that more firstborns are finalists for the National Merit Scholarships and are usually overrepresented in *Who's Who*. The firstborn child may lack personal security because he measures himself against adult levels of accomplishment. He may not hold up well under stress and turn to others for support. Like the only child, he may be the most serious, the most conservative, and the most fearful of change. In order to understand the firstborn child, it may help us to consider the following points:

1. This child was an only child for a period of time and during that time has had the undivided attention of his parents.
2. As a firstborn, this child feels threatened by the advance of the sibling that follows him. He must maintain the position of being "first," in the sense of holding superiority over any other children.
3. With the birth of a second child, a firstborn, having been an only child, now becomes a "dethroned" child. He may draw the conclusion that now his parents do not love him as much as they did before and that they now neglect him because they are so preoccupied with the newborn baby.
4. He sometimes strives to protect and help others in his struggle to keep the upper hand as the big brother or the big sister.
5. He may express death wishes or hate directed toward the second child.

6. If the second child is precocious, developing fast and catching up to the firstborn, it may threaten the firstborn's position. This would be enhanced if the second child is a girl and the first is a boy in a male oriented family where more is expected of him, not only because he is older but because he is male.
7. If the first child is a girl and the second is a boy over whom the family fusses and if she draws the conclusion that boys are preferred, she may develop a feeling of inferiority and may try to overcompensate through achievement, charm, cooperation, and so on, or she may become a tomboy and in this way hope to find acceptance.

The Second Child

The second child has somewhat of an uncomfortable position in life. Mostly, the child takes a steam-engine attitude, trying to catch up with the child in front, and feels as though he is under constant pressure. It is not unusual to see these youngsters move right on past their older and more perfectionistic-minded first-borns.

The parents, however, are more calm and relaxed with a second child, less strict, and less preoccupied with child rearing. The second child is usually more socially oriented. He is also apt to be more aggressive and competitive, and quite often rejects rules and regulations.

The second child may exhibit these characteristics:

1. The child never has his parents undivided attention.
2. The child always has in front of him another child who is more advanced.
3. The child feels that the first child cannot be matched, which disputes his claim of equality.
4. The child often acts as though he were in a race—hyperactive and pushy.
5. If the first child is successful, the second is more likely to feel uncertain of himself and his abilities.
6. The child usually is the opposite of the first child (if the first child is dependable and "good," the second may become undependable and "bad").
7. The child may be less concerned about winning adult approval than about winning peer approval.
8. The child may frequently be a rebel. (Supposedly, a high percentage of hippies were second born children.)

The Middle Child (Family of Three)

The middle child in a family of three has an uncertain place in the family group and may feel neglected. He may have the following characteristics:

1. The child may feel that he has neither the privileges of the youngest nor the rights of the oldest child.
2. The child may hold the conviction that people are unfair to him.
3. The child may feel unloved.
4. The child may become extremely discouraged and a problem child.
5. The child may replace his family if they do not feel as if they belong by becoming overly involved with a peer group.

The Youngest Child

The youngest child has quite a special place in the family constellation. He may become a speeder because he has been outdistanced and may then become the most successful, or he may become the most discouraged and feel inferior to the others. The youngest, being last,

1. may get more attention from the family
2. may not get as much parental pressure as his older siblings
3. may be punished less
4. may retain the baby role and place others in his service
5. feels often like an only child
6. usually has things done for him
7. has most decisions made for him by others and responsibility taken from him
8. may not be taken seriously
9. may become the "boss" in the family
10. often allies himself with the first child
11. may attempt to excel and overtake his older siblings.

The Middle Child (Large Family)

Children who come in the middle of a large family usually develop a more stable character, and conflicts between the children tend to be less fierce. In our experience, we observed that in a larger family, there is usually less conflict and strife among the children. We attribute this to the fact that the parents have less time to be involved, to pamper, and to serve the children. In large families the children depend upon each other. They are also forced by necessity to cooperate and to assume responsibilities for themselves.

Generalizations

If there are five to six years of spacing between the birth of children, each child may have some characteristics of an only child. In such a situation there may be more than one family constellation.

The direction that the child will pursue will depend on the family's values. If a boy grows up in a highly male-oriented family and if he feels inferior as a male, he may acquire *feminine* characteristics. In contrast, a girl who grows up in such a family may emulate the behavior of boys. Both of these children lack confidence in themselves with regard to their sex roles. This feeling of not measuring up may prevail through their entire lives unless they have received insights into their misconceptions of what it means to be a boy or a girl and unless they are encouraged to accept their roles.

Family traits develop out of values of any kind that are held by both parents. Values include feelings on such things as education, money, health, success, honesty, religion, hard work, obedience, and so on. If a value is held by both parents, then every child in the family is bound to take a stand. Children who conform usually accept the family values and adopt them as their own, but some children rebel. Rebellious children turn their backs on the family's values, because they realize that this is one way to defeat their parents. It may happen that one child may side with one parent against the other if the parents disagree. But one thing is certain: no child can remain neutral.

Competition

Competition accounts for the degree of differences between children in the same family. Sibling rivalry can occur even when there are no fights on the surface, even when children seem to be getting along well.

We found two distinct kinds of sibling rivalry: quantitative and qualitative.

1. Quantitative competition is found in children within the same family who pursue the same goal but who are each striving to outshine the other.
2. Qualitative competition is found in children who stay out of the areas in which their siblings are successful. Each child tends to stay out of the other child's territory, however, each child strives to be successful in his own area. One noteworthy observation is that a child who has been very successful in a certain field often will give up the moment a sibling becomes interested in the same area, especially if the sibling meets with success.
3. Every child looks for his area of significance.

Every brother and sister has some pleasant feelings and some unpleasant feelings about each other. They are likely to have pleasant relations when they satisfy one another's needs. Since each child feels differently toward each brother and sister, the relationship of any two of them is very special. As each member strives for his own place within the group, the competing opponents watch each other carefully to see the ways and means by which the opponent succeeds or fails. Where one succeeds, the other gives up; where one shows weakness or deficiencies, the other steps in. In this way competition between two members of a family is always expressed through differences in character, temperament, interests, and abilities. Conversely, the similarity of characteristics always indicates alliances. Sometimes the two strongest competitors show no sign of open rivalry but rather present a close-knit pair. Nevertheless, their competitive striving is expressed in personality differences: One may be the leader or the active and powerful protector, whereas the other may be dependent and seek support by weakness and frailty.

Each sibling develops his own area of success and trains himself in it, while considering himself a failure in and tending to neglect those areas in which his competency is unsuccessful One child may surrender and give up in an area in which another child is successful. This may occur especially with the first two children.

Often we have noticed that if the younger of two children believes himself to be unable to compete with an older, successful sibling, he may turn his interest in an entirely different direction, since competing on the same ground with his older sibling is bound to put him in the latter's shadow. For instance, if the older child succeeds as a student, the younger may seek success in areas in which his older sibling has not ventured or has failed. Such a youngster may seek to make his mark in sports or through charming people and becoming popular socially.

Although Adler strongly supports the points made in this chapter, we would like to emphasize that these characteristics may not always apply. However, because these points apply in most situations, we strongly advocate that the teacher study and be aware of the characteristics of the family constellation.

Part 2
Effective Democratic Methods

Chapter 8

The Democratic Versus the Traditional Classroom

The basic cause of conflict in the classroom is social inequality among individuals and groups. If the social relationship among people is unstable, it inevitably leads to conflict and disharmony. Equality alone, the foundation of democracy, can provide social harmony, peace, and stable social relationships.

A democratic atmosphere does not imply anarchy and permissiveness; nor can order be established by domination. In a democratic society both freedom and order are necessary, unlike an autocratic society in which the two are mutually exclusive. Permissiveness invariably leads to anarchy, whereas force and power often induce rebellion. It is autocratic to force, but democratic to induce compliance.

Equality

Some people think that equality means equal opportunities, with equal rights to vote, and equal rights in education. Our reference to equality includes *social equality*, where every person, regardless of religion, wealth, education, heritage, physical appearance, or age enjoys the same dignity and the same respect. Although many adults agree with these concepts, they have difficulty accepting a child as an equal.

To most adults it seems preposterous to consider a child as an equal. The adult views the child as small in size, limited in physical ability, limited in capability of responsibility, and too unskilled and unsophisticated to be given the stature that equality and respect imply. Lack of qualities or abilities should never deprive a person of respect and of equal voice. Unfortunately, the adult frequently believes that he can maintain this attitude only as long as he is not threatened in his own status. Furthermore, few adults treat the child as they would treat another adult. The mere assumption that children should be treated as their equal is an absurd idea to them.

Cooperation in the democratic classroom is based on consideration for the other's rights and interests while standing up for one's own rights. In such an atmosphere, one does not concern himself with what others do but accepts responsibility for what *he* has to do. Neither imposing on others nor letting others dictate is the formula for equality.

Mutual Respect

The principle underlying this type of classroom implies that there should be mutual respect—respect for the dignity of others and respect for oneself. Mutual respect means treating every person with respect, recognizing the worth of his ideas, accepting his plans and contributions, and also, when necessary, rejecting his contributions as having no value in a particular situation while at the same time not rejecting him as a person.

Respect implies the recognition that the other person has something to offer, as well as the right to offer it. Mutual respect is based upon acceptance of the equality of human beings, independent of individual differences, knowledge, information, abilities, and position (Dreikurs, 1971).

Respect for oneself implies not letting oneself be put into another person's services forcibly, standing up for one's beliefs without getting into a fight, not abusing those who are weaker or younger, or punishing others for not accepting one's ideas.

To live as equals with our fellow humans, we must cooperate with them. Cooperation in a democracy must be based on consideration for others' rights and interests while standing up for one's own rights. This is the formula for equality; mutual respect is its premise.

Respect for another's rights is the prerequisite for harmony and for a peaceful solution of conflicts. Reaching voluntary agreement requires a total reorientation in our attitudes and approaches. The principle sounds simple enough, but its application is complex.

The primary prerequisite for a proper relationship implies an expression of respect in words and deeds, in the tone of voice, in the willingness to *listen*, and in our acceptance of other people's feelings. Showing respect implies being a good friend, undemanding, trusting, not bribing. We can respect others if we respect ourselves, and we can trust life only if we trust ourselves. Everyone has the *right* and the *obligation* to say what he thinks and also the *obligation* to listen to what others say and to try to understand what the other fellow feels and thinks.

We need training in cooperative techniques. We can become sensitive to the needs of others; we can feel worthwhile, respected, and appreciated. We can learn to alleviate others' problems, not by words but by actions.

We must work for the general establishment and recognition of human dignity, mutual respect, and mutual assistance to truly have a "democratic society."

What Characterizes a Democratic Classroom?

In a democratic classroom the pupils and the teacher are united in planning, organizing, implementing, and participating in their common activities. The teacher, as the expert, provides a broad base. She has the duty and the responsibility to give direction, to help each child to increase his ability to take part effectively in group settings, and to be able to make and carry out group decisions.

Essential to a democratic classroom is a combination of firmness and kindness expressed in the teacher's attitude toward her class. *Firmness* implies self-respect; *kindness* implies respect for others. Neither one alone achieves a harmonious relationship of equals. We can resolve our conflicts without either fighting or yielding, by both respecting others and respecting ourselves. This is the foundation upon which satisfactory classroom relationships are built.

Children need to be trained in order to work effectively in a democratic classroom. The teacher should take a few days at the beginning of the school year to talk over democratic methods with the students and to get to know how they think and what their values are. A teacher who takes time at the beginning of the year to train her children and to involve them in planning will find that as time goes on she will need to spend less and less time fighting with the children. She will also find that most of the children are willing learners and become more self-motivated. So, although training does take time in the beginning, it pays off in the long run.

The teacher may start with a group discussion about what democracy is. She may lead them to realize that democracy implies shared responsibility, shared decision making, and cooperation. She may help them to understand that cooperation is a two-way street—that they must cooperate with each other and not just, as some believe, that the children have to supply all the cooperation. In this way, the students and the teacher can have their first discussion about democratic living. Every time a child behaves in a manner that violates democratic principles, the teacher should take time to review those principles (see Chapter 13).

The question is often asked whether a teacher can have a democratic classroom in a school system that is essentially not democratic. The answer is yes, she can, provided she believes in it and provided she possesses the skill to implement it. A desert can have an oasis. The authors have taught in nondemocratic school systems and have been able to create a democratic spirit in their own classes, but it required that the students accept the democratic principles. This is possible only if they are helped to stop competing and measuring themselves against others. Many teachers who follow our suggestions have succeeded in establishing a democratic classroom although they work in an undemocratic school. This shows then that even in an autocratic school system, the teacher can proceed with democratic methods.

Another question arises whether students should be given the right to decide whether or not they will learn and what they will learn. This is no longer a question, because the children have already taken this decision upon themselves, and the teacher is in no position to force a reluctant student to learn.

Shared Responsibility

Once the principle of sharing responsibility is understood by the teacher, she will not find it difficult to apply it. At the present time, teachers vacillate between imposing their will on the children and letting the children dominate them. Some say that we should teach the children what they like to learn. Such an approach means abdication. Then there are others who try to force the children to learn what they are supposed to learn. This is autocratic education. Neither of the two approaches will achieve satisfactory results. We suggest that teachers motivate the children to enjoy and to learn what they ought to learn. Children are more than willing to accept guidance from adults if ideas are not imposed on them and if they feel that their opinions and suggestions are taken seriously. This does not necessarily mean that the teacher is obligated to do what they suggest. It does mean that teacher and students come to conclusions by considering the issues from all sides. The curriculum should, however, be flexible enough to give students and teachers a chance to follow the inclination and interest of each class.

Children should have a voice in determining the curriculum and the rules of their school. Democracy is best learned by living it. Children who attend a school in which they are asked to take responsibility for the curriculum and rules discover democracy; they also discover that in a democratic school, as in a democratic country, many problems have no clear-cut solution. Rather they learn that they have a responsibility for finding the best alternatives to a series of difficult problems, problems that they themselves help to pose. (Glasser, 1969)

At the present time, the curriculum is usually imposed on the teacher. Even under these circumstances, she still can have a democratic class if she shares her obligations and her frustrations with her pupils.

In a class for seniors, the teacher and the students decided to change the order of the units of work that were required by the State Board of Education. The students and the teacher cooperatively planned which unit would be studied first, second, and so on. They also figured how much time should be allotted for each unit and the scope of each one. Their involvement in the planning contributed to their enjoyment of their work.

A teacher may find it difficult to win her students as equal partners in all activities because of a general tendency on her part to underestimate the ability of the children, their intelligence, and their capacity for responsibility. Planning and decision-making cannot be left solely to the teacher or her allies in the class. All pupils can participate in the planning of activities that meet both the needs of the curriculum and of the students. They can work creatively on all school problems, provided they know that they have the respect, cooperation, and support of their teachers. The critical point is that every member of the class and that all classes within the school should participate in the planning of the entire educational process.

Sharing responsibility is possible when the teacher is confronted with certain demands from the administration that contradict her democratic procedures. Usually, teachers are inclined to pass the pressure that they receive from the principal on to the children. We recommend that the teacher ask the children to join her in carrying out her obligations by accepting reality as a given fact. Whenever she appeals for help to the students, she is more likely than not to get it, particularly when she has demonstrated her sincerity and proven to be trustworthy and not an enemy.

It was the teacher's first day of facing her class. She thought that she would make an impression and instill fear into her students by coming on strong. The kids looked at each other and knew what to do, and they gave her the 1–2, especially one girl. After several unsuccessful attempts to establish order, the teacher asked this girl to come with her to see the principal. After leaving the class, the teacher became frightened. She did not know the principal or what he would think of her, and she burst into tears and shared her fears with the girl. The girl took the teacher into her arms and consoled her. They both went back to class, and the girl announced to the class, "She's O.K., and she needs our help."

Teacher's Versus Student's Rights

Although some teachers claim that they have a democratic atmosphere in their class and that they treat their students with respect, they are often not aware of how they violate this principle the moment their prestige is at stake. The following two examples illustrate this point.

A teacher had to see a principal of an elementary school. They talked about the present dilemma of the schools. Mr. X seemed very enlightened: he suggested that students should have a bigger say in policy making, that we should listen to children more than we do, and so on.

The bell rang, and the children were going home for lunch. Mr. X excused himself, stating that he always liked to stand at the foot of the stairs as the students came down. The teacher went with him. The children came down in a very orderly fashion, single file, with their hands folded across their chests.

Suddenly Mr. X pulled a boy around 9 years old out of the line and held him firmly by one shoulder until all the children had passed. He then turned to the boy and asked, "How many feet apart from the child ahead of you must you be?" Keeping his hands in his pockets and without looking up, the boy replied, "Three." Mr. X went on, "Hands out of your pockets when you talk to me! Understand?" The child mumbled an "O.K."

Mr. X became angrier with each answer. At this point, he shouted, "When you talk to me, you say 'Yes, sir,' and not 'O.K.' Understand?"

While we do not condone impudent behavior by a child, we cannot approve of the manner in which this principal handled the situation. If he accomplished anything, he probably provoked this uncooperative boy to feel even greater resentment against him. In his heart he may have wished the principal to be dead or to break a leg while his lips were saying, "Yes, sir."

The playground where teachers stand around watching their students while they play is usually the place where teachers discuss their experiences of the day and express their feelings.

While one of the authors was standing on the playground, watching her class, she observed the following. A teacher who was just coming out of the building shook a child by his shoulders, repeating over and over, "How dare you?" It turned out that this boy, having noticed that the teacher was munching on a cookie before leaving the classroom, reminded her that chewing in class was against school regulations. He reminded her that she had often taken cookies away from, and even punished, children who were caught eating them. The teacher shook a threatening finger at him and shouted, "Don't be fresh or I'll send you back to your room!"

The child shrugged his shoulders in complete lack of understanding. The teacher then turned to the author and remarked, "See what I have to put up with?"

This example is not an unusual one. Teachers who insist that their students never eat in class, often munch on something themselves when they feel hungry. They believe that the children will not notice if they eat behind the door of their coat closet or in a corridor. Children are very much aware of what the teacher is doing. They often discuss this practice by the teachers among themselves.

Teachers have the right to go to the teacher's lounge and smoke a cigarette or to have a cup of coffee—rights that the students do not have. Can we imagine what would happen if a student, feeling the urge to drink milk or a coke, were to go to his locker and proceed to drink whatever he brought from home? In the following group discussion we can see how a similar experience was handled.

RANDY: I'd like to bring up something that the teacher and the teacher's aide do that disturbs me.

TEACHER'S AIDE: What is it?

RANDY: Well, after we have our bathroom break, you two guys drink coffee in the classroom. We can't drink coke or other soft drinks, and I don't think that's right.

OTHER CHILDREN: That's right; that's not fair.

TEACHER: I can understand that. Could I explain something to you, and then we'll see if you still think it's unfair?

OTHER CHILDREN: Sure, what is it?

TEACHER: As a class, you have a snack break at 10:00. Is that correct?

KIM: That's right. We have peanuts and fruit juice and ten minutes of free time.

TEACHER'S AIDE: What do Mr. T. and I do during this time?

MICHAEL: You stay with us 'cause you're on duty.

TEACHER: And what happens next—at 10:10?

DAVE: We have a bathroom break.

BARBARA: Yeah—and one of you have to go with us 'cause the principal says so.

TEACHER'S AIDE: Right. Then what happens?

JASON: The other one of you goes and gets coffee, and brings it back to the classroom.

RANDY: Then you drink it while we're working, and that's not fair.

TEACHER: Does anybody have any idea why we drink coffee at that time?

PAUL: I think that you two really don't have a break.

TEACHER'S AIDE: That's right.

DAVE: Oh, I see. The only time you can go to the teacher's lounge for coffee is while we're in the bathroom!

TEACHER: You figured it out, Dave.

DAVE: Well, when you look at it like that, it's only fair to work it out that way.

TEACHER: What do the rest of you have to say?

RANDY: Well, I brought it up, and from the way it was explained I think it's fair.

KIM: Yeah, I feel better about it and I think it's O.K. It seems like we kids get a break but you don't.

TEACHER: Does anybody else have anything to say?

BARBARA: Well, I'm glad we talked about this. I guess we were all feeling kind of resentful about it but not anymore.

RANDY: How about it everyone—is it O.K. with us if they drink coffee? I think they deserve it.
CHILDREN: We agree.

The teacher should have an understanding with her students and administrators that at a certain time of the day she can go to the teacher's lounge to have some refreshment while the children are allowed to have a snack in class. This is possible only after the class has been well trained in decision-making and where the students assume responsibility for their behavior. Before such time, students and teacher may agree on a snack time for all who want it.

The Student Council

School administrators argue that their school is democratic and that the students' rights and opinions are represented through the student council. But which students are chosen to serve on the student council? The students who are eligible have to have specific prerequisite qualities to be on the student council. They are students who have distinguished themselves either academically or in sports. The rebel and the poor student are left out in this process. It is precisely these students that need representation. At present the student councils foster a merit system in which the good student becomes better and the bad student becomes worse. Those who need encouragement the most get it the least. In addition, the student council sometimes is used by the administration to implement their own decisions.

Creative Thinking Versus Exact Answers

In a traditional school setting children realize that they have little part in making decisions. They also learn that doing original and creative thinking may only get them into trouble, as the following example will show.

A fourth-grade class was studying the history of Chicago as part of a social studies lesson. The teacher asked a girl to recite two factors that contributed toward the development of the city. The girl answered, "The lake and the cow that kicked the bucket and started the big fire." The teacher looked at the girl quizzically, as if she did not believe what she had just heard. "And what has the cow to do with it?," she asked. The girl explained, "Well, after the city burned down, they had to build it up again, and they made it bigger and nicer." The teacher said, "Where did you read that nonsense?" The girl answered, "I didn't read it; I just thought of it." To this the teacher replied, "Next time, don't think but read your book."

The teacher then asked another student to give two factors. This student said, "The lake and two Indian trails that ran through the territory." The teacher praised him for reading the textbook.

There are other prominent educators who support our point of view. William Glasser (1969) states:

Little emphasis is given to critical thinking. Education does not emphasize thinking and is so memory-oriented because all schools and colleges are dominated by the "certainty principle." According to the certainty principle, there is a right and a wrong answer to every question; the function of education is then to ensure that each student knows the right answers to a series of questions, questions that educators have decided are important.

As long as the certainty principle dominates our educational system, we will not teach our children to think. Memory is not education, answers are not knowledge."

To go back to the preceding example, an imaginative teacher who is not concerned with getting the exact answers to her questions would have used the opportunity to encourage the girl to be independent in her thinking. She might have said, "I never thought of this, but it's very plausible. I'm glad you thought of it. Can you think of another factor to add to the two you gave me?" She probably would have won over this child.

Teachers who insist on exact answers that they have prepared or that come from a book are dull teachers, responsible not only for the boredom of their students but for many discipline problems that come up because of their rigid, stale, and antiquated method of teaching. It is not uncommon to find children who because of such teaching decide that they do not like certain subjects.

Democratic Versus Autocratic Leadership

Kurt Lewin (1948) in his Iowa Experiments experimented with three different "social climates" in boys' clubs, which are of crucial significance for our present predicament. He trained leaders in three basic approaches: autocracy, democracy, and laissez-faire anarchy. The autocratic leader told the boys what to do, and the boys did it; the democratic leader helped the boys to design and to carry out projects, and they became independent; and the laissez-faire leader let the boys do what they wanted, and chaos reigned. The results are of profound importance. Clearly, the experiment points out several lessons.

The first of these is that democracy should not be confused with anarchy. The second important fact involves the differences in how the democratic group functioned when compared with the autocratic group. The autocratically governed group could only work when the leader was present.

Without the leader the boys became undisciplined. They could function only under control. In contrast, the democratically led group continued their work when the leader was absent and got along with each other. They had inner control.

The most striking and significant observation was made when the leader changed his role. When the democratic leader became autocratic, nothing happened. Both groups were cooperative, but for different reasons. Why? The democratic group cooperated out of self-motivation, whereas the autocratic group cooperated out of fear. But what happened when the autocratic leader was told to be democratic? Bedlam broke loose. Why? The group was not trained for self-direction. It took the leader some time before the boys settled down and became a democratic group.

When the autocratic pressure on a group stops, anarchy sets in. Then people become free to do what they want, without any sense of responsibility. In the case of Lewin's boys, they had a leader who helped them to become democratic. In our society often we do not have such leaders. Consequently, children as well as adults often misuse the freedom that the democratic evolution has provided for them. This is one of the problems of our time.

This observation has far-reaching significance for our entire culture. Whenever people move from an autocratic setting into a democratic setting, they become "free," but they do not know what to do with their freedom. Freedom carries with it certain responsibilities. This holds true for adults as well as for children. Many of the events of our time—the confusion, misused freedom, and lack of responsibility—validate the observations of Kurt Lewin.

The following list explains the difference between an autocratic leader and a democratic one.

Autocratic	*Democratic*
Boss	Leader
Sharp voice	Friendly voice
Command	Invitation
Power	Influence
Pressure	Stimulation
Demands cooperation	Wins cooperation
"I tell you what you should do"	"I tell you what I would like to do"
Imposes ideas	Sells ideas
Dominates	Guides
Criticizes	Encourages
Finding fault	Acknowledges achievement
Punishes	Helps
"I tell you"	Discusses
"I decide; you obey"	"I suggest and help you to decide"
Has sole responsibility of group	Shares responsibility of team

The left column of the chart indicates pressure from without, and the right indicates stimulation from within. This list of democratic and autocratic approaches could probably be enlarged. It permits each teacher to use it as her own "democratic index" if she takes the description of procedures as a guide to evaluate her way of handling her class.

A teacher who shares the responsibility for conducting the class with her students does not need a personal display of authority. Unless she can create a team spirit, she cannot integrate the class or unite its members in cooperative efforts. Only by integrating everyone into one unit can all be influenced and advanced.

This is the reason that the competitive spirit has to be replaced with one of cooperation that serves the common interest. In such a setting each child is important, a prerequisite for harmonious function within the group. Competition makes one student feel superior and another inferior. In such a situation, no cooperation or team work is possible.

Grading

Let us examine the question of grading. Grades are a typical system of reward and punishment. They are neither needed nor effective. Because of this system, today's children do not learn out of a desire for knowledge; they work for grades, as evidenced by the questions students are usually asked when they receive their report card—"What grade did you get?" (not "What did you learn?").

The only children who respond to grading are the good students who could be stimulated without a grading system. The poor students often shrug them off as a new proof of their hopeless condition and as spoils of war. The more discouraged a child is the worse he is treated.

What can an individual teacher do to offset the detrimental and discouraging effects of poor grades? The teacher can refrain from presenting them as her "verdict." She can make the present grading process, which is unpleasant and humiliating, a common task. All can work together, not only on what grades each child should get, since the teacher is obliged to grade, but on helping the poor student to avoid low grades.

In one class the students turned in a written evaluation of their own work a week before the grading period. During the following week, brief conferences were held with each student, and agreement was usually reached as to a fair grade.

Prior to this time the slow or poor student had been encouraged both by the class and by the teacher. The faster students served as tutors to the slower students. The entire class benefited from this arrangement. Not only did the slow student learn faster, but the faster student learned more and the course grew in depth and scope.

This is in sharp contrast to most classes where the good students lord it over the poor and push them further down in esteem, status, and achievement.

In a cooperative atmosphere being a good student or being very bright and ahead of everyone else does not ensure glory; rather, it entails a responsibility to help others and to be of service.

Training for Leadership

The schools should train the students in cooperative leadership. Leadership qualities consist of more than popular support. They are the ability to resolve conflicts and to reconcile opposing interests. Differences of interest and opinion will always exist. Furthermore, without such differences, progress would not be possible. The democratic process requires leaders. Without them we have no democracy, only anarchy.

The recognized function of the school is to prepare children for life, for responsible adulthood. This requires more than teaching a particular subject matter and increasing the knowledge of the students. Since there is no other agency in society that has the same potential, the school needs to concern itself with the values on which students operate. This is done primarily through group involvement. Leadership training is one aspect of the development of values needed in a democratic society. We have to recognize the obligation of schools to be a value forming agency.

Throughout this chapter, we have discussed various methods and techniques that a teacher could use in order to provide a democratic classroom. Briefly, the ground rules are as follows:

1. Order is necessary under all circumstances. A group cannot be run democratically without order and ground rules.
2. Limits are necessary. School rules and school policies may not be correct or adequate and may need revision, but as long as they exist, they must be followed. They are reality.
3. Children should participate in establishing and maintaining any rules necessary for functioning in an orderly group.
4. The teacher needs to know how to exert democratic leadership.
5. Without trust and faith in each other a class cannot function democratically. Efforts may be required to establish mutual trust between students and teacher.
6. The teacher must know how to solicit the help of the students. She cannot demand it.
7. A spirit of cooperation has to replace competitiveness in the classroom.
8. A warm, friendly classroom atmosphere is essential for solving problems.

9. The teacher needs the skills necessary to integrate the class for a common purpose.
10. The pattern of relationships existing in a class is usually established during the first few days. It requires the full attention of the teacher to give each child a feeling of belonging.
11. Group discussion is essential in a democratic setting.
12. The democratic school requires a school council in which all segments of the school population are represented.
13. The teacher needs to learn not only teaching methods but also principles of motivation.
14. The teacher should not be concerned with personal prestige.
15. The teacher must establish limits and give the children freedom within those limits.
16. There can be no equality without equal rights and mutual respect.
17. Children should be encouraged to experiment and to learn from mistakes.

REFERENCES

Dreikurs, Rudolf. *Social Equality: The Challenge of Today*. Chicago: Henry Regnery, 1971.
Glasser, William. *Schools Without Failure*. New York: Harper & Row, 1969.
Lewin, Kurt. *Resolving Social Conflicts*. New York: Harper & Row, 1948.

Chapter 9
Discipline and Order

Discipline is without question the most essential and the most difficult aspect of education, for without discipline there can be no effective teaching. Unfortunately, many people have a distorted view of what discipline really is and a misleading concept of why there is a lack of discipline in our schools.

Discipline, as love, as respect, or as the acceptance of responsibilities is not a subject that can be taught out of a book or that can be obtained by sheer demand. All aspects of discipline grow out of social relationships. Discipline is an inner process; an integrated part of one's values. Therefore, we cannot discuss discipline without emphasis on the importance of values. We may question: "Whose values?" and "Do we have a right to impose our values on others?" Since we advocate a democratic educational process, it stands to reason that we also advocate training children in the basic, democratic values that stress not only equal rights for all people but also mutual respect and cooperation. Without mutual respect and cooperation, we are bound to have difficulties obtaining from our students a *discipline* based on convictions.

The teaching of discipline as a basic value is an ongoing process and is not something to be resorted to only in times of stress and misbehavior.

One of the reasons for the present dilemma concerning discipline is that most people, educators and parents alike, use the word "discipline" to mean control through punitive measures. To many people it signifies physical punishment; to others, rigid control of rules and regulations and autocratic authority. The individuals who are disciplined are completely left out of the process of making these rules and are never consulted about the enforcement of them.

In school the teacher or the principal confronts the child with the consequences that they have decided upon, regardless of whether this makes sense to the child or not. Some teachers argue that the child knows why he is being punished, and they usually view the consequences as being fair, in spite of the child's protests. Defiance, sulkiness, and secret resentment are usually the result of the child not understanding or agreeing with the adult decision. Some teachers argue further that punishment is good for the child because he learns to distinguish between right and wrong and he learns that wrong behavior does not pay off. They disregard the fact that the child may begin to hate authority. He feels that being punished gives him the right to punish too, and retaliation aimed at other children usually is more effective than retaliation aimed at adults.

Discipline should not be regarded as synonymous with punishment, especially not with corporal punishment. Punishment is what some people use when training fails or in place of training. Punishment may mean isolation, removal, denial of privileges, and so on. Punishment teaches the child what not to do but fails to teach the child what to do. In this chapter we would like to consider discipline, not imposed by any teacher but rather imposed by the individual himself or by the group, and we would also like to consider the development of intelligent self-control rather than blind obedience out of fear.

We have found that the application of logical consequences (Chapter 12) is effective when children choose to disregard accepted rules and when they are provoked. For the most part, teachers who maintain discipline through autocratic, punitive means instill a fear of punishment into their students. Since this kind of discipline is not based on an inner conviction and belief, chaos breaks out in such classes when the teacher leaves the room or when the class has a substitute teacher.

Maintaining Discipline

Discipline, as discussed in this book, relates to the kind of behavior through which the child experiences acceptance by others and consequently greater acceptance of himself. The establishment of self-approval is the strongest form of control.

When thought of in this manner, discipline ceases to be a restriction. As teachers, we should no longer think of discipline in terms of an authority figure who rules with an iron fist. We need to think of discipline in terms of a leader figure who permits freedom within certain limits.

Early training in the home influences the child's attitude toward discipline and his acceptance of responsibility. The better the relationship among the family members and the greater cooperation between the parents themselves, the more likely will the child accept the limits that the parents have set for him and the more likely will be his concern for their approval. As the child grows older, he is confronted with more situations in which discipline is necessary and where some leadership should be present to guide him.

The moment the child enters school, his social horizon broadens as he is confronted with teachers and students. Here he is exposed to new kinds of disciplines, such as listening to the teacher and to his classmates, studying, completing assignments on time, and so on. The more cooperative he is at home, the more cooperative the child will be in class, provided that the classroom atmosphere is, in a broader sense, a continuation of the home atmosphere. If the child in school is faced with different values and different disciplinary measures from those that he has experienced at home, he may have difficulties adjusting. This applies to both kinds of home backgrounds—democratic or autocratic. In order to help this child make the adjustment to his new environment and the new expectations, the teacher should acquaint herself with this child's previous experiences in terms of responsibility and cooperation. The teacher is then in a better position to help the child make the proper changes, if changes are necessary, and to develop behavior patterns that are conducive to learning.

It is necessary to think of learning experiences that the teacher can use in her class, which will help to develop self-discipline. These experiences should be determined by the stage of growth of each individual child and the behavior that he needs to develop. The decision as to which experience should be used should be made cooperatively by the child and the teacher. Children need areas of freedom to discover the world, to express their feelings, to develop their own ideas, and to test their own self-discipline. These experiences should vary from the relatively simple to the more difficult and complex. They should provide experience in solving problems and should help to establish desired behaviors.

The following example demonstrates a very simple exercise in learning to plan cooperatively within certain prescribed limits:

At the beginning of the school term, the teacher listed the units to be studied for the years as prescribed by the curriculum department. The children and the teacher discussed what units should be taught first and the order of the other units. Through this process the children were given the limits within which to make decisions and choices.

In this next example, we can see the more complex experiences that would help a child to grow towards self-discipline:

In health class we were studying the unit, "Is able to discuss problems and growth changes." The general topic to be dealt with was the realization that people of all ages have emotions, concepts, and intentions. The specific topic under study dealt with *anger*.

The class had decided there were three areas that needed exploration. Consequently, three groups were formed to research and report on the three areas. Each report was to be followed by discussion.

The first group reported on "What makes you angry." A listing was written on the blackboard that was added to and discussed by the entire class.

The second and third groups discussed "For what purpose did you get angry" and "Different ways to overcome angry feelings." As part of their report, the third group did some role playing.

In the general discussion afterward, such points were brought up as, "Why it is difficult to talk with someone with whom you are angry" and "Why I get mad when my parents don't let me do what I want."

The teacher and the group discuss the amount of work the class will have to cover in mathematics during the week. The children can choose to work page by page and hand in the work each day or to skip around instead of following the pages systematically. Each child is then responsible for completing the assigned chapter or number of pages at his own pace and according to his own decisions. He may decide to do all of the work in one day, in which case he has a certain number of minutes each day to use as he decides.

At the end of the week there should be an evaluation by the teacher and the entire class group. Children who, for instance, decide to leave most or all of the work for the last day and then cannot finish may have to accept the logical consequence of doing a definite number of pages each day until such time as they are ready and willing to budget the work themselves and have all work in by the end of the week.

Children often write, direct, and produce their own plays. Usually this is done in the classroom after they have completed their work or during recess. The director chooses the actors, and all remain in the classroom, rehearsing, preparing costumes, and so on. These children must then give a report to the class with regard to their accomplishments for the day. Children who act up instead of working on the assignment are first encouraged to help do their part, but if their wrong behavior continues, they are replaced by other children who are interested in being in the play and willing to exercise the self-discipline expected by the group and by the teacher. These children are left in class on their honor. There is nobody there to supervise or discipline them.

The Role of Discipline in the Teaching Environment

Discipline in the classroom, then, means teaching the child a set of inner controls that will provide him with a pattern of behavior that is acceptable to society and that will contribute to his own welfare and progress.

Teachers need to set aside time for training the child in essential skills. There are times when a teacher may have to explain a lesson more than once or may have to go back to a lesson that was already taught and review it. However, the teacher will have to differentiate between listlessness (which is a demand for additional service from the teacher) and a true inability to comprehend a new lesson after one explanation. This understanding will help the teacher in the process of training. It is advisable that she discuss a child's negative attitude and his bid for attention, or his disregard of the teacher's presentation of a lesson with the child or during group discussion. Constant nagging and reminding will fail to teach the child, for he looks upon such tactics as criticism and humiliation. It is our job to correct and to guide children in developing a sense of responsibility and consideration for other people.

In order for cooperation to take place, the teaching environment should be of a positive, accepting, and nonthreatening nature. It is important for the teacher to remember that growth takes place in one direction when the child is having something *done to* him and in another direction when things are being *done with* him. This type of classroom atmosphere calls for the incorporation of teacher-child planning. Children will approach the educational task with an altogether different attitude when they have been consulted about what they are going to do. They then have a feeling of personal involvement, are committed, and feel responsible for success or failure of the venture. The teacher needs to be willing to share the responsibility of developing plans with the class and to give support and approval in carrying out the plans.

In such a climate, the children will recognize the need for limitations that are placed upon them and upon the teacher by the reality of school policies. As youngsters grow up in a society, they have to curb many of their personal desires and impulses because of regulations necessary to group life. Every school has rules and regulations that must be followed. Children are more likely to respect them if they have discussed them and understand them.

Sometimes it is difficult for children to understand the necessity for some school rules or regulations, as is shown in this example:

One week we had a great deal of snow, which was unusual in our part of the country. All teachers received notices from the principal that we were to read to our classes. The note stated. "The southwest area of the playground has been reserved for snowballing. No snowballing is to be allowed on any other part of the grounds. There is to be no snow brought into the buildings. Offenders will be dealt with."

Upon reading the announcement, there were many audible groans among my sixth-grade students. We then discussed the "snowball ruling." At first the students viewed the situation as, "He never lets us have any fun." After some discussion, however, the class could understand and accept the ruling. Several of the boys and girls were really relieved, because they had been pelted with hard-packed snowballs when they entered the building. As the discussion progressed, the class came to realize that it was a "fair" rule. Those who wanted to had the privilege of having the fun of snowballing while those who did not want to did not have to protect themselves. (But the wording of the ruling was provocative: normally, it would incite the disobedience of the students.)

During group discussion (see Chapter 14) the teacher should explain to the children why she must make certain decisions that affect the entire class, for instance which tables in the cafeteria are to be reserved for her class. Through this process the children find out what the class is expected to do.

Setting Limits

Setting limits with children is a form of training in discipline. Training children in the everyday routine of living is basic. Whenever teachers induce children to wash their hands before lunch, to complete their assignments within the allotted time period, and to get permission to use another child's property, or when they help them to recognize that mowing the lawn is sharing family responsibility, that keeping the bathroom straight is everyone's responsibility, that being ready for school on time is the child's responsibility, and so on, then they are really training in discipline. Discipline in this sense means teaching the child that there are certain rules in life that people live by and that it is expected that the child will become accustomed to these rules and adopt them for his own. The goal that needs to be kept in mind in the daily teaching of children is progress toward self-discipline and self-direction.

The following example illustrates how a child was able to work directly on self-discipline.

Mason, a 10-year-old boy, was in a special adjustment room because of his educational deficiency and his behavior pattern. After being in this room for a couple of months, he had become quite cooperative, was interested in learning, and was really a delight.

However, he still had a problem of talking out in class without raising his hand. The teacher invariably found herself answering, even if he didn't raise his hand. She told Mason that since she was not able to help him with that problem he would have to take care of it himself. She asked, "What do you suggest?" He said, "Each time I talk out without raising my hand, I will have to leave the room for two minutes and make up my time later." They agreed on this procedure and within a week Mason was no longer talking out.

Some teachers will say that discussing such issues with children is pointless. "Children should obey without questioning" or "You are teaching them to argue," they say. However, if we want our children to become thinking adults, the problem solving discussion approach not only teaches them fairness, it also teaches them to consider the alternatives of various issues and situations.

Teachers who make the basic assumption that children are trustworthy are more likely to teach them to have attitudes of dependability and responsibility. If regulations are to be observed, the child should be stimulated to want to conform. If the children share with the teacher what they consider to be acceptable behavior and unacceptable behavior, and if the teacher's response is consistent, they will not feel that she is being unjust, as shown in the following example.

> The teacher was assigning homework. There was a restlessness and rumbling among the students. Upon inquiry, the students said that the title soccer game was being played that night and that they wanted to watch it, since their hometown team was in the play-off. The teacher considered the request a fair one and consented.

In consenting to the students' request the teacher set a good example of consideration and cooperation. In such a class, the teacher can expect to get equal consideration and cooperation from her students. Children will respond in a positive way to those who are kind but firm, fair, and consistent in maintaining discipline and order.

Cooperative Discipline

The rules for classroom behavior, arrived at through the cooperative efforts of the class, not only give the children an opportunity to increase their understanding of some of the laws of our society, but they also help build respect and obedience for them. Discussing such matters as borrowing personal belongings, using the audio-visual equipment, playing with other children on the playground, table manners in the cafeteria, calling other children names, bicycle rules in general as well as on the school grounds, and getting help from other classmates, is all part of training in discipline.

One of the best ways to insure that the class works cooperatively is to help the children discover and share mutual interests and concerns. Getting acquainted during the first few days of school helps to prevent hostilities from building up and brings the group closer together. When a child knows that his classmates are his friends, that they are interested in him for himself, then he does not have to show off or act up to get attention. Children have vast influence over each other, and peer approval or disapproval can play a major role in helping the child behave positively. The teacher who has the cooperation of her class can be effective in most situations, with the children as her allies when isolated cases of misbehavior occur. Quite often, the children themselves will provide the control without the intervention of the teacher.

> One day Randy was transferred back into my class after being across the hall for a couple of months. He was sitting at his desk humming away and gazing out of the window. Dennis leaned over to him and said, "We work in this

room and we don't make noise 'cause it bothers us." Randy looked surprised, stopped his humming, and started to work.

In many of the chapters we discuss factors that deal largely with the prevention of discipline problems and with understanding the child in terms of his goal, his need to have status in the group, and his response to encouragement and to natural and logical consequences as compared to punishment. Still, it may happen that in spite of our careful planning we may run into behavioral difficulties with some children.

Here are some of the principles that foster individual growth in discipline and responsibility.

1. The structure of the learning activities should leave room for the child to grow. He needs time to correct mistakes, to think, and to understand. This implies that children should be allowed to work at their own pace.
2. The teaching environment should be of a positive, accepting, and non-threatening nature.
3. Children should find that spontaneity and enthusiasm are associated with their experience.
4. Children need limits to help them develop their own capacities, as well as to curb their impulses, but they also need freedom to explore, to discover, and to use their initiative and imagination.
5. The children and the teacher should plan together.
6. The child needs help in developing a concern for and an awareness of all human beings.
7. Children need to realize that there are certain rules that both they and the teacher cannot change.
8. Children need to accept the responsibility and the consequences of their own behavior.

If children are to become autonomous adults, they must gain independence by being encouraged to find their own solutions, to have creative ideas and independent views, as well as to carry out assigned tasks. By so doing, self-management can be integrated into meeting the needs of the child and those of the situation.

The children and the teacher should have an inner freedom, which is the result of positive and free cooperation with one another. This is the freedom to choose, to be responsible for their choices and their behavior, to say what they are thinking, to have mutual respect and trust for each other, to analyze, and to make decisions different from the pattern of the typical school. Included must be:

1. responsibility for what you are doing
2. respect for yourself and your work

3. respect for others and their work
4. tolerance for the behavior of others
5. responsibility to influence the behavior of others
6. understanding of what is happening around you
7. developing a "we" feeling.

The Do's and Don't's of Discipline

What can a teacher do in order to have the kind of classroom order that is satisfactory to her and to the students? Are these two possible? They are if discipline and order are used as a cooperative enterprise, with understanding on both sides and team spirit. In order to achieve this end, the teacher must know what not to do as well as what she must do in a given situation. Let us consider first what she should *never* do.

1. A preoccupation with one's authority may provoke rather than stifle defiance and resistance to discipline. The teacher should not be concerned with her own prestige.
2. Refrain from nagging and scolding, since it may fortify the child's mistaken concept of how to get attention.
3. Do not ask a child to promise anything. Most children will promise to change in order to get out of an uncomfortable situation. It is a sheer waste of time.
4. Do not give rewards for good behavior. The child may then work only in order to get his reward and stop as soon as he has achieved his goal. What's more, this will only strengthen his belief that he must be paid every time he acts civil or makes a contribution.
5. Refrain from finding fault with the child. It may hurt his self-esteem and may discourage him.
6. Avoid double standards—one for yourself and another for the students. In a democratic atmosphere everybody must have equal rights. This includes the chewing of gum, swearing, tardiness, unnecessary visiting, and talking with members of the faculty in class when the children are working, sitting when the class pledges allegiance, checking papers or doing any kind of work that prevents the teacher from looking at the child when he is talking to her.
7. Do not use threats as a method to discipline the child. Although some children may become intimidated and conform for the moment, it has no lasting value since it does not change their basic attitudes.
8. Do not be vindictive; it only stirs up resentment and unfriendly feelings.

Let us now consider some of the effective measures that a teacher can use in the disciplinary procedure.

1. Because problem behavior is usually closely related to the child's faulty evaluation of his social position and how he must behave in order to have a place in the class group, the teacher's first concern must be to understand the purpose of his behavior (see Chapter 3). Only then will she be in a position to plan more effectively for this child.
2. Give clear-cut directions for the expected action of the child. Wait until you have the attention of all class members before you proceed in giving directions.
3. Be more concerned with the future behavior of the child rather than with past behavior. Refrain from reminding the child what he used to be or do.
4. As soon as a child misbehaves and tends to threaten the general atmosphere in the class, give him the choice either to remain in his seat without disturbing the others or to leave the classroom if possible or go to the back of the room.
5. Build on the positive and minimize the negative. There is much good in every child, but if you look *only* for academic achievement, you may never find it.
6. Try to establish a relationship with the child built on trust and mutual respect.
7. Discuss the child's problem at a time when neither of you is emotionally charged, preferably in the regular class discussions.
8. Use natural consequences instead of traditional punishment. The consequence must bear a direct relationship to the behavior and must be understood by the child.
9. Be consistent in your decisions. Do not change a decision arbitrarily just because it suits your purpose at the moment. Inconsistency confuses the child about what is expected of him at a certain procedure.
10. See behavior in its proper perspective. In this way, you will avoid making a serious issue out of trivial incidents.
11. Establish cooperative planning for future goals and the solution of problems.
12. Let children assume greater responsibility for their own behavior and learning. They cannot learn this unless you plan for such learning. Teachers who are afraid to leave the room because of what might happen prevent the children from taking responsibility. Responsibility is taught by giving responsibility. Be prepared for children to act up at first. Such training takes time.
13. Use the class as a group to express disapproval when a child behaves in an antisocial manner.
14. Treat the child as your social equal.
15. Combine kindness with firmness. The child must always sense that you are his friend, but that you would not accept certain kinds of behavior.
16. At all times distinguish between the deed and the doer. This permits respect for the child, even when he does something wrong.

17. Guide the individual to assume independence and his own self-direction.
18. Set the limits from the beginning, but work toward mutual understanding, a sense of responsibility, and consideration for others.
19. Admit your mistakes—the children will respect your honesty. Nothing is as pathetic as a defeated authoritarian who does not want to admit her defeat.
20. Mean what you say, but keep your demands simple, and see that they are carried out.
21. Children look to you for help and guidance. Give them this security, but make cooperation and eventual self-control the goal.
22. Keep in mind your long-term goal: an independent, responsible adult.
23. Children need direction and guidance until they can learn to direct themselves.
24. Close an incident quickly, and revive good spirits. Let children know that mistakes are corrected and then forgotten.
25. Commend a child when his behavior in a situation shows improvement.
26. Work cooperatively with the children to develop a procedure for dealing with infractions of the rules.
27. "Do unto others as you would have them do unto you."

As teachers we need to exercise kindness but also firmness so that the children will know what to expect from us; thus mutual respect between students and teachers will be the result of the democratic educational process. In this way the child will be able to project the inner order that exists in him out into his environment and will be able to make order in his own way, find his own place, and develop self-discipline.

When the students understand what is expected of them, when they have been accepted and respected as equal partners, when the teachers no longer feel threatened, then and only then, will they be ready to move into the process of learning in its true sense.

Order

Lack of respect for order is one of the most common complaints of teachers today. Usually the complaint goes like this: "I just don't know what to do. I spend half of my time trying to keep order in the room. It seems like all I do is discipline the kids and try to keep order."

Let us now look at the word "order." It has many meanings and we often get confused as to what order should mean in the classroom. Too often it means sitting in nice neat rows, feet flat on the floor, eyes straight ahead, no talking or working in groups, no moving around the room, and most of all—silence. It may also mean lining up and marching down the hall to the restrooms, to the cafeteria, or to the gym. Order may also mean that children do not ask questions, that they only do their assignment and do not use their creativity, initiative, or curiosity. Their classroom must be immaculate, every book must be in its right place, and the art work must be arranged in neat rows across the bulletin board with each design the exact replica of the one next to it.

It would be more meaningful if we could substitute the word "orderly" for the word "order." Order usually means rigidity. An orderly room could be one in which there is flexibility and also a proper arrangement or sequence of things to do such as keeping the floor free from litter, arranging a variety of art works in an artistic fashion, or grouping the children in small groups and working on unit projects. In such a room there is an animated look on the children's faces and they are free to move about and explore their environment. Chairs are shifted from one activity to the next and children work together and talk quietly about their project; there is evidence of teacher-pupil planning and cooperation.

It is the responsibility of the teacher to set up a schedule in which the children can function and to establish and maintain a daily routine and let the children fall into line. This sets the basis for self-discipline, the guidelines one must live by in adult life.

A child needs definite limits in order to develop a sense of security and discipline. Order cannot be maintained by pressure from without in the form of punishment but only by stimulation from within.

Learning can and does take place in a classroom where discipline and orderliness prevail.

If an individual is to become a useful person, he must adapt himself to some orderly pattern of living, learn to think and act in line with social regulations, adjust to his environment, and develop a sense of responsibility. Individuals cannot live with other persons unless they are guided by certain rules and regulations necessary for happy, peaceful living. It is this process that we call discipline.

In an autocratic society, freedom and order are mutually exclusive. Order means doing as you are told, and there is no freedom of self-determination. In a democratic society, freedom and order are necessarily complementary; one cannot exist without the other. Freedom alone leads to anarchy: anyone can do what he wants. Each one has to restrain his own freedom to permit optimum freedom for everybody else. Without order there can be no freedom, and without freedom there can be no order in a democratic setting, because imposed order is rejected.

We need to help young people learn to live successfully in a changing world that involves them in many different kinds of human relationships. They must be able to set up a pattern for living within a reliable frame of reference. This frame of reference must lead beyond absorbing subject matter into developing attitudes, establishing values, realizing the extent of one's own freedom and self-determination, and accepting responsibility. A set of rules that guarantees success or excludes conflict cannot be devised, so each child will have to make decisions according to his own perception of himself and others.

Chapter 10

Winning Over the Child

One of the most fundamental and often neglected principles in winning the child is the recognition that a person cannot influence another person unless he has first succeeded in gaining his cooperation. If a good relationship exists between the teacher and her students, the latter will be less inclined to create serious disturbances. This fact is often overlooked by teachers. They try to influence a child and to correct his behavioral deficiencies without paying any attention to the kind of relationship that they have with the child. Without this understanding, the teacher, in her effort to remedy a child's misbehavior, often upsets the already deteriorated relationship even further.

We find that a good personal relationship is the basis on which educational influences can be exerted successfully. Its establishment and maintenance require deliberate thought and consideration. A friendly yet firm teacher can win over her pupils without too much conscious effort. The requirements and pressures to which the teacher is subjected make it necessary for her to watch carefully her relationship with her students and to reevaluate the situation whenever the slightest friction arises. A sensitive teacher will be aware that her pupils do not function well when she gets upset. However, occasional emotional irritation with a child is almost unavoidable; therefore, each educator must make deliberate efforts to ameliorate the situation, otherwise an occasional regression may lead to the vicious game of mutual retaliation.

The technique of how to win over a child requires considerable study and consideration. There are no shortcuts for this training; it cannot be accomplished on the basis of past prescriptions. Too much depends on the individual personality of each teacher, on intangibles, on subtle expressions of attitudes, on emotional dynamics, and on values. Everyone has to find his own personal approach. Sincerity is the only means to win over children. Children are keen observers, and they know who is sincere and who is not. When anyone tries to put up a front, most children will sense this and resent or ridicule it.

Warmth of personality, kindness and friendliness of feeling are very important, but these qualities cannot be learned. They must come from within; there must be a sincere belief in and an appreciation of other people. These qualities require a proper relationship based on mutual respect, on a sense of equality, despite all individual differences of knowledge, power, and position. Any action that induces, expresses, or implies humiliation of a child greatly disturbs the relationship. The teacher who has the proper respect for the child and treats the child with dignity can induce this child to accept the order and the regulations necessary for any social function.

It is important that the teacher give her full attention toward establishing the right personal relationship when she first meets a new class.

Before school starts in the fall, children become anxious about their new teachers. Frequent comments from children are, "Who will be my teacher?"; "I hope I get Mr. Andrews; I heard that he's nice"; "I sure hope that I don't get Miss Stone. The other children don't like her; they say that she's mean." Changing teachers may be a great relief to those children who have had bad experiences with a teacher the previous year, or it may cause great anxiety lest a previous bad experience repeat itself. This is less obvious in older children; they may discuss their new teachers among themselves, but they do not betray their fears as readily as young children do. It is not uncommon to see a child clinging to his mother's hand, crying, and afraid to let go of her. Sometimes a parent expects a different teacher for his or her child and may openly show disappointment upon meeting the new teacher. The parent may even ask if it is still possible to change teachers. The teacher should not let her pride stand in the way of doing what the parent has requested. To such a parent the teacher may say something like: "I am sorry you feel this way and that you are disappointed. I don't know if it is possible to change classes at this point. Why don't you go down to the office and try? I am sure that they will make the change if it is still possible. However, if not, I will do my best to make Betty comfortable in my class." Such understanding and friendliness on the part of the teacher may dispel any doubts that the parent may have had and may win this parent over.

The first contact that the teacher has with her students is of great importance, since it lays the foundation for their future relationship. The teacher may succeed in winning over a student immediately or within the first few days, or without being aware of it she may antagonize a student and then need weeks or months to repair the damage.

If the teacher has some information about the child, she may be in a position to make the first contact personal and meaningful to the student. She may greet a student in the following ways:

"I recall you from last year. I used to watch you on the playground, and I noticed the way you shared the ball with the other children."

"Miss Kordova spoke very highly of you. She enjoyed having you in her Mathematics class last year. Is Math your favorite subject?"

"I heard that you lost your dog last June. I hope you finally found it."

To a student who is new to the community she might say:

"I believe that you are new to this school. It may feel a little strange at first, not knowing any of the children, but you will soon get to know them."

These examples illustrate how initial contact may be made with an apprehensive child. Light, friendly but sincere conversation and interest may help to soothe the student and make him feel welcome.

With older students the teacher may say the following:

"My name is Robert Holz. I am your science teacher. May I know who you are? How do you do, Mary. I am glad to meet you."

"Yes, I know you are Mary Berg, the girl who writes for the school paper. I often read your reports. I am glad to have you in my class, Mary."

It is a bad policy for the teacher to be working at the blackboard or at her desk when the students first come into her class. Some students may interpret this as indifference, and it may result in a bad start. The teacher has a better chance of winning the students over the first day of school if she stands by the door and greets each student personally.

In the first edition of this book the authors suggested that the teacher acquaint herself with the background, personality traits, and behavioral patterns of each student before she meets her class. This information is often found in the student's individual record. However, it has since come to our attention that many teachers become apprehensive and prejudiced against students whose records contain mostly reports of disruptive behavior. They expect the worst from these students, and, as often happens, these students live up to the teacher's expectations. Had the teacher not been familiar with such a student's past behavior, the student might have received different treatment and might have had a chance to start the school year with a more positive attitude. We therefore recommend that the teacher refrain from looking into the personal folders of the students until she has formed her own opinions. Then she can compare her opinions with what others have said. The teacher may discover that the previous evaluations no longer apply to the individual students. This is an encouraging experience for a teacher, because it indicates that she may have had a very positive influence on the student. It is not a good policy to tell students about their previous bad records, even if they have changed for the better. Reminding people of previous mistakes may be discouraging.

It may happen that a student who had difficulties in school and who took pride in his ability to defeat a teacher may ask the new teacher,

> "Didn't you hear any bad things about me? I did some very awful things last year."

This may be more than just a question; it may be a challenge, designed to test the new teacher's response to his provocation. The teacher should be careful not to fall into this type of trap. A possible reply might be:

> "To be honest, I am not concerned with what you did last year. Why should I worry about last year?"

We must remember that only a younger child may resort to such provocation. Mostly such incidents end in laughter. However, sometimes a child will question such a reply. Since the first morning is not a proper time to get into a long discussion, the teacher could suggest that this matter be discussed with the entire class at a later time. This promise should be carried out.

A humorous remark may take the edge off a challenging situation, as shown in the following example.

> Paul, a junior, was angry when the English teacher refused to accept his book report because he did not follow specific directions. As she returned the paper to Paul, explaining the reasons, he remarked, "Oh, you are full of sh——!" To this, the teacher answered, "Prove it!" Everyone laughed, and the tension disappeared.

To gain and maintain the child's full confidence requires constant deliberate thought and consideration on the part of the teacher. The initial contact is usually the basis for future relationships, for the child often evaluates his new teacher and establishes an attitude toward her based on his first impressions. If the child's attitude is a negative one, it may take months before the teacher can change it and establish a good relationship. On the other hand, if the initial contact is favorable, the teacher has her foot in the door. Her chances of success are much greater, and the child's chances of learning are increased.

The technique of winning a child over takes in many considerations: the age of the child, the general atmosphere of the classroom, any previous encounters the teacher may have had with the child (directly or indirectly), the amount of time she can devote to the child during the first day of school, and any knowledge she has as to the child's general attitude toward school, to mention but a few. If the teacher has some previous knowledge about the child, she can plot the first encounter with considerable assurance that it will be pleasing to the child. But, generally speaking, there is no definite technique for winning over a child. Each teacher must find her own technique. What may work for one teacher or with one child may not work with another. Winning a child over does not depend solely on the words but also on the inflection of the voice, the facial expressions, the physical proximity of the teacher, the timing, others who are present in the class, and her general personality.

The First Day of School

The first day of school may be just as frightening to the new teacher as it is to the child. The teacher, as well as the children, need time to adjust to the new situation. She needs to help the children to establish satisfying interpersonal relationships with each other, as well as with herself.

Since the teacher does not know her students and their immediate interests, it helps to have a number of activities of light nature prepared for the first few hours. The students should be allowed to move freely and to look at a display of books, art material, workbooks, and so on. The teacher may mingle with the students and answer questions. When the class settles down, the initial organized program should be light and pleasant. At no time should a teacher allow the situation to become disorganized and out of hand, for this may be a green light for some students to become disruptive or may suggest to some that in this class they can do as they wish. This would be a very bad start. Should this happen, the teacher should stop the activity and say something like this:

> "Class, I want very much for you to be happy here, and I will do everything in my power to help you enjoy this class, but I hope that you will do the same for me. We can only be happy here if we consider each other. We can not have a happy class if you run around and if you disturb everyone else. We cannot allow this. So, please, let's go back to what we were doing and enjoy it."

The teacher must convey friendliness but also firmness. One without the other does not work well.

Teachers should acquaint themselves with the proper pronunciation of each child's name. Children are often sensitive to mispronunciation of their names, especially younger children.

It is important for the teacher to establish control of her class and some kind of routine on the first morning. As children plan with the teacher, they will learn to accept some responsibility for their own behavior, and the teacher can relax and enjoy the children.

Inviting Trouble

Some teachers believe that they can avoid trouble if they tell a problem child that they are familiar with his history and that he had better watch his step. With this approach, the teacher may evoke resistance and open defiance from the child. If the child feels humiliated, he may be determined to defeat her. If his antisocial behavior is a means to get status in class, she may have helped him achieve his goal the minute he enters the class-room. He now must live up to his reputation. The following example illus-trates such a case.

> During the second or third year of teaching, I thought that I would avoid difficulties by taking the bull by the horns. I told Anthony that there would be no monkey business in my class and that he had better watch his step. As it turned out, it was I who did not watch my step, for a few minutes later he tripped me as I walked through the aisle, and I fell. The class roared. I sent Anthony to the principal, who in turn sent for his parents. Thus, I antagonized Anthony, his parents, and the principal on the first day of school.

Avoiding Discouragement

The teacher should not become discouraged if all the children do not rally to her side within a few days. Children who have had unsatisfying rela-tionships with adults will be quite distrustful. These children are usually the ones everyone has heard about from year to year. When a teacher is faced with this type of child, it is possible to discipline herself and to trans-form resentment into positive action, as the following example indicates:

> I knew for two-and-a-half months that I was going to have Larry in my class when high school opened. I thought of resigning, getting sick, or moving away. Then I thought of Larry. How must he feel? He really must be miser-able to make life such a hassle. What could I do to help him so that we both could survive and maybe even have some fun? I planned a course of action:
>
> 1. Be certain he had some successful experiences.
> 2. Let him know that I liked him by my actions, attitudes, and words.
> 3. Give him a trustworthy job in a matter-of-fact way.

4. Raise my expectations of Larry and of myself.
5. Arrange time for weekly conferences with Larry.

Larry and I both learned slowly, step by step to build on our successes together. It was a difficult task but a rewarding one. I shudder to think what might have happened if I had not plotted and planned!

A good relationship between teacher and student calls for mutual respect and confidence. Children who are treated with dignity and friendliness (not just at the moment but consistently) respond sooner or later and accept order and cooperation, which is necessary for any social existence.

Winning over the Teenager

Winning over the teenager sometimes is more difficult than winning over younger children, because his ways and his beliefs are more set. Furthermore, he is usually more dependent on the opinion and the acceptance of his peers than the young child is. If he has established a reputation of being tough and unafraid of teachers, he may feel threatened in his position if he gives in to the friendliness of a teacher, no matter how much he might want to. He may provoke the teacher at the first meeting in order to impress the group with his unchanged attitude and courage. The understanding teacher will refrain from putting this student "in his place" or from making a great issue of the situation. The teacher may say things such as:

"I think that you have made your point, Ricky. The class is impressed and so am I. You have a lot of courage."

"I hope that you can relax now that you have impressed everyone with your courage. And I hope that your opinion of me will change once you get to know me."

"Are you trying to shock me, Ricky? I am impressed with your courage. What do you expect me to do now?"

The approach has to shift from an individual to a class discussion. The teacher may ask each student to fill out a prepared questionnaire that will help her obtain information about how each individual student feels about school, about himself, and especially about her class. At the same time, most students appreciate the teacher's attempt to accommodate the class and her willingness to cooperate with them wherever possible. The following example may be of help to teachers.

At the first meeting of the class I asked the students to fill out a form and answer the following four questions:

1. What induced you to take this class as an elective?
2. How would you like this class to be run, and what would you like your part to be in helping the class to function in this manner?
3. What do you expect from the teacher?
4. What do you expect from yourself?

Most of the answers were concerned with questions two and three. They wanted the class to be orderly, to be able to hear, and to have some freedom. They wanted the teacher to be kind, considerate, fair, affectionate, obedient, punctual, understanding, friendly, and to give them a break. For themselves, they expected to come to class and act as seniors should. As a group, we explored what they meant by an orderly class. Since very few had included on their paper what they felt their part was in relationship to the organization and operation of the class, we discussed this problem. The group clarified their responsibility for maintaining an orderly class. We then discussed their expectations of the teacher, stopping to define in their own terms the meanings of the various qualities with particular attention to the words "fair" and "give them a break." After this was accomplished, we looked at their expectations of themselves. It was a real eye-opener to them to realize that they were asking many things of the teacher but not much of themselves. They concluded that perhaps it was the teacher who really needed to be given a break, and they decided that it was the students who needed to be fair! As one boy laughingly said, "What a revolting development this is!" The students were cooperative, responsible, and receptive.

The teacher may fill out a similar questionnaire herself.

1. What do I expect of this class?
2. What would I like this class to be?
3. What can I do to make my students feel that they are respected and that they belong?
4. What is my overall goal for this class?

The questionnaire should be designed so that after each question there would be a space large enough for the student to write his answers.

The answers to these questions should then be discussed with the class and clarified in order to avoid any misunderstanding. The teacher and students must come to certain agreements based on what is realistically possible for a teacher to do. Students often have distorted ideas about the teacher's power. For instance, if a student wants more time for recess, a change of textbook, or whatever, which is not within the jurisdiction of the teacher, it must be discussed honestly.

Children readily accept an adult's superior experience and skill, provided the adult does not flaunt his superiority or take special privileges that are denied to the children. All of us probably remember overhearing a child complain to his friend: "She always talks to another teacher during assembly, but when *we* do, she punishes us. Why can't we talk if she can?"

A teacher who sets aside special rights for herself has little chance of getting the children to trust and respect her. They recognize her double standards, and they resent it.

We must not confuse kindness and understanding with indulgence or giving children free rein. The former are related to the basic rules of respect, trust, and cooperation, whereas the latter are based on disorder and lack of self-respect. To be effective, a teacher must be kind and firm.

The teacher of young children could also write on the blackboard, "Sh-h-h, teacher has a headache." By so doing, she can often prevent misunderstandings. Nevertheless, misunderstandings may occur, not just on days when the teacher is out of sorts, but at any time. The following example illustrates how much on the alert a teacher has to be in order to avoid misunderstandings.

> I recall an unfortunate experience that I had with a student some time ago. Mitzi was a withdrawn child when she entered my class. It took me months to gain her confidence, and then I ruined it with one sentence. One day she asked me why I never wore anything brown. I replied that brown was not "my color," meaning that it was not becoming to me. Mitzi took it that I disliked the color. As it happened, she had on a new brown dress that day, which I had not noticed. Mitzi cried bitterly and pushed me away when I tried to console her. I could not reach her for weeks.

It is not enough to show occasional interest in a child. Children's needs are ever present, and teachers must be aware of them. If the teacher had noticed Mitzi's new brown dress, she would not have had to renew her energies and devote so much time to winning Mitzi over again.

Children usually test each teacher, especially during the first week or so of school, to find out what the limits are and what the consequences of transgression are. She should avoid making a value judgment of a child. The child will interpret this as "You don't like me," "You hate me," or "You really don't care." It is important for the teacher to help the child distinglish between. "I like you" and "It is your behavior that is unacceptable."

The teacher needs to look at this testing period as an academic exercise rather than as a personal affront, and then she will be more able to cope with the situation.

Chapter 11

Encouragement

The process of encouragement or reinforcement is paramount in building the child's learning ability and in developing his commitment to the learning process. All children need approval and seek approbation, regardless of the status that they occupy in the group. Lack of appreciation may easily discourage even a very gifted child, and he may withdraw from participation.

If the teacher expects failure and is convinced that the child will have to be coaxed or punished to learn, he will most likely succeed in these expectations, which, in turn, will convince her that she was right in the first place.

On the other hand, if the child has been helped to have the courage to take chances, even at the risk of failure, he will probably do better than he expected. For a discouraged child, even the slightest proof of success is a great booster, for he may have never experienced success and may be convinced that he never would. Even a little success can be a tremendous help to the teacher and to the group to build on, for it is really the foundation on which all can stand firmly without feeling hypocritical; in giving recognition.

Teachers who lack this understanding tend to discourage children by means and gestures that they think are encouraging but really are not.

Encouragement Versus Discouragement

Every misbehaving or deficient child is discouraged. As long as he has confidence in his ability, he will use constructive means to find a place in the home or in school. He deviates only if he finds himself blocked in his endeavors. Discouragement is at the root of mistaken approaches. Every child would like to be good and is "bad" only if he sees no chance to succeed. Parents and teachers don't realize how they, unwittingly, constantly discourage children. They sincerely believe that the child will be spurred on to do better if they humilate, shame, and punish him for disobedience or for not having done a job according to the adult's expectations. They do not realize that criticism and humiliation do not add to a child's self-confidence and to his courage, yet the two qualities are the basis for social adjustment and academic progress. They alone provide a sense of security.

We must realize that many teachers are confronted with children who are already handicapped by their home training. The teacher, provoked by the student, often continues the discouraging methods used by the parents. It requires a great deal of understanding and patience to resist a child's unconscious schemes.

The teacher is in a crucial position in the child's life. She is often the first person besides his parents who exerts deliberate educational influences. Furthermore, she is the first to emphasize work, duty and responsibility. If her influence is discouraging, she may permanently block a child's function in a social relationship or in some field of endeavor. Many people suffer from unnecessary deficiencies as a result of their first experiences in school, because their teacher convinced them of their inability in a certain field. Many people retain a strong distaste for any formal education because of the discouraging experiences of their early school years. Undoubtedly their teachers had the best intentions of developing the student's knowledge and intellectual capacities, but they operated on false premises.

A realization of the importance of encouragement, and a knowledge of the methods of its implementation, are an absolute prerequisite for any teacher who wants to exert constructive influence on her pupils. Unfortunately, teachers have misconceptions about how to encourage children (Dreikurs, 1951).

The teacher who does not know how to influence a child is inclined to blame him for her own ineffectiveness. Even when she tried to assume an encouraging attitude, she may do it in a discouraging manner. An example of this follows.

Telling a child that he could do much better and that he could be such a nice child if he would only try is meant to encourage the child. However, these words may actually discourage a child who has been trying, and he may think that the teacher is not aware of his efforts. He may say to himself, "So what's the use of trying?" and give up altogether. The teacher's words may convey to a child, "You are not a nice child as you are." This may be regarded by the child as an accusation, and the child may be angry or his feelings hurt.

It is difficult to define the exact method of encouragement, as everything depends on the child's reaction. The same words spoken to two different children may have two different effects. One child may feel discouraged while the other child may see this as the teacher's confidence in his ability and feel encouraged.

What Is Encouragement?

Encouragement is a complex process; its development is dependent on a number of gross and minute circumstances that shift continuously. As a result, a precise definition is impossible to give.

At best, we can say that it is an action that conveys to the child that the teacher respects, trusts, and believes in him and thinks that his present lack of skills in no way diminishes his value as a person.

An effective process of encouragement demands continuous alertness for the right moment, tone of voice, and choice of words. Constant opportunities for encouragement appear in many areas of a student's efforts, whether the efforts are altogether successful or not.

Recognition must be given for real trying, even if there has been no visible accomplishment. A teacher may say, "You have been working so hard on spelling this morning. I have been watching you, and I am happy to see your determination." Or she may say, "Would you like to rest for a few minutes? You have been working so hard that you deserve it." Recognition should never be overdone. A few words will suffice.

A teacher may encourage a child without using any words. For example, a child's paper is checked as soon as he completes the assignment. Each correct answer is marked with a capital C. Each incorrect problem is left unmarked. The paper is immediately returned to the child, who then reworks the incorrect problems. Then an *O.K.* is written on the correct response. Thus, the completed paper has only positive markings, which is encouraging to the child, and another step has been taken in bringing even more academic performance to full strength. Minimizing mistakes will have an encouraging effect if the child is still struggling. This does not imply that a teacher must overlook them or even deny that the child has made mistakes. The following will illustrate this.

A math teacher gave his class an assignment of ten problems. One of the students worked out six without making a mistake. The teacher marked the paper −4 and gave this boy an unsatisfactory grade.

This teacher missed a wonderful opportunity to encourage this student honestly and convincingly. The teacher might have given this boy a +6, which is in itself encouraging, and she might have said: "Since you worked out six problems without making an error, I know that you understand how to do these exercises. There must have been a reason why you did not complete the assignment. Would you mind telling me what happened? I did not grade you, as you must have noticed, because I wanted to talk to you first. You missed a passing grade by one point. Would you like a chance to finish your paper?"

The teacher would have won over this child by giving encouragement at a point at which the child was feeling discouraged. Encouragement builds on the child's strength.

Encouragement can be applied systematically to the slow child by dividing the assignments into many short tasks. This type of programming provides experiences that are "built in" to stimulate the child's positive attention. His concentration span is lengthened, his enjoyment of the tasks is raised, and his self-respect is enhanced. These results have the effect of eliminating many of his old forms of misbehavior. With this method, during a 45-minute period a child can accomplish 10 to 15 items. It also produces a spiral effect in learning, since the teacher is able to reprogram the problem and the child is able to mark his paper correctly and thereby reinforce his learning of that concept.

When to Begin Encouraging the Child

Encouragement is most effective if it starts at the very beginning of the school year. No doubt a sudden change in the teacher's attitude will have an effect on the child's response, particularly if the teacher is persistent in her approval. However, she can save herself a great deal of time and energy if she demonstrates her belief in the child from the first encounter she has with him. This presupposes the teacher's genuine belief in children and in the process of encouragement.

Since no two children are alike, the teacher will need to be sensitive to the feelings of each member of her class in order to know when and how to encourage him. The effect of her encouragement will also depend on the child's relationship within the group. A child may well be skeptical of the teacher's recognition if he had been in her class for a considerable time and she has never before expressed any appreciation or belief in him. The following example illustrates this point:

> Doug, a senior in high school, in four months had never received attention or recognition from his teacher in drafting class. Although Doug never completed an assignment, the teacher merely gave him a failing grade without commenting on it. One day the teacher passed his table, gently patted him on the shoulder, and said that he was doing a good job on his project. Doug was too startled to respond, but after class he was overheard making the following remark to one of the boys: "Did you hear what old B— said to me today? What do you suppose he wants?"
>
> It never occurred to Doug that the teacher was serious in his compliment.

The Overambitious Teacher

Some teachers may start out during the year using encouragement, but if they do not see immediate results, they themselves may become discouraged and either revert to autocratic disciplinary measures or lose confidence in their own ability to exert an influence on the child and let him do as he pleases. How often do we hear teachers say, "I have tried everything but all in vain. I give up, because I don't know how to get through to this child." Such a reaction is very unfortunate for both the child and the teacher. A teacher has to develop techniques and abilities together with patience and self-confidence in order to help the child overcome his difficulties. This may require that the teacher alter her own viewpoint. Instead of seeking academic accomplishments, she may have to look for commendable performances in the everyday activities of the child. He may be a good runner or good at sharpening the teacher's pencils.

A teacher can discourage a child by her actions, perhaps even more so than by her words. She may act as if he were ignorant, stupid, or incapable.

Miki was working on a sixth-grade Social Studies assignment. He asked his teacher for help in locating the answer to a particular question. The teacher helped him to locate the material and hovered over him until he had written the answer. She then read the next question aloud and began to look through the book for the answer. At this point Miki said, "Go away, I can do these by myself. Do you think I'm stupid or something?"

The act of hovering has a discouraging effect in itself, because it tells the child that the teacher does not think he is capable of continuing alone. To another child it may seem that the teacher does not trust his reasoning or thinking abilities or thinks that he cannot do the work correctly.

One of the most frequent and deadly means of discouraging a child is pointing out to him how much better he could be. Instead of spurring him on to greater efforts, it usually stops him from even trying. This is the worst thing she can tell a child.

The way in which a teacher asks a child to do something may have either an encouraging or a discouraging effect. Usually, she will get better cooperation if she refrains from negative commands: "Try to hold your pencil like this and your hand won't get tired" instead of "Don't hold your pencil at the top. Whoever writes like this?"; "Don't you think it would be better to do the workbook first since your group is going to check it soon?" instead of, "I told you to do the workbook first. Why don't you do as you are told?" "Please" and "thank you" are always helpful.

The Danger of Competitive Encouragement

The teacher must be very cautious in using the term "better than others." Many children get the impression that they are important only if they are better than others. Such misconceptions are often fostered by parents and teachers. It is preferable to say, "I like the way you sharpen my pencils" rather than "You're the best pencil sharpener I have ever had."

Consistency in the Relationship

Inherent in the process of encouragement is the concept of developing a basic mutual trust between the teacher and the child, because mutual trust is the foundation upon which good interpersonal relationships are built. A child's trust often precedes confidence in himself. Trust implies that the child has learned to rely on the sameness constancy of the teacher and to trust himself in his transactions with the teacher. Then he is able to consider himself trustworthy enough so that the teacher will remain constant in her relationship. A child's trust in his teacher implies reliance on her integrity and sincerity.

The development of a child's abilities may grow at varied rates. His learning experiences change with time, as well as his views of his relationship with the teacher. As a result, some children will test the relationship constantly, whereas others will test it only occasionally.

A child who has not learned to trust others quite often will not trust himself in his relationships. He will relate to very few people, and his academic progress may become stymied. The establishment of trust is a necessary step in the process of encouraging this type of child.

Barry was an 11-year-old boy who trusted no one, who did not like himself, and who refused to try anything academic. He was not allowed to go through the halls alone, because he constantly bothered the students in the other rooms. I had Barry for several days and had been instructed to accompany him through the halls, which I did.

One day Barry asked to leave the room, and I talked with him, saying that I believed that I could trust him to go to the bathroom and return alone and would give him a pass so he would not be questioned. Big tears came into his eyes while he said to me that no one had ever trusted him. He asked if I was going to stand at the door and watch him, "No," I said, "you can go to the bathroom and return alone. I can trust you to do this."

Barry lived up to my expectations. Then Barry and I discussed other ways in which he might be trusted. I told him that I would make no promises and would not ask him to make promises, since there might be an oversight and one of us might forget and break one. This was important to Barry, because many people had extracted promises from him that he usually broke. For the first time, Barry found an adult who maintained the same kind of relationship with him during his good times as well as his bad times—a person who accepted him as he was and who let him grow and develop at his own pace.

Rigidity as an Obstacle to Encouragement

There are always exceptions to every rule. What is said is often less important than how it is said. Anything that strengthens the child's belief in himself, without damaging his relationship with others, is highly recommended. Let us examine this more carefully. It would be perfectly in order to fuss over a child who has at last mustered up enough courage to participate in some activity, academic or other. For example, if a child has been afraid to play ball because she may get hurt while catching it, but she has at last decided to join in a game, it would greatly encourage her if everybody, and not just the teacher, would show appreciation. However, the teacher may have to maneuver the situation in order to stimulate or influence the group to praise the child for her action. The teacher may say, "Look, children, Sally is playing ball with us today. I am so glad, aren't you? Let's show her how glad we are." The class may applaud or they may give her the ball to throw first. There are numerous other ways by which other children can express their confidence and their pleasure. Most children will have compassion for those who are not successful if the class is cooperative and not competitive. It is necessary to develop in children the ability to be aware of other people's needs and of the power they have to help others.

Children must be helped to understand that people are different and that this is good. Then the teacher can help them to accept their own personal capacities and difficulties and to understand that others have talents as well as troubles. To encourage a child by comparing him with another defeats such efforts. If another child, like Sally, was frightened of playing ball and had not yet made an attempt, the child would be discouraged if the teacher pointed out Sally to him as an example. It would be better to help Hank by letting him carry the ball or perhaps throw it to someone and by commenting on his throwing.

Sibling Rivalry as Discouragement

What can a teacher do if she realizes that a child is discouraged because of a sister or a brother who is a better student in school? She can use various approaches. She can help the child through discussions with the entire class about the differences that can be found in people. She can stress that all of us have problems and that we are not alone in our difficulties and feelings of inferiority. She might also speak to the parents and point out the mistake they are making by comparing the two children.

Most important is the teacher's constant alertness to situations that present chances to raise the child's self-esteem. She must provide opportunities to make him feel important and respected by the group. Janek's case might well illustrate such a situation.

Janek was the second child in a family of four. His older sister, as well as his younger brother, were excellent students. The parents, who had little education, placed great value on academic knowledge and were determined to give their children an education. They depended on their oldest daughter to do all the writing for them and promised to send her to college because she was doing so well in school. They loved Janek, but they were disappointed and hurt because of his poor performance in school. They were constantly holding up Sonia, his sister, as an example.

In spite of all the affection he got from his parents, Janek was convinced that they did not love him and that he had no place in their hearts. It was difficult for the parents to understand what they should do, especially how to encourage the boy. Janek had never known any adult who took a genuine interest in him. He was withdrawn in class and showed no interest in any activity except music. He had a lovely voice, but he would hold back in group singing. My first break with him came when we were discussing the different kinds of names people have. Someone asked me what name I liked best. I replied that one of my favorite names was Janek, that it had a musical sound, and that it looked interesting when written. Everyone's eyes turned to Janek, who blushed, but for once he looked straight at me. I added casually, "Sometimes we like certain names because they remind us of people we like. Maybe that's another reason why I like the name Janek." He said goodbye to me when he left school, something he had never done before.

Soon after that, I asked him if he sang in the church choir, and when he said he didn't, I told him that they would be delighted to have someone who could sing as he could and that he should join. When I asked if he would like to, he shrugged his shoulders as if he were indifferent, but I could detect a gleam in his eye. I asked him if he would object if I tried to find out how he could join, and he replied that he didn't care one way or another. At least he did not say "No."

The parents were not aware of Janek's voice; he seldom sang at home. I was very glad to learn that nobody else in the family could sing well. They were less impressed with the discovery of their son's voice than with the possibility that he would sing in the church choir. Both parents understood that this would give Janek prestige and that they should make some fuss over his talent. Soon after, Janek sang in the church choir. This was the beginning of his general change toward better adjustment at school and at home.

Janek was now willing to sing for the class, and he even agreed to sing by himself at a school party at which his parents were present. During group singing in class I asked him to sit next to children who had difficulty carrying a tune, so that he could lead them. He accepted readily. He was easier to talk to, because he did not hang his head as he did before. He was willing to read his compositions to the class and often volunteered to lead in an activity. As Janek improved in school, it was also easier for me to direct his parents in their handling of the boy, for now their belief in him had also grown. Thus it happened that Janek established a closer relationship with his teacher, the group, and his parents.

Encouragement Versus Praise

It is crucial that teachers recognize the difference between praise and encouragement. Praise is usually given to the child when a task or a deed is well done, or when the task is completed. Encouragement is necessary when a child fails. Encouraging the child during the task or for trying is as important as giving the child recognition upon completion of the task. If the child is once rewarded with praise, then the withholding or lack of praise signifies failure. Flattery may promote insecurity since the child may become frightened of the possibility of not being able to live up to expectations or may not be certain he will get the same kind of praise again. The child has the mistaken idea that *unless he is praised, he has no value* and therefore he is a failure. Praise puts emphasis on the child; encouragement puts emphasis on the task.

Most of us have grown up believing that praise is desperately needed by all children in order to stimulate them into "right" behavior. If we watch closely when he is receiving praise we may discover some astonishing facts. Some children gloat, some panic, some express "So what," some seem to say, "Well, finally!"

We are suddenly confronted with the fact that we need to see how the child interprets what is going on rather than assume that he regards everything as we do.

Examination of the intention of the praiser shows that he is offering a reward: "If you are good you will have the reward of being high in my esteem." Well, fine. What is wrong with this approach? Why not help the child learn to do the right thing by earning a high place in parental esteem?

If we look at the situation from the child's point of view, we will find the mistake of this approach.

How does praise affect the child's self-image? He may get the impression that his personal worth depends upon how he "measures up" to the demands and values of others. "If I am praised, my personal worth is high. If I am scolded, I am worthless." When this child becomes an adult, his effectiveness, his ability to function, his capacity to cope with life's tasks will depend entirely upon his estimation of how he stands in the opinion of others. He will live constantly on an elevator—up and down.

Praise is apt to center the attention of the child upon himself. "How do I measure up?" rather than "What does the situation need?" This gives rise to a fictive-goal of "self-being-praised" instead of the reality of the reality-goal of "what-can-I-do-to-help."

Another child may come to see praise as his right—as rightfully due him from life. Therefore, life is unfair if he doesn't receive praise for every effort. "Poor me—no one appreciates me." Or, he may feel he has no obligation to perform if no praise is forthcoming. "What's in it for me? What will I get out of it? If no praise (reward) is forthcoming, why should I bother?"

Praise can be terribly discouraging. If the child's effort fails to bring the expected praise, he may assume either that he isn't good enough or that what he has to offer isn't worth the effort and so give up.

If a child has set exceedingly high standards for himself, praise may sound like mockery or scorn, especially when his efforts fail to measure up to his own standards. In such a child, praise only serves to increase his anger with himself and his resentment of others for not understanding his dilemma (Soltz, 1967).

When we encourage the child we must be alert to his response. We must move from a premise of "How good am I?" to "What can I do to help?" Anything we can do that will help a child feel better about himself and increase his self-esteem and that will show him that he can contribute is encouraging to the child. Encouragement assists the child in finding the inner strength and the courage to handle the difficulties of life.

Let us look at some differences between praising and encouraging statements:

Praise	*Encouragement*
You are the best student I ever had.	You are a fine student. Any teacher will appreciate and enjoy you.
You are always on time.	You sure make an effort to be on time.
You have the highest score in the class on this exam.	You did very well on this exam.
I am so proud of you.	You seem to really enjoy learning.
You're the best helper I ever had.	The room looks very neat since you straightened the bookshelves.
I'm so proud of your artwork.	It is nice to see that you enjoy art.

The following comparisons are from Taylor (1979).

Praise	*Encouragement*
stimulates rivalry and competition	stimulates cooperation and contribution for the good of all
focuses on quality of performance	focuses on amount of effort and joy
evaluative and judgmental; person feels "judged"	little or no evaluation of person or act; person feels "accepted"
fosters selfishness at the expense of others	fosters self-interest, which does not hurt others
emphasis on global evaluation of the person—"You are better than others."	emphasis of specific contribution—"You have helped in this way."
creates quitters	creates triers
fosters fear of failure	fosters acceptance of being imperfect
fosters dependence	fosters self-sufficiency and independence

A teacher often tends to put her faith mainly in the child's intellectual potentialities, which she measures by his performance. If he performs well, she is pleased with herself as well as with the child. Her attitude has a very definite influence on the child's regard for academic achievement per se, for he senses that the degree of his performance may determine his position in the class.

> A teacher recalled a conversation with a boy who was not her student. He was extremely nasty to other children on the playground. When she confronted him with this fact, he replied, "I know. My teacher always calls me a pest, but she never does anything to me because I am the best student in her class."

This boy felt protected because of his scholastic standing in the class. However, his need for belligerence indicates a lack of confidence in himself, at least in social relationships. His academic success obviously was not helping him toward a better social adjustment.

The teacher must not confuse encouraging a child with inspiring him to show courage. Showing courage does not always imply self-confidence. A child may show courage if his desire for approval is very strong.

> A student who was afraid of playing ball because he might get hurt climbed the outside ledge of a window on the second floor, causing everyone to look at him.

A child may force himself to show courage in order not to be called a sissy. Many people believe that such daring acts are indications of courage and do not realize that this child may be really frightened and insecure. It is not unusual for a teacher to hear a parent say, "How can you say that my child is discouraged? You should see him climb trees and ride his bicycle without using his hands." This same child may lack the confidence to participate in academic work or in any other group activity. He may feel that nobody likes him and that the only way to get attention is to do daring deeds. Encouraging such displays of bravado may even become dangerous, for the child may become foolhardy or belligerent.

A child does not feel encouraged if the teacher gives with one hand and takes away with the other. Complimenting a child with a "but" kills any encouraging words. "Buts" can easily slip into our good intentions: "I'm very proud of your reading, but you must watch your punctuation." "Your spelling is improving, but you're neglecting your English." Acknowledgments must stand by themselves, with nothing to mar them, if they are to be effective.

Comparing children is another important factor to be considered. Parents and teachers often believe that they can induce a child to do better if they point out how much better another child is doing or how much better in school his sibling was. How many times do we hear, "John is doing better and we are pleased, but at his age Michael, his brother, was much further along in school than he is." Or, "Why don't you do as well as your brother? I had no trouble with him when he was in my class." Comparing children unfavorably creates defeatism, adds to sibling rivalry, and lowers the child's self-respect. Always keep in mind that each child is different and that each must get respect for what *he* is.

What a Teacher Can Do

An important factor in encouraging a child is the teacher's understanding of the goal that the child has set for himself in a particular situation (see Chapter 3). In most cases, recognition of a child before the entire class carries more weight, because peer approval often is more important to the child than the teacher's approval.

Dinkmeyer and Dreikurs (1963) made up a list of nine things that the teacher and parents should keep in mind when they are encouraging children.

1. Place value on the child as he is.
2. Show faith in the child and enable him to have faith in himself.
3. Sincerely believe in the child's ability and win his confidence while building his self-respect.
4. Recognize a job "well done" and give recognition for his effort.
5. Utilize the class group to facilitate and enhance the development of the child.
6. Integrate the group so that each child can be sure of his place in it.
7. Assist in the development of skills sequentially in order to insure success.
8. Recognize and focus on strengths and assets.
9. Utilize the interest of the child to energize constructive activity.

To illustrate further, Reimer (1967) offers a list of words that are encouraging to a child.

1. *"You do a good job of. . . ."* Children should be encouraged when they do not expect it or when they are not asking for it. It is possible to point out some useful act or contribution in each child. Even a comment about something small and insignificant to us may have great importance to a child.
2. *"You have improved in. . . ."* Growth and improvement is something that we should expect from all children. They may not be where we would like them to be, but if there is progress, there is less chance for

discouragement. Children will usually continue to try if they can see some improvement.

3. *"We like (enjoy) you, but we don't like what you do."* Often a child feels that he is not liked after he has made a mistake or has misbehaved. A child should never think that *he* is not liked. It is important to distinguish between the child and his behavior, between the act and the actor.

4. *"You can help me (us, the others, and so on) by. . . ."* To feel useful and helpful is important to everyone. Children want to be helpful; we have only to give them the opportunity.

5. *"Let's try it together."* Children who think that they have to do things perfectly are often afraid to attempt something new for fear of making a mistake or of failing.

6. *"So you do make a mistake; now, what can you learn from your mistake?"* There is nothing that can be done about what has already happened, but a person can always do something about the future. Mistakes can teach the child a great deal, and he will learn if he does not feel embarrassed about having made a mistake.

7. *"You would like us to think you can't do it, but we think you can."* This approach could be used when the child says or conveys the impression that something is too difficult for him and when he hesitates to even try it. If he tries and fails, he has at least had the courage to try. Our expectations should be consistent with the child's ability and maturity.

8. *"Keep trying. Don't give up."* When a child is trying but not meeting with much success a comment like this might be helpful.

9. *"I'm sure you can straighten this out (solve this problem), but if you need any help, you know where to find me."* Adults need to express confidence that children are able to and will resolve their own conflicts, if they are given a chance.

10. *"I can understand how you feel (not sympathy, but empathy) but I'm sure you'll be able to handle it."* Sympathizing with another person seldom helps him; rather, it suggests that life has been unfair to him. Understanding the situation and believing in the child's ability to adjust to it is of much greater help to him.

Sometimes children have such a poor self-image that they do not believe that they can be liked or can do anything that is acceptable to adults. Therefore, we must give them as much encouragement as possible.

Other Things a Teacher Can Do to Encourage a Child

1. If a child expresses doubt in his abilities in spite of the teacher's reassurance, she may show him reports of other teachers concerning him, if they are favorable. She may say, "I don't do this very often, but I should like you to see for yourself that I am not the only one who believes in you. Listen to what Mrs. X has said about you."

2. If a child is unsure and therefore does not start an assigned project, the teacher may sit down next to him and do part of the work with him. This may, in some cases, be enough to motivate the child. However, we must caution the teacher to be careful not to make a habit of this procedure with this child. It may encourage dependency. We must remember that what we do always depends on the kind of child we are dealing with.

3. Let a child teach the entire class something he knows how to do well, no matter how insignificant it may be.

4. If the teacher senses that a child is unhappy because he is too big or too small for his age, she may read to the class about the achievements of great people who had the same problems. In this way the child learns to evaluate himself and others not by their size but by their personality.

5. Let a poor speller be the spelling teacher now and then, and allow him to use the book. The same may apply to any subject from which the child shies away.

6. Find special jobs for the child—jobs that give him status.

7. Let a child with poor writing habits write the teacher's assignments on the blackboard.

8. Ask a child who feels rejected to be the master of ceremonies at a party.

9. Invite to speak to the class a member of the child's family who might make an impression on the others in class, if, for example, the child's father or brother is a policeman, firefighter, or does work that is usually admired by children.

10. If the teacher knows of some special contribution a child has made at home, tell it to the entire class.

11. Display the child's work for everyone to see.

12. Invite the parents to the class, and say in his presence something positive about the child to them.

13. Send a note home commenting favorably on the child's behavior, performance, or both. Teachers tend to send notes home only when children have difficulties.

Teachers must provide opportunities for children to experience success. Merely telling a child that "he can if he tries hard enough" is not enough.

The child can succeed only if the teacher plans situations in which he can succeed. It entails planning, which is work for the teacher—additional work to the already heavy load that teachers carry. However, in the long run, such work is rewarding, not only because the children do better but also because it cuts down the amount of time that the teacher will have to spend on children because of their antisocial behavior.

Some teachers may argue that despite their best intentions they cannot find any area in which a certain child can do well or experience even minute success. If we assume that these teachers refer to academic work, it may be true. However, we cannot be concerned merely with academic success if we are trying to raise a child's self-esteem or self-evaluation.

> Merril was a first-grader who had difficulties with his visual motor skills. In order to help him to obtain better coordination, a part of each day was devoted to teaching Merril to play jacks. Day after day, Merril practiced bouncing and catching the ball and picking up jacks. After several weeks, the teacher noticed that Merril was able to catch the ball and pick up the jacks at the same time. What a happy time that was! The class applauded because they wanted to show Merril that they valued his achievement.

If the child in question is a troublemaker, a teacher can always utilize his ability to defeat teachers and parents as a means to uplift the child. However, this must be done in a very specific way, because the goal of the teacher is to help this child see how powerful he is and the possibilities that he has to use his power constructively.

Therefore, any situation that allows the teacher an opportunity to put in a good word for a particular child should be utilized. He may be a good whistler or even a good bubble-gum blower. If the teacher realizes this, the child should be given an opportunity to show off his skill and to be recognized for it. We must remember that this is just a stepping-stone toward further achievement. In time, as the child feels more accepted, he will become interested in other achievements.

Teachers must always remember that no technique in itself is applicable to every situation. Each child and each situation are unique.

REFERENCES

Dinkmeyer, Don, and Dreikurs, Rudolf. *Encouraging Children to Learn.* Englewood Cliffs, N.J.: Prentice-Hall, 1963.

Dreikurs, Rudolf. *Understanding the Child, a Manual for Teachers* (monograph), 1951.

Reimer, Clint. "Some Words of Encouragement," in Vicki Soltz, ed., *Study Group Leader's Manual.* Chicago: Alfred Adler Institute, 1967.

Soltz, Vicki, ed. *Study Group Leader's Manual.* Chicago: Alfred Adler Institute, 1967.

Taylor, John F. "Encouragement vs. Praise," unpublished manuscript presented at a workshop in Portland, Oreg., January 1979.

SELECTED READING

Canfield, Jack, and Wells, Harold. *100 Ways to Enhance Self-Concept in the Classroom.* Englewood Cliffs, N.J.: Prentice-Hall, 1976.

Chapter 12

Logical Consequences Versus Arbitrary Punishment

In order to live and to function in society, we must respect the logic of social living. A society cannot function without basic rules that include respect and consideration for others. These rules can be a valuable ally to a teacher in getting the child to see the relationship between his own actions and the results of those actions. The social order consists of a body of rules that operates on an impersonal level and *must be learned* and *followed* in order for the child and the adult to function adequately. Without such social order, we have chaos and anarchy.

The home is the child's first "society," and it is there where he learns to recognize the logic of the respect for social living and its rules. The degree to which he accepts these rules will depend upon the manner in which the parents present them to him. In an autocratic society and classroom, parents and teachers have no difficulty teaching rules and regulations. It is accepted that "a child should be seen but not heard." Children know this and present few problems. This does not hold true, however, in a democratic society or classroom, as we saw in Chapter 8.

Today parents and teachers no longer can make the child behave. Reality demands that we apply new methods to influence and to motivate children to cooperate. Punishment such as spanking, slapping, humiliating, depriving, and generally putting children down are outdated and are ineffective means of disciplining children. As previously explained, children retaliate because they see no relationship between the punishment and the crime.

Therefore, we need to use different techniques to motivate the child toward cooperation and more acceptable behavior. We need to win the child's cooperation. We propose that the teacher let the child experience the logical consequences of his behavior, which he can associate with his transgressions and with his defiance of the social order. It is possible to stimulate children to proper and acceptable behavior through the use of natural, applied, and logical consequences. This chapter will discuss the issues concerning these consequences in detail.

Natural Consequences

Natural consequences represent the natural flow of events in which a person is faced with the unexpected effects of his behavior. For instance, if a child runs and falls, he bruises his knees; if the child does not tie his shoes, he may trip over them and fall; the child plays with a knife, he may cut his fingers. These consequences are not arranged or imposed by anyone; they just occur. The adult does not threaten the child, argue with him, or concede to him but rather permits the child to discover on his own the advantages of respect for order. He replaces stimulation from without with stimulation from within. By experiencing consequences the child develops a sense of self-discipline, responsibility, and internal motivation.

We do not advise parents and teachers to add punishment to the child once he has experienced the natural consequences of his behavior. Punishment would only add insult to injury, and the lesson that the child could learn from the natural consequences may be diminished or even lost.

Ward flew a model airplane and let it fly in the direction of the street over the school fence. The teacher had made Ward aware that flying the plane over the fence might result in losing the plane. The child paid no heed. The plane landed on the street and a car ran over it and smashed it. Ward cried, but he could blame no one but himself. The teacher did not threaten, scold, argue, or preach but expressed her sincere regrets.

Applied Logical Consequences

Applied logical consequences are those consequences that the teacher applies when a child provokes her, another child, or the class. The teacher has not previously discussed the consequences with the class. The consequence is logical in that it relates to the behavior but is decided upon by the adult. Two examples follow.

Joe spills paint on the floor. The teacher tells him to clean it up.

Drexel changes the TV channel while the class is watching the program. He is given the choice of leaving the room or not touching the TV.

Applied consequences are usually a one-time procedure. At a later time the adult and the child discuss the misbehavior and agree on the consequences. In this way the same application to such a situation that before was an applied consequence now becomes a logical consequence. The class discusses what to do when the paint is spilled on the floor, to use one of the previous examples. The students decide on a logical consequence.

> Joe spilled paint on the floor, and he is responsible for cleaning it up.

Even though the application is the same as before, it is now a logical consequence.

Logical Consequences

Logical consequences are guided and arranged. They must be *discussed* with, *understood*, and *accepted* by the child, otherwise the child may consider it punishment. When logical consequences are used, the child is motivated toward proper behavior through his own experience of the social order in which he lives.

The technique of logical consequences can be used effectively only when a good relationship exists between the teacher and the child. In a power conflict they become punishments. Although the teacher is responsible for what is taking place, she acts not as a powerful authority but as a representative of a social order that affects all children alike. In using this technique, the teacher allows the child to experience the logical consequences of his own behavior, as is shown in the following example.

> In Home Economics class the girls, together with their teacher, had decided on the rules for cooking class. Anyone who did not bring an apron would be unable to cook or to share the goodies. Jessie forgot to bring her apron and, consequently, could not cook. She remembered to bring her apron to school for the rest of the food unit.

Consequences will be effective *only* if they are applied consistently. If teachers apply them once or twice only and then allow the *same* situation to go by unnoticed, the child will soon take advantage of the teacher's inconsistency. The student will gamble on the teacher's good mood and on his good luck, for he sees a chance to get by with his misbehavior. The teacher needs to be alert and not fall for a side issue if she wants to impress the child with the consequences of his behavior. Consequences must be applied so that the child becomes convinced that they will follow his misdemeanor, just as he is convinced that if he were to put his hand in water it would come out wet.

The use of logical consequences is one of the most important techniques that adults can use to improve the behavior of children in order to ensure their cooperation and to have good relationships with each other.

> Rafael did not answer to my roll call on the first day of school. I called his name a second time without getting any response. I decided to ignore it and went on with the roll call. The next day when Rafael did not respond when I called his name, I ignored the issue again. On the third day I omitted his name. When I had finished, Rafael called out, "You did not call my name, teacher." I told him that I thought that he wouldn't mind, but if it mattered, I'd call his name the next day. The following day when his name was called, he shouted at the top of his voice, "present." The class laughed so hard that it took a few minutes to quiet them down. The following day when I omitted Rafael's name again, he stood up and yelled, "You did not call my name again." I ignored his outburst and continued with the roll call. I omitted calling his name for several more days. Rafael watched me but said nothing. After a week of this procedure, I decided to try once more. When I called his name, he looked pleased, and in a pleasant way he responded with, "here." I had no trouble with Rafael again on that score.

Logical Consequences Applied Universally

Sometimes the teacher may have to face the consequences of her own behavior. If a democratic spirit is to prevail in the class, the teacher must take such consequences graciously. Two examples may illustrate such a situation.

> Once after having hastily written an assignment on the blackboard, I left the class alone for a few minutes. Upon my return, I found several words on the board had been circled with colored chalk. At the bottom was written, "Careless writing, please do over." I made the corrections without any comment. Since there was no reaction from the class, it was obvious that the children took this as a matter of fact.
>
> At another time I forgot to announce that a movie would be shown in the afternoon. Since my class missed it, they asked for a 20-minute activity period as compensation.

With regard to the examples above, we must remember that the class had discussed the logical consequences of careless writing, as well as the breaking of agreements. When the teacher mentioned these incidents to some of her colleagues, they were horrified at what they felt was insolence on the part of the students. In their views such permissiveness leads to disrespect and disorder. We cannot share this pessimism. Children have greater respect for adults who do admit their mistakes, who respect a child's opinion, and who share equally in privileges. Furthermore, children are prone to accept the logical consequences of their behavior if the teacher sets herself up as a model.

Logical Consequences Involve Choices

Logical consequences take in the following considerations:

1. The consequences must be related to the misbehavior.
2. In using logical consequences, the child must be given a choice.
   "You have the choice to walk down the stairs without pushing or I have to hold your hand until we walk down the stairs and the class is dismissed. You choose."
3. Do not use logical consequences where you cannot, for example, in the following cases:
   a. Where safety (life or death) or danger is involved.
   b. When the child uses power, revenge, or displays inadequacy.
4. Understand the goal of the child.
   a. Logical consequences work best on attention getting behavior.
   b. When a child is seeking power or revenge, the child is so busy asserting his superiority over the adult or in getting even with the adult that he often does not care what results his actions incur.

Specific Classroom Situations

Let us consider two situations that often come up in class and that may be baffling to the teacher as to the kind of logical consequence she should apply.

Pushing on the Stairway: In such a situation the teacher may give the child a choice of not pushing or of going back to class, waiting until everyone has gone, and then going down by himself.

Handing in Sloppy, Dirty Papers: In such a situation the teacher may ask the child if he wants to have his papers checked. If he does, she can tell him that she would be glad to do this if he would rewrite his paper. She may add, "All I want you to do is to hand in a clean paper. Anytime you hand it in I will correct it."

Adults who have little confidence in the child's basic integrity may argue that the child will not rewrite the paper. This may happen once or twice, mainly because the child is testing the teacher or is punishing her. A teacher who ignores such provocations, yet at the same time plans activities in which the child will experience the logical consequences of his behavior, will find that most children soon cooperate. This may be done in one of the following two ways.

After correcting the students' work, the teacher should return them to the prospective children and discuss whatever problems they had with the work; she should take children to the blackboard and practice with them on problems or tasks that they did not understand. She may ask one of the students who knows the work to come up to the blackboard and work with individual children who need help. Thus, the entire class becomes involved in the process of helping or tutoring one another. The student who did not turn in any work is left out in this class project, since he has no paper to correct. He should, however, not be ignored. The teacher must remain friendly but not solicit his help in the tutoring process.

If the assignment lends itself to being checked by the students themselves, the teacher could distribute the papers to them in such a way that each of them gets another child's paper to be checked. The teacher reads the answers while the students check and mark the papers. Most children enjoy checking other children's papers. The student who does not hand in his work is left out of this process. Often, such a student is eager to get a paper and asks the teacher why he was left out. The teacher may say to this student, "I am sorry, but I must give only someone who handed in his work a paper to check. I have nothing for you, but, perhaps next time." She should make no further issue out of the incident.

Writing on the Walls: Writing on the walls, especially in the bathrooms, is a frequent occurrence in schools. Mostly the teacher or the janitor approaches the class in an angry, threatening fashion, demanding to know who the culprit is.

We suggest that the teacher refrain from asking the class to tell who is guilty. This encourages tattling and competition. If she happens to know who is guilty, she may give him the choice of either washing or erasing the writing from the wall or paying the janitor to do it. If she does not know who is guilty, she should put the entire class into the same boat, including herself, and hold everyone responsible. She may say:

"Since we don't know who is responsible for the writing—and I appreciate that those who do know are not tattling—we will all have to assume the responsibility of getting the wall clean again. We have a choice of each contributing a certain amount of money to have the janitor do the work or of each of us taking a turn to clean the wall. Which do you prefer?"

If they choose the latter, she may ask who will volunteer to start. They should decide on how many minutes each must work. They may have to ask the janitor for instructions. The children who did not get a turn to help (if it does not require many helpers) will have a turn next time if this incident should recur. Each person's allotted time should not be very long—five to ten minutes, at the most. If a child refuses to participate, then the teacher may have to do the work for him. Some teachers may object to this proposal, claiming that they will not assume a responsibility for something they did not do. This is exactly the argument of the student who refuses to help. The teacher's willingness to participate in the solution of the problem stimulates an atmosphere of togetherness. Usually when the teacher tells the child without making a fuss, "Since you refuse to help, I will have to do the work for you" the child responds favorably and assumes his responsibility.

Often it also happens that the guilty child sees that the class is concerned with solving the problem of the dirty wall and not with who did it, volunteers to help, and confesses that it is his fault. If this should happen, we suggest that the teacher tell him that it took courage to make such an admission.

Being Late for the School Bus:

Jim was frequently late in catching the school bus. At times he enjoyed playing games and having the bus driver look for him. The teacher, the bus driver, the parents and Jim all discussed the situation and decided that Jim could either choose to be at the bus stop at the proper time or to walk home. The emphasis is on Jim's decision and choice. (Should the child refuse to make a decision, then the adult can say, "You are putting me in a position of having to make a decision for you.)

Being Late from Recess: Give the child a choice of returning with the others or standing by the teacher during recess until it is time to return to class.

Tardiness for Class: Give the child the choice of coming in on time or waiting by the door until the teacher has finished giving instructions. The student can then be seated. However, he cannot disturb other children concerning the assignment. If he complains that he does not know what to do, the teacher may say, "I'm sorry."

Some teachers may argue that this gives the child permission not to do the work. This is true. We should not force children to do their work, because then they think that they are working for the teacher. We must help children to realize that whatever work they do it is for themselves and for their own growth.

As we already pointed out, before we apply a consequence, we must consider the particular child, the goal of his behavior, and his method of obtaining it. Then we must apply the kind of consequence that will most likely be effective in his specific case. Sending a child out of the room for a few minutes may be a very effective consequence for the child who seldom disturbs the class, but if it concerns another child who is constantly disturbing the class, then sending him out of the room for a few minutes may be only a feather in his cap. What then should the teacher do with the second child? One thing is certain—we cannot and must not allow him to disturb the class. There are several consequences that may impress him. Let us consider some of them:

1. The teacher and the child can discuss how often he wants to interrupt the class.
2. The teacher may use paradoxical intentions which is doing the opposite to what he expects, reminding him to talk out whenever he is quiet. She may say "Sam you've been quiet for some time, wouldn't you like to say something?"
3. The teacher can give him permission to answer questions that are posed to other students. (Our experience is that giving the child permission to do what he does in order to provoke takes the fun out of his defiance.)
4. The teacher can discuss the situation with the class and expose the child to feedback from the other students.

Consistent use of logical consequences is extremely effective and usually results in less friction and an increase in harmony in the classroom, in the home, with one person, or with a group.

In many group situations, the other children will take care of an incident, as shown in the following example:

During a group discussion the children and the teacher agreed that persons who splashed other children at the water table would have to leave that particular activity. Two days later, Tony splashed water at Steve while they both were at the water table. Steve reminded him of the previous discussion. Other children joined Steve in the verbal discussion and told Tony that he would have to leave and go to another area. Tony put the water toys down and left.

The best consequence can be turned into punishment through misapplication or by talking too much. Most discipline is done by coaxing, reminding, threatening, and punishing, which may destroy the effect of consequences rather than allow children to experience the unpleasant results of their actions.

Punishment

Punishment is imposed by adults with no direct relationship to the misbehavior (see Chapter 9). Very frequently, the child does not associate the punishment with his action but with the punisher. Since the child's main objective is to emerge the winner in every situation, he refuses to associate his action with antisocial behavior; all he can see is that he has been caught and it is humiliating. His entire thinking then resolves around means to win the upper hand in the situation. Not only does he want to continue his offensive behavior despite any form of punishment, but very often he tries to assume the role of the punisher. If others can punish him, then he feels that he has the same right to administer punishment to those who have punished him.

> A 12-year-old boy was accused by his teacher of loitering in the hall. In spite of his protests and denial of the charges, the teacher demanded as punishment that he write a composition consisting of 100 words on any subject.

This example illustrates that the punishment bears no relationship to the offense. Here are some other examples:

> A child talks in class. The teacher sends him to the corner.
> A child is caught chewing gum in class. He is denied watching a movie.
> A child gets into a fight. He is sent to the principal.
> A child sasses the teacher. He is required to stay after school.

These and other transgressions sometimes are met with physical punishment. Such arbitrary punishment makes no sense to the child and the child may begin to fantasize retaliatory actions.

Retaliations frequently take on very subtle forms. The child may refuse to do any work, may become belligerent, may stop listening, may abuse or destroy property, may start to steal, and may even engage in serious delinquent crimes.

Children are quick to find an adult's Achilles heel and strike out where it hurts most. Unfortunately, adults often do not see the connection between their own behavior and that of the child's.

Logical Consequences Versus Traditional Punishment

How do we teach children to understand the difference between logical consequences and traditional punishment? This is a question that often comes up when we talk to teachers. Usually when we ask the class what to do when a child trangresses, the children propose punitive measures. The teacher needs to help the children to understand the subtle differences between logical consequences and traditional forms of punishment. Children of all ages can learn this within a short time. Some examples follow.

A Montessori school teacher noticed that one of the children secretly sneaked up to the shelf where she kept candy and took some for himself. This candy was distributed to the group at a certain time during the day.

The teacher discussed the problem with her class and asked them for suggestions. She did not mention the name of the child but instead discussed it as a general problem. One child suggested that a child who takes candy in this way should be sent to the corner for an hour.

TEACHER: What has the corner to do with candy? Let's think of something that has a connection with the candy.

CHILD: Tell his mother.

TEACHER: His mother has nothing to do with the candy. Besides, this is our problem, and we must find a solution. His mother should not get mixed up in our problems. See if you can come up with something that has to do with a child's behavior, namely, that he took candy that was meant to be distributed to the entire class.

After some more punitive suggestions, one child came up with the idea of leaving this child out in the receiving of candy on the day he already had his share. This was discussed with the entire group until they all came to a consensus.

It helps if the teacher asks a number of individual children, including the particular child, "What do you think of this suggestion? Is this a good solution?" When the time arrives to distribute the candy, the teacher may either ask a child to give out the candy but skip the guilty child or she may distribute it herself and skip the child. If the children should ask why the child was left out, the teacher can say, "I think you know why," and make no further comments.

The teacher of the previous example reported that she had to use this logical consequence only once. We can see from this example that even at a very young age the children understand the concept of logical consequences. We can also see that the young child already depends on group approval, although it is by far not as pronounced as it is with older children.

The following is an example that will show how a teacher can avoid fighting and use logical consequences *instead* of punishment.

If the teacher does not permit John to draw during the period when other children are drawing because he was dawdling when he should have been working on his arithmetic, John may well feel abused and that he has been deprived of his right without any good reason. If, on the other hand, the class as a group establishes the rule that anyone who chooses to dawdle during the time when others work must do the work assignment during art time, then John no longer has the right to feel resentful toward the teacher, who is only putting into practice the very principle that he helped to establish.

There is no pat formula for applying *logical consequences*. What will work in one situation may not work in another. The child who likes to go outdoors, for example, will be differently affected by being kept in during recess than a child who hates to go out. Therefore, by treating these two children in different ways similar results can be obtained. And since they have participated in setting up the logical consequences, they do not feel that they are punished by the teacher. It must be remembered that the use of logical consequences requires an understanding of the child and of the situation. *When* to do *what* and to *whom* requires judgment about many inponderables because every situation is unique.

Reward

The notion of reward is rejected by the Adlerian point of view because of its connotation of bribery. Through bribery we reinforce the terror tactics of the unmanageable child, which clearly puts him in control of the situation.

Reward as well as punishment induces false values in the child. Many children desire to do well only because of the reward that parents or teachers promise. If no reward is foreseen, the child's incentive toward doing well may disappear. We often hear of parents who promise their children money, toys, or grant them special favors for good grades or good behavior. Both parents and teachers bribe the child instead of encouraging him to take pride and pleasure in his functioning. The case of Paul may well illustrate such a situation.

> Paul did very poorly in school until his mother promised him money for every good grade he received on his report card. As long as he expected the reward, Paul did extremely well at school (which indicated his ability). Yet, when this reward was no longer offered, he not only became worse in his school work than he had ever been before but he came late to school, fought, scribbled in his textbooks, and so forth. Prior to his mother's promises, he had only been a poor student.

This example takes into account the following points: (1) Paul had the ability; (2) he worked only for the reward; (3) he had to get even, as many children do, by punishing his parents through his failure in school; and (4) his parents set high goals for the child.

Rewarding the child for a task that the situation requires is an indirect

Table 12–1   A Comparison of Consequences Versus Punishment

Natural	Applied (Logical)	Logical (Agreed)	Punishment
Natural result of an act	Situation centered Training begins	Reality of the situation Training continues	Arbitrary exercise of power by the adult No training
No adult intervention the consequences—child falls, bruises knees	Logical, but results imposed by adults the first time the behavior occurs "If you disturb, you'll have to leave"	Related logically to the behavior, but has been discussed, understood, and accepted by child after first time behavior occurs	Power of authority dominates— "Do as I say, no questions asked" Child may lose respect for order
Child associates the consequences with his behavior	Separates the deed from the doer	No element of moral judgment —"You are O.K., your behavior is not"	Some moral judgment—usually "bad" or "wrong" May stimulate defiance
Deals with present behavior	Deals with present behavior	Deals with present and future behavior	Deals with past, present, and future behavior
Has no choice— consequences occur	No choice	Gives child a choice to be responsible for own behavior	Gives no choice and implies adult is responsible for child's behavior
Child learns inner discipline	Sets the stage for developing inner discipline	Develops inner discipline	Imposed discipline is maintained May encourage misbehavior Child behaves out of fear and not out of inner conviction
No adult interference	Adult remains friendly Voice conveys good will	Positive attitude maintained Child feels mutual respect	Adult displays anger Antagonistic atmosphere is perpetuated, which creates resentment in child

Developed by Floy C. Pepper and Bernice Grunwald from a chart by Floy C. Pepper, John Platt, and Ann Platt.

admission that the child is being asked to do something that is so unpleasant that it merits a reward. However, even in situations in which the task may be unpleasant the child has to be helped to realize and to accept that in life now and then everyone has to do something that they do not want to do. Children who are constantly rewarded do not develop a sense of responsibility; they feel entitled to receive a pay-off for everything they do.

Some readers may argue that the positive reinforcement that we have discussed in this book is a form of reward. We are not concerned with the terminology but with the avoidance of tangible rewards and with the reinforcement of intrinsic rewards.

A Correctional Method

We must remember that the concept of consequences is only a correctional method for dealing with the immediate situation; it is not an end in itself. In every case the child must be helped to understand *why* he is behaving as he does, how this kind of behavior has brought him "success" (from his point of view) until now, how it affects other people, and finally, how he can obtain status through more acceptable methods of behavior.

Teachers and parents often expect that miracles will take place after they have applied natural and logical consequences for a day or two. In most cases it takes much longer than a few days for a child to give up a pattern of behavior. Teachers and parents may become discouraged when they see no drastic changes, and they may then resort to their old methods of dealing with the child. To them, the method of using consequences appears an unworkable form of discipline.

This is unfortunate. Adults must have perseverance and determination if they hope to be successful. They may lose some time in the process, but in the long run it will be rewarding.

Logical consequences must be used with no strings attached. If the teacher or parent uses logical consequences with the intention of forcing the child to give in to her wishes, if she is unwilling to accept the child's own choice, or if she attempts to manipulate the situation through the use of logical consequences, the child will perceive this. Instead of a positive change in behavior and lasting results, the child will respond with fortified resistance. Perhaps an easier way to see the comparison of the three types of consequences and punishment is in the form of a chart (see Table 12–1).

Chapter 13

The Structure of the Group

Humans are social beings. All their personal characteristics express social movement and interaction. As a social being, the child lives and grows in a group. The child tries to find his place first in his family group and then in his peer group. He develops individual ways to integrate, to find a place in accordance with his concepts of himself and of life, and to assume specific roles within each group.

New Aspects of the Peer Group

With the development of democratic social patterns in our society, the peer group gains increasing significance and importance for the child. The approval of his peers becomes more important for the child than that of adults, parents, or teachers. For this reason, the child's relationship to the classroom group and his interaction in it deserves careful study. The use of the group to influence the child not only constitutes an effective way to teach and to exert corrective influences on the child but also has become imperative in our democratic atmosphere. The group is the reality in which the child lives and operates. Through corrective feedback, it establishes and reinforces his attitudes and behavior.

The Role of the Teacher in the Group

The teacher must consider that she is working not merely with a given number of individual children but with the whole class group and its various subgroups. In a sense, the teacher is a group worker. Because of her training, the teacher thinks of children in terms of individual differences, in isolation from the child's functioning in the group setting. The teacher often believes that the child's problem is isolated from his position in the class group and from the general classroom atmosphere. This conviction is often an obstacle to the teacher's efforts to understand the dynamics of the existing problems, and consequently the teacher may meet with failure in spite of her good intentions and efforts. We must remember that behavior has to be examined and understood in its social setting. A child may behave altogether differently when he is alone from when he is in class. It also depends on how this child perceives his social position in the class. For instance, when we ask children who are serious behavior problems if they would behave in the same manner if they were transferred to a different community where nobody would know them, invariably they reply that they would not. When they are asked why they would not act up in a different community, they almost always tell us that they would be afraid that the children in the class might not approve of their behavior. It is not the teacher they fear, only the class group. This supports our belief that behavior has to be examined in its social setting. Whatever the child does, the way he functions is part of his social interaction with the other children and is not merely based on his relationship with the teacher.

Teachers are often unaware of how their relationship with one student affects their relationships with other students in the class. One of the frequent occurrences of this nature can be seen when a teacher and an individual child have a confrontation and another child makes comments or tries to get involved in one way or another. The teacher usually tells this child to mind his own business without realizing that for this child this *is* his business because of his strong alliance with the child whom the teacher is scolding. There may be more than one child in class who is allied with this particular child. Thus, a fight between a teacher and an individual child may affect many children in class, and the teacher runs the risk of antagonizing these children. This is certain to color the atmosphere of the class. For this reason, it is essential for teachers to acquaint themselves with the dynamics operating in the group. The knowledge of psychodynamics, the psychological processes occurring within the child that are responsible for his motivation, needs to be supplemented with the knowledge of group dynamics.

Subgroups

In every classroom group we find subgroups. Understanding these subgroups enables the teacher to grasp fully the significance of a disturbing child who plays up to the group or of the defeatism of the isolate who sees no chance to establish himself in a peer group. Without this knowledge, the teacher may unwittingly intensify existing, detrimental intergroup relationships and fail to rearrange the subgroup structure to facilitate influences on the class and on an individual child.

The class can be an extraordinary help or a dangerous accomplice. Some teachers who do not know this or lack the skill to evoke group pressure in favor of their educational goals, permit a troublemaker to get the class on his side. It is, therefore, important to spot these leaders as quickly as possible and to recognize the methods that they employ to get the class on their side. The teacher must aim to win the support of these children. The sooner she wins them over to her side, the quicker will exist a change of atmosphere in the class. She can win these leaders by recognizing the power that they wield in class and by providing opportunities for them to remain leaders and use their power constructively. The following is a sample conversation between the teacher and such a child.

TEACHER: Gill, you are a very clever boy. Do you know that?

GILL: I am?

TEACHER: You sure are. Do you think that anyone who is dumb could keep so many people occupied with him?

GILL: What do you mean?

TEACHER: Look how many people you manage to keep busy with you and who don't know what to do with you. There are the teachers, the principal, the counselor, your parents, the police, and many of the children in class. Why, it takes brains to do that. You have the brains. And you know what else?

GILL: What?

TEACHER: You are a natural leader. The children follow you. They do what you tell them to do. They don't do what I tell them or what the principal tells them to do. Not many people have such leadership qualities. You could be of such help as a leader, if you decided to be one. But, as you know, there are good leaders, and there are bad leaders. You would have to decide what kind of leader you would want to be.

GILL: What kind?

TEACHER: I can't tell you what kind of leader you should be. You must decide this for yourself. If you should decide to use your influence and help others, I would be very happy because you would be helping not only the other children but also me. Think about it, and tell me what you have decided to do as soon as you have made a decision. Then we can talk further.

We must always keep in mind that the pattern of interpersonal relations in class has many subtle movements and that it defines the roles and the activities of the individuals with respect to each other, with respect to the subgroup, and with respect to the group as a whole. An individual child may have a role assigned to him by the others or he may have one he has chosen for himself because it facilitates obtaining his goal. Basically these two amount to the same thing. For instance, if the class laughs and enjoys the clowning of a child, this child may draw the conclusion that the group appreciates him for his behavior, and he is bound to continue clowning.

In the group, some individuals have status and are admired while others may be completely ignored or rejected. Some individuals are loners by choice, whereas others are loners because they have been rejected by the group. It becomes the teacher's and the group's task to integrate such children.

Billy, going on 11, was one of the oldest students in his third-grade class. His appearance was that of a mentally retarded child. The teacher had to call his name several times before he responded. Billy did not seem to be interested in any of the children or they in him.

Billy spent most of the school day daydreaming. He showed no interest in any of the school activities, not even in art or in physical education.

Billy had failed twice in school. During his four years at school he had learned virtually nothing, for he could not write his full name, did not know the letters of the alphabet, and could not count in successive order.

Billy never replied directly to any question. When he was asked, "Billy, where is your father?" he would reply, "Sometimes my uncle buys me candy." When the teacher replied, "Oh, you have an uncle? Does he live with you?," he would answer, "Sometimes he lets me ride on his shoulders." It was impossible to get a straight answer from him, since he continually followed his own train of thought.

One day the teacher noticed that Billy was watching two boys playing checkers. She asked him if he knew how to play, and he said that he didn't. When she asked him if he would like to learn to play checkers, he seemed eager. The teacher presented this situation to the class during group discussion. It was decided that the teacher should play checkers with Billy for ten minutes every day and that one of the students would then play with him for ten more minutes. This pleased Billy immensely. The next morning, he came straight to the teacher and asked her when she would play with him. She asked him to watch the clock until the big hand pointed to a certain number and then to call her. (He could not tell time.) Billy's eyes were glued to the clock, and the moment the hand pointed to the specified number, he reminded the teacher that it was time.

Billy did not learn easily, but he seemed very happy in the process. After a few days, he understood the fundamental principles and could move his checkers along the black squares without getting off onto the red. (This principle helped him later in understanding to keep on the line when he was writing.) Melvin, the boy who played checkers with Billy most of the time, was very patient and very encouraging. He encouraged Billy by pointing out his progress. It was in response to Melvin's comments that Billy summoned the courage to thank Melvin in front of the class for his help. This was his first real contact with the entire group.

One day Billy asked the teacher if he could sit next to Melvin. Melvin said that he would like to have Billy as a neighbor and that he would like to help him with his work. The teacher was pleased with this new development, because nobody had chosen Billy in the sociometric test that the class had taken a few weeks before. Thus, a new chapter started in Billy's life. He practiced writing, and when he could write legibly, he began working on simple spelling and arithmetic. Melvin helped him by checking his work and by practicing with him on the blackboard. The teacher devoted time to helping Melvin with his reading.

As Billy progressed in his studies he became more outgoing and learned to make friends. This was especially noticeable during recess. He was no longer isolated but participated in activities with the other children.

Characteristics of the Group

Every class has its own particular qualities. Although in many respects the group resembles other groups of similar size, each class has its own unique characteristics. These characteristics explain why teachers express astonishment at the differences in the children that they had the previous year when they compare them with those that they have this year. One group may be a delight to work with, while another may be impossible. What makes the difference? The children come from the same community and have similar backgrounds. They are equally intelligent and yet, when compared with the previous year's children who were cooperative and eager to learn, they fight and show no interest in learning

The class reflects the characteristics of the individuals, who play a leading part. Everyone in his own way, through his behavior, contributes toward the particular climate that eventually prevails in the classroom. There are those who promote easy contact with others and who are peacemakers, the lazy, the overambitious, the industrious, the heroes, the rejected, the beautiful, the unattractive, and a score of others. Each one of these has a strong impact on the structure and the atmosphere of the group. Thus, we may find an altogether different group behavior in a class in which there is a great deal of mutual attraction, while in another group, we find that antagonism prevails. The tone of the class usually is decided by a few who are the natural leaders. An example of this follows.

Three second-grade boys were regarded with horror by the others in class, including their teacher. They were noisy, beat up any child who did not go along with their demands and beat up those who were admired because of their academic achievement. These boys dictated to their class and literally controlled it. When they entered the third grade, they had a new teacher but the same class group. The old atmosphere that had prevailed in second grade was automatically passed on to the third grade. Had these boys been separated and assigned to different rooms, the situation might have been altogether different at the start of school, and it would have influenced the initial setting of the classroom climate.

This example illustrates that the pictures the children have of one another are important for the class. The same types of behavior of two different children may be seen and interpreted differently by the members of the same class. It is the attitude that the group takes toward the behavior of the individual that will determine the individual's position in the class. It may bring him status and satisfaction, or it may develop or increase his loneliness and unhappiness.

The skilled teacher, who is sensitive to the group atmosphere, will sense the type of atmosphere that her new class has and plan a constructive program through which she can gradually change the children's attitudes. The climate of the classroom reflects the personal characteristics of all and influences in turn the development of each child emotionally, and socially. Therefore, the teacher must know not only the individuals in the class but also how they interact with one another, since this determines how they feel in the class. Without some knowledge of group dynamics, a teacher cannot have the necessary insight into the group's problems. She can understand the functions of the group only by examining the interactions that take place and the perceptions, goals, and frustrations of the individual students.

When a teacher is faced with a class that does not respond or cooperate, she needs to remind herself that it is not she alone who determines whether the group will be satisfactory or chaotic. There are other factors that make the integration of a group difficult. Of major importance is the presence of leaders of various cliques within the group. The teacher needs to ask herself these questions: "Is there a clique structure in the group?" "What values do the cliques hold?" "Is there a hierarchical leadership structure?" "Is there a pattern of clique rivalry and competition?" The teacher who is confronted with such a class may very well wonder how she will be able to teach these children to live together, to share together, and to use their varying abilities and interests for the common good.

How can a teacher learn to know each student as an individual as well as a member of his group? How can she learn about the antagonisms and competitions among cliques and other such groups? A great deal can be learned from direct observation in the classroom and on the playground. It is important to observe who plays with whom, who takes the lead, who refuses to participate unless he has his way, who teases (and how the others respond to it), who is left out at all times, who is left out just in certain activities, who appears clumsy, who gets easily angry, who retaliates, who deliberately withdraws, who runs to the teacher for help, who disregards the rules of the game, who is boasting, who fights other people's battles, and scores of others. The teacher needs to be aware of who sets off contagious behavior, who eggs others on in their misbehavior, and who starts enthusiastic volunteering.

Equally important is knowing who walks home with whom, who plays with whom after school, who goes to the same Sunday school, who visits whom at home, who eats lunch together, who whispers or sends notes to whom, and who copies his work from others.

Sociometric Methods

Sociometry is the study of the relationships among people. A sociogram points to the attractions that individuals have toward each other, and it discloses the role they occupy in the class. H. H. Jennings (1948) refers to the sociogram as a test of friendship constellations. It tells us how individuals perceive themselves in relation to others. A sociometric test allows each child to express his personal feeling for others in the form of choices for functioning with them and within the group of which he and they are members. After the tests are given, the data need to be tabulated. Two methods that are frequently used are the grid system and sociometric matrix, which is a diagram used to show clearly the network of acceptance and rejections in a graphic way.

There are various forms of sociometric methods. Some are complicated and require a lot of work. Teachers quite often discard them because it takes too much of their time. The authors have designed a simple method that is shown in Table 12–2. Such a method will provide her with the information needed to deal with children's problems effectively. The teacher who collects sociometric information is well equipped to plan for desired cooperation.

A sociogram will help the teacher to know the child's position in the group. Knowing who the individual chooses to associate with may provide a clue to his attitudes and to his values, which may explain any difficulties he has in class. In addition, it provides insight into the kind of position the child wants to occupy. Thus, the teacher can find out which classmates can influence the behavior of a particular child. Seating the child next to children whom he chooses will help him to gain greater acceptance among the class members and to change his past poor associations for better ones. The child gains increasing ability to establish mutual relationships with other children to whom he is drawn.

Through this sociometric device, for example, a teacher may discover that timid Larry wants to sit next to boisterous, bullying Jim. Evidently, Larry considers Jim strong, powerful, and worthy of admiration. This permits the teacher to plan activities that may induce Larry's independence and get him to join children with healthier values. In new contacts he can come to a reappraisal of himself. Furthermore, the teacher can use her understanding of their relationship to help both Jim and Larry.

She may assign a project to these two boys for which each would be required to give a report. The chances are that Jim's support would help

Larry, who is always afraid to talk in front of the group, to get up the courage to face his ordeal. He may do better than he expected. The group could then give Larry real encouragement by showing their understanding of his problem and their appreciation of his delivery.

Jim, on the other hand, might be helped in a reversed way. Larry's admiration for him may help him feel more secure in his social relationships, and he may, as a result, have less need to be boisterous. The chances are that he may give his report in a manner in which the effectiveness of Larry's report will not be diminished. The group has a wonderful opportunity to give Jim attention by admiring his modest and considerate manner.

In the same class the teacher may discover that a gentle child is regarded with the highest favor by a number of problem children. This would give the teacher a clue to the inner wishes of many of the tough ones, and this relationship could be used to influence them.

The information necessary for making up the sociometric matrix in the following example can be obtained by asking each child to indicate which classmates he would like to have sit next to him in the classroom. Two choices are allowed each child. They are asked to indicate with a number 1 their first choice and with a number 2 their second choice (see Table 12–2).

The individual's choice must be taken seriously, regardless of how the teacher may feel about this particular constellation. Teachers must give special attention to those students who were not chosen by anyone, placing

Table 12–2   Sociometric Table

Choosers	Chosen Ann	Gary	Tom	Helen	Susan	Peter	Barbara	Keith	Danny
Ann		X		1	X		2	X	
Gary		X	2		X	1		X	
Tom		X			X	1		X	2
Helen	1	X			X			X	
Susan	1	X			X			X	2
Peter	X	X	X	X	X	X	X	X	X
Barbara	2	X		1	X			X	
Keith		X			X	1		X	2
Danny		X	2		X	1		X	
Totals	3	0	2	2	0	4	1	0	3

X = Not chosen or the child made no choice himself.
Not chosen: 1. Gary. Put him next to one of his choices—Peter or Tom. 2. Keith. Put him next to Peter or Danny. Helen chose only one girl, but she was chosen twice. Peter chose no one, but he is most popular in class. Why? Probably an operator. If he were popular for being kind or for being a good student, most likely he would have chosen someone. Telling somebody that he likes him is beneath Peter, or a sign of weakness, but he succeeded in impressing this class with his "strength." Next popular is Danny. Ann is the most popular of the girls. No one chose Susan. Put her next to Ann or Danny. Notice she is the only girl who picked a boy. Could she be showing too much interest in boys, and could this be the reason the girls don't want her? Observe her and observe the attitude of the girls toward the boys. Barbara is not popular. Why are she and Helen not popular?

them with one of their own choices. Since the unchosen ones are usually discouraged and unhappy children, putting them together with members whom they admire and envy automatically raises their self-esteem, as well as their status in the group. Each sociogram is only a starting point for further investigation to gain understanding of the motives and values underlying the choices and rejections.

Sociograms should be given at specific intervals, for attractions and rejections change as the class works together. These changes occur more frequently in the lower grades, where children are more easily influenced. Such tests may be given once a month during the first three months of the school year and later reduced to every two months. However, there is no set pattern as to how and when to give a sociometric test. Each teacher must know her group and use her own judgment.

There are times when a teacher is very much tempted to separate children who show a great interest in each other because it interferes with the work. Separating these children may be a temporary solution to the teacher's problem, but it is not an effective method that will help them toward self-discipline and learning.

Usually, seating arrangements, working committees, and other groupings are set up without consideration of the children's wishes. Although such arrangements are made with the best intentions in the belief that this will produce the best working atmosphere, the opposite is often the case, for the best conditions for learning are thereby destroyed.

The following example illustrates how a sociogram helped the teacher understand the problem a child had and how it helped the child as well.

Leo entered the seventh grade during the middle of the school year. His parents moved from California to the Midwest. This in itself required a considerable adjustment. What added to Leo's difficulties was his appearance, for he was very tall and skinny. He walked with a slight stoop and with downcast eyes. Leo had been a loner for a long time. He kept to himself both in class and on the playground. He was an average student, except for mathematics and science, in which he excelled.

When the teacher gave the sociogram, Leo received one first and two second choices. He was very much surprised that anyone had chosen him. As it happened, all of the students who chose Leo were poor in mathematics, and their choice of Leo may have had selfish motivations. However, this did not prevent the development of sincere friendships. Leo became more outgoing and, in time, more involved in class activities.

Without the application of the sociogram, it might have taken Leo much longer to become integrated into the class group. Integration of students is of primary importance, since it is the basis for any successful classroom teaching.

Proposed Seating Arrangements

Since several children want to sit next to Peter, as we can see in Table 12–2, the teacher must arrange the seating in such a way that they are near him either on his sides, in front, or in back where they can turn to him or he to them. The children who sit right next to Peter should change seats with those who sit in front or behind him after a week, and each week they should exchange seats until the next sociogram is done.

For Teachers who cannot obtain a commercial seating chart, we suggest that they make their own. Instructions are given below.

How to Make a Seating Chart

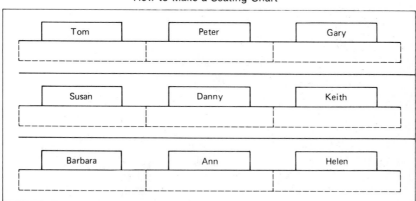

Key: ———————— = Stitch or staple

Material: poster board
Cut one sheet big enough to put as many names on as you have students (approximately 8½ x 11 inches).
Cut strips of poster board, about 1½ inches wide and as long as the width of your big sheet.
Stitch or staple each strip on the board.
Divide the strips into sections (pockets) to hold the names of the students.
Cut strips of poster board and divide them into small rectangular cards the size of the pockets.
Write the names of your students on each card and insert them into the appropriate pockets.
When students change seats, all you need to do is to exchange the name cards.
For those who find sewing too much work, use a stapler.

It is not always possible to seat both choices next to the child. However, if even one of the children whom they have chosen is to sit next to them, they are always pleased. The following chart should help the teacher understand the seating arrangement.

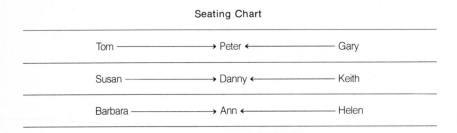

Seating Chart

Tom ⟶ Peter ⟵ Gary

Susan ⟶ Danny ⟵ Keith

Barbara ⟶ Ann ⟵ Helen

The sociogram must be carefully studied and analyzed after it has been tabulated. Who are the leaders, and what do they have in common? Who are the children who were left out, and what do they have in common? How might these two groups of students affect the classroom atmosphere? The teacher may find that all of the leaders are bullies, which would help her to be on the alert and plan activities that would counteract and avoid or diminish disturbances. Or, she may find out that the leaders are basically pleasant, cooperative children, which would help her engage their support in the process of exerting positive influences on the group. The teacher may become aware that the subgroup that has been left out consists of all good students or well-dressed children, which would throw light on the overall values of her class, namely, that they look with disdain on learning and on compliance. Possibly the teacher fusses over these nice students, and the others feel inferior to them. Sometimes, two or three special students may put a damper on the classroom atmosphere. It may happen that some of the other students come from foreign countries and speak English poorly or live in a poor section of town. All this information will help the teacher to plan her activities and to work toward a specific goal.

The Child Who Is Not Chosen

The chances are good that a child who has not been chosen by anybody has chosen someone, and then there is no problem. The teacher should seat this child next to his choice. If the child has not chosen anyone and if no one has chosen the child, it becomes more difficult. We suggest that the teacher speak with this child privately, find out the reason that he has not chosen anyone, ask him where he would want to sit, and honor his decision. However, it becomes important for the teacher to find ways to encourage such a child and to integrate him through activities that he enjoys or in which he excels. In most cases, this child will indicate choices when the next sociogram is administered.

Talking and Disturbing the Class

The question of what to do when the children who choose one another talk and disturb the class occurs frequently. This is a reason why so many teachers separate children. However, separating children who attract each other destroys a good learning atmosphere. Most children enjoy school more when they like their neighbors, and if they enjoy school, they are bound to learn more. Talking is a problem only at first. The teacher should discuss with the class how to handle talking and disturbing the class. We should, however, distinguish between constructive and destructive talking. Children who like each other help each other: they compare their work; they ask questions like, "How do you do this problem? Can you help me?" Such talking, if done low and with restraint can easily be tolerated. Teachers who insist on absolute quiet have distorted concepts about what constitutes a good learning climate. A teacher can train herself to distinguish between talking that is aiding the learning process and talking that is gossiping or not relating to the work.

How Often Should We Give Sociograms?

At the beginning, sociograms should be administered at least once a month. This helps the teacher to see what chain of interaction has taken place, what new attractions have developed, and it gives the students an opportunity to change seats if they are not happy with their previous choice or if they have made new friends in the meantime. As the group becomes trained in discussing their problems and in participating in decision making, the class will decide when they want a new sociogram or if they want to leave it up to the individual students themselves to change seats when they want to.

Are Sociograms a Great Deal of Work?

The kind of sociograms that we advocate do not require a great deal of work on the part of the teacher. The teacher needs only to do the work once. We suggest that the teacher use a piece of light cardboard, which can hold up for the entire year. She should leave enough space between the names of the children and the upper numbers, so that she can indicate new choices by using a different color pencil right next to the previous choice. This also has the advantage of allowing the teacher with a glance to observe the changes that have taken place.

When Should Children Change Seats?

Must children wait until the next sociogram is given before they can change seats? There is no "must" in this. Each situation requires careful study. In some cases, it may be better for the class to change seats before the next sociogram is given. The use of sociometric methods gives the teacher insight and knowledge as to the composition of her classroom and the subgroups therein. It allows her to succeed in breaking down the antagonistic forces and to build on the positive elements, so that isolated children and oppositional leaders are integrated into a cooperative, cohesive classroom.

The power of the peer group and its influence on the individual members in a class are recognized by many educators and psychologists. For those who are interested in the writings of others who advocate the group process, please see the References and Suggested Readings at the end of the chapter.

REFERENCE

Jennings, Helen Hall, *Sociometry in Group Relations: A Work Guide for Teachers*. Washington, D.C.: American Council on Education, 1948.

SELECTED READINGS

Berenda, R. W. *The Influence of the Group on the Judgment of Children*. New York: Teachers College, Columbia University, 1950.

Bonney, M. E. "Sociometric Study of Agreement Between Teacher Judgment and Student Choices." *Sociometry*, vol. 10, no. 2 (1947).

Corsini, Raymond J. *Methods of Group Psychotherapy*. Chicago, Ill.: William James Press, 1964.

Jennings, Helen Hall. Sociometry in Group Relations. Washington, D.C.: American Council on Education, 1951.

Richardson, J. E. "Group Dynamics and the School." *British Journal of Educational Studies*, vol. 4, no. 2 (1956).

Sonstegard, Manford. "Interaction Process and the Personality Growth of Children." *Group Psychotherapy*, vol. 11, no. 1 (1956).

Young, D. "Everything Under Control; Trusting the Group for Working and Planning." *Child Education*, vol. 20 (1951).

Chapter 14

Group Discussions in the Classroom

Increasingly, more psychologists, counselors, and teachers recognize the impact that the group has on the individual. We hear more and more of group approaches to influence people toward corrective behavior.

Alfred Adler was among the pioneers to use the class group in the educational process, and today we find many known educators who advocate group dynamics, especially the use of group discussions for training children to understand behavior and to unite them toward common goals.

The peer group has always had a strong influence on the individual child but not to the same extent as it has today. Peer pressure and the need to belong to a peer group are so strong that even the good child will often do things imposed by the group that he would normally never do. To illustrate this point, let us consider the following case:

> Gail, a freshman in high school, asked to be admitted to a fan club. In order to be accepted, she had to swallow a small worm. She obliged, even though she felt sure that she would throw up.

A strong subgroup can sway an entire class to undo everything an effective teacher is trying to accomplish. In fact, it takes only two or three students to make teaching impossible if they are united against the teacher.

Group discussion in the classroom is a necessary procedure in a democratic setting. It is the means by which children can integrate themselves into the class as a unit with status, responsibility, and active voluntary participation.

The Purposes of Group Discussions

Using group discussion not only helps children to develop better inter-personal relationships but also enhances learning through accumulated information. Effective communication of ideas leads to problem solving. Children learn through discussions to explore controversial matters and to deal with people of different backgrounds.

In a discussion group children form attitudes and set values that may influence them for their entire life and may affect their behavior inside and outside of school. Group discussions provide opportunities for emotional and intellectual participation and reassurance that one is not alone. Difficult tasks seem lighter when ideas, aspirations, successes, problems, and anxieties are shared. The child learns to evaluate and profit from another classmate's experience as well as from his own. He feels supported and becomes more responsive. He can learn constructive ways of handling frustrations and of working through upsetting problems.

Through effectively directed group discussions, the teacher can succeed in raising the morale of the group and change the atmosphere of the room. In this way, the learning process is facilitated by a common goal of all the students. The teacher learns what each child feels and thinks, how he relates to others, and what his attitude is toward school. For many children, talking in an atmosphere of mutual understanding stimulates thinking. As a child mulls over and talks about some problem, he may find a solution. Quite often the child will realize that there are a number of solutions to the same problem.

One task of group discussion is to stimulate each child to listen to others. Frequently, people do not listen to others who express different opinions. In the group discussion everybody has the right to say what he thinks. Everybody is equal and treated with respect. Children usually listen to others in such a setting.

Sometimes there are children who would like to participate in group discussions but since they have never experienced friendly talking with others they do not know how. They need help from the teacher and other students.

Preparing Students for Group Discussion

The children should respect the confidentiality of their peers. The teacher should not discourage the children to tell their parents what has transpired in the class. On the contrary, we suggest working toward the student's acceptance of discussing with his parents those areas that concern him personally. The teacher should, however, discourage children from discussing sensitive personal topics in class, such as their parents' habits— drinking, gambling, sex abuse, and so on. If the teacher senses that the child has a great need to talk to someone about one of these, the teacher can offer to talk to this child in privacy or refer him to the counselor or social worker. It helps if the teacher and the class understand and agree before group discussions are started that there are topics that do not belong in class discussions.

Children are helped to become aware that through group discussions, they will gain an increased understanding of themselves, as well as a respect for each others needs, feelings, and viewpoints. The teacher and the group need to decide on some guidelines, which should include the following.

1. Help each other; do not hurt one another.
2. Establish how to take turns and listen to everyone.
3. Establish trust and mutual respect.
4. Cooperate with each other.

Guidelines help to protect the rights of everyone and to prevent unfair members from interfering with the rights of others.

The Role of the Teacher

A teacher cannot be a good leader unless she has inner freedom and unless she can admit that she herself has made a mistake without feeling threatened by it. If a teacher can accept being human, which means making occasional mistakes, her students will have an easier time of accepting the fact that making mistakes leads to learning. This will depend on how a teacher reacts to her students' mistakes.

The teacher cannot be passive if she wants to have effective group discussions. She must be directive, involved, and even manipulative. Since the purpose of group discussions is not only to change behavior but to change values, manipulation may sometimes be necessary. When we say "values," we refer to the teacher's objectives for the child and for the class. The objectives that the teacher sets are based on universal values. They include accepting oneself and others, helping those who are in need of assistance, encouraging others, learning for oneself and not for the parents or teacher, finding one's place through positive rather than through negative behavior, and so on.

Leadership Is Sometimes "Manipulation"

Some readers may find manipulation of a situation questionable, if not offensive. This comes from a lack of understanding of what manipulation entails. Therefore, we would like to illustrate our suggestion with the following example.

TEACHER: Can you imagine that a teacher may not like a student?

STUDENTS: Yes.

TEACHER: Suppose this teacher decides not to work for this student—not to check the student's papers and not to call on him when he raises his hand. How do you feel about this?

STUDENTS: That wouldn't be right. A teacher cannot neglect or refuse her responsibilities to the student no matter how she feels about him.

TEACHER: Why not?

STUDENTS: This is unfair. Her feelings should not interfere with her responsibilities.

TEACHER: Does anyone have an idea why I brought up this question? (No one comes up with an answer.) A while ago you agreed that we should all have the same rights. Have you changed your minds?

STUDENT: But this is not the same situation. A teacher gets paid for teaching, whereas a child doesn't get paid for learning.

STUDENTS: That's right.

TEACHER: Are you saying that learning is for "nothing," that you do this for the teacher out of the goodness of your hearts?

The students will start examining this question from a new point of view. They should be helped to realize that in the process of education they carry as much responsibility as the teacher. It is true that the teacher's responsibility is to teach, but by the same token, the student's responsibility is to learn. Whether the teacher or the students live up to their responsibilities is their decision; they have the right to decide what they want to do, but they both have equal rights. The discussion should focus on the children's misconception of why they learn. They should be helped to realize how they use learning as reward or punishment for parents or teachers.

Without leadership, group discussions often turn into griping sessions centering on who is right and who is wrong. In such an atmosphere nothing is accomplished in terms of insight and of unification of the class. Such discussions often end in chaos. As a result, the teacher becomes discouraged and discontinues group discussions.

Group discussions can be compared to the conference table where teachers and students confront each other and where they come to agreements. It is a necessary procedure in a democratic setting. It is the means by which children can integrate themselves into the class at a unit with status, responsibility, and active voluntary participation. It is particularly important that the child should be able to discuss his problem without fear of ridicule. The group explores the causes of friction and how it can be avoided or solved when it occurs. Through group discussion the spirit of competition becomes one of mutual sympathy and concern. The child who is often subject to ridicule becomes a challenge to the group who is trying to help him. Let us consider such a situation.

In a fifth-grade class the children enjoyed making fun of Alan, laughing at him, and mocking his behavior. The teacher talked to the class and even punished the children for their shameful behavior but to no avail. It became so bad that the only recourse she saw open to her was to have Alan do his work in the principal's office. He spent most of the day there.

A consultant to this school carried on a discussion with the class while Alan was in the principal's office. The consultant started the discussion with the question of who should have more rights, in order to help the children become aware of the rights that they grant to themselves but never grant to others.

LEADER: What kind of class are we?

STUDENT: We are in the fifth grade.

LEADER: I mean, are you a friendly class, and do you get along with others?

STUDENT: We get along all right, except for one kid. We don't get along with him.

LEADER: Why not?

STUDENT: He's a funny kid; we can't help it. He always does such funny things.

LEADER: What about the others? Do you see this situation the same way?

STUDENT: You should see him. By the way, his name is Alan. He's in the principal's office now. You could see for yourself.

LEADER: You say he is funny. What does he do?

STUDENT: Well, he walks in a strange way, as if he's pushing along. You know what I mean.

STUDENT: Yeah, and he also talks in a funny way, not like the rest of us.

STUDENT: Even in gym he is so clumsy, he can never throw a ball straight.

LEADER: Does he ever hurt any one of you?

STUDENTS: No. He's not that kind of kid.

LEADER: Why is he in the principal's office?

STUDENT: As we told you, we don't get along with him.

LEADER: Just what do you do exactly?

STUDENT: Well, I guess it isn't nice, but we do it, and I do it also, but I know it isn't nice.

LEADER: Do what?

STUDENT: We laugh at him. Sometimes we call him names, and sometimes we kind of push him around, but we don't really hurt him. We just have fun.

LEADER: I would like to ask you a few questions. May I?

STUDENTS: Sure.

LEADER: Suppose I were to come here with five hats, wearing each one on top of the other. (laughter) Would I be hurting anyone?

STUDENTS: No.

LEADER: Do I have a right to be funny?

STUDENTS: Yes.

LEADER: Does anyone have the right to punish me if I am funny but do not hurt others with my behavior?

STUDENTS: No.

LEADER: Suppose I were to come to school with one red shoe and with one black shoe. Nobody dresses that way, and I would look strange or funny. Am I hurting anyone? Does anyone have a right to punish me?

STUDENTS: No.

LEADER: Suppose I were to talk funny, walk funny, and never throw a ball straight. Would I be hurting anyone?

STUDENTS: No.

LEADER: Does anyone have a right to punish me?

Through such discussion the children are being helped to see what they are doing. It must be pointed out that in many situations in which this kind of discussion is used the students always answer with "yes" or "no" when they are asked, "Do I hurt anyone? Does anyone have the right to punish me for my strange behavior?" Let us continue now with the consultant's discussion technique.

LEADER: Is Alan a happy boy, in your opinion?

STUDENTS: No.

LEADER: Does this concern you? How do you feel about people who are unhappy and not just Alan? In your opinion, should we just let them suffer or even add to their unhappiness?

STUDENTS: No.

LEADER: This is what we must think through very carefully. I don't think that you have ever thought about it. Here is a person who is miserable, and why? How would you feel if you walked funny or were not able to throw a ball?

STUDENT: I really think that we did wrong. I wish I hadn't done what I did. I think that we can help Alan. I think that many of us feel different now.

STUDENTS: I do. I think that we should help Alan.

LEADER: Those of you who want to help him—how could you do this?

The discussion now can center around how to help Alan. Without a directed group discussion, this would not have been accomplished. This may be regarded as manipulation, but it is done for constructive purposes.

A few weeks later, the consultant received a thank-you letter from the principal, telling how Alan's life in school had changed and how many of the children now tried to teach and to help him.

The topic of equality surfaces frequently with the teacher's interaction with students, and teachers often maintain that they do not know how to teach the concept of equality to students. We should like to illustrate this technique through the following example which may also be a form of manipulation.

Most students tell us that they do not work for a teacher they do not like. They see nothing wrong with this behavior.

TEACHER: Do you believe in equality for all people?

STUDENT: What do you mean by "equality"? Do you mean that we are all the same?

TEACHER: No, we can't all be the same. You are you, and I am I, but as human beings we are the same. Should we have the same rights?

JOHN: I don't think so. I think that teachers are grownups and that they should have more rights than kids.

TEACHER: In order to understand this, I would like to ask if you are saying that I, as a teacher, should be allowed to chew gum in class when none of you are allowed to do this?

MANY STUDENTS: No, never. That would be unfair.

TEACHER: What about you, John. Do you still think that I should have this right while you don't have it?

JOHN: No, I don't think so.

TEACHER: If we have a school rule that nobody is to push others out of line or on the stairs, should I, as a teacher, be allowed to do this?

JOHN AND OTHERS: No.

TEACHER: Well, then, what you all mean is that we should all have the same rights. Do I have this correct?

STUDENTS: Yes.

Asking the right question is probably the most difficult technique in leading group discussions. Many teachers ask how they can learn this. There is no prescribed way of learning how to ask questions except through trial and error.

Difficulties with Group Discussions

Some teachers have difficulty with group discussions, mainly because they doubt their own abilities to be effective. Some believe that they are having a group discussion when in actuality they are using the opportunity to impose their own ideas, to preach, and to hold lectures about what the students should or should not do. Children usually turn a deaf ear to such preaching, as the following example illustrates.

> TEACHER: Put your work away, and we will have a discussion.
>
> CHILD: I have something I want to bring up.
>
> TEACHER: First, there is something I want to talk to the class about. This morning when you went to the gym, I was utterly ashamed of you. You know better than to run down the stairs. We've talked about it dozens of times. How often have I told you that you must not run through the corridors and on the stairs? Honestly, one would think that I had never talked about it to you. I don't ever want to see this again. Do you understand? And if this happens again, I just won't let you go to gym. I don't like to have to punish you like this, but I'm sure that you will agree that you're forcing me to do this.

A trained leader in group discussions might have conducted this incident in the following manner:

> TEACHER: Class, I would like to discuss with you what happened this morning on the way to gym. I'd appreciate it if you would carefully consider this matter and comment on it.

With such an approach, the chances are that most of the children would want to talk about it. Should no one respond, the discussion might be channeled in this direction:

> TEACHER: I need your help, children. I don't want to make any decisions without discussing it with you first. In fact, I hope that you will make suggestions as to what we should do. Does anyone know what I'm referring to?
>
> CHILD: I think you are talking about the way we went to gym this morning.
>
> TEACHER: That's right. How do you feel about the way the class behaved? (The child may say that the class ran and shouted.)
>
> TEACHER: I recall that we have discussed this matter before. How many of you remember?
>
> CHILDREN: (Hands go up.)
>
> TEACHER: What do you think we should do now? This kind of behavior may get us into trouble with the principal and with other teachers.
>
> JIMMY: Next time our class should walk quietly down the stairs.
>
> TEACHER: How do the rest of you feel about Jimmy's suggestion?
>
> CHILD: Most of us walk down in an orderly fashion, but there are some who won't.
>
> TEACHER: What shall we do about these children? Please don't think of punishment but try to think of a solution that would give these children some choices.

CHILD: Maybe they ought to be given a chance to walk down with the class, but if they run or shout they should return to class. They shouldn't have gym that day.

TEACHER: How many think that this is a good solution to this problem? (If the children agree to this solution then it should be tried.)

TEACHER: Let's try it, and if it doesn't work out, we'll have to try something else.

This is only one of a number of possible approaches by which the teacher and the class can try to find a solution to a problem. The teacher's appeal to the children for help raises their feeling of importance and unites the class toward a common goal. The teacher who uses the class to help her with whatever problem she may have will find that most children will respond in a positive manner.

The following example is especially typical of how teachers use group discussions to talk to children.

TEACHER: I'd like to talk to you about the basketball. I repeat, "basketball," not "football." I am sure all of you know the difference. A basketball is meant to be thrown into a basket. That's why it is called "basketball." This afternoon I saw some of you kicking it. Do you know what may happen when you kick it? It may get a hole in it, and then we'd have to get it repaired. Do you know how much it costs to have such a ball repaired? It's not cheap, and the school will not pay for it. You know who will have to pay for it? You will. I know that you enjoy playing basketball and wouldn't want anything to happen to the ball, so let's all be very careful about how we use it. Alright? (Children nod their heads.) I knew you'd see it my way, and I'm very proud of you.

In this example the teacher is trying to convey friendliness and confidence in the children. However, she still is resorting to preaching. The chances are good that the children will pay little attention to what she has said. She might have had the following discussion:

TEACHER: I must talk to you about the basketball. I know that you enjoy playing with it, but before we can take it out again, we'll have to make some decisions. Whose ball is it?

CHILD: Ours.

TEACHER: I am afraid it is not.

CHILD: It belongs to the school.

TEACHER: That's right. We may use it, but we are responsible if anything happens to it. How can we prevent this? (The children discuss various possibilities of how to use the ball so that no damage will occur to it.)

TEACHER: What should we do if any of the children kick it?

The children will then suggest a number of consequences that will make sense to the possible offenders. They may suggest that these children should not be permitted to play basketball for one or two days, or they may suggest that these children should pay for any damage they have done. The important thing is that the students need to be involved in the discussion and decision making.

Another pitfall for the teacher to avoid in conducting a discussion is allowing the discussion to become a free-for-all, for when things get out of control, the teacher often resorts to autocratic means and becomes overpowering.

Some teachers voice other objections to the use of group discussions. They have the mistaken idea that children are not capable of understanding the behavior of others, the roles they play within the group, or the ways in which they influence each other.

Other teachers, concerned with covering the subject matter, find that they cannot afford to give time to group discussions. Although their concern is understandable, it is misleading to think that because of group discussions they will lose teaching time. Those who have used group discussions will attest to the fact that, actually, the teacher gains more time. It stands to reason that children will not only cooperate with the teacher but enjoy the subject she teaches if they are happy in class.

Getting Discussions Started

Group discussions should start as soon as the teacher becomes acquainted with her class and the students feel comfortable with her. This may be the very first day of school (see Chapter 10).

She may invite the class to suggest how the room should be decorated or how they would like to spend the first two days in class. Most of the children will respond favorably to suggestions that do not involve them in a personal way. A discussion develops during the process of planning, organizing committees, and assigning responsibilities. Planning bulletin boards is a suggested beginning. The project should be planned for the following day. The next two examples illustrate a discussion held on the first day of school. The first is for children in primary grades, and the second is for children in the upper grades.

TEACHER: As you see, our room is pretty bare. I was wondering if I should put up pictures, but I thought I would wait for you to help me decide how we should decorate our classroom.

NANCY: I brought a geranium last year.

ALEX: I think that we could draw some pictures and put them on the wall.

TEACHER: Both of you have good ideas. But let's first see how the rest of you feel about plants and then we will talk about pictures. Alright?

HELEN: Maybe everyone can bring a plant to school.

JOE: I can't bring a plant, because we have only two plants and my mother will not let me have one of them.

TEACHER: I understand that not everyone can bring a plant. But let's see if most of you like the idea of having plants. How many of you would like to have plants? (Many hands go up.) Find out if you can bring a plant to school. You can tell me in a day or so.

TOMMY: I don't know if I can bring a plant, but I have a fish bowl with five guppies that I can bring.

TEACHER: Who would like Tommy to bring his guppies? (Many children raise their hands.) Tommy, do you know how to take care of the fish? I don't have much experience with fish.

TOMMY: Oh, I know what to do. I always take care of the fish.

JIM: I can help him. We have an aquarium at home, and I know all about it.

TEACHER: Maybe I'll learn from both of you. Somebody mentioned pictures. What kind of pictures should we have?

The class then discusses whatever else they would like to decorate the room with. This is an informal discussion, not aimed at specific training but at creating an atmosphere of togetherness.

Some children may want to change the arrangements of the desks. If this is possible, the decision can be made by the group. Now we can look at a discussion held with upper-grade students.

TEACHER: Class, perhaps you know that every teacher has to submit a lesson plan to the principal each week. I haven't made mine yet because I was hoping that we might make some of these decisions together. Could we take a little time and talk about it?

PAT: What do you mean?

TEACHER: I teach spelling, reading, and social studies in the morning. It's entirely up to me to decide when to teach what. I could start the morning with reading, followed by spelling, and then go to social studies, or I could reverse the order. I could also change the procedure each week. It would depend on what you like. It seems to me that we could plan our time better if we do it together. What do you think?

TONY: You mean we can decide such things?

LESTER: You're not kidding?

TEACHER: I mean that we can decide together.

ALEX: Could we leave out spelling? I don't like that subject.

TEACHER: What do you kids think? Can I leave out spelling?

JIM: Yes, let's do that.

TEACHER: That isn't what I meant. I meant, is it up to me to teach or not to teach spelling?

JANET: I guess not. You have to teach spelling. Everybody has to learn how to spell, and teachers must teach it.

TEACHER: You're right. I must teach it whether I like it or not. The question is whether you want to start the morning with spelling rather than with reading or social studies.

HELEN: I'd rather start with reading and have spelling later.

TEACHER: How do the others feel?

JANE: Let's see and find out.

TEACHER: Good idea. How many of you would prefer starting the morning with reading? (Most hands go up.) Most of you seem to prefer it, so we'll start that way. If we don't like it, we can always change. What do you want next?

JANET: I'm always through with spelling before anyone else. I don't need that much time for spelling.

LESTER: Me neither. (Many children voice similar opinions.)

TEACHER: Perhaps we ought to discuss what those who finish early can do while the others finish.

LIZ: Are we allowed to take dictionaries to our desks?

TEACHER: Yes.

TOMMY: Maybe we could look up new words and add them to our spelling list of words for that day.

JOE: I don't want to do this.

TEACHER: How many of you would like to work with the dictionary? (Some hands go up.) Those who like it, may use the dictionary. Would you care to hand in your additional work for me to see or would you rather not do it?

The discussion continues until the students and the teacher are pleased with the arrangements.

It is recommended that the teacher help the class to realize that she is not always free to do what she wants to do. In this way, the children can see that the teacher also is subject to certain rules and procedures.

Training the Class

Children need specific training for participation in group discussions. During the training period it is necessary for the teacher to participate actively as the leader of the group. Gradually, she will relinquish the role of leader to the students as they become proficient. However, it is important that she remain alert and direct the discussion whenever it strays or does any harm. She may remind the discussion leaders of time limits, to refrain from becoming personal, to focus on the problem at hand, to talk louder, and so on.

Handling Touchy Problems

The teacher must keep the discussion focused on constructive thinking; she should not allow nonproductive or meaningless discussion. Never should she permit a child to humiliate another. If a child does make a derogatory remark, the teacher may

1. point out that problems are not solved by hurting others
2. discuss with the class the purpose of humiliating remarks
3. help the student realize that he could handle critical situations in a different manner.

When the discussion strays, the teacher can lead it back to its original purpose by interjections such as "We were discussing why Larry is getting into frequent fights. Some other time we may discuss the fights that you, Harry, have with your brother" or, "Could it be that Richard felt left out and therefore he changed the subject?"

If a child talks forever without getting to the point, the teacher can bring him back to the original problem. An example follows.

Karl tells the class of a fight he has had with his brother and his report goes something like this: "My brother called me stupid, and so I said, "You are stupid yourself." Then he said, "No, you are stupid." At this point the teacher may interrupt, asking, "Karl, how often do you fight? Where are your parents, and what are they doing when you are fighting?"

Gradually, the children will learn themselves how to handle touchy problems and carry on a discussion.

Stimulate Ideas

As the students gain experience in group discussion, as well as some freedom of expression and skill in the processes of problem solving, the teacher may suggest that they discuss problems encountered outside the class, such as getting along with brothers and sisters, getting along with parents, getting along with friends, fighting, and so forth. She may also say, "Sometimes, you may wish to talk about something that you don't like. Unless you tell me, I'll never know about it."

The following are examples in which the class is critical of the teacher.

JOAN: I'd like to bring up something that you do that sometimes disturbs me. Everytime a teacher comes into our room, she stands by your desk, which is right in front of mine, and you talk and disturb me. I can't do my work.

PETER: I have noticed this too.

JOAN: Maybe you could go outside the room and talk there. That wouldn't disturb us.

TEACHER: I'm so glad that you brought this to my attention. I should have realized this myself, but I didn't. I am truly sorry if I disturbed you, and I'll remember to walk out whenever somebody from the outside comes in to talk to me.

RANDY: I'd like to bring up something that you and the teacher's aide do that disturbs me.

TEACHER'S AIDE: What is it?

RANDY: Well, after we have our bathroom break, you two drink coffee in the classroom. We can't drink coke or other soft drinks, and I don't think that's right.

MANY CHILDREN: That's right, that's not fair.

TEACHER: I can understand that. Could I explain something to you, and then we'll see if you still think it's unfair?

MANY CHILDREN: Sure, what is it?

TEACHER: When the class has a snack break at 10 o'clock, we have to stay with you because we are on duty. Our only chance to have a cup of coffee is the time when you come back to the room.

DAVE: Well, when you look at it like that, it's only fair that you do it that way.

TEACHER: What do the rest of you think?

RANDY: Well, I brought it up, and from the way it was explained I think it's fair.

KIM: Yeah, I feel better about it, and I think it's O.K. It seems like we kids get a break, but you don't.

Children are basically fair. Once they realize that teachers too have needs, they show understanding.

Group Decisions and Evaluation of Progress

In discussions children are constantly making decisions. The teacher needs to be aware of how these decisions will affect all the class members and also whether the consequences are of a punitive nature. The group must be able to tolerate and appreciate differences of opinion. Sometimes a minority opinion is the most valuable contribution and can stimulate a reassessment of the majority opinion.

Group decisions are hard to undo. Sometimes it may be necessary to reconstruct the discussion in order to understand how a decision was reached. In this process, the group may see implications of their previous decision. At this point, the group may wish to withdraw their decision and initiate another course of action. Reviewing what the group has done helps to give the group a feeling of accomplishment. The use of direct questions is one way to get the group to evaluate itself: "What have we accomplished?" "Has it been of value? In what way?" "Did we leave out anything?" A teacher also could say, "It seems as though we understand and agree about ___." "We seem to need more discussions about ___." "We seem to be working well together on ___." As a teacher works with her group, she will find other ways of stock-taking that will fit into her particular needs.

Changing Attitudes Through Discussion

Letting the children determine why a problem exists helps them gain insight into the purpose of behavior. For instance, a teacher may say to the class:

> I'd like to discuss with you a problem that I had last year. One of my students was always late coming into class after we returned from recess. Let's take a moment and think about this problem. Why, in your opinion, would a child behave this way? Of course, we can only guess, but guessing is fun, and it helps us think through a problem and come up with some very good explanations as to why a person behaves in a certain way. Who would like to start this discussion?

The following discussion is based on this kind of technique. The problem was that a boy had taken money out of his mother's purse without telling her and then had bought candy, which he gave to other children.

> TEACHER: Let's take a few minutes and think about this problem. We don't know much about this boy, yet I'm sure that we have some feelings about him and his behavior. Why would any child do such a thing? Let's guess and see what we can come up with.
>
> MIKE: I think that maybe the children asked him to get them some candy, and that's why he did it.
>
> BOB: I think that this boy probably was afraid of the children, and that's why he did it.
>
> TEACHER: What do you mean?
>
> BOB: I mean that maybe they told him that they would get him after school, and he was afraid.
>
> TEACHER: Do you mean that they threatened to beat him up unless he gave them candy?

BOB: Yes.

TEACHER: How do the rest of you feel about this?

JUDY: Maybe this boy promised them the candy, and he had no money, so he had to take it from his mother. Maybe his mother didn't want to give him the money.

BILL: He stole the money, and that's not right.

TEACHER: Do you mind if we don't discuss now if what this boy did was right or wrong and talk only about the reasons he did such a thing?

SANDRA: Maybe this boy wanted to make friends with these children.

ANN: I think that he was probably a lonely boy and he wanted friends. I agree with Sandra.

JOHN: I think that probably his mother wasn't home and then he is the boss in the house, so he doesn't have to ask his mother for permission to take the money. He probably had only 20 cents of his own, and it wasn't enough, so he took what he needed.

BETSY: He must be a very spoiled boy.

MARY: John said that he is the boss when his mother isn't home. Is this boy grown up—like a man, I mean?

TEACHER: This boy is 10 years old. John, did you think that he was already a grown man?

JOHN: Well, I think it makes no difference. I mean, when his mother isn't home, if he is the only boy in the family, then maybe he is the boss—when his father isn't home, I mean.

HELEN: I don't agree with you that he is the boss just because he is a boy and his father isn't home. Why should he be a boss when he is only a child? Anyway, he should ask permission before he takes money from his mother's purse.

JANE: I agree with Helen. Maybe there are other children, and even if they are girls, I don't think that they would like it if he made himself the boss.

ANN: If you let him be a boss in the family, then maybe he would like to be a boss all the time.

TEACHER: Can you explain what you mean by that?

SANDRA: Well, if he thinks that he is a boss at home, he may want to be the boss when he is outside or in school.

BILL: I think that John said this because he is the only boy in his family, and maybe he is the boss when his father isn't home.

TEACHER: Please, children, we are not discussing John now. We are discussing somebody's problem—a boy we don't even know. Let us try and discuss the problem.

PETER: I think that he is trying to make friends. He probably has no friends.

TEACHER: Do you have friends?

PETER: Yes.

TEACHER: Do you have to give them candy or other presents to be your friend?

PETER: No.

(The teacher asked several children if they had friends and if they made friends by giving them candy or other presents. All the children said that they did not.)

TEACHER: All of you tell me that you have friends and that you do not have to bribe them. Peter tells us that this boy tried to make friends. Let's discuss this a little further.

JIM: If he tries to make friends this way, the children will like him only for a little while, and then they won't be his friends anymore.

TEACHER: Why not?

JIM: Because they will always want him to buy them candy, and if he doesn't always have the money, they won't be his friends.

FRANK: That's right. They won't be his friends. He would have to buy them candy all the time.

TONY: He should play with them and maybe ask them to come over sometime and play at his home. Then he can make friends.

TEACHER: Why doesn't this boy have any friends? Let's see if we could guess what some of the reasons might be.

MARY: Well, if he is like John said, the boss, I don't blame the children if they don't want to be his friend.

KEVIN: Maybe he is not very friendly.

LINDA: He could be a nasty kid, and that's why he doesn't have friends.

PATSY: Maybe he is new in the neighborhood, and that's why he has no friends.

BILL: But even then he could make friends without taking money from his mother.

SANDRA: I think that maybe he wants his way all the time, and that's why he has no friends.

TEACHER: You have come up with some very good ideas. Everything you said may be the reason why this boy behaved as he did. We are not sure, but this is not important. You see how many different reasons there are why some people behave in one way and others behave in a different way in the same kind of situation. Each one of you has friends, yet each of you has made friends in a different way than this boy did or tried to do.

Some readers may wonder why the teacher did not discuss the moral and ethical aspects of this problem. This can be done at another time when the focus of the training is on values. In this discussion the focus was on understanding behavior. It would take too much time, and it would be too confusing if the teacher were to concentrate on both morals and training at the same time.

During the preceding discussion, the teacher may have observed that some children lowered their heads or listened with an expression of extreme intensity. This is usually a recognition reflex. Probably these children identified with the action and motivation behind the behavior of this boy.

In the case of John, the teacher gained great insight into his position at home—that he is the only boy of 11 children. Although the teacher discouraged the group from discussing John's position in his family, John was indirectly exposed to the children's feelings of such behavior, and, we may assume, that he gave this some thought.

From this example, we can see that any discussion that is thought provoking, if it is skillfully led by the teacher, has possibilities for training children to understand behavior and to draw conclusions about it. The teacher must be on the alert to know when and what kind of questions to ask in order to promote further logical thinking. Interpretations must come from the children themselves. If none are forthcoming, she may bring up some of the comments made by the children with regard to this problem and continue the discussion at another time.

From the examples in this chapter you can see that teachers have to become sensitive to what goes on in a group. One of the greatest benefits of group discussions is that children lose their fear of revealing themselves when they see that many other children also have problems.

The Values of Group Discussion

Group discussion is probably the most effective technique a teacher can use to unite the class for a common goal.

1. It helps children to develop better interpersonal relationships.
2. It enhances learning through accumulated information.
3. Children learn to explore controversial matters and to deal with people of different backgrounds.
4. Children examine problem areas and face unpleasant facts that they normally ignore or push aside.
5. Children learn to form attitudes and values that may influence them for life and that may affect their behavior inside and outside of school.
6. It makes difficult tasks seem lighter when ideas, aspirations, successes, problems, and anxieties are shared.
7. Children feel supported by their peers and are more responsive.
8. Children learn constructive ways of handling frustrations and of working through upsetting problems.
9. The teacher may raise the morale of the group and change the atmosphere of the room.
10. Talking in an atmosphere of mutual understanding stimulates thinking.
11. The teacher learns what each child feels and thinks, how he relates to others, and what his attitude toward school is.
12. As children mull over and discuss a problem, they may find one solution or they may find a number of solutions to the same problem.
13. It unifies all children into a group for a common purpose. They are

working on the same problem at the same time and usually have good
results.

14. It helps the child to feel accepted and as if he belongs.
15. The children gain increased self-direction, self-management, and
    decision making abilities.
16. It helps children to see the value of structure and order within group
    living.

SELECTED READINGS

Bates, Marilyn, and Johnson, Clarence D. *Group Leadership.* Denver, Colo.:
Lane Publishing Company, 1972.

Dinkmeyer, Don C., and Muro, James J. *Group Counseling.* Itasca, Ill.: F. E.
Peacock Publishers, 1971.

Dreikurs, Rudolf. *Psychology in the Classroom.* New York: Harper & Row,
1957.

Gazda, George M. *Group Counseling.* Boston: Allyn & Bacon, 1971.

Lindgren, H. C. *Educational Psychology in the Classroom.* New York: Wiley,
1956.

Ohlsen, Merle M. *Counseling Children in Groups.* New York: Holt, Rinehart
and Winston, 1973.

Sweeney, Thomas J. *Adlerian Counseling.* Boston: Houghton Mifflin, 1975.

Chapter 15

Specific Techniques:

Group Discussions

In this chapter we intend to give practical suggestions on how to implement and how to facilitate discussions in the classroom.

Group Discussions, Class Meetings, or Class Councils?

Group discussions, class meetings, and class councils have many things in common. Teachers who use the discussion method quite often use these terms interchangeably. In order to clarify our thinking and writings on this matter, let us define the three terms.

A group discussion is a meeting in which the group discusses and makes decisions concerning the operation of the classroom, discusses the actions and feelings of group members, explores alternatives to help change a child's behavior or to alleviate a child's feelings, and gives encouragement to a group member who is in the process of making a change. A group discussion is similar to a subject in social living, and in some schools grades are given for participation in the group. The teacher may be the leader, a student may be selected as the leader, or the group may function without a designated leader.

A class meeting includes taking care of the business of the class, such as milk or lunch count, field trips, room arrangement, planning for interclass sports, parties, picnics, and so on. There are usually class officers who conduct the regular meetings and who take care of the class business. They also act as discussion leaders.

The class council usually is a combination of group discussions and class meetings but usually has an added dimension. The class council usually is composed of two members who serve for about six to eight weeks and who are representatives to the regular school Student Council. They take information from their class council to the Student Council and bring back information, which they relay to the class. In this way, the council members are aware of what is going on in the mainstream of the school and keep the class informed. They also are the leaders of the class discussions.

It really does not make much difference what a teacher and her class decide to call the discussion time. However, what goes on in the discussions is very important.

Electing Leaders for the Class Council

The teacher should first find out if the class wants to have a leader. In kindergarten to the sixth grade there are usually two leaders. In the upper grades, there is usually one leader or chairperson. The teacher may prepare a chart with all the children's names on it. The children are told that each child will have a chance to serve as a leader, unless he declines, and that nobody can serve a second time until all the children have had their turns. The teacher may ask for nominations of two children who will serve together. The class then proposes four or five couples. Their names are written on the board. The teacher asks these two children to put their heads down while the class votes by a show of hands. The couple who gets the most votes are the coleaders until the next election. The names of these two children are then crossed off the list. And so it goes to the end of the year.

Training Leaders for Class Meeting or Student Council

Children need to be taught how to be effective leaders. In the lower grades the teacher can give the leader a notebook in which they write the names of the students who want to talk during Student Council meetings. It makes the leader feel important, and it helps him to get started with the discussions. Any child who has a grievance or a suggestion asks the leader to sign him up for the next meeting. Or, the agenda can be placed in a certain spot in the room so that the children can sign up. The agenda has merit in that heated arguments or fights between children must wait until the next meeting. By then, they have calmed down. The leader starts the meeting with a call to order and then reads the names of the children who wish to talk. If there is time, children who did not sign up but want to talk can be given a chance. If there is not time, those who have signed up have the floor. However, after the student presents his problem or suggestion, one of the coleaders invites the group to respond. In this way, many children partake in the discussion whether they have signed up or not.

The teacher, as an equal member of the group, must sign up if she has something that she wants the group to discuss. She must also hold her hand up each time she wants to talk during the discussion and wait for the leader to recognize her.

During the first few weeks, the teacher sits between the coleaders and guides them. For instance, a child may say, "I have a home problem. My sister always hits me. The teacher (speaking softly) says to one of the leaders, "Find out how old the sister is." After the leader poses the question and receives an answer, the teacher again speaks softly to him: "Find out if any of the parents are involved in this fight." Again the leader complies. The teacher may now speak softly to the leader and say, "Ask the class what they think about parents getting involved in children's fighting?" In this fashion the teacher trains the class until such training is no longer necessary.

The teacher may ask the coleaders to stay for a few minutes during lunchtime so that she can discuss with them the procedures used or their shortcomings. She may make them aware that one of them is taking over and does not share responsibility with the other, or that they tend to call again and again on their friends and ignore the hands of the other children, or she may ask them to speak louder.

At the end of their service as leaders the class evaluates them and makes suggestions for the leaders to follow. There is always an evaluation.

Setting Goals for the Week

After discussing whatever problems that come up, the class sets goals for the entire class to work on until the next election. The goal may be any of the following: to walk down the stairs; to use one paper towel when washing hands; to talk softly when the teacher is out of the room, and so on. Before the next election the class evaluates the achievement of the goal, and if they feel that they have been successful, they set new goals. If they feel that they have not been successful, they may continue working on the same goal for another week or longer. If this still remains a problem, the class will have to discuss why this is so and reevaluate the goal.

Questions Concerning Group Discussions

Teachers who are interested in group discussions often ask a great number of questions. We would like to deal with each of these questions, not just from a theoretical point of view but also from personal experiences with effective group discussions that have spanned more than 20 years.

1. *Can a teacher have effective group discussions in a large class?* The size of the group is not a determining factor in the learning process. We have had over 40 students in a class, and the size did not interfere with the effectiveness of the discussions. A large class may, however, determine the time that the teacher wishes to allot to regular group discussions. (The more students there are, the more clerical work there is for a teacher, the more parent-teacher conferences there are, the more grades there are to record, and the more reports there are to write.) Teachers often sacrifice group discussions for time to attend to other responsibilities. This is unfortunate. Precisely because the teacher is so pressed for time, she needs the class to help her waste less time on discipline and learning problems. Through good group discussions, a teacher gains time.

2. *What about children who sit in the back and cannot hear?* We suggest that the children and the teacher sit in a circle whenever possible. This enables her to have eye contact with each student, and it helps with hearing. We further suggest that the teacher sit next to the troublemaker. Her physical closeness exercises control over the student's possible misbehavior. If desks are fastened to the floor and forming a circle is not possible, the students can form a circle by sitting on the floor, or the last row of children can double up with children in front.

3. *How does a teacher handle children who manipulate the discussion?* If a child manipulates the conversation, which may happen, the teacher or the leader can remind this child that others are waiting to speak, so would he, please, come to the point. The class can decide on how many minutes a person should be allowed to talk.

4. *When do you start?* Start on the first day, if possible. This should be a very informal group discussion. The teacher and the class can discuss such things as how they want to decorate the room or how they want to handle going to the washroom or the water fountain.

5. *How long should the discussions last?* The length of the discussions should depend on the age and the intellectual level of the group. In kindergarten and first grade, it should not exceed 20 minutes. In the second through fifth grades it may last 20 to 30 minutes. Older children should have 40 to 50 minutes. The discussion should never drag and become boring to the class. They must not necessarily solve all the problems during a meeting. Some problems may be tabled for next time, if need be. Trainable-mentally retarded (TMR) or developmentally disabled children should have 5 to 10 minute group discussions daily. We have found that they are very capable of handling short discussions.

6. *With what age groups can a teacher have group discussions?* Group discussions can be held with children who are as young as 4 or 5 years old.

7. *What should the teacher do with children who refuse to participate?* No child should be forced to participate. People learn from listening. But children should be invited to express their feelings and opinions. A teacher, or the leader, may say to a quiet child, "We haven't heard from you,

Dennis. How do you feel about what we have just discussed?," or "I have the feeling that you have something that you would like to say, Dennis. How about it? We would like to hear your opinion."

8. *What does the teacher do with children who disturb the discussions?* If children disturb a discussion, the teacher would do better to stop the discussion for that day without getting angry or making the disturbing children feel guilty. She may say, "We cannot have a good discussion with people disturbing. Therefore, we will have to postpone our discussion for tomorrow. It will be at the same time." If the children get angry, they will deal with the culprits on their own.

The following day, the children should be invited to try again. If there is further disturbance, the teacher should go through the same procedure and postpone the discussion once more. It is very important that the teacher remain calm. It rarely happens that there will be any further disturbance after several postponements. Should there be a child that persists in disturbing, the teacher can suggest that he go to another teacher until the discussion is finished. (This must be arranged with a teacher beforehand.) She should assure this student that he will be called back as soon as the class has finished the discussion. He should also be given the option of returning to class whenever he decides not to disturb it. In our experience class discussions are the highlight of the week's activities, and the children always want to be part of them.

9. *Is everything handled by the group?* There are very few things that are not handled by the group. Everything that pertains to the particular class should be handled by the group.

10. *Does the class follow a majority decision?* We prefer having a general consensus to majority rule. When the class cannot reach a consensus, we then try to negotiate with the dissenters to gain a consensus. If this fails, then we ask those who are in opposition to live with the decision until the next discussion. Usually the opposition agrees.

11. *Can the class discuss a problem when it occurs, or must the class wait until the regular discussion time?* Whenever possible we prefer to wait to solve problems until the class has its meeting. There are, however, times when this is not possible and when a matter has to be discussed on the spot. For instance, should a child continue to disturb a class to a point where teaching and learning is impossible, the teacher may stop everything and have a group discussion right there and then. She may ask the class to help her find a solution to the problem. She may say something like the following: "As you have noticed, Gail has not let me teach. I wonder what she expects of me? What do you think she wants me to do? In your opinion, why has she such a need to disturb us? Where do we go from here? I will not fight with Gail, but neither will I be able to teach as long as she is disturbing us." This is bound to develop into a group discussion.

12. *What does the teacher do about very personal problems such as drug addiction, alcoholism, or parents who have a jail record?* Children

may bring up problems that are of a very personal nature like, "My old man came home drunk and he beat up my mother." The teacher should very tactfully suggest that this should be discussed with her privately. A big issue should not be made of it, but it should not be ignored either. At a later time the teacher can ask the child if he would like to discuss his problems with her and explain that his parents may resent or may even be hurt if he were to discuss their problems with the class.

13. *How does the teacher handle children who resent being discussed by the class?* Now and then we run into a child who demands that the group should never talk about him. Usually, this is a child who takes all rights for himself and never grants the same rights to others. Often, this child has serious behavioral problems.

We have found a very effective way of dealing with such children. We use a story or a report of some kind to pave the way for effective discussion. The teacher may say to the entire class.

"Class, I would like to discuss with you a certain situation, and I would like for you to tell me how you would handle this problem if it were your problem. Let's imagine that all of you are parents and that you have a child that has a toothache. What would you do?"

Children invariably tell us that they would take the child to the dentist. The teacher must then ask a number of children if this is what they would do in this situation, including the child for whose benefit the teacher is discussing this problem. This is very important. A sample dialogue follows.

TEACHER: How about you, Stacy, would you take your child to the dentist?"
STACY: Yes.
TEACHER: But suppose your child objects and refuses to go because it hurts. What would you do then?"
STACY: I would still take the child.
TEACHER: But why would you do this? Don't you love your child?"

The children claim that precisely because as a parent, they would not want their child to lose his teeth, and because they love the child, they would take him, no matter how much he objected.

The teacher goes through her questioning once more, to make certain that this is what Stacy would do. After the children gave their approval of taking the child in spite of his objections, the teacher may say:

TEACHER: Alright, Stacy, into the dentist's chair! I like you and am concerned about you. Therefore, I must discuss the problems we are having with you. Just as the parent would take the child to the dentist because the parent cares, so I must discuss the problems we are having with you because I care.

14. *What should the teacher do about parents who demand that the class never discuss their child during meetings?* It may also happen that the child goes home and tells his parents that he does not want the class to talk about him, and so the parent comes to school to voice his objections. The teacher may try to help this parent see how she or he is unwittingly reinforcing the child's antisocial attitude and behavior. The teacher may say: "I appreciate your concern. I would not want to hurt Stacy for anything. As you know, Stacy has been having problems in school for years. I would hate for her to leave this class at the end of the year and continue to have problems in school. I care very much about her behavior. You give her the green light to continue behaving as she does. Indirectly you are allowing her to disturb us, to beat up other children, and not to do her work, but you won't give us the right to talk about it. I don't question that you want to protect your child, but this is going to hurt her more. Please, allow the class to handle this problem. It will be much more effective than if you or I were to handle it on our own."

Should the parent still insist that the class should not discuss Stacy's problem, the teacher should honor this request if she feels that she can reach Stacy in spite of it. If she feels that this is the only way to reach Stacy, the teacher may have to go against this mother and in the process make an enemy of her, at least until such time that Stacy's behavior changes.

15. *Why should the teacher discuss home problems in school?* Many school problems have their origins in the home. Parents often are no match for their children, and the latter are successful in their manipulation of their parents. This can be brought to the child's awareness. Many home problems have been solved through discussions that the teacher has held in class. Furthermore, some children may have few problems in class, but they may have problems outside class and nobody to discuss them with. For instance, a child may have complained that she is afraid to walk home from school because some dogs attack her on the way home. The children can come up with all kinds of solutions to this problem. Another child may have no friends to play with after school. Again, the children can help with this problem.

16. *What kinds of topics or problems can the class discuss?* One cannot possibly suggest all the problems that might arise in the classroom. The following questions would be pertinent to any class discussion.

Why do children act up when they have substitute teachers?
How would children manage a day without a teacher?
Why are rules and regulations necessary in the home, in school, and in society?
For what purposes do some people break rules?
Who should have more rights—adults or children?
How does a child make friends?

Should people have equal rights?
Why do children act up and disturb the class?
When two children fight at home should parents become involved in it?
Why is it that some bright children do not learn?

The following is a list of general topics for discussion that the teacher can bring up.

having courage to do things
having courage to make mistakes
doing a job well
helping around the house
respect for order
cooperation
respect for self
respect for others
manipulation of others
respect for one's own property
respect for others' property
problems with friends
doing a job completely
how students annoy teachers, parents, peers
power struggles
getting "set up" in certain situations
doing a job for the enjoyment of doing it
being of equal value
doing the unpopular thing
accepting responsibility
always showing off
being different from others
does one *have* to like school?
responsibility for or to others
students are *not* stupid
students are *not* lazy
family constellation
sibling problems
rights of others

helping others
parental problems
concern for others
helping each other
temper tantrums
crying and reasons for crying
getting along with people you do not like
helping one's brothers and sisters
getting recognition in a positive and constructive way
doing things one does not like to do
helping someone who is discouraged
handling anger
stories for self-understanding
discouragement
feeling sorry for oneself
putting people down
jealousy
boasting
stealing
competing; having to be first, best, or right
social interest versus self-centeredness
yielding to group pressure versus doing what one thinks one should do
clowning around
role playing problems
keeping promises

These are some suggestions. The teacher may want to discuss other situations that may have a more direct bearing on problems she has in class.

17. *Should the class always talk about problems during discussion sessions?* No, the class should not always talk about problems. The teacher must bring this to the class's attention or they will only discuss problems.

She can suggest that they discuss a student's improvements, the good things other class members do, encouragement, and so on.

18. *How often should the class have discussion meetings?* The class decides on the day or days that they will meet. We suggest two meetings a week in the lower grades and one meeting a week for older children.

19. *How does the teacher train children to encourage others during class councils or group discussions?* It is of greatest importance that the teacher train the class in encouraging others. Children respond to the encouragement they receive from their peers. The teacher may tell the class, for example, that she is very pleased to see that a child is now coming to school on time. She may ask if anyone else has noticed this. She may suggest that children should be watchful of any progress made by anyone in class, including the teacher, and indicate that they have noticed the change.

The teacher can ask one of the children to comment on a child's progress during group discussion. She may say: "Did you notice that Stanley wasn't in a single fight all week? This was not easy for him. I believe he would be very encouraged if one of you were to mention it. Would you mind? It would carry more weight and be more meaningful to him if one of you were to mention it instead of me." Gradually, the children learn the importance of encouragement and they eagerly respond to it.

With the older children, the class may elect a chairperson each time the group meets. The children hold up their hands, and the chairperson calls on them. The teacher can guide this leader with questions such as the following.

"Harry said that he hates doing arithmetic. You did not follow this up, and we did not help him. Would you mind going back to this problem?

I would appreciate it if you did not allow the students to mention names of teachers who are not here to defend themselves. Let's leave out names of people altogether."

Here, as in the lower grades, each student has a chance to be a leader. The leader is discussed, and suggestions are made before a new chairperson is elected.

20. *Should the teacher allow strangers to sit in during class meetings?* She can invite anyone who is interested in the group meetings to come in as a silent observer. Often teachers from other classes like to observe. Sometimes they send students to observe and then report what they have learned to their respective classes. Many a teacher did not start group discussions with her class before she had a chance to observe first. We suggest that teachers new at leading group discussions should not invite visitors until they have had more experience and feel more comfortable.

The teacher may assign a student to serve as the host and to greet the guests as they come in and escort them to a chair.

21. *What is the role of the teacher?* The teacher must take on a leading position and teach and train the group until such time as she can step back and participate as a group member without excessive direction to students. But for some time, the teacher guides the class by means of suggestions and mostly through pertinent questions that lead the students to think logically. Without such training, the class discussion develops into a bickering session and there is chaos.

Everyone may be mainly concerned with complaining and with punishing. If this happens the discussion session ceases to be a democratic procedure. Without adequate training the children do not gain any insight into their behavior and they do not change their values. We have no qualms with teachers who allow their students to talk about whatever they want to without any leadership. Such talking should not take the place of guided group discussions, however. Most teachers who claim to have had group discussions but experience bad results, used group discussions to express their own ideas, to explain, and to preach. Others conducted their discussions as free-for-all's in an unrestrained and unstructured way. Some consider show-and-tell time and magic circle as group discussion; others believe that a debate is a group discussion. The group discussions that we propose have meaning. They serve a purpose; they are aimed not only at changing behavior but at fostering healthy values.

22. *What skills should a teacher have in order to lead an effective group discussion?*

a. Understand the four goals of misbehavior (see Chapter 3).
b. Understand the private logic and hidden reason behind what a child is saying (see Chapter 4).
c. Learn how to reveal the psychological goal of the child (see Chapter 4).
d. Know how to phrase questions (especially with teenagers) in order to get to the hidden reason, which is the justification for their actions (see Chapter 4).
e. Be aware of cliques or subgroups in the classroom (see Chapter 13).
f. Be alert to detect feelings and attitudes that are implied but not expressed.
g. Help the children to express their thoughts, feelings, and attitudes more clearly.
h. Encourage quiet members to participate.
i. Link the thoughts and feelings of group members.
j. Sense the group atmosphere and be willing to discuss it.
k. Encourage group members to cooperate in learning a new process rather than competing.
l. Help the group to establish its own limits
m. Encourage the group members to see both the strengths and the assets of individual members.

n. Help the group to make guesses about the purposes of each other's behavior.
o. Help the group members to summarize and evaluate what they have learned.
p. Have the ability to confront the group with what it is doing and produce feedback.

To be a leader of a group discussion requires considerable self-assurance, spontaneity, and inner freedom. These qualities permit a teacher to function without fear and without concern for her own prestige or of what the children may say. The teacher must know how to draw the children out and to help them feel free and unthreatened to discuss their feelings and their ideas. It is a subtle leadership. Teachers must also remember that group discussions are used for psychological and corrective purposes. They help children understand what makes them tick, why they have problems, and what they can do to solve them.

Classroom discussions can counteract delinquent tendencies, and they can also foster general improvement, both in learning and behaving.

Despite the many favorable comments published about group discussions in the classroom, we must consider that many teachers lack training in leading them and that they are prone to make mistakes. This should not discourage them. We suggest that teachers who are considering having group discussions should get the support of the principal and of the parents in order to forestall possible disapproval.

Case Studies: Adolescents

The following case study can be used by the teacher in group discussions with adolescents. The teacher should read only the case study to the class and use the analysis to assist her in leading the discussions in the right direction.

Charles, 16, dropped out of high school. He has a part-time job and lives at home. He bought himself an old car, drives fast, and has had several minor accidents. In one such accident his friend was badly hurt. He was arrested by the police, but his father bailed him out.

Charles and his father fight frequently. Now and then his father hits him. Sometimes Charles does not come home for several days and does not let his family know his whereabouts. Charles's mother died two years ago.

Charles has a number of friends who also dropped out of school. They all hang around a pool hall. They smoke grass, drink beer, and complain about their parents and about society.

Charles has three siblings. Steve, 14, is a freshman. He is very athletic and involved with sports. He is an average student. He is very popular and is often invited to parties. He and his father also do not get along. Steve is sloppy around the house and is not involved with anyone except his friends.

Peggy, 11, is in the sixth grade. She is very pretty, an A student, very kind, and "a joy to have around," as her father puts it. She helps with household chores. She is very critical of her two older brothers and often complains about them to her father.

Anton, 8, is in the third grade. He is an average student. He is a very good-looking child, charming, always in good humor, likes to sing, and he is pleasant to everyone. He resembles his father, whose name also is Anton.

TEACHER: Let's see how you understand this boy.

STUDENT: He's got problems all right.

STUDENT: He sounds very irresponsible to me. He drives too fast, has accidents, and gets into fights.

STUDENT: Now wait a minute. This boy has problems, as you said, but do we really know enough about him to condemn him?

STUDENT: We do know something, and we can have an idea about this, Charles. I, for instance, think that his father may have a lot to do with it. His mother died when he was only 14. Who takes care of him?

TEACHER: It's true, we don't know who takes care of all of the children, but we know something about them. I wonder if you have given any thought to Charles's siblings and how he might feel about them?

STUDENT: His brother, Steve, is no better than he is.

STUDENT: Wait a minute. He is an average student, which I doubt that Charles is. Also, he is talented—good in athletics. Do you think that this might have an influence on Charles? I know that I don't like it when my brother is excelling in something. I wouldn't say that I don't want him to excel, but I am jealous, and I admit it.

STUDENT: But why doesn't Steve get along with his father?

STUDENT: I was wondering the same thing.

The teacher gets the class involved in the understanding of the family constellation and how the other children may have affected Charles's self-evaluation. She must lead the class to examine the qualities of each of the children in the family. For instance, Steve is popular and good in sports. Peggy is the only girl, which in itself gives her a special place in the family. She is good and gains her place through pleasing. Anton is the baby, good looking, and charming. He resembles his father. It is possible that Charles, being the oldest, is expected to assume responsibilities toward the younger children. Possibly this was even increased after his mother died. We may speculate about whether his behavior is directed against his father as punishment for the unfairness that Charles feels in the situation.

The teacher must focus on how this boy can be helped. Since Charles does not understand his behavior and his need to get even with his father, he may need counseling. This discussion may then revolve around the student's attitude toward counselors.

The goal of the teacher is also to help her class realize how important it is for Charles to get even with his father, with the school, and perhaps even with society, and how he is willing to sacrifice his own happiness for it.

Since he is already allowed to work, he may be encouraged to take a full-time job, with the assurance (by his father) that he can go back to school any time he wants to. The emphasis should be on encouragement from everyone, including his peers.

Using case studies with adolescents is more complicated than using case studies with elementary school students, especially if the teacher teaches math or science or any subject that does not require reading. Teachers of literature should have no problem. Most novels, short stories, or plays lend themselves to character analysis. For teachers who do not teach literature, we suggest that they bring into class and discuss newspaper reports about youngsters who have gotten into trouble. If possible, the teacher can find out something more personal about the character in the article: some background material; the family constellation; how the child behaved in school; or the neighborhood he grew up in.

We must always help children to understand that antisocial behavior stems from discouragement. We must also help them to realize that everything they do is by their own decision, that nobody makes them do anything, since they themselves decide what they will or will not do, and that they usually have alternative ways of behaving. We must discuss these alternatives when we present a problem. It requires that the teacher lead the discussion in a challenging way or else it will become dull and will not be interesting.

Chapter 16

Training Children to Understand Behavior Through the Use of Stories

If the teacher feels that the class is not yet ready to discuss its own be-havior problems, she can train the class to analyze and to understand behavior through the use of stories. Stories are a link in the transitional process from discussing general problems to dealing with personal ones.

Almost every story lends itself to a discussion that involves social rela-tionships and to an analysis of the character's motivation to behave as he does. The teacher should focus the discussion on the basic points that deal with the problem, always emphasizing the purpose of the behavior. It often happens that a student associates his own behavior with the story's char-acter and openly admits this. Once one child makes such an admission, others follow and talk about their own behavior. Such discussions should never become personal but should focus on the situation and how it is handled. The situation should be discussed from a general point of view, such as why some people always argue. We must remember that each story is used for a very specific purpose. The teacher discusses the problem with the class from a psychological point of view without fear of putting a specific child on the spot. As she and the class talk about behavior in general, the child learns to accept that everyone has some kind of problem. The following example (Bullard, 1963) will illustrate this point.

BO, THE BALL PLAYER

TEACHER: Class, I will read to you a story about a French poodle. Later we will discuss how you feel about this little dog.

(This story lends itself to children in kindergarten up to the second grade. The purpose of the story is to help children realize how Bo manages to keep the attention focused on him.

Bo was a beautiful, young, silver-gray French poodle. He was friendly, liked to play ball, and quickly made friends with everybody.

Bo had two very nice masters, father and mother Johnson. They had many friends who often came to visit. Bo was a fine ball player. He could catch a ball that was rolling across the floor on the first bounce or that was even high in the air. He would carry it back in his mouth and toss it into the lap of anyone who looked like a ball player. Bo thought everyone looked like a ball player.

Whenever father and mother Johnson's guests met Bo for the first time, they always said, "What a cute dog, and how clever he is to catch and bring the ball." Bo would wag his short tail. No matter what direction they threw the ball, Bo would scramble and catch it. Everybody admired Bo.

But Bo never seemed to get tired. Nobody could quit playing ball because Bo wanted everybody to see how well he played. He would play for ten minutes, a half hour, or even a whole hour. Everybody got tired of playing with Bo. They came to talk and have fun with father and mother Johnson, but Bo would toss the ball on their laps, wag his tail, sneak up on the ball, and even turn half circles in the air when he jumped for the ball.

TEACHER: Well, what do you think of Bo?
Who likes him? Why?
Who doesn't like him? Why?
What exactly does he do?
Why does he do this?
What happens when the people don't want to pay attention to him any more?
How does Bo feel when nobody pays attention to him?
If any one of you were Bo, what would you do in his place?
Are dogs the only ones who need so much attention?
Do you know any people who do things that are similar to what Bo is doing?
How do they do this?
How does a person who wants constant attention behave at home? How about school?

The group will discuss Bo from various points of view. Most of the children usually see him as a very lovable dog, one they would love to have themselves. But, after some discussion, they pick up the clue that Bo behaves in a way that many of them behave at home or in class. Such a discussion should always take into consideration that there are other possibilities for Bo to get attention without making a nuisance of himself.

A similar story may be used for discussion at a later time. Gradually, the children begin to identify the problems in the stories with those that they have themselves and they start to talk about them.

An excellent story for a group discussion is "Ricky Goes Fishing" (Hartley, Sterl A., Gray, William S., Monroe, Marion, 1958). It is a story of a young boy who promises his father not to fish from the pier while his father goes deep-sea fishing. This discussion usually takes the following form:

RICKY GOES FISHING

TEACHER: What do you think of Ricky?

CHILD: I like him.

TEACHER: Why do you like him?

CHILD: Because he does not disobey his father.

CHILD: I like him too for the same reason. His father told him not to fish from the pier, and he doesn't.

TEACHER: Doesn't he want to?

CHILD: Yes, he wants to very much, but he promised his father that he wouldn't do it.

TEACHER: Couldn't he fish anyway? After all, his father is too far away to see him and may never find out.

CHILD: But that wouldn't be nice if he gave a promise.

CHILD: I don't think that he should do this just because his father isn't there to see him.

CHILD: What's the use of giving a promise if you're going to break it?

TEACHER: How many of you agree with these children that promises should be kept? (Most children raise their hands.)

TEACHER: Could we apply this example to a school situation?

CHILD: I don't understand what you mean. We don't fish in class.

TEACHER: Let me explain what I mean. Is there ever a class situation that is similar to Ricky's? (No answer) Let's assume that this class is a family. Who in class could take the place of Ricky?

CHILD: Do you mean one of us?

TEACHER: Is one child my class?

CHILD: You mean that we are in class the same as Ricky is in the family?

TEACHER: Exactly.

CHILD: Then we, all of us, are like Ricky to you.

TEACHER: Right. Who is the father?

CHILD: You are.

TEACHER: Do all of you follow this?

CHILD: How can you be a father?

TEACHER: We are just trying to set up a similar situation. You may think of me as the mother if it will help you.

CHILD: But you don't go deep-sea fishing.

TEACHER: The father in the story goes away and leaves Ricky behind. Right?

CLASS: Right.

TEACHER: Doesn't a teacher ever go away and leave her children behind?

CHILD: Yes.

CHILD: I see what you mean. You go away, just like the father does in the story, and you leave the class, just like he does.

TEACHER: That's right. Let's recall what happened between the father and Ricky before he left.

CHILD: The father asked him not to go fishing from the pier.

TEACHER: And what did Ricky say?

CHILD: He said that he would not go.

CHILD: I know what the teacher means.

TEACHER: What do I mean?

CHILD: When you go out you ask us not to talk and not to leave our desks.

TEACHER: And what do you say?

CHILD: We always promise not to do it.

CLASS: I understand now, too.

TEACHER: And what happens when I leave?

CHILD: We start talking, and sometimes we get out of our seats.

TEACHER: Do you think that Ricky is a likeable boy because he keeps his promise to his father but that you don't have to keep your promise? (No answer) We call this a "double standard," which means that we don't stick to our opinions or we think that other people have to behave in a certain way but we don't have to. What do you think of this?

CHILD: I think that we mustn't leave our seats if you leave the room.

CHILD: We mustn't promise to be good if we don't intend to keep our promise.

CHILD: I agree. If we promise, we should keep our promise.

TEACHER: Think about it. A teacher has to leave the class many times. So there will be plenty of opportunities to find out how you really feel about this situation now that we have talked about it.

Such a discussion should end right there. No references need to be made to any specific child in class. At a later time, the teacher may, in connection with a specific child's problem, bring up Ricky's case. We suggest that after discussing this story the teacher leave the room for a few minutes and put the children to the test. This is a good opportunity for her to show appreciation and reinforce positive behavior.

A number of stories indirectly touch on problems that many children will recognize as their own. "Whizzer's Purple Tail" (Curren, 1958), for example, is an excellent story to use as a basis for a discussion of people who will go to any length in their behavior in order to maintain a special position in the family or in any group.

WHIZZER'S PURPLE TAIL

This is a story in which a young mouse receives more attention than the others in his family by disregarding the wishes of his parents. He receives the status of a king in the family when by accident he dips his tail into purple paint. Purple is the sign of a king, according to his father. When the paint begins to wear off, Whizzer is mortified lest he lose his royal status, so he deliberately dips his tail into the paint again.

Whizzer's position in the family could be discussed from an objective point of view. Questions could be asked, such as, "Would you like to have him for your brother? Why not? Why is it so necessary for Whizzer to be different in an unpleasant way? Is this the only way he could get attention? Did Whizzer believe that he could be liked and accepted by others if he were not any different?" The extent to which Whizzer behaved in order to maintain his position of being something "special" could be discussed. The group could be asked if they know people who behave similarly to Whizzer and for the same reason.

Now and then a child offers voluntarily that this is precisely what he has been doing. Many children occupy "royal" status because they are different from their sisters and brothers in one way or another: they may be the only boy or girl among siblings of the opposite sex; they may be an only child; they may be the oldest or the youngest, more talented in some area, and so on. They too have fears of losing their status and become difficult the minute they sense any threat. Once a child makes such an admission, other children have the courage to speak about their faulty behavior. These discussions never fail to have an effect on children, and they do bring results.

Other stories that can be used include: John Steptoe, *Stevie*; Charlotte Zolotow, *The Quarreling Book*; and C. Berghoff, *Where Is Daddy*?

Almost every story lends itself to discussion that involves social relationships and analysis of the character's motivation. The teacher who is skilled in conducting discussions will succeed in bringing out the points that would touch upon the problems existing in the class without putting any student on the spot at that time. She should focus more on the problem as it affects everyone and less on the individual child.

Through the discussion of characters in stories, students can be trained to question and to understand their own and other children's behavior. As they learn to accept the fact that everyone makes mistakes, that mistakes can be rectified, that they should not feel embarrassed to discuss their problems, the teacher can start bringing up for discussion specific problems of specific children in the class.

When a problem needs discussing but the teacher cannot find a story that deals with such a problem, she can write her own story. The following story was written by a teacher to train children to understand a specific behavior.

CARMEN

Carmen was in the second grade. She was a very smart girl according to everyone who knew her. She liked to go to school, but she did not do any work in class. She spent most of her time drawing, walking about the room, or talking to other children. This made the teacher angry, and she often scolded and punished Carmen for her behavior. The parents also were very angry with Carmen. They could not understand why she behaved this way, since they were always very good to her and gave her everything she asked for.

TEACHER: What do you think of Carmen?

A CHILD: Well, she sure doesn't act right.

TEACHER: What do you mean?

CHILD: She is not nice.

TEACHER: Why not?

A CHILD: She should be doing her work in class, just like everybody else.

TEACHER: Yes, she should, but she doesn't. Why doesn't she?

CHILD: Maybe the work is too hard.

TEACHER: Do you believe that the work is too hard for Carmen?

CHILD: Maybe not.

CHILD: I don't think it's too hard for her.

TEACHER: How do we know that the work isn't too hard for her?

CHILD: She is very smart, and everybody thinks so.

CHILD: Yes, she is smart, but I think that she is just stubborn.

TEACHER: What do you mean by that?

CHILD: Well, she wants to have her way.

TEACHER: How do the rest of you feel about what ___ just said? (Many children agree that Carmen probably wants to have her way.)

TEACHER: Why is it so important to Carmen to have her way?

CHILD: I think that she is spoiled.

TEACHER: Could you explain to the others what you mean by "spoiled"?

CHILD: Well, at home she gets everything she wants.

TEACHER: Is there anything wrong with this? (Many children say "no" and many say "yes." This develops into a discussion concerning family inter-relationships and merits and disadvantages of being spoiled.)

CHILD: I think that she thinks that she must get her way in everything because if she doesn't, she thinks that people don't love her.

TEACHER: Do you think that people could love Carmen and that she could get attention in a different way—a way that would make living with her more pleasant?

CHILD: Yes, I think she could.

CHILD: She could if she tried.

TEACHER: What could she do?

CHILD: She could help her mother and get attention that way.

CHILD: She could even help other children who are not as smart as she is.

CHILD: Yes, and this way she would be helping the teacher too.

TEACHER: I see that you all have very good ideas about how Carmen could get attention. There is nothing wrong with wanting attention. We all do. It's a question of how we go about getting it. How should we get attention?

Invariably, someone will mention that we must get attention in a way that is pleasant to us yet does not hurt others. As the teacher listens to the individual members of her class, as she begins to understand their problems and their concepts of how they can solve them, as she gets a picture of the relationships among the students, she can plan more successfully for the individual student, establish shared values, and raise the morale of the entire group. This requires confidence in the group, self-assurance, and inner freedom, so that the teacher can function without concern for her own prestige. Only then will she succeed in guiding the child to the successful development of his innate abilities and his social potential.

Following are examples of illustrative stories written by teachers for use in their classes.

Stories for Kindergarten Through Primary Grades

GARY, THE SNATCHER

Gary is a little boy of 5 who is always getting into mischief. He especially enjoys snatching something from other children or from his father, running off with it, and laughing. Of course, the children and the father run after him and try to get back what he has taken. Gary only laughs. When he thinks that he will not be able to hold on to the object, he throws it away and laughs still harder.

Gary seldom takes anything from his mother. Once when he took her slipper and tried to run off with it, she threw him the other slipper too and kept reading her book, never even glancing up. Gary stood for a while, not knowing what he should do. Then he took both slippers and put them by his mother's chair.

QUESTIONS
1. What do you think of Gary?
2. Why is he taking things from everybody except his mother?
3. What does he get out of this behavior?
4. What would you do if you were his father or a child from whom he likes to take things? How could you stop him without getting into a fight?
5. Do you know of any behavior that is similar to Gary's but is happening in this class?
6. What could we do in such a case?

QUIET JANICE

Janice never got in anyone's way. She always saw to it that she was the last in line for recess, for lunch, or for the library. Of course, if someone else wanted to be last she didn't care.

When Janice came to the reading group, she would wait until all the other children were seated before she would slide silently into her chair.

One day the teacher asked Janice to read. She began to read, but as usual she read so softly that no one could hear her. The teacher and the children did everything they could think of to get Janice to read loud enough for them all to hear, but they just couldn't get her to do it.

QUESTIONS
1. What do you think of Janice?
2. Why do you think she was always so quiet?
3. Could she have read louder?
4. Why didn't she read louder?
5. Was she getting people to notice her?
6. How did she do it?
7. Do you know people like Janice?
8. In what other ways could Janice get attention that might be better?

LUCKY AND LUKE

Lucky and Luke are two dogs that live with the Apple family. Lucky is a little white poodle with fluffy, curly hair. Luke is a great, big German shepard, who is sleek and black.

Lucky often bites people, and then he runs to Luke for protection. Luke barks and snaps at people who try to punish his little friend. This frightens the people away, but it doesn't take long for Lucky to attack other people. When Luke stands up for him, Lucky sits on his hind legs and watches. An observer has the feeling that if Lucky could talk, he would probably want to say, "You see, there is nothing you can do to me."

This story focuses on behavior that we often find in the youngest children. They provoke and then expect that their parents will protect them from suffering the consequences. Many "good" children provoke their "bad" brothers or sisters in order to get them into trouble and then run to their parents for protection. They may do this also in school and expect protection from the teacher.

Children should be led to realize that such a child must fight his own battles and that nobody should get involved even if he gets a bloody nose in the process. He will learn not to provoke or to take the consequences if he does provoke.

MIMI

Mimi was a beautiful kitten with bright blue eyes. She loved to climb trees or high places. Once up, she would start crying for someone to take her down. Usually, her mistress would bring a ladder and take Mimi down, but one day everyone in the family decided to let Mimi cry and see what she would do. After an hour of crying, Mimi came down by herself.

Mimi uses water power (crying) in order to put others into her service, even though she is very capable of doing things for herself.

Stories for Third and Fourth Grades

PAUL

When Paul entered his house, he called, "Jane, hey Jane, where are you? I need you, Jane, come here!"

"Not so loud, Paul," said his mother, "Dad is taking a nap."

Paul yelled even louder, "Jane, I'm calling you. Come here this minute. I'm in a hurry." At this moment, Jane came up from the basement. "All right, Paul. What is it you want?"

"I can't find my bat, Jane, and the boys are waiting outside for me. Find it quickly. Hurry up!" He ran into the kitchen and yelled, "Mom, make me a sandwich to take along. I haven't any time to eat it now. Don't give me cheese, like you did yesterday. I hate it. Give me ham."

Jane came in with the bat. "Honestly, Paul, I wish you would find your own things. You never even try." Paul grabbed the bat and ran out of the house.

QUESTIONS
  1. What do you think of Paul?
  2. What's wrong with doing what he did?
  3. What is his attitude toward other people?
  4. What would you do if you were his sister?
  5. How do you think he behaves with the boys when he plays with them? Let's guess.
  6. How many children do you know who behave just like Paul?

BE NICE

"Did you do your workbook?," asked George. Samuel shook his head. "That darn workbook. I haven't touched it in days." He pulled out the workbook and opened it. "So many questions," he said to himself, "and so many different answers to each question! How am I to know which is the right answer?"

Without reading any of the questions, Samuel started to underline the answers. After a while, he turned to George. "Hey, George," he said, "is this right?"

George shook his head and pointed to the line below. "Thanks, George," said Samuel, as he erased his own answer and underlined the one George had pointed out.

Next he tapped Pamela on the shoulder. "Hey, Pam, what's the right answer to question number 2?" Pamela opened her workbook and showed him her answer. "Oh, thanks," said Samuel, as he drew a line under the same answer.

He noticed that Jimmy who sat in back of him was also working on the same page. He turned around and looked at Jimmy's workbook. At this, Jimmy covered his page with a piece of paper. "Do your own work, Samuel," he whispered. Samuel stuck his tongue out at Jimmy.

The focus of the discussion about this story should be on people who depend on others to do the work for them. If anyone refuses, they get angry, as Samuel did when he stuck his tongue out at Jimmy.

QUESTIONS
1. What do you think of Samuel?
2. Who likes him? Why?
3. Who doesn't like him? Why?
4. What's wrong with what he is doing?
5. What does he get out of this behavior?
6. Why isn't he doing his own work?
7. What do you think of George and Pamela? Are they good friends of Samuel? Why "yes" and why "no"?
8. What would you do if your neighbor acted like Samuel?
9. What should a teacher do?
10. How many of you agree with this suggestion?
11. Shall we try to do this in our class if this problem ever arises?

The teacher should use each story for a specific purpose. Before using a story the teacher, in preparing for the presentation of the story, needs to make certain that she knows the purpose of using each story.

Stories for Grades Three to Six

RUDY AND CANDY

Rudy was nervous and was switching his lunch box from one hand to the other as he was standing in front of the school building, waiting for his younger sister, Candy, to come out. Children were streaming out of the building, pushing and screaming. One small boy bumped into Rudy and almost knocked him to the ground. "Watch where you're going, Buster," yelled Rudy, and he gave him a shove. The boy fell to the ground.

At this moment Rudy saw Candy come out of the building. She was with her two friends, Jeannie and Barbara. The three stopped to talk while Rudy was waiting. "I wish mother wouldn't insist that I wait for Candy and bring her home," he mumbled to himself. "First thing she'll tell me is how much the teacher likes her and how she was first to finish her work." "What's the matter, Rudy?," asked Stefan, who was standing nearby. "Are you talking to yourself?" "None of your business," replied Rudy, and then he shouted, "Hey, Can, quit your yacking. Let's go."

When Candy noticed her brother, she left her friends and slowly walked toward Rudy. "Hi," she said, but he did not answer and started walking ahead of her. Candy quickened her pace and caught up with him. "Guess what I got in the arithmetic test, Ru?," she asked. Without waiting for an answer, she continued, "I made the highest score in class again. Mrs. James said that nobody, but nobody, can beat me in fractions. You know Quin? Well, Mrs. James almost went out of her mind trying to explain to him how to multiply fractions. But Quin is so dumb. You should have seen what he did when Mrs. James called him to the blackboard. I thought I'd die laughing." Rudy started running as fast as he could. "What's the matter with you, Ru? Why are you running away? Mom said that we must go home together. Wait until she finds out that you left me. Ru, Rudy!" She started running after him, but when she realized that he was too far and that she could not catch up with him, she gave up.

Rudy ran across the street and then took off up the alley, although his parents had told him many times not to walk through any alleys. As he ran, he kicked the garbage cans that were in his way.

QUESTIONS
1. How do you feel about these two children?
2. Whom do you like? Why?
3. What could we guess about Rudy that this story does not tell us?
4. What can we guess about Candy?
5. What do you think is going on at home?
6. Who might be tattling?
7. How does Rudy feel?
8. How well do you think Rudy does in mathematics? Why?
9. How does Rudy get attention?
10. How did he treat the boy who ran into him? Why?
11. How can we help both of these children, assuming such children are in our class?
12. What can the teacher do?
13. What can the students do?

The children should learn from this story that children in the same family compete and that a child may give up when a sibling is doing very well in a subject, because he may think that he can not do as well as his sister or brother. Actually, this child does not know how well he can do, because he does not give himself a chance to find out.

JEAN

Jean was 11 years old and was still in the fourth grade. Sometimes the children teased her about this. Only this morning, Sandra, who sat in front of her had said to her, "You know, Jean, I think that you'll still be in grade school when I graduate from high school." Jean did not answer, as she never did when anyone indicated that she was not very bright. She never said unkind things to anyone. In fact, she spoke very little of anyone. In school, Jean spent most of the time looking out the window or playing with some object on her desk. She was often lost in her daydreams and did not hear what the teacher said. Everybody seemed to accept the fact that she was a bad listener and a lazy girl who never touched her work.

At home, it was not much different. Her older sister, Brenda, called her "stupid." She had done this for so long that Jean got used to this name. Whenever Brenda called, "Hey, stupid," Jean looked up and sometimes asked, "What do you want?" Jean thought that Brenda was very smart and that she could do anything. The day before yesterday, when her mother was sewing kitchen curtains, she let Brenda do some of the sewing on the machine. Her mother thought that Brenda was very good at it. Jean wanted to try also, but her mother would not let her. She said, "No, Jean. I paid too much money for this machine, and I can't afford to let you break it."

QUESTIONS

1. How does Jean feel when children tease her?
2. Why would children do things to make others unhappy?
3. What child might do this and what child would not do this?
4. Does Jean believe that people like her?
5. Does Jean believe that she is as smart as the other children are?
6. From what we know about her, do we really know how smart she is? (Whatever answer the teacher may get.) What makes you think so?
7. In your opinion, who discourages Jean the most?
8. How do you feel about her sister, Brenda?
9. Do you like her?
10. Who could help Jean feel happier?
11. Sometimes, we find children in class who feel and act like Jean.
12. Should the children and the teacher be concerned about helping this child? How could one help such a child?

Stories for Junior High and High School

HOWARD

Howard is 12 years old. He is in the sixth grade. He is painfully thin, and his whitish-blond hair and pale face give him a "washed-out" appearance.

Howard is constantly on the go. His teachers are sure that he is hyperactive. However, this has not been confirmed by the psychologist, who has tested him. Some of the teachers, claiming that he misdiagnosed Howard's case, are angry with the psychologist. They share their opinions with Howard's parents and insist that they should put him on tranquilizers.

Howard usually is jumping, tapping, running, making funny noises, and so forth. His movements are jerky and fast, which add to his grotesque appearance.

Howard never misses an opportunity to be funny. When the teacher takes the roll call, he yawns so loudly that many children turn to look at him and then burst out laughing. He mocks the teacher behind her back, making sure that the children notice it. He draws funny pictures on the blackboard when the teacher is not in class.

Howard changes the words in songs, and he sings them above the voices of the other children, making it impossible for the teacher to continue her lesson.

Howard is often sent to the principal's office. Sometimes he spends the entire day there. At other times, the teachers (he has four) send him out into the corridor, although normally this is not allowed. Invariably, Howard has to return to class or go to the office because he makes such a racket in the corridor that the other teachers complain.

Howard is an only child. His father died when he was 3 years old. His mother works as a saleswoman in a department store. Howard spends his time after school at his aunt's, who has four children of her own. His aunt constantly is complaining to his mother about Howard's behavior and is threatening to throw him out. Howard's mother then cries and threatens to send him to a military school if he does not change his behavior. She also threatens that some day he will end up in a reform school. When she is desperate, she beats him with a stick.

The teacher should guide her students to realize that Howard has talents. He is a good comedian; he can draw cartoons; he can make up words to songs. With the help of the students, Howard could be given a special place in class so that he would get the class's attention in a constructive way.

The class should be helped to realize that Howard's aunt and mother discourage Howard. His mother does it out of desperation, not out of rejection. In a sense, the school does the same. Howard could be encouraged by the other children, and this would help him, not only in class but also in his relationship with his mother.

J. J.

The sixth-grade boys were restless on this sunny Tuesday morning. It was difficult for Mrs. Berban to keep their attention on what she was saying and on what they were supposed to be doing. She noticed that their eyes kept wandering to the window and that they exchanged knowing smiles. She learned that Mr. Hayes, the gym teacher, had promised them that they could play baseball outdoors the moment the weather would permit. Since today was a sunny day, this would be the day.

J. J., a heavy-set boy, watched the others with a frown and a sullen expression on his face. Nobody paid any attention to him, but the teacher noticed that J. J. was unhappy.

At one point J. J. got up and headed toward the window. He walked backward, humming softly but audibly, because a number of children turned around and looked at him.

"Watch out!," yelled a few of the children, because they noticed that J. J. was walking straight into the fishbowl. But it was too late. He had knocked it over, and the water and the guppies spilled all over the floor. J. J. just stood there, looking at the children, not saying a word.

The questions that the teacher should raise in order to develop a discussion of what happened and the purpose of J. J.'s behavior is of great importance. It is a very good story for behavior analysis, but the unskilled teacher may have difficulty developing its fine points. The questions must be challenging, provocative, and even manipulative.

TEACHER: This story tells us only what happened, but it tells us nothing about the kind of child that J. J. is, how he might behave in general, or his position in the class. The story does tell enough, however, for you to make guesses about certain possibilities. Let's review what really happened in the story. (They go over the story) What did the story tell us about him that would help us guess how he felt that day?

CHILD: It said that he had a frown on his face. Maybe he was unhappy or angry.

CHILD: It said that he was heavy. Maybe he is not very athletic.

CHILD: I was wondering about that also. The story said that Mrs. Berban noticed that he was unhappy. So we know how he felt.

CHILD: He was also very clumsy.

TEACHER: How do you know this? The story said nothing about clumsiness.

CHILD: But he knocked down the fishbowl. He may have been clumsy.

TEACHER: Maybe. Does anyone see other possibilities concerning why he may have knocked down the fishbowl.

CHILD: No, I don't. I don't think that he would have knocked over the fishbowl if he hadn't walked backwards. He didn't watch where he was going.

TEACHER: Are you saying that he was clumsy or that he was not clumsy?

CHILD: I don't think he was clumsy. He just didn't see the fishbowl. Anyway, why did he walk backwards? Didn't he know what might happen?

CHILD: And he was humming and looking at the others while he was doing this.

TEACHER: Does his humming have any significance?

CHILD: Yes, I think so. I think he did it on purpose.

CHILD: Me, too. I think he wanted everyone to pay attention to him.

TEACHER: What do you all think?

CHILD: I am beginning to agree with ___. I also think that he did it in order to have everyone notice him.

TEACHER: Why, in your opinion, did he want attention at this particular time?

CHILD: If he is not good at playing baseball, he may have felt jealous of the others, and this is why he wanted to be noticed.

CHILD: How did the children feel before J. J. knocked over the fishbowl?

CHILD: Excited.

CHILD: Real happy.

TEACHER: How do they feel now?

CHILD: Upset and angry.

It is not important for us to go into details here about the discussion, except to mention that it should help the students realize how this incident changed the mood of the students in J. J.'s class, because now they had to be concerned with saving the guppies, mopping the floor, and being angry with J. J. J. J., in fact, stole the show.

The teacher can pursue the reason for J. J.'s behavior. She can ask the students to crawl into J. J.'s skin and talk about how they feel there. In this fashion, she can get them to understand how others feel and how some handle their feelings. The children may feel that J. J. is not liked because of his looks, that he is bad in sports, that he is jealous, or that he wants to get even with the other children because they do not have his problem.

Next the teacher may ask how the class could help J. J. Usually, when we use this story, the children suggest the following things.

1. Somebody can teach him how to play ball, but this must be done with patience, and the person should practice with him. J. J. should be encouraged.
2. The children and the teacher should make J. J. feel good about himself by noticing things that he can do. Maybe he can sing; maybe he is good in science or math; maybe he can help another child who is not as good in this subject as he is.
3. Children must not ignore him but must talk to him on the playground, eat lunch with him, invite him to their homes, and invite him to join in whatever they do in school or outside of school.

A trained teacher may notice recognition reflexes on some students' faces as this discussion is going on. Many children may identify with J. J., and it will show on their faces. In this way, the teacher can indirectly help some of her students in the class. She has, at least, planted a seed of self-awareness.

The teacher may ask if anyone in class has J. J.'s problem and if he would like to talk about it, but she should not become personal with any student even if she has noticed a recognition reflex. She should leave the decision to talk or not to talk up to the student.

There are many details that a teacher must consider when she tells a story for the purpose of self-awareness. The teacher may discuss the problem of a girl when she really has in mind one of the boys in class. She may make the girl younger or older but not the same age as the boy. She may have to use a setting outside of school if the boy's problem is in school.

The timing of the discussion is important. It is advisable not to discuss a case study right after an unpleasant incident with a child, especially with an older child. The teacher should wait a few days or a week. Timing is very important in anything the teacher does, and she has to become sensitive to it.

The ages of the children must be considered. Very young children (preschool or kindergarten) may or may not sit quietly while the teacher tells a story. They may be painting or doing another quiet activity while at the same time they are listening to the story. We should not be rigid about such things. The moment we force a child to listen without doing anything else, the child may resist, just as this child may resist any academic subject toward which he has developed unfriendly feelings.

In the lower grades, if the teacher has a specific child in mind when she is telling a story and if this child is inattentive, the teacher may do well to move her chair next to this child and casually ask this child questions about the story. Encourage the child to talk, regardless of whether his answers are to the point or not. Get him to talk first and then come back to the question. Gradually, this child will learn to respond. This gives the teacher a chance to use positive comments, like: "I am glad that you felt like talking about the story" or, "I am glad that you answered my question." She may get the other children involved by asking, "Tommy made me very happy now. He did something that shows that he is one of us. Does anyone know what I mean?" If no one has noticed, the teacher may tell the class that he did not avoid answering the question but answered it and participated in the discussion.

Goals for Using Stories

The goal of using a story is to get the children to listen and to talk to each other. There are people who are never involved with anyone and who are disinterested in anything that has no direct connection with themselves. Many children are, therefore, disinterested in stories. Teachers may find children who cannot be motivated to like reading for the same reason: the stories in the book do not concern them personally; this is something that happened to somebody else, so who cares? We find many children with this kind of attitude who are not interested in social studies. However, these children may be motivated or interested in a story told in a dramatic manner. This is the reason they enjoy TV: it is a visual thing that does not necessarily require attentive listening. (Such children are often poor listeners.) Teachers who have access to television could use this media for specific training of listening and discussing the program, especially if the program lends itself to analysis of social interaction and to problem solving.

Getting Children Involved in Participation

The teacher can train children to become involved in participation through challenging questions and encouragement. The following are some examples of challenging or encouraging statements and questions.

1. "You have a point there that we should consider."
2. "I am glad that you feel stimulated by the story."
3. "I am glad that you expressed your feelings."
4. "I am glad that you are aware of what is going on."
5. "You seem to understand this character."

When a child is quiet and lost in his thoughts, the teacher can challenge him with questions such as

1. "What is your opinion?"
2. "How would you handle this problem?"
3. "What advice do you have for this character?"
4. "Would you want him as a friend? Why?"
5. "Would you want to help him? How?"

If the child cannot give any answers, the teacher may say

1. "That's all right. I will call on you again, and you will probably help us then. Your opinion is very much valued."

Determining Which Stories to Use

Each story is used for a specific purpose. It may be to get the class to understand behavior in general, or the teacher may have a specific child in mind. A story can be used to understand the goal of certain behaviors, for instance, the goal of the bully, the disruptive child, the overly sensitive child, the child who likes to hurt others, and so on. Stories also may be used to change children's values.

Whenever a story is used for such purposes, the teacher must be sensitive to a number of things: the age of the child, the length of the story, the number of characters involved, and the specific incident that describes the problem. For instance, "Bo, the Ball Player" works beautifully with younger children who require a lot of attention, who interrupt, and who show off, but this story is not effective with older children. The story of "Howard," on the other hand, works with junior high school students, whereas "Charles" can be used very effectively with high school students.

REFERENCES

Berghoff, C. *Where Is Daddy?* Englewood Cliffs, N.J.: Prentice Hall, 1969.

Bullard, Maurice L. *The Use of Stories for Self-Understanding.* 1320 N.W. 13th Corvallis, Oregon, 1963.

Curren, Polly. *Whizzer's Purple Tail, The New Streets and Roads* (Third Grade). Chicago: Scott, Foresman, 1958.

Harley, Sterl. "Ricky Goes Fishing" *The New Streets and Roads.* Chicago: Scott, Foresman, 1958.

Steptoe, John. *Stevie.* New York: Harper & Row, 1969.

Zolotov, Charlotte. *The Quarreling Book.* New York: Harper & Row, 1963.

In the literature taught at the high school level, we have found many characters whose personalities can be analyzed from the point of view of their "social interest," that is, their concern or lack of concern for others and the underlying goals of their behavior. Newspaper articles and movies also make excellent topics for group discussion.

RECOMMENDED STORIES FOR GROUP DISCUSSION

Andersen, H. C. *The Emperor's New Clothes.* New York: Oxford University Press, 1945.

——— *The Princess and the Pea.* New York: Oxford University Press, 1955.

——— *The Ugly Duckling.* New York: Oxford University Press, 1955.

Bollinger, Max. *Joseph.* New York: Dell (Delacorte Press), 1967.

Elkin, Benjamin. *The Loudest Noise in the World.* New York: Viking Press, 1954.

Epstein, Samuel. *George Washington Carver.* Champagne, Ill.: Gerrard Press, 1960.

Geisel, Theodore Seuss. *Horton Hatches the Egg.* New York: Random House, 1960.

——— *Horton Hears a Who.* New York: Random House, 1954.

——— *Thidwick, the Big-Hearted Moose.* New York: Random House, 1958.

Grantoff, Christian. *The Stubborn Donkey.* New York: Aladdin Books, 1969.

Gudrum, Thorne-Thomsen. *The Giant Who Had No Heart in His Body. A Book of Giant Stories.* New York: Dodd, Mead, 1926.

Moore, Lillian. *The Terrible Mr. Twitimeyer.* Eau Claire, Wis.: E. M. Hale & Co., 1952.

Part 3
Coping with Special Academic Problems

Chapter 17

Learning Disabilities

Learning disabilities seem to have replaced open classrooms as the most talked about aspect of education today. Because learning disabilities affect so many children and because they are of such great concern to teachers, we are devoting a chapter to the learning disabled child.

Definition of a Learning Disability

The fact is that up to now, no one has discovered what constitutes a learning disability. A few years ago a number of well-known educators from all over the country met at the University of Maine to discuss and to compare opinions. They came up with no specific diagnosis or definitions of learning disabilities.

According to Hardman, Egan, and Landau (1981), psychology uses the terms *perceptual disorders* and *hyperactivity*; medicine uses descriptors such as brain damage, minimal brain damage impairment; and language specialists use the terms *aphasia* and *dyslexia*. From such a variety of opinions coming from recognized professionals in the field, it is difficult to get a true definition of learning disabilities. Compton (1974) defines learning disabilities as *anything* that prevents a child from achieving in the classroom, including psychological factors.

The Education of All Handicapped Children Act. PL 94-142, 1975, states:

Special learning disability means a disorder in one or more of the basic psychological processes involved in understanding or in using language, spoken or written, which may manifest itself in an imperfect ability to listen, think, speak, read, write, spell, or to do mathematical calculations.

We do not deny that there are children who have learning disabilities. Our concern is the children who have been misleadingly classified as learning disabled. These children often behave in a manner which may well give the impression that they have a learning deficiency. We found that these very children gain self-confidence and start to enjoy learning when they are encouraged by the teacher and the peer group and when they feel respected and wanted.

We want to emphasize that we are referring only to the misclassified children and do not refute that there are children who suffer from a pathological disability. Furthermore, we hope to make the teacher aware of the possibility that a child may have been incorrectly diagnosed. Therefore the teacher should not accept the present classification of the child as fact, but should observe the child carefully in various kinds of situations and activities to be certain that the child's diagnosis is correct. To give an example:

A boy was diagnosed as multiply handicapped and because of the severity of his problems he was legally withdrawn from school. One day when he was fifteen, the boy went to high school to meet his sister. While sitting in front of the school building, the counselor came out to see why he was there. While talking to the boy, the counselor learned about the boy's past history. The counselor was impressed with the boy and he encouraged him to return to school. He told this youngster that if he would consider returning to school, the counselor would see what he could do to get the boy re-entered, and that he and the other teachers would do what was in their power to help him with his work and to become a regular class member. The boy agreed, finished high school, and is presently attending college.

We might well imagine what might have become of this youngster had he not had the fortunate meeting with this encouraging counselor.

Psychological Aspects

If we accept the premise that a great many children have difficulties in learning because of psychological factors as well as organic deficiencies, we can understand why the present form of corrective educational practices so often fails. Such children are so convinced that they will fail that they refuse to try and may even oppose and sabotage efforts at instruction. These children's attitudes can be changed if we help them realize their discouragement and their decision to operate on "I can't" rather than to admit (even to themselves) "I don't want to."

Therefore, we believe that we need to look at the deficits in a child's learning as a teacher's "teaching disability" rather than concentrate on physical aspects of the child's failure to learn. We believe that these children can learn and achieve (each according to his innate potential) and it is up to the teachers to find the proper methods and techniques to allow learning to take place. When the deficits are viewed as a teaching disability rather than a learning disability, then the educational system becomes accountable for the success or the failure of the child.

The average special educator has not been prepared to understand the child's resistance to learning and the psychological dynamics that play a decisive role in the child's attitude.

Teachers usually regard handicapped children as "special" and they have a "special" attitude toward these children and different expectations of them.

Being "special" because of a physical or mental handicap, or being different implies in our culture not merely a difference in individual characteristics, but also a difference in social status. With rare exceptions, there is a social stigma attached to people who are different. In the competitive society of our times, the yardstick of superiority and inferiority is applied to any outstanding difference, such as being wealthier than . . .; being more educated than . . .; being more successful than . . .; and so on.

Almost any deviation based on a deficiency evokes unfavorable reactions. It is our contention that success or failure becomes insignificant if we stop measuring and comparing people. Only then can we stimulate children in their development and function, not toward becoming a success, and in this case, becoming a successful student, but toward becoming a social being who has a secure place in the group, home, or school, regardless of what he is and how much he can do. For this reason any clarification of children based on comparison with others is damaging.

A child may be in a regular classroom yet feel isolated, different, inferior, and lonely. It is unfortunate that organic or physiological factors often lead to an underestimation of the psychological factors that contribute to the child's difficulties in life.

Without an understanding of the psychological factors it will be difficult if not impossible to take corrective measures to help the handicapped child.

The handicapped child needs to be helped to a more positive attitude toward themselves. This is possible only if the social milieu in which the child lives and functions takes a positive attitude toward this child.

The tasks of encouraging these children, of restoring their sense of adequacy and optimism is not an easy one. It cannot be done merely by giving them pep-talks and telling them how able they are.

The emphasis on each child's ability to be useful and to participate is the only means to bring the best out in the child. The teacher must attempt to provide an atmosphere in her class where the child experiences a sense of accomplishment and of belonging. This does not imply that these children should not receive special instruction or that they should never leave the regular classroom for special instruction. But they should spend as much time as possible in the regular classroom and be taught that this is the class where they belong.

The resource teacher or the teacher with special education training and the school counselor should work hand-in-hand with the regular teacher. They need to form a partnership approach so that the most effective instructional program possible will be directed to the handicapped child.

In conclusion, we want to emphasize that we are not critical of teachers who are not effective with children that have a learning disability or any other handicap. We realize that it is extremely difficult to distinguish between a true learning disability and one that may appear as a learning disability but has psychological underlying factors.

REFERENCES

Compton, R. "The Learning Disabled Adolescent" in B. Kratoville, editor, *Youth in Trouble*. San Rafael, California: Academic Therapy Publications, 1974.

Hardman, Michael L.; Egan, M. Winston, and Landau, Elliot D. *What Will We Do in the Morning?* Dubuque, Iowa: Wm. C. Brown Co. Publishers. 1981.

SELECTED READINGS

Bryan, T. S. "An Observational Analysis of Classroom Behaviors of Children with Learning Disabilities." *Journal of Learning Disabilities*, vol. 7, 1974, pp. 226–234.

Katzman, A. "From the perspective of Albert Katzman." In N. Ramos, ed., *Delinquent Youth and Learning Disabilities*. San Rafael, Calif.: Academic Therapy Publications, 1978.

Murray, C. *The Link Between Learning Disabilities and Juvenile Delinquency: Current Theory and Knowledge*. (U. S. Department of Justice, Law Enforcement Assistance Administration), Washington, D.C.: U. S. Government Printing Office, 1976.

Reynolds, Maynard, and Birch, Jack. *Teaching the Exceptional Child in All American Schools*. Reston, Va.: Council of Exceptional Children Publications, 1977.

Waugh, Kenneth W. and Bush, Wilma Jo. *Diagnosing Learning Disorders*. Columbus, Ohio: Merrill, 1971.

Williams, Jessie Francis. *Children with Specific Learning Deficiencies*. Elmsford, N.Y.: Pergamon Press, 1970.

Chapter 18
Reading Difficulties

A conservative estimate is that between 15 and 20 percent of our school children are nonachievers and are especially deficient in reading skills. This exists in spite of the fact that they have no mental or physical handicap and that their intelligence is normal and often above average. Parents and educators are very apprehensive about this alarming situation and are looking for explanations of and remedies for it. This awareness has brought forth numerous books and hundreds of articles dealing with reading difficulties. New theories concerned with teaching methods as well as with the causes of poor reading habits arise every few years. They become popular for a few years only to be displaced by a new theory a few years later.

About Reading Difficulties

1. Some claim that the kindergarten is to blame for the poor preparation, because the children do not receive reading readiness and are not prepared for reading in first grade. They claim that reading readiness is either not taught at all, is taught before the child is ready, or is taught poorly and that this is responsible for the child's poor attitude toward reading and toward learning in general.
2. Some claim that the root of the problem lies in the poor reading instructions that children receive in first grade and that these children are sent to second grade in spite of their lack of fundamentals at the first-grade level. This continues year after year until the child reaches junior high school, at which time teachers and parents become alarmed and begin

applying "remedies," but at this stage it is exceedingly difficult to help the child.

3. There are some who believe that phonics are the key to the teaching of reading and that the schools of today do not emphasize the technique sufficiently.

4. There are some who are convinced that the child is not motivated because of the poor textbooks that schools use, the content of which is either not stimulating or completely foreign to the child's experience.

5. There are those who attribute reading failures to a bad experience during the child's first attempts to read, either at home or at school. They contend that the first experience has discouraged the child to such a degree that he wants no part of reading from then on.

6. Many believe that the child's learning retardation stems from a socially and culturally disadvantaged or deprived background.

7. Many believe that the child's difficulties stem from mysterious pathological reasons, which make them either uneducable or slow in learning. They are diagnosed as suffering from a learning disability, a perceptual retardation, dyslexia, neurogenic learning disability, sidedness, minimal brain damage, asphasia, and so on.

8. There are those who see a high correlation between reading difficulties and an emotional disturbance in the child. This theory has been much emphasized during the last decade, although it has been pointed out by a number of people at an earlier time.

9. Finally, there are teachers who insist that the child is just plain dumb, and they use the child's intelligence quotient (IQ) to justify their feelings.

No doubt there is an element of truth in all of the above stated arguments, but we question whether we can attribute reading difficulties to any single factor. Although we do not dispute and although we certainly deplore the fact that in some cases these diagnoses are valid, there is evidence to suggest that a great percentage of children who have been thus diagnosed are literally being sacrificed because of a faulty and misleading diagnosis. Studies and our personal experiences give ample proof that we cannot rely on single factors as a sure indication of why children learn or do not learn. For one, a disability, if it does exist, does not necessarily indicate incapacity but rather that the child is not using his potential abilities and resources. From an Adlerian point of view, underachievement cannot be understood in isolation but must be considered as one among a number of factors, such as purpose of behavior, position in the family, family atmosphere and values, acceptance of the child by the teacher and by the peer group, grade placement, physical condition, and social position in the community, to name but a few. Each child would have to be studied individually in order for us to understand the underlying causes that prevent him from learning.

Reading and the Child's Personality

Many studies indicate that the method of teaching reading is less important than the child's individual personality and his attitude toward learning and that the reasons for his difficulties are applicable to him alone, although there may be others who have similar difficulties. It becomes a matter of understanding the child's problem from a holistic point of view, which takes in his emotional, physical, and social development in order to understand the underlying reasons of his problem. Without this understanding, the teacher is in no position to help the child overcome his handicap. Unfortunately, many teachers cannot understand or accept the theory that there is a relationship between a child's lack of learning and his personality development. More deplorable still is the fact that the teachers who abide by this theory have a hard time conveying it to the parents, who are often the source of the child's problem. This lack of understanding, both by the parents and by the teachers, prompt them to push harder, force the child to read, to drill, and often punish him for his lack of progress.

We know that children who are underachievers in one area are usually also underachievers in other areas, especially in their social adjustment. Many are failure oriented and fail in almost everything. Most of these children are lonely and isolated from the achievers, the group that they hold in high esteem and to which they would like to belong. Often they join other children who are in the same boat, thus reinforcing their attitudes and behavior.

Most young children are eager to learn, and they look forward to going to school and to learning. Yet we see many children who resent school after a couple of weeks and refuse to go or attend school. It often happens that these children have been poorly prepared by their parents toward social living and independent behavior, but the problem is not just with their upbringing; more often it is the teachers' lack of understanding of such children and their inability to motivate them. Children who feel happy in school and who feel that they are accepted and respected by their teachers and their peer group will be motivated to learn by any method, although we do not deny that some methods may be more effective than others for some children. Certainly, the books that attract the child's interests are preferable to those that do not stimulate him, but this alone will not determine his willingness to learn.

If a child is promoted to the next grade, despite his lack of academic preparation for the next grade, we have found this does less harm to the child, to his emotional state, and to his attitude toward school than does failing the child. The teacher who understands the child's real problem, who knows how to win the child and is skillful in engaging the class group in the process of helping the child overcome his difficulties, will succeed in pulling the child out of his present state of resistance to learn. The child then is more apt to catch up with the others.

Blaming instructional methods for the child's difficulties in learning deals only with the mechanical part of the instruction. No method of instruction, not even the most attractive books will motivate the child as long as he feels unfriendly toward school and especially toward the subject. We must realize that his failure to learn is only one aspect of his general failure in his adjustment to life and to an acceptance of social responsibilities. There are experimental schools in which children are taught to read at the age of 3 or 4. Not only do these children learn, but they enjoy the experience. As for readiness, it does not just come with age, but it is a process of stimulation and encouragement. It requires a sincere belief in the child's innate potential. Unfortunately, teachers are not only misled in their training of why some children cannot learn, but, indirectly, they are excused from assuming responsibilities toward these children and expect little or no progress from them because of a prevalent belief in causes that preclude failure.

Perpetual Difficulties

In recent years many underachievers, especially those who are deficient in reading, have been classified as either having perceptual problems, a learning disability, dyslexia, minimal brain damage, neurophrenia, aphasia, disgraphia, intrasensory and intersensory disabilities, deficiencies in auditory perception, disorders of auditory comprehension, problems with visual imagery, special visual distortions, and many other similar disorders.

The fundamental principles that experts suggest to the teacher for consideration are the integrities, deficits, tolerance levels, number and types of sensory modalities to be activated, types of involvement, levels of involvement, relationship between reception and expression, nature of verbal and nonverbal disturbances, state of readiness, and the need for assistance with total integration. They conclude that the teacher must develop the greatest possible degree of balance among the behavioral functions by individualizing the program for each child or each group of children. Teachers are often expected to "diagnose the nature of the learning problem, the deficits, the integrities, the levels of function in spoken, read, and written language, and the nonverbal and medical aspects" (Johnson and Myklebust, 1967).

At a time when too few teachers understand the problems of the normal child who is disturbing the class or who is deficient, how can we expect in the foreseeable future to train sufficient teachers in the diagnosis and specific remedial procedures for the 20 percent of all our school population who supposedly are afflicted with dyslexia and other physiological problems?

Fortunately, we hear from many people who object to this trend. "The methods in perceptual training and visual-motor coordination have not yet been proven to have any direct effect on the learning of reading. The various methods are presented sometimes with the partisanship and finality that seem to preclude alternatives" (Money, 1966).

According to Eisenberg (1966), "competent investigators have been led to contrary conclusions about the role of handedness, heredity, perceptual handicap, and the like. Incomplete cerebral dominance does not account for reading problems. The determination of laterality is not so simple a matter as what one thought, nor is brainedness so readily to be inferred from handedness."

All the assumptions of neurogenic learning disabilities and similar organic explanations for reading disabilities will continue and probably increase in number and kind as long as teaching techniques do not catch up with the way young children can learn at a very early age—even before they enter school.

Nobody denies that children may have brain damage, but brain damaged children do not behave in the same manner as minimal brain damaged children. Their hyperactivity is not a result of brain damage, which cannot be proven, but a behavior problem. It can be stopped through firm but kind restrictions. Still worse is the assumption of perceptual handicap. We know of children with a form of aphasia in which they cannot identify what they see. However, this is a rare condition. Today the diagnosis of perceptual handicap is made for thousands of children. In those children with whom we have worked and who were diagnosed as brain damaged or perceptually handicapped, we found such evidence in a very small percentage of children.

A 14-year-old girl who was diagnosed as suffering from perceptual difficulties was placed in a special class. This girl could read on a fourth-grade level when she was in the third grade. Suddenly she stopped progressing both in reading and in comprehension. Upon investigation it was found that at that time a baby boy was born into the family. This girl had been an only child up until then. It was also found that this girl was always a good child, never causing her parents any aggravation and always being held up as a model child. Such a child could not rebel openly, as this would make her bad in the eyes of her parents, but she could avoid taking the risk of being thought of as bad by assuming an inability to read. This was the worst thing she could do to her sophisticated and cultured parents.

The counselor felt that the girl could read as well as before, if not better, and he conveyed this to her parents. The parents suddenly recalled that their daughter spent much time reading mystery stories. This confirmed the counselor's suspicion, for how could this girl read a mystery if she had no comprehension?

When the girl was asked if she could read, she replied, "Yes, when I am interested." The girl was helped to understand what she was doing and why.

Her teachers and her parents were advised to make no fuss over her behavior but to leave her alone. The school was advised to take her out of the
special class and to put her into the class where she belonged. The girl soon
regained her ability to read and to comprehend.

Here is another example.

Ten-year-old Rudy was classified as suffering from auditory perceptual retardation. He was placed in a special class. At home his parents and siblings
assumed all responsibilities for him. Everyone served him.

When the counselor questioned him about his behavior, he looked into
space, giving no answers. When asked why he did not reply, he answered
that he did not understand what the counselor was saying. Only when the
counselor told Rudy that he advised his parents to stop doing so many things
for him and to let him assume some responsibilities for himself did he look
at the counselor and say, "They won't listen to you." Obviously, he heard and
understood. The counselor asked, "Why not?," and Rudy replied, "Because
they know that I can't do things for myself." Again, the counselor asked,
"Why not?," and Rudy said, "Because I am different, and I can't do things
as others can." The counselor proceeded to explain to Rudy why he didn't
want to assume responsibilities for himself, but Rudy started to shout, "You
get out of here. You have no right to tell my parents anything, and they
won't listen to you."

Rudy's parents, who were present at the counseling session, suddenly
realized that "they had been had." Through a process of counseling his
parents, teachers, and Rudy himself, the boy gradually started to assume
responsibilities and in time was integrated in a regular class.

Both of these examples show us how careful we must be before we accept an explanation of pathological reasons that a child does not learn.
Organic or physiological concepts lead to an underestimation of the psychological factors of reading difficulties. Without comprehension of goals,
the significance of the child's dysfunctions and deficiencies cannot be determined. Corrective measures require an understanding of the child's concepts and his private logic (see Chapter 4). Even if he is physically deficient
or culturally deprived, it is the reaction to these conditions that explain
his behavior. What a child has is less important than what he does with it.

Resistance to Order and Learning

We have found that the retarded reader often lacks the willingness to
cooperate with others, especially with adults. He often displays disdain
for and defiance of order. He is often unwilling to follow directions, for
this means cooperation, and he refuses to cooperate. The reading difficulty

appears then as merely one facet of disturbed interpersonal relationships resulting in social maladjustment.

Reading and writing are the two subjects most affected by a child's reluctance to accept rules and to conform to them. No other subject is as closely related to order. Arithmetic, for instance, also requires the recognition of rules and order, but a child who has difficulties with arithmetic is less impressed with the aspect of order than with the need to solve his own problems. He feels unable to deal with his problems on his own, because he is too dependent on others to solve his problems for him. In contrast, spelling is most difficult for a child who has not been trained to accept order. He does not like anyone to tell him what to do or to restrict him. Such a child spells as the spirit moves him; at times he spells a word one way, and at other times, he spells the same word differently. Poor handwriting also reflects defiance of order, unless there exists poor motor coordination. Reading deficiencies, however, are the strongest rebuff to the academic demands of adults.

Too often the reading disability is not regarded as a symptom but as the real problem. As long as the teacher does not understand the child's psychological dynamics, she is in no position to realize that the child's reading deficiency is only a symptom of a deeper problem and, therefore, does not direct her efforts toward changing them. In this way, the teacher is involved in an uphill struggle. Her own discouragement puts an additional handicap in the way of the child's progress. Instead of relieving the child's apprehensions and fears, the teacher only adds to them through the tedious and often torturous practices imposed on the child. This is also the case when the teacher falls for the child's demands for special attention and service and indulges him with sympathy and pity. This only deters his progress.

Corrective Approaches

The elements necessary for an adequate corrective approach are self-evident. Remedial teaching requires not merely a specific teaching technique; it also must stimulate a change in motivation. Instead of involving the child in the laborious practice of reading, the teacher has to use corrective measures of a psychological nature. Three such measures are listed below.

1. The teacher cannot ignore the faulty values on which the child may be operating, like the fallacy of constantly comparing himself with others or of being more concerned with success than with learning. Such distorted ambition often leads the child to assume that he is a failure. The child may need a better concept of order and usefulness. The teacher can and should enhance the child's comprehension of social living. Such teaching should not be incidental to the practice of reading but rather should

be the essence of remedial teaching. This can be achieved through individual and particularly group discussion, since most students in remedial classes share similar deficiencies in their value system.

2. The basis for effective educational endeavors is proper interpersonal relationships. Children in need of special instruction have not been able to establish such a relationship in their families, otherwise they would not be academically and socially deficient. The teacher will be put in the same role as the child's mother, father, and other authority figures, unless she makes deliberate efforts to recognize such faulty patterns and to correct them. This collusion of adults against the child is only fortified if the teacher tries to involve the mother in supervising the child's reading efforts.

3. The teacher has to free herself from the assumption that the child's difficulty with reading permits any conclusion about the reading *ability* of a child. Presently, the real ability of children in this regard is grossly underestimated by the majority of teachers.

The following are cases of children who made no progress in reading in spite of years of remedial help but who learned how to read within a comparatively short time once their resistance to learning was removed and after their self-image had been changed.

Peter was an only child of elderly parents. He was small and underweight until the age of 4. Both parents constantly worried about him and gave in to him in order not to upset him. When he couldn't have his way, Peter screamed and threw anything that was near at hand at his parents. When they gave in to him, he was lovable and very affectionate, which both parents adored.

Peter was not sent to kindergarten. His parents were afraid that he might catch diseases from the other children. They were equally afraid of letting him go out and play with other children. One of his parents would take him to the park every afternoon, where he'd sit on a swing while his parent pushed it. His mother insisted that Peter loved it this way because he never asked to be allowed to play with other children.

When Peter entered the first grade, he cried and would not let go of his mother. She promised to stand outside where he could see her through the window. After some time, the teacher insisted that the mother go away, which she did, only to wait for Peter around the corner. She would bring him to school and pick him up at noon and after school every day for two years, in spite of the teacher's appeal to allow the boy to walk home alone or with other children.

Peter made no progress in first grade. He was promoted to second grade in spite of the fact that he had not learned how to read or write. Thus, he was promoted again into the third grade. Here he spent most of the time either at the window, or going back and forth to the washroom or to the drinking fountain. He seemed not to hear when the teacher spoke to him.

While he was still in the third grade, Peter's mother had a fatal accident. This changed his entire life. His father worked during the day; he left the house before Peter had to leave for school. Not being able to afford a house-keeper, Peter was forced to shift for himself. He had to walk to school either by himself or with other children. After school, he waited for his father in the home of a neighbor who had young children.

The first few weeks were, indeed, pitiful. Peter was too stunned. He understood that tantrums would not help him now. He walked as if in his sleep. For a while, the children in class overprotected and pampered him. They took him to the cafeteria, where they sat with him; they walked with him to and from school; they invited him to their homes to wait for his father. Gradually, he formed relationships with them, and he discovered that he could hold his own quite successfully. This change carried over into his attitude toward everything that concerned school and school activities. By the end of the school year, he could read and write as well as many of the students in his class.

Although this is an unusual case, nevertheless, it helps us to see how overdependency affects a child's attitude toward school.

Percy was the younger of two children. His parents were divorced when he was 3 years old. Each of his parents took one child. Percy remained with his mother.

Percy's mother ran a small grocery store, where he stayed all day. He was a very fearful child, afraid of lightning and thunder, of the dark, of animals, and of strange people. He refused to ride a tricycle because he might fall off. He slept in the same bed with his mother until he was 11, at which time she was helped to understand that she was holding him back with her overprotection.

Percy's school attendance was very irregular. Usually he skipped school in the mornings, and often he did not show up for many days in a row. In class he was usually well behaved and showed considerable interest and knowledge in science. He lacked the most rudimentary reading skills. Whatever he learned in his remedial reading class, he forgot within minutes.

When Percy was 11 years old his mother became alarmed about his reading disability, and she went to the teacher for help. This was unusual for this woman, because up to this point she had never kept any appointments for conferences with the teachers in any grade.

Percy's mother was helped to understand how she had deprived Percy of a normal development by making him the center of her life, by giving in to him, and by serving him as though he were incapable of learning to be responsible for himself. She was helped to see the connection between what she did and his school retardation. She was an intelligent woman and desperate enough to follow the teacher's advice. It was a very difficult task for all of them—his mother, Percy, and the teacher. Although Percy was prepared for the changes that would take place at home, he threw tantrums, broke dishes, refused to go to school, and so forth. His mother was desperate and ran to the teacher for help almost daily. Her biggest difficulties consisted of knowing how to show love and affection for the boy without being his slave.

Both of them required frequent counseling. In this way, both of them were reeducated and slowly formed a new relationship. Percy's school attendance became more regular, and he began to form social relationships with some of the children. The teacher assigned to him the lead in the Christmas play. This required the memorization of lines. Percy had to depend on other children to read the lines for him, which he did, but in the process he developed a feeling for reading for the first time. Reading seemed to make sense to him, and he could see the need for it. It was then that the remedial instruction that he had received for over two years took on importance and meaning. He made fast progress.

Jerry was classified as a nonlearner after four years of individual instruction. At the age of 11 he still looked like 8, and people who did not know his age would often ask him if he were in the first or second grade. He never answered such questions but hung his head or looked away. Whenever he was confronted with such a question in front of his mother, she would reply quickly that he was in the fifth grade, which was not true, and she added that he was very shy.

Jerry was the second child of five children. His older brother died when he was 3 years old. His other three siblings were born after he was 5 and were already in kindergarten.

After the death of his brother, Jerry's parents doubled their vigilance and protection not only of this boy but of all of their children. Jerry was kept at home on rainy days and whenever the weather changed for the worse. He was never allowed to join the class on field trips or in activities in the gymnasium.

In class Jerry was very talkative but in a sly, underhanded manner. When the teacher looked at him, he assumed an angelic expression, but the moment she took her eyes off him, he started talking to his neighbors. Usually, he brought some object to school and would show it off or play with it under his desk. Whenever the teacher called on him, he got up as if he were in a daze. He hung his head so low that it would almost touch his desk. He often remained in this position in spite of the teacher's invitation to sit down. Mostly the children looked at him with pity, and those nearby often pleaded with him to sit down.

Jerry could never find his pencil or his scissors. His desk was crammed with unwritten papers and with the various objects that he had brought from home. He could neither read nor write, and he showed no interest in any subject. Whenever the teacher tried to help him, he shook his head and mumbled, "I can't." Nevertheless, Jerry never missed going to his remedial reading class. He never had to be reminded.

During an interview with Jerry's mother, it became obvious that his parents accepted the belief that Jerry was retarded physically as well as mentally and that he needed their protection.

It was impossible to persuade his parents to try a different approach. They were not only convinced of Jerry's retardation but reproached themselves for having had children altogether, since one of the father's brothers was mentally retarded and in an institution. They blamed Jerry's condition on heredity.

During one class discussion, it was brought up that sometimes it pays for children to play dumb even if they are quite intelligent. Jerry, who had never taken obvious interest in these discussions, raised his hand for the first time. He asked the class to explain what anyone could possibly get out of playing dumb. He said, "If you're dumb, you're dumb. You don't play like you're dumb, because you get nothing." The group disagreed with him. They gave him many examples of how it could pay off for somebody to play dumb; of how people are forced into the person's services; of how nobody expects anything of such a child; and of how the child gets out of assuming responsibility for himself. One child said that it might pay off while the person is young, but when that person grows up, he will have a hard time because he will not know how to do anything for himself. Nobody mentioned Jerry's name, but he suddenly got up and in a clear voice announced, "But I'm not playing dumb." The teacher asked him to explain this comment, but all he could say was, "I'm not playing dumb" over and over. For several seconds they could hear a pin drop. Nobody said a word, but everyone looked at Jerry. Finally one girl remarked, "How do you know, Jerry? Maybe you're much smarter than you think, but you never try to find out. You don't even try to walk home by yourself like the other kids do."

After class was dismissed, Jerry stopped at the teacher's desk and timidly asked if she would speak to his parents and ask them to allow him to walk to and from school by himself. This was Jerry's first step toward independence. After he learned to walk to school by himself, he asked to be permitted to walk to the park by himself. Next the teacher induced his parents to get him an alarm clock and to let him get up in the morning without being awakened by them, and then to get ready for school by himself. Each time Jerry made the slightest progress, his parents were instructed to show appreciation. In class the children complimented Jerry and showed their interest in all of his achievements. As his parent's and the children's attitude toward him changed, so did his self-evaluation. When he was asked a question, he no longer hung his head but answered without fear. He did not always know the answers, but he showed no sign of fear or shame of saying so.

Jerry's progress in school was unbelievably fast. His dormant ambitions now came to the fore, and he set for himself high goals, like completing a reader within one month. He did. At the end of the year, he had successfully covered three years' work.

In this case we see a reverse process, namely of a child changing the attitudes of his parents. This is possible only when the teacher understands how to redirect the child's wrong concepts and how to use the group to encourage the child. Without the help of the group, this would have been impossible.

REFERENCES

Eisenberg, Leon, and Money, John. *The Disabled Reader*. Baltimore, Md.: John Hopkins Press, 1966.

Johnson, Doris J., and Myklebust, Helmer R. *Learning Disabilities*. New York: Grune & Stratton, 1967.

SELECTED READINGS

Johnson, Doris J., and Myklebust, Helmer R. *Learning Disabilities*. New York: Grune & Stratton, 1967.

Spache, George D. *Diagnosing and Correcting Reading Disabilities*. Boston: Allyn & Bacon, 1976.

Chapter 19
Culturally Deprived Children

One of the accepted causes for children's failure in school is that they come from culturally deprived or disadvantaged homes and, therefore, learn at a slower rate or not at all. It is very disheartening and highly deplorable that so many children live under such sad and discouraging conditions. We do not minimize the effect it may have on some children or the fact that this would make it more difficult for the school to motivate these children. We question the assumption that these children lack the ability to learn because of their backgrounds and that they, therefore, cannot be motivated. Precisely because the home and society failed them, the school must not also let them down. These children need to be helped to change their own faulty assumptions that they are inferior to others—a prejudice that they have against themselves, which includes the feeling that learning in school (they do learn many things out of school) will not alter their inferior position in society. We have yet to see a child fail to make progress if he feels good about himself, if he respects himself, and if he feels that he is amongst friends who are concerned about him and who have confidence in him.

The sad fact is that we have used tags such as "culturally deprived" as an alibi for our own inadequacies and lack of understanding of children who perform poorly or not at all. The authors are especially unhappy with the term "culturally deprived." None of the "culturally deprived" children are deprived of their culture, we feel. Rather, we think it means that they are "deprived of our culture," the one that most people admire and respect. This is misleading and inconclusive. This is a reference to a middle-class culture that many people recognize and respect. Many people who come from other cultures feel that they are described as inferior beings. They feel insulted and are resentful of this terminology, which does not encourage them to feel friendly and trusting toward our schools.

If we are sincerely concerned with helping children whose cultural backgrounds have not prepared them to feel secure in a culture that they have to function in, we must change our own beliefs. Our attitudes, feelings, and expectations have a lot to do with the attitudes that these children develop toward school and toward learning. It is not enough to love these children, as teachers often tell us, if deep down in their hearts teachers do not believe that these children can be as successful as the other children or that their background is an unsurmountable and detrimental handicap. In most cases, in spite of the teacher's liking for the child, the teacher would rather not have the child in class, if she has a choice. Children are very quick to pick up these feelings and attitudes. If they sense that teachers do not expect much of them, they will get very little from them. Teachers who say, "What can I do with a child who comes from such a background?" are bound to get just what they expect—nothing or very little.

The moment teachers believe that these children are doomed from the beginning, they accept a "force majeur" over which they have no power. This has two dangerous pitfalls. They do not assume the same responsibility toward these children as they do toward those who they believe are capable of making progress. Secondly, they believe in an unproven myth that these children cannot learn. It is either a conscious or an unconscious prejudice against people of another culture—an acceptance that a member of a minority group is not their equal.

Adler tells us that the experience of the child is less important than his interpretation of his experience and how he then reacts to it. We know that not all children who come from culturally deprived homes fail in school or in life. Why then do some succeed while others fail? This would not be possible if the home environment and the social background were the prime causes for the child's intellectual development. In order to understand this, we cannot ignore the interplay of social forces, as well as the individual child's conclusions that he has drawn from his experiences, and the conscious or subconscious decisions consequently he has made, which determine his attitudes to school and to learning. One child may conclude that he does not have a chance, while another child, even in the same family, may become determined not to let his background stand in the way of his success in life.

Teachers often ask us, "What can we expect of these children?" The mere phrase "these children" already indicates doubts about their potential. What can we expect of any child? Each child is different and must be viewed in the light of his whole development.

We suggest that teachers look at themselves and their own attitudes and practices. Frequently there is a great discrepancy between what they believe and what they actually do. They should be careful not to fall into this category.

Teachers claim that many children who come from socially different backgrounds are serious disciplinary problems and have learning problems. As long as these children are placed in a socially inferior environment, they may well become discipline problems. It becomes a matter of helping them feel worthwhile and accepted both by teachers and by their peers, of helping them toward some realistic success, which is often not on an academic level, and of accepting the probability that such changes will not occur immediately, but will take time.

Teachers sometimes ask, "Should we accept antisocial behavior in children from different home environments?" Such a question in itself indicates a kind of prejudice. If we are to create a democratic environment for all children, we must assume the same attitudes and practices toward all. We should not accept or ignore the behavior of children who come from impoverished backgrounds any more or any less than we do of children who come from any other background. All children have to learn that rules are necessary in a democratic setting. Without them we have chaos.

Another question often posed to us is, "How can we change the attitudes of parents of children from deprived areas?" Teachers often claim that these parents are basically not interested in the school or the education of their children. This is not our experience. This is a generalization that has no real basis in fact. We have found parents of all kinds of children who are not cooperative, for whatever reason, and some who are not interested in their children's education. However, there are very few such parents. Our experience points to the contrary; most of the parents are very interested in the education of their children.

Many parents hope that the school can be an instrument for realizing their own aspirations. This is especially true of parents of young children. Parents of older children will get into deeper trouble if they talk to them or make demands that they stay out of their way and leave them alone. This is often the reason why they do not come to parent-teacher conferences. However, even these parents could be reached if the schools were to contact them and give them professional guidance in ways in which they might deal with their children. They need to be helped to improve their relationships with their children first before they can have any influence on them. It becomes the responsibility of the school to help these parents, not only for the children's sake but also for society's sake.

However, a teacher can do a great deal for these children even if there is no cooperation from the parents. Through group discussion, we have helped many children understand their parents and to accept them in spite of their limitations.

We must remove the barriers that lead to failure. Although we cannot change the home situation, we can change our attitudes toward the children of impoverished homes and the culturally different. We could help each child succeed in some area. Only success brings further success. We must give them courage and self-respect.

SELECTED READINGS

Baca, Leonard, and Lane, Karen. "A Dialogue on Cultural Implications for Learning" in *Exceptional Children*. May 1974 published. Reston, Va.: Council of Exceptional Children, 1974.

Baldwin, Alexinia Y., Gear, Gayle H., and Lucito, Leonard J. *Educational Planning for the Gifted: Overcoming Cultural, Geographic and Socioeconomic Impediments*. Reston, Va.: Council of Exceptional Children, 1978.

Bereiter, Carl, and Engleman, Siegfried. *Teaching Disadvantaged Children in the Preschool*. Englewood Cliffs, N.J.: Prentice-Hall, 1966.

Bransford, Louis, Baca, Leonard, and Lave, Karen. "Cultural Diversity and the Exceptional Child," in Highlights of the Proceedings from the Council of Exceptional Children Conference on Cultural Diversity. Reston, Va.: Council of Exceptional Children, 1973.

Frost, Jan L. *Disadvantaged Children—Issues and Innovations*, 2d ed. Boston: Houghton Mifflin, 1970.

Henderson, George. *Understanding and Counseling Ethnic Minorities*. Springfield, Ill.: The as, 1979.

Jones, Reginald L. *Mainstreaming and the Minority Child*. Reston, Va.: Council of Exceptional Children, 1976.

Chapter 20

Pseudoretardation Referred to as Stupidity

Amazingly, often children who have been classified as retarded and therefore stupid perform tasks of substantial complexity. We may ask ourselves, "How is this possible?" No one has yet come up with a satisfactory answer to this question. We know that unhappiness, humiliation, and disregard for special talents are a result of society's attitude toward what is considered to be normal intellectual development on the one hand and stupidity on the other hand. Stupidity is automatically equated with "failure." We refer here mainly to school intelligence, which, in a sense, is a special kind of intelligence and only one form of intelligence. Yet we know of people who were considered stupid in school and who were extremely bright and successful once they left school. We must take this into consideration if we want to understand the impact that a diagnosis or a label of "stupid" has on an individual.

In our society it is not uncommon for children to be punished for being stupid. Often these children are ridiculed, rejected, insulted, and treated with disdain. "Don't be so stupid." "How can anyone be so dumb?" "Can't you think a little faster?" "You're as dumb as an ox." are remarks that the so-called stupid child often hears. We can imagine the effects on a child who is regarded as stupid by his parents, his siblings, and the school. We must consider what this child feels and what he perceives. In most cases the child starts to believe himself that he is stupid, and he withdraws into his own shell, afraid of giving answers lest he should say the wrong thing and afraid of coming close to people lest he be rejected. In order to help such a child develop his innate potential, it is not enough for the teacher to believe in him and treat him with respect; the peer group must also believe in this child and help him feel secure and liked. It is only after the child has been exposed to an encouraging environment for some time that the teacher will be in a position to know whether this child has intellectual potential or not. We can see this in the following example.

> Jeanette was a very shy and withdrawn child of 8. All her life she had been regarded as dumb, and her parents often told her that she was too stupid to learn. According to her I.Q. score of 66, Jeanette was a mentally retarded child. She was to be placed in a special class for the mentally retarded, but one of the authors suggested that Jeanette and a few other children who were regarded as retarded be placed in her class and retested at the end of the year.
>
> Since the students were encouraged to be concerned and to help one another, they took the retarded children under their wings, played with them, invited them to their homes, helped them with their work, listened to them, encouraged them to talk up, and so on. At the end of the school year, Jeanette's I.Q. went up considerably, and none of the children were now eligible to attend the special class for the retarded.

Stein and Susser (1963) felt that discouragement in school is partly responsible for their observation among backward students who are clinically and physically normal.

Many people are familiar with the Pygmalion Experiment by Lenore Jacobson and Robert Rosenthal, two psychologists in San Francisco, California. According to their findings, children's I.Q.'s went up considerably when the teacher was misled into believing that these children had normal intelligence. She expected them to learn, and they did.

> A principal who had heard of this experiment decided to test it. He gave a teacher a group of children all of whom had tested low or were at borderline level. He told the teacher that according to the tests these children would do well, and they did. When the principal complimented the teacher for a job well done, she said, "I have always said that if kids have something upstairs, they do well in school. I'm glad you didn't give me a slow group."

We wonder how these children would have fared if the teacher had known the truth.

Arthur Combs (1966) pointed out that students who were diagnosed as retarded when followed up as adults did very well on their jobs and seemed quite intelligent. As children in school, they lacked confidence in themselves, resented schooling because they were subjected to a basically meaningless experience and to frequent ridicule. As adults, they discovered areas in which they could perform adequately or above average—areas in which they had always possessed skills but they were never discovered or recognized by adults. In consequence, as children, these students learned to take pains not to get involved in the educational process for fear that they might expose themselves in their stupidity.

For those who are genuinely retarded, being treated as inferior persons because of their retardation can hardly encourage them to love learning or to find out what they are capable of learning.

Slow as well as retarded behavior has to be understood in terms of the purposes so many children use this type of behavior. Some use stupidity deliberately as a way to avoid responsibilities, and in this way they manage to have others assume their responsibilities for them. Consider the many parents who spend hours and hours each day sitting with their children who claim that they cannot understand and, therefore, cannot do their homework unless their parents help them. Consider the teachers who spend hours giving individual instruction to children who claim that they cannot understand the teacher's explanation when she gives it to the entire class. The following example of a counseling situation is a typical illustration of how children can manipulate their parents and teachers and put them into their services.

COUNSELOR: Fred, your teachers tell me that you require special attention when they explain a lesson. Is this correct?

FRED: Well, if you say so. I don't need special attention, but I want them to explain the lesson to me again, to make sure that I understand.

COUNSELOR: What happens when you feel that way? What do you do?

FRED: I tell the teacher.

COUNSELOR: And what happens?

FRED: The teacher comes over and explains the lesson to me and then I understand what to do.

COUNSELOR: Why does the teacher have to come over to you? Couldn't she explain it at the blackboard?

FRED: I don't understand it as well when she explains it at the blackboard.

COUNSELOR: Tell me, Fred, if you really wanted to, could you understand her directions while she is giving them to all children?

FRED: Maybe.

COUNSELOR: Then why don't you? Why should the teacher have to explain a lesson to you personally?

FRED: (no answer)

COUNSELOR: Could it be that you like this special attention and make sure that you get it?

FRED: Maybe.

COUNSELOR: What would happen if the teacher refused to explain it to you personally?

FRED: I don't know.

COUNSELOR: Would you do the work then?

FRED: No.

This example needs no further explanations. The counselor had to help the teacher realize how she reinforced Fred's attitude toward acceptance of responsibilities and how cleverly he manipulated all his teachers by playing dumb.

However, by and large, all people are subject to the fear of humiliation. The school and society in general makes such a fuss over the bright and the gifted and puts high intelligence on such a high pedestal that the average child, and certainly the one with below average intelligence, is automatically put into the position of a second-rate school citizen, deserving less consideration and less respect. Parents, even more than teachers, dread the possibility of having a child who brings disgrace upon them. No matter how hard these parents try to conceal their feelings, the child invariably picks them up. The fear of being thought of as stupid is a great factor in the child's self-evaluation and in his ultimate withdrawal from any situation that threatens him with disgrace and failure.

REFERENCES

Combs, Arthur. *Professional Education for Teachers*. Boston, Mass.: Allyn & Bacon, 1966.

Chinn, Philip, Winn, Joyce, and Walters, Robert H. *Two-Way Talking with Parents of Special Problems*. St. Louis, Mo.: Mosby, 1978.

SELECTED READINGS

Gallagher, Patricia. *Teaching Students with Behavior Disorders*. Denver, Colo.: Lane Publishing Company, 1979.

Stein, Z., and Susser, M. "The Social Distribution of Mental Retardation." *American Journal of Mental Deficiency*, vol. 67, no. 6 (1963), pp. 811–821. N.Y., N.Y.

Chapter 21

Gifted Children and Homogeneous Grouping

People sometimes ask, "What about gifted children? There is so much concern for the slow and the learning disabled that we neglect the development of the gifted." This is not quite true. Many schools have extensive programs for gifted children. We do not support the belief that bright children have to be separated from not-so-bright children in order for them to develop their potential. We do not support the belief that an ordinary classroom cannot challenge them to excel. The entire concept of gifted children and of special classes for them must be carefully examined. The notion of having to treat children differently has to be examined. We are not questioning the concept of understanding each child individually and of helping him solve his individual problems. What we mean is that teachers must teach efficiently and effectively, and this means that they have to adjust to individual differences, but this does not imply that they must teach children separately.

The schools have devised new systems of education that separate children of different intellectual capacities. Taking gifted children out of the classroom and expecting them to perform at a high rate is often very harmful to them.

Some parents and teachers claim that the gifted child becomes bored in a regular classroom and that he then loses interest in learning. Children themselves rarely make such complaints. Complaints almost always come from the adults.

In a sense, the gifted child may find himself in a similar situation as the slow or the retarded child. In the case of the gifted child, however, adults often make too great demands and have too high expectations of him. Often this discourages him, and he does nothing. Thus, both are challenging situations and must be carefully examined by the school.

Separating children through homogenous grouping does not solve the problem of the underachiever or help the overachiever. The argument that the gifted child is held back in his progress because he must wait for the slow children becomes a matter of how well or how poorly a teacher handles such a class. A gifted child would not feel bored in class if he were stimulated into finding intellectual outlets and interesting activities within the classroom. In many respects, if the child were on his own or with other children of similar interests and could explore and make his own discoveries, which he would then share with the others, this would stimulate his independence and his creativity. In the long run this has greater value than the teacher directed activities that are often found in the special classes for the gifted. Bright children should be stimulated to develop a sense of responsibility toward the less gifted children by tutoring those children who need help. In this way the teacher stimulates the gifted child to operate on the horizontal plane (Chapter 3) and to develop social interest, which is the basis of good adjustment in life.

The drive and the competition in a class for the gifted often is more than some can easily endure. Many children become tense and nervous, whereas others actually break down under the strain. In this respect, the school system fails them just as much as the impoverished program does the slow child. School then becomes a drudge for both.

Some people argue that mixing gifted children with slow children is bad for the latter; it produces anxieties and feelings of inferiority, because they compare themselves with the brighter children, which adds to their discouragement. This may happen in a highly competitive class where the teacher encourages such competition. This may even happen to gifted children who are in a special class. Here, too, they will encounter other children who do better than they do, and this may discourage them to a point where they give up or get ill, are unhappy, or work without any enjoyment in learning. An example of such a discouraged child follows.

Melany was placed in a special class for gifted children when she was 10 years old. Her parents and all of her relatives celebrated this event by giving her a big party. Melany did very well at first, but suddenly she lost interest and produced hardly any work. After a while, she feigned illness and refused to go to school altogether. It was extremely difficult to find the reason for Melany's change. It was difficult to counsel her because she gave no answers.

One day the counselor asked the teacher if there was another child in class who worked as well as Melany did before. The teacher suddenly realized that just shortly before Melany's change a new student had entered the class. This girl was an extremely bright child, and she outshone all of the others.

When the counselor asked Melany what she thought of this girl, Melany started to cry. She cried through the entire session. She had to be helped to understand how overambitious and how competitive she was and how this discouraged her. Gradually, Melany went back to participation and doing her work as before.

Such discouragement is not likely to occur in a class where a democratic atmosphere prevails and where children are guided to respect individual differences on all levels. This requires unification of the class toward positive social interaction. In such an atmosphere, the self-esteem of the slow child is bound to be raised by the acceptance of those whom he admires.

Children who are grouped according to ability are deprived of the stimulation derived from interrelationships with other children who come from different socioeconomic and cultural backgrounds. Such stimulation broadens their horizons; it helps them to see others in a different light, and respect for them is bound to grow. It helps them develop healthy values, and it prepares them for life far better than an enriched program in subject matter where they are together with children of the same background and of the same interests.

We are not saying that schools should do away with enriched programs. On the contrary, every class should have an enriched program, but we need not separate children for this purpose. It is a pity that so many children come in contact only with other children of the same background and the same values as their own. How often do we hear teachers say about a child, "He is a fine student, but he is poorly adjusted." What good is his intellectual achievement if he is not well adjusted?

Some people argue that the school cannot afford to be concerned about and cannot accept the responsibility for children who cannot make the adjustment and who cannot learn. This is taking a very limited and an undemocratic approach to this problem. All children need to be our concern. To take a passive attitude is to admit failure from the very start. If we have failed so far, we should try with a different nontraditional approach, not only in our teaching techniques but in the entire school structure—from top to bottom. So far, we have resisted changes and deviations from the old established ways.

Bruno Bettelheim (1978), a well-known psychologist and a professor of educational psychology at the University of Chicago, made the following observations:

The gifted child in the ordinary classroom reaps another benefit. Because he learns easily, he becomes confident.

If the gifted child is put into a special class where learning is not easy for him, where he is only average among a group of extremely gifted youngsters, he may feel his abilities are only average and later lack the courage to take on difficult problems.

By putting a gifted child in a special class and by demanding high achievement from him, we may also push him beyond what is good for him. . . .

Special schooling teaches him at an early age to look down on the rest of the population as inferior. And this is my greatest fear, that by separating the gifted from the rest, we may well end up with something like what George Orwell predicted in his novel, *1984;* a world of big brothers who hold little brothers at their mercy because the little brothers can't speak their language or even hold the same view of the world.

The identification of gifted children is often left to the classroom teacher. Studies suggest that many children are then selected who are not gifted while many truly gifted children are overlooked. One study by Pegnato and Birch found that 31.4 percent of teachers' choices of gifted children were in error and that the teacher missed more than half of those who had superior ability in the area of academics, as well as in the arts (music, dancing, drama) and mechanical areas. (Gallagher, 1975).

It is a well-known fact that many adults who are now famous and who wield world respect for their exceptionally high abilities and contributions to society were regarded as dunces in school.

REFERENCES

Bettleheim, Bruno. "Stop Pampering Gifted Children." Albany, N.Y.: Speak Out Publishers, 1978.
Gallagher, James J. *Teaching the Gifted Child.* Boston: Allyn & Bacon, 1975.

Chapter 22

I. Q. Tests

One myth concerning learning is the matter of the child's intelligence, which is measured by intelligence tests. Generally speaking, we rely too much on I.Q. scores, believing that intellectual activity and intellectual potential are the same. Today we find many people in education and psychology who warn us about the validity of I.Q. tests. They are convinced that we are not the *victims* of but the *creators* of intelligence (Rosenthal, 1968).

Postman and Weingartner (1973) indicate that intelligence tests are reliable. Their validity depends on whether or not you accept the definition of intelligence that they use. However, no reputable psychologist would claim that an intelligence test measures a "thing" called intelligence.

Our I.Q. tests are not yet conclusive in measuring the child's potential if he is exposed to rich and meaningful experiences and if he is encouraged to learn and to enjoy learning. At present the most we can say about I.Q. tests is that they tell us how the child performed at the moment; it does not tell us how the same child may perform if properly guided and motivated and under different circumstances. I.Q. tests are valid only when they are given to well-adjusted, cooperative children. Children who have bad relationships with adults, especially with school people, who are defeated, angry, or uncooperative will cooperate in a testing situation just as little as they do in other situations.

Walter, an eighth-grade student, read only at a fourth-grade level, according to his Achievement Test. He was, therefore, placed in a special class for students with reading problems. Walter was referred for counseling. During the interview, the counselor learned that Walter was an expert on the Far

East and that he read avidly all books that dealt with this region. When the counselor questioned how he could read such difficult books if his reading was only at a fourth-grade level, he replied, "Oh, you probably refer to the test I took. Well, I did very poorly because, frankly, I never read the test except for a paragraph or two. It was so boring that I didn't bother reading it." He then answered the testing questions the best he could.

Walter's case is an excellent example of children who do not cooperate in a testing situation. Unfortunately, neither teachers nor school psychologists who administer tests realize the attitude that such children take when being tested.

Michael, a third grader, was taken out from class to take an I.Q. test. When he returned, he grinned from ear to ear as he announced, "Hey guys, you know what that stupid man asked me? He asked how many legs a horse has. And you know what? I told him five, and you know what? He believed me, because I saw him write it down. Cross my heart."

Michael felt very superior in this situation, as do other children who deliberately give wrong answers. When Michael's test evaluation was given to the teacher, it said, among other things, "Michael is not very observant for a child his age."

We feel that poor performance, academically or other, has little to do with tests. Often children appear slow or stupid in order to avoid tasks or to draw others into their service. Some children use poor performance as a subconscious means of getting even with overambitious parents or with teachers who push and make them work. Still others have been so beaten down by their previous experiences, which always spelled "failure," that they gave up trying.

Betty's I.Q. was 68, and she was to be placed in a special class for the mentally retarded. At the suggestion of her teacher, she was allowed to remain in a class with normal children, and she was to be retested at the end of the school year.

There were six children in Betty's family. The oldest two were married and lived away from home. A 12-year-old sister was in seventh grade and a good student. Betty was 10 years old and in third grade. (She had repeated the first grade and was then promoted because of her age.) Her 9-year-old sister was also in the third grade. She was an average student, but she was an accomplished tap dancer and had appeared on television twice. The youngest child, a boy of 7, was in the second grade. He was asthmatic and was frequently absent from school. From this family situation, we can see that every child, except Betty, occupied a special position in the family. She was squeezed out by two successful sisters.

Betty's mother told the teacher that at home her daughter kept to herself. She helped with the chores, but she was not very smart.

Betty was also withdrawn in class. She liked to draw and to paint, so she spent most of her time with these activities. Many children knew her from previous classes, and they accepted the fact that nothing could be expected of her. She was ignored.

As the class became aware of the differences in people, of the problems that some children have, and of how they as a group could help to solve some of these problems, the children started to pay attention to Betty. Those who lived close to her walked home with her; some invited her to their homes; still others offered to help her with her school work. Gradually, Betty began to show attentiveness, especially during group discussions. Now and then she offered a suggestion or asked a question.

One day after a lesson on the characteristics of mammals, she asked why an elephant was not smarter than a human being, considering that the mother elephant carried her baby much longer than the human mother. She reasoned that the elephant's brain would be better developed, because it would have had more time to do so. Since the brain determines intelligence, it would follow that the elephant would be more intelligent.

This was the first time that Betty had expressed an opinion in more than just a few words. The other children were very impressed with her reasonings, and they told her so. The fact that she was not right in her conclusion did not diminish their impression.

Betty lost her fear of saying something dumb. When she was retested her I.Q. had gone up to 97.

Robert was a mentally retarded child, his I.Q. being under 70. He was the oldest of three boys, all of whom had spent most of their lives in foster homes. Robert's parents had abandoned the children when Robert was 5 years old. He could not remember them. Robert lived with a family of many children, all younger than he. He had to help with the household chores, babysit for the children, and take frequent punishment for not having done the right things at home or for neglecting one of the little ones. His nickname at home was "moron."

Robert spent most of his time in class daydreaming or looking out of the window. He was not a behavior problem. He was very attentive during class discussions, but he never participated.

One day a boy asked the class to help him with a personal problem. He said that his parents' tenants complained that his family was too noisy and that they must stop making so much noise. This boy felt that since it was his parents' house, they had a right to make all the noise they wanted, and he wanted to know how the rest of the children felt about this problem. Suddenly Robert got up and shouted, "You have no such rights. Nobody has a right to make others unhappy. I don't care if this is your house or who you are, or how smart you think you are."

Everybody stared at Robert. Suddenly they saw a different boy in him. Many children agreed that Robert was right, but they asked him why was he so angry. One child said that perhaps Robert felt the class had not treated him right, and he was angry not only because of the problem discussed but because of his own situation. Other children expressed similar opinions. A new life in class had started for Robert. At the end of the year his I.Q. had gone up to 91.

Intelligence can be increased. We know that children who spend many years in institutions for the mentally retarded only get worse as time goes on. The longer they stay in the institution, the lower their I.Q. is likely to get. When the child is taken out of the institution and put into an enriched and caring environment, his I.Q. usually goes up. As we have previously pointed out, we have seen children whose I.Q. went up as much as 30 points. But even if their I.Q. rose only 10 or 15 points (which it did in most cases), their intelligence level had changed significantly enough for them to be placed in a class with children of normal intelligence.

Intelligence and self-concept cannot be separated. How a person feels about himself is a great factor in the person's overall development. The more the person sees himself in a positive way, the better adjusted he will be to life, and a well-adjusted person is more creative, more daring, and less afraid of making mistakes. Maladjusted people see themselves in the opposite way: as unwanted, unacceptable, and inferior. They are afraid to move ahead. People with a positive view of themselves are likely to be more intelligent than those who feel inferior. Therefore, teachers should, in the first place, do everything to help children feel better about themselves. Unfortunately, this is not what they get paid for. They get paid for teaching.

Another factor detrimental to good education is the idea that all learning should be solitary; that children must learn by themselves. The most effective learning is social learning, in which ideas are discussed and exchanged and children learn from each other.

We look for purposes in all behavior. If a child has difficulties with regard to behavior or learning, we always look for the reasons behind these difficulties. How does it pay off for the child to behave in a certain way or have this problem? For people who are not familiar with the Adlerian philosophy and with purposive behavior, this may sound strange and unbelievable. Why would a child, especially a basically cooperative and bright child, want to have a learning disability? It just doesn't make sense. It makes no sense to us, because we are looking at it from our point of view using our own logic. We should be trying instead to understand the child's logic without the child being aware of it. The payoff lies in the adult's reaction to the child's behavior.

We may ask, "What factors contribute to intellectual growth?" Whatever enhances and strengthens a person's feelings about himself; whatever contributes positive experiences to his life; whatever encourages the person; and whatever makes him feel valuable contributes to his intelligence, his self-confidence, and self-concept.

REFERENCES

Eysenck, H. J., "The I.Q. Argument." 1971.

Featherstone, Joseph. "Liveright." *Commonweal,* vol. 95, pp. 42–45, Oct. 8, 1971.

Hoffman, Banesh. *The Tyrant of Testing.* New York: Macmillan Co., 1964.

Hunt, J. McV. *Intelligence and Experience.* New York: John Wiley & Sons.

Postman, Neil, and Weingartner, Charles. *The School Book.* New York: Dell (Delacorte Press), 1973.

Rosenthal, Robert. "Self-Fulfilling Prophecies." *Psychology Today,* vol. 2, 1968.

Part 4

Coping with Special Behavior Problems

Chapter 23

The Adolescent

Adolescents have become a major problem, not only for teachers, parents, and society, but also for themselves.

Adolescence is a period of major change; it is the third phase of childhood. In his preschool days, the child finds his place in his own family by developing definite patterns to his personality. As he enters school, which is the second phase, he joins members of other families and integrates himself into the community by recognizing the general rules of behavior, work, and order. In adolescence, he becomes part of society at large. He strives for intellectual and personal freedom and independence, and he looks critically at the values of adult society. He then chooses the reference group with which he shares values and ideals. He undergoes a period of psychosexual upheaval through which he sets his pattern of sexual behavior.

In the past, during this period, the teenager had one foot in adolescence and the other in adulthood. He slowly became an adult. He got a job, drove his own car, contributed to the family income, and took on the responsibility for his younger brothers and sisters. All this has changed. At present, teenagers are at war with adult society. Their freedom from responsibility induces them to continue their adolescence far beyond the age customary for this period of life. They do not want to assume the responsibilities of adults. Teenagers have become a powerful subgroup, living in a different world, distinguishing themselves from adults through their long hair, untidiness, odd clothing, noisy music, and use of drugs.

Generation Gap

The rebellion of youth is the basis of what we call the generation gap. Adolescents and adults do not see eye to eye because they live in two different worlds. This warfare is so insidious that it penetrates almost every family and expresses itself in the most divergent ways. The young idealist is in the same opposition to adult society as the juvenile delinquent. What distinguishes each is his form of rebellion. At the present time, we have no evidence of any effort on the part of either camp, adolescents or adults, to come to a meeting of the minds. The generalized warfare gives the youthful rebels continuous fuel. The teenager and the college student, who form a group of antiadults and antiestablishment, join the other rebellious groups. Probably the major battle against the establishment will be fought between adolescents and adults.

This warfare will worsen before it gets better. It will penetrate every family and every community, until we finally give up the traditional methods of dealing with adolescents and have the courage to start a new era and give young people a voice in all affairs in which they are involved.

With exceptions, adults rarely listen to young people. A good many have literally no use for adolescents. As one parent said, "They ought to be buried at 11 and dug up again at 25." Adolescents, for their part, blame parents and teachers for everything and claim that it is their fault that they dress differently, use different language, and behave differently.

Basically, adolescents do not trust adults because they do not think that adults will understand them. Adolescents feel that adults cannot help them because "they are old-fashioned; they have forgotten what it feels like to be young; and they always want to have their way." Whereas adolescents are very critical of adults, they see nothing wrong with their own behavior and how it affects adults.

They have become critical of their elders and question adults' values, social amenities, "good manners," dress, material values, attitudes toward marriage and sex, and the school system, to name a few. There are very few older people after whom adolescents want to model themselves. This is a great departure from the past when most youngsters had a hero or older person whom they looked up to.

Adolescents embrace anything that adults detest. This makes them feel like they belong to the youth culture and are "in." Adolescents complain that adults manipulate them, but they fail to see that they perceive any person who tells them what to do as autocratic and their enemy. Young people fail to realize that we manipulate each other: they manipulate adults no less than adults manipulate them. It is difficult to say who is more successful in the process.

Refusal to Do Schoolwork

Adolescents say that they cannot work for a dull teacher, and so they refuse to work for such a teacher. Let's face it, all students are not always stimulating to teachers. Can we imagine the opposite—a teacher who refuses to work for a dull student? When we confront them with such a question, they almost always get angry. They claim that teachers have no right to refuse to work with a student, no matter how they regard that student. At the same time, they demand "equal rights for all."

We suggest that adolescents should be helped to realize their part in the situation and that learning or not learning is an attitudinal question. While a student may not enjoy a dull teacher or a dull subject, in the final analysis, whether he learns or not depends on his decisions. Unfortunately, counselors often reinforce this attitude by agreeing with them. No teacher should be boring, but this is not the issue. We must pinpoint the real issue for the student who claims that he cannot learn from a boring teacher and help him realize that he himself decided that he would not learn because the teacher was not to his liking.

Are Adolescents Free?

Often adolescents who complain about their families escape by substituting their peer group for their family. Influenced by their peers and reference group, they believe they are running away from the "establishment"— parents, teachers, police. But "establishment" means something entirely different to different people. For instance, to black people the establishment is the white race; for labor it is management; for women it is men; and for children, it is adults.

Adolescents believe that they are free when they do not listen to adults. But are they? They are now dependent on the acceptance of the peer group, and they often do things in order to feel accepted, which they would previously never have considered doing. They drink, smoke, and often deliberately do poorly in school. We will illustrate this with an example.

> Melinda, a freshman, felt rejected by her peer group because she was not "hip," and she was told that in order to be accepted she would have to steal something from a store. This would have to be done in the presence of two students who would then vouch for her honesty. Furthermore, she was told to repaint a small monument and to change three "no parking" signs to "parking" signs.

To cite another example:

> A 16-year-old boy stole a car and was caught by the police. He needed a car because he had promised his girl friend that he would drive her to a party. When his father refused to let him use his car because he needed the car himself, the boy looked for an open car, and when he found one, he just drove off.

Since the incident with the police, this boy blackmails his parents with his threats of what he will do whenever they refuse him the car. It does not disturb the boy that his father often has to use public transportation when he gives up his car.

Although here we are dealing with parents who need guidance in how they respond to their son's threats, the fact remains that some adolescents take rights that they would never grant to adults. This must be brought to their attention when they discuss equal rights. Both adults and adolescents need to know what they do to each other and the games that each side plays.

The most pronounced rebellion is found in juvenile delinquents and in drug users. The drug trip with its fantasies is their concept of the height of excitement. This desire for excitement is a major factor in their behavior. Excitement is also obtained when they defeat adults.

The rebellion against autocracy unites all young people against adult society. This rebellion may be expressed in idealistic ways such as with posters, songs, poems, demonstrations, or in destructive ways. This is not a new phenomenon. The war between the generations is age old. Whenever one group sets itself up as superior and dominates another, then resentment and rebellion exist. However, the resentment of open expression had to be limited in an autocratic society that upheld the dominant power of one group over the other. In an autocratic society youth had to obey. This was the establishment rule.

It is only in our democratic society that the rapidly increasing status of equality for all brings the conflict between the previously subdued and the superior groups into the open.

Today's youth dares to defy more openly than in former times. They are sensitive to the changing times and are aware that they have rights.

More than anything, the adolescent wants to be independent and free to make his own decisions. This is most difficult for adults to accept. Many problems at home and in school would not exist if parents and teachers recognized these needs and made it possible for their children to make all decisions, even if they were wrong, and let them learn from their mistakes.

The Role of the Adult

Adults need to be educated to understand how they, unwittingly, create tension between them and adolescents. Adults instill feelings of insecurity and of worthlessness in young people, which make them feel unappreciated and unwanted. They need to realize that they give children platitudes and moralistic lectures instead of treating them as equals, with respect, concern, trust, and confidence.

Students often complain that teachers are only concerned with subject matter, that they have no time to listen to them, and that they do not care about their feelings. They say that authority figures expect teenagers to be humble, obedient, submissive, polite, respectful, all of which are one sided, because adults never accord this courtesy to them.

> A teacher reported a student for smoking in the bathroom. The principal suspended this student for several days because he broke a school rule. But this same teacher is often seen smoking in the boiler room. The student confronted the teacher with this fact; he argued that the rules and regulations should be the same for all, especially since in class they talked so much about equal rights. The teacher argued that when they were older, they too would have the same rights as he had now. This provoked the student even more.

The student felt that the teacher's response was a put-down of youth; that being young automatically placed them in an inferior position; and that this was contrary to what he preached.

> TEACHER: I want you to do pages 20 to 25 and hand the work in by tomorrow.
> STUDENTS: Gee, why so many pages? It will keep us busy all afternoon.
> TEACHER: I am sorry, but I know how much practice you need and what you must do. I want no further arguments.
> HOWARD: But I know the subject already, and I don't see why I should have to do so much homework.
> TEACHER: I said "no arguments."

Teachers are not aware of how they systematically discourage children by instilling in them the idea that they are not good enough as they are. The examples we have given are very typical of what goes on between teachers and adolescents. Gradually, the adolescent withdraws from them. He feels completely misunderstood and mistreated, so he then withdraws and tells them nothing or he lies. This is referred to by many as a breakdown in communication. This is an unfortunate term, since there is no breakdown, because each individual communicates exactly what he wants to communicate.

The Games We Play

We are always communicating to others our feelings and our intentions, and it is up to others to respond to them or not. The moment a person responds, he is establishing communication. If a discussion ends with arguing or with fighting, people often say, "I can't communicate with him." What the person really means, however, is "It must be my way or I won't play the game."

This is extremely important for us to understand. It is equally important to help adolescents to understand their part in reaching their goals. They often accuse adults of not communicating with them when adults do not see things their way. The students need to understand the roles they play in such situations and that they are out to defeat adults no less than adults are determined to keep an upper hand, even if in the process they have to put the students down, or humiliate, criticize, and threaten them.

Is this situation hopeless? Are there any avenues open to us to improve, if not change entirely, the relationships between adolescents and adults? Many of the proposed suggestions have already been mentioned, but there are many more things adults can do, especially teachers and counselors.

Teachers and parents need desperately to learn new methods to influence adolescents and to regain their confidence. This requires that adults accept some radical changes in their dealings with young people. We are often asked, "Is it possible for adults who have been raised in an autocratic family and educated in an autocratic school to give up their own values and adopt such radical ideas?" This is a fair question. It is not easy for us to give up our values and beliefs. It calls for a thorough investigation of what is threatening us in these new ideas and of why we hold on to our old ones. It also calls for an analysis of whether such changes would intensify our feelings of insecurity and fear of failure. The change may be threatening, because we may be overly concerned with being in command and in control and of losing our prestige.

We cannot support the belief that we are what we are and that we cannot change. This is a defeatist attitude and is discouraging. If we grant ourselves this privilege, we would have to accept the student's argument that he cannot learn from a boring teacher or that he cannot help getting into a fight when someone disagrees with him. The decision of what we can or cannot do rests with us and is not determined by causes beyond our control. We cannot change *what was*, but we can change *what is*.

Democratic Practices

Any teacher can establish a democratic classroom by saying to the students:

"Let's discuss things and decide together what we will do. I will not make any decisions without first discussing them with you and without coming to a mutual agreement. I can, however, share decision making only in areas in which I have the right to do so and only in matters that concern my own class. I cannot change the curriculum or the hour you have to come to class. I wish I could, but I myself must follow what was decided by those who make policy. Still, this leaves us many areas in which we are in a position to make changes. For instance, we can decide if the class has to be absolutely quiet at all times or if some low talking may be allowed. We can also decide how much homework individual students should do."

Probably the most single way by which we can change the class atmosphere and the relationships between teachers and students and between students themselves is through the establishment of the *democratic classroom* (Chapter 9) and *group discussions* (Chapter 15) through which all decide what *they* are going to do about the interruptions in class, about fighting, about students who are discouraged and give up, about vandalism, and so on. In this way, students are helped to realize that what happens in class is the result of what everyone is doing and not of what just the teacher is doing.

Some teachers claim that the peer group is so strong that many students, fortified by the values of the peer group, use group discussion for the sake of arguing and killing time. The teachers feel that they have no chance to influence these students and therefore refuse to have group discussions in class. This is sometimes true, but in each class there are bound to be a few students who will listen and participate, and these few may gradually pull others along. In a group setting there is a possibility of driving a wedge between the participants, splitting them up, and this is bound to weaken their power. The moment the teacher wins one or more of the students, it fortifies her position.

Academic Tests

Since students's resistance to tests is often a factor in poor relationships with teachers, we should like to propose some possibilities for change.

Tests are threatening and provoke anxiety in teenagers. Many students accuse teachers of being unfair, because they ask questions on the tests that were not discussed in class and they do not grade them objectively.

We suggest that teachers ask students to accept the responsibility for their own tests by submitting weekly questions relevant to what was being taught in class that week. These questions would then be discussed and clarified. Out of these questions the teacher may select a certain number for a class exam, or the teacher may give each student his own questions to which he must write the answers. No student can then complain of the unfairness of the exam. This method has been used successfully by some teachers.

The question is sometimes raised of what to do with students who either refuse to submit questions or who cannot pose any intelligent questions. The teacher who has had regular group discussions may get help from her class with such a student. It becomes a matter of helping this student realize his fictitious goal—to show his power and to defeat the teacher.

Such a student cannot be forced to take the test but must be confronted with the logical consequences that will follow. More than anything, the teacher and the class would have to find ways to help this student feel important and fully accepted as a person. This does not mean that they should accept his behavior. Together, they may find solutions to the problem.

As for the student who cannot raise intelligent questions, the teacher may examine how she has taught the subject. Perhaps it has not been presented in a manner that was understandable to some students. If the student is truly incapable of raising intelligent questions, the teacher may allow him to take the test over after someone in class has worked with this student for some time. In other words, she can give this student an "incomplete" rather than a failing grade.

Self-Awareness

Ida Harper Simons (1968) developed a very helpful technique that aids the teacher in understanding her students better and in discovering important factors that hinder the student from feeling happy at home or at school. The technique indicates the student's hidden ambitions, resentments, and fears.

One of the techniques suggested is a sentence completion exercise in which the student is asked to complete a sentence.

EXAMPLE
1. I have learned about myself _____.
2. I wish _____.
3. If I could I would _____.
4. I hope to _____.
5. I like people who are _____.
6. When I don't like someone I _____.

We can appreciate the effectiveness of such an exercise if we examine how students completed these sentences.

1. I have learned about myself

that I can have friends when I don't insist on having my way
that I cry, not because it hurts, but because I want people to feel sorry for me
that I won't do anything unless I am absolutely certain that I will do it well
that I am not as dumb as I thought

2. I wish

   that they would do away with school and that I would be free to do
       what I want
   that Mr. Hochberg would stop picking on me
   that the coach would let me play in the next football game
   that my father would be less stingy
   that I shouldn't be so afraid of the next English exam

3. If I could I would

   ask Sarah to come and stay with us because she is unhappy at home
   run away from home and go to California
   skip math and science
   want to have all the money in the world

4. I hope to

   become a great doctor some day
   get a job and quit school when I am 16
   graduate from high school
   show my parents how wrong they are about me and make them feel
       sorry for how they treat me

These examples indicate self-awareness, hopes and dreams, resentments, fears, and unrealistic daydreams. The exercise will help the teacher plan for the individual student who needs reassurance and encouragement to feel more important than he does at present. The teacher is in a better position to structure the class discussions and to lead the students to realize that it is not enough to make a value judgment such as, "I think that studying social science is stupid"; they must find a better way to do the things that are inevitable and must be done and to give up those that are doing them harm. The students must then commit themselves to their choices. For instance, a student could make a commitment based on judgment that smoking grass or sniffing coke may be harmful and that he will not gamble and take chances. Only then would there be a possibility that the student would stop smoking and taking drugs.

The teacher would now be in a position to find out who feels at ease in expressing feelings and ideas and who has difficulties. Knowing this, the teacher can focus the group discussion around such subjects that would encourage the students to express their feelings without fear of appearing stupid and of being ridiculed.

5. I like people

   who are kind
   who are tough

who are sincere
who like me

6. When I don't like someone, I

have nothing to do with him
like to bug him and make him mad
feel good when he gets into trouble
don't talk to him

Shock Techniques

Some students may complete a sentence in order to shock the teacher ("*I wish* you would break a leg" or "*I wish* I could see you in the nude") or hurt the teacher: "*I wish* that they would fire you and that you should never get another teaching job" or "*I wish* to never have to set eyes on your ugly face again."

This is done consciously, with the expectation that the teacher will now retaliate in some fashion. Usually, the student who challenges the teacher in this way is prepared to show this teacher, "I dare you. Now, what will you do about it? See how unafraid I am of you. There is nothing you can do to me." They shock the teacher through negative behavior and provocation in order to show their power and, in many instances, in order to impress the class with their courage.

If such a situation occurs, we suggest that the teacher ignore such challenges for the time being. A teacher may even return the "shock" by thanking the student for being so honest. At a later time the teacher can discuss with the class the purpose of such provocations, without mentioning the names of the students who tried to provoke her. However, the teacher should examine what she is doing that provokes such angry feelings in a student and possibly should change her behavior. The teacher may discuss with the student why he has such hostile feelings toward her and what she could do to change the relationship. This should be done in privacy. Some teachers insist that they should not have to become involved in the reeducation of their students, that they have not been trained to counsel students who have difficulties, and that they want only to teach. They suggest that students who have problems should be handled by the school counselor.

Unfortunately, this is an unrealistic and (to the student) detrimental way of looking at the situation. The teacher is in a much better position than the counselor to help the student, because the teacher has the group to help her in the process of reeducation. This already has been discussed in Chapter 15.

Counseling Adolescents

It is a sad fact that school counselors are burdened with the responsibility of counseling adolescents with regard to the subjects they should take and finding the right college after they graduate from high school. When counselors do psychological counseling they often reinforce rather than help students understand their destructive behavior. Some counselors are no match for the students who are sent to them and do not know what to do; therefore, they are afraid to confront them with their behavior and goals.

EXAMPLE

THELMA: I just can't stand that old witch, Mrs. Spence. I would like to tear her hair out each time she says "Now, class do this. . . ."

COUNSELOR: I know how you feel. I remember when I felt that way toward a teacher.

THELMA: One of these days I am really going to let her have it.

COUNSELOR: I can just imagine.

THELMA: So what do you want me here for?

COUNSELOR: I want to know how you feel.

THELMA: I have just told you.

COUNSELOR: So you did; that's right.

We regard this kind of counseling as no more that "chit, chat." Thelma has gained no insight into her need to feel superior and perhaps to be admired by the other children for her daring provocations, and how in the counselor's office she is challenging the counselor.

A well-trained counselor would help Thelma evaluate her feelings and her behavior. The counselor might ask any of the following questions:

Could it be

that you feel this way toward Mrs. Spence because she does not treat you as special?

that the teacher showed no respect for you?

that you feel misunderstood by the teacher?

that the teacher shows no respect for your judgment?

that you feel that the teacher is pushing you around by telling you what to do and what not to do?

that you resent all people who tell you what to do?

that you must show adults "I can do what I want and you can't stop me"?

that you believe that the other students in class admire you when you show such brazen behavior?

that you came here to shock me?

that you are testing me to see what I will say or do now that you have told me what you would do to Mrs. Spence?

When the student feels understood, even if the realization is unpleasant, the counselor is in a position to help him realize that he has set fictitious goals for himself. The student believes that by doing only what he wants he will be a big-shot and admired by others or feared by them, and that being overambitious discourages him and he often gives up or uses destructive means to achieve his goal. The student needs to understand how important it is to him to show the parents or teachers "I can do only what I want," disregarding the high price he may have to pay for this. The teacher is now in a position to show him that he has choices, and that together they can find ways through useful behavior for him to be important and to feel accepted. The teacher must help the student realize that through his behavior he does not change the teacher or the parent, just as they do not change him through their behavior.

The counselor may guess the hidden reason for his behavior, his resistance, and his defiance (see Chapter 4).

COUNSELOR: Ben, do you know why you don't answer my questions? May I tell you what I think is going through your mind right now? Could it be that you intend to make me look foolish, and that it is important to you to show me how much stronger you are and how stupid I am for trying to get you to talk to me because you won't talk no matter what I say?

BEN: (grinning) Not exactly.

COUNSELOR: Well, I was wrong. May I be wrong sometimes, Ben?

BEN: I don't mind if you are wrong all the time.

COUNSELOR: That's an honest answer. Could it be that you won't mind because then you are "right"?

BEN: Not all the time.

COUNSELOR: How about right now? How important is it to you to be right?

BEN: I don't know. Maybe it is not as important as it was before.

Communication has been established in this dialogue. The counselor has zeroed in on Ben's motivation for his behavior. This can be discussed further, not through criticism and accusations but through reevaluation. Had this counselor accused Ben of wasting his time and said that there is nothing any one can do for students like him, it is very doubtful if the visit with the counselor would have had any value. When students realize that the counselor or the teacher does not sit in judgment of them but rather is concerned with the situation and is eager to help, they often lessen their resistance and are then willing to listen and to talk honestly.

Group Discussion with Adolescents

The class decided that they wanted to discuss dropping out of school during one of their group discussion sessions.

JOAN: I would drop out of school if I weren't afraid that I would hurt my parents.

TED: What would you do?

JOAN: I don't know. I would look for a job, I guess.

HELEN: How would you get a job? You think it's easy for us to get jobs? Have you ever tried to look for a job?

BILL: Take it easy, Helen. Why are you getting so excited?

HELEN: Because you kids who think that you can get jobs without at least a high school diploma are stupid.

BILL: O.K., O.K.

TEACHER: Why do you want to quit school, Joan?

JOAN: Because I am sick and tired of it.

STUDENTS: Here, here. Me too; you said it.

TEACHER: I still don't know why you are sick and tired of school.

JOAN: School bores me, and if you want to know, this class bores me.

JEFFREY: I still think that you should finish high school. I agree with Helen, because my brother is a high-school dropout. He's been home since last June, and he still can't get a job.

JOAN: If I want your opinion, Jeff, I'll ask for it.

TEACHER: Joan, is there any class you like?

JOAN: No.

TEACHER: Is there anything at all that you enjoy in school?

JOAN: I can't say.

TEACHER: Is there anything you enjoy outside of school?

JOAN: Lots of things.

HELEN: Come on, Joan, there must be something you enjoy here. Don't give me that. I know that you enjoy some things, even in this class.

JOAN: So you know more about me than I do.

TEACHER: May we shift the emphasis from a personal attitude to a general one. What makes students drop out of school? Why do they drop out? And what can be done about it? Is it alright if we talk about this problem, since it affects so many young people?

BILLY: I can sympathize with Joan. I often feel the same as she does.

MARGARET: I agree with Mrs. Starr; let's not keep it personal.

BILLY: I guess, you are right. I am sorry.

TEACHER: You know kids who dropped out and many in our school who want to drop out. Joan said that she is bored. I would like to hear from the rest of you. How do you see this problem?

STEVEN: Well, boredom is a big factor. You can't learn if the subject bores you. That's pretty clear to anyone.

TEACHER: Not to me, it isn't.

STUDENTS: Huh?

ANN: I know that I can't learn when a teacher or a subject bores me.

TEACHER: You say that you and many others can't learn when the subject or the teacher bores you. Would you mind talking about this?

TED: I don't know if it is a matter of "I can't"; it's more than that. How can I explain it? When I am bored, I am not stimulated to learn, and then I don't learn.

CANDY: I can only talk for myself. I want to learn, and I can learn from any kind of teacher. I think that when you really want to learn, you just make up your mind that you are going to learn, and you do. It's as simple as that. Mr. Howard is not a very stimulating teacher, and I can see how someone could get bored in his class. I know I do, but I still learn in his class.

TEACHER: Class, please, let's leave out names and keep this discussion impersonal.

JOAN: You are such a good girl, Candy. Why would you have a name like Candy if you weren't so sweet?

TEACHER: Shall we postpone this discussion for some other time? You seem to be too eager to attack one another. Maybe when we discuss this problem next time, we can just stick to the problem itself.

STUDENTS: No, no, let's continue the discussion.

JOAN: O.K., I won't say another word to anyone personally.

STEVEN: I take back what I said. I agree that you can learn from a boring teacher if you want to.

TEACHER: Who decides whether we can learn or not? Do outside forces compel us to make decisions?

HELEN: Sometimes. Sometimes, outside forces do compel us to make a decision that we wouldn't make otherwise.

TEACHER: Are you referring to learning or not learning?

HELEN: No, but there are situations in which we are compelled.

TEACHER: May we first finish discussing our feelings about when we learn and when we don't?

STEFAN: I would agree that everyone decides for himself whether or not he is going to learn, and this does not depend on the subject but on himself.

TEACHER: In other words, it is an attitude toward learning that you are talking about.

STEFAN: Right.

TEACHER: How can we apply our conclusions about learning from boring teachers to dropouts?

CANDY: They would rather drop out than learn from a boring teacher. It's as simple as that.

DAVID: Kids who drop out of school don't like to be told what to do. They want to be free and do what is fun for a change. They get very tired of following rules, spending hours studying, and being nagged at school and at home about what they must do. It's not just being bored.

TEACHER: I am glad you brought up the issue of "wanting to do what the kid decides himself" and wanting to be "free." I wonder what some of you think about this?

HELEN: But you aren't free to do what you want just because you drop out of school. This is exactly what I meant when I said that other forces do compel us to do things, whether we like it or not.

TEACHER: Could you give us an example of what you mean?

HELEN: Let me see. It's difficult to find an example when you need it. Well, for instance, you need money. You probably need more money when you are out of school than when you are in school. Where are you going to get it? You may have to depend on your parents for a long time. So, are you free?

JOAN: But you can sleep late, and you don't have to worry about home-work and such.

HELEN: Joan, I think that you're trying to be funny. I think you know very well what I mean.

TEACHER: How do the rest of you feel about this? Are we really free when we can do what we want?

TED: If you can do what you want, then you are free. I don't think that many people can do what they want, but when they can, they are free.

BILL: You are certainly more free when you are out of school than when you are in school, and I think that's why kids drop out. So you don't have money for a while, but sooner or later, you get a job and you don't have to depend on your parents.

TEACHER: Chris, you haven't said a thing. What is your opinion?

CHRIS: (Shrugs shoulder.) I have no opinion. I just mind my own business.

ANN: But how do you feel about school?

CHRIS: It's something you have to do. There are things I like, and there are things I don't like. It all depends. But since you ask, I don't believe that dropping out of school is a wise thing to do. I don't care how much you hate it, it's not as if you decide that you don't like playing tennis and so you stop. It's a much more serious thing. I know that I must finish high school even if I don't like some things.

TEACHER: For someone who had nothing to say, you sure have a lot to say. I am glad that you said it. We were talking about freedom. Imagine that everyone could do only what he wanted to do because he thought that this was being free. He could go to school whenever he wanted to or not at all. The police officer, the teacher, and everyone else who renders a service would feel as some of you do. They would want to be free and do only what pleased them. Have you ever thought of this? Is this possible?

TED: That's what I was talking about before. It's not just that you have to consider what your parents feel but also what others feel. I am thinking of what Mrs. Starr said. We might include the fire fighter, the doctor, or even the president of the United States. My father and I talked about this problem some time ago, and I really understand it much better.

HELEN: This is exactly how I feel. What do you mean by "free"? I feel that I am free. Going to school is something that is for my own good, and I appreciate that the freedom of going to school is given to me.

MARY: I haven't said anything, but I want to make one statement. I believe that the school and the parents should not force kids to attend school if they don't want to.

TEACHER: I believe that we have touched upon this already, or am I wrong? Did we talk about this or about boring subjects? What I hoped we could clarify today is the reason for dropping out and the purpose of it. And so far, we seem to have reached only one conclusion—that most students drop out because they want to be free. Some of you seem to feel that this is not freedom, that we all have responsibilities toward each other, and that nobody is completely free.

BILL: But if you do something that hurts no one except yourself, why shouldn't you have the right to be free to do what you want?

HOWARD: I think that most dropouts hurt society in the long run. Just look around you. Take the kids from our school who have dropped out. Where are they now, and what are they doing? Mike was picked up by the police for being drunk, and Melony Fitch from last year is now living with a guy because her parents threw her out. Some are home and don't have a cent to their names. Sure, there are a few who have jobs and are alright, but most of them are not any happier now that they are out of school.

JOAN: I have two good friends who are dropouts, and I see them often. They did not finish high school for the same reason that I don't want to finish. These kids are both working and are doing O.K. I see them sometimes at work, and I know.

TEACHER: Would you want to talk to some kids who have dropped out of school and hear from them how they view their situation now that they are free? I think that this might be interesting and worth our time. What do you think?

STUDENTS: Sure; let's; O.K.

BILLY: I know some guys I could invite.

OTHERS: Me, too.

TEACHER: Let's have a show of hands from those of you who would want to invite to class a few young people who have dropped out of school and have them tell us what it is like now? (Class indicates by a show of hands.) Let's see who knows people who might come. (Show of hands.) For what day can we invite them?

BILLY: Those who are working won't be able to come during the day, and I think that we should listen to them also.

TEACHER: You are right. I didn't think of that. How can we get them to come?

CHRIS: Why don't we ask them first? Maybe some can take off for an hour?

HELEN: Yes, let's first ask them and see who can come?

TEACHER: Our group meets next Thursday. Could you report then who can come? We can then decide on a day. Is there any other business for today?

PETER: I feel that you are giving us too much homework.

TEACHER: I do? Do others feel this way also?

ANN: Yes, I do, and I think a number of us feel this way.

HOWARD: Every teacher thinks that she is the only one who assigns homework, so each one loads us with homework in her subject. As a result, we go home and can't do anything else but homework.

BILLY: Yes, I agree. Couldn't you give us a little less homework?

TEACHER: Well, I'll have to think about it. I don't give you work just to keep you busy. I feel that you need the practice if we are to finish all the work for this year.

BILLY: I don't need any practice. I know the subject without having to do homework. Why should I have to do this stupid homework? I am sorry if I hurt your feelings, but why do I have to? You know I know it.

CHRIS: That goes for me too. I see no sense in all of this busy work.

TEACHER: But there are others who don't know the subject. What about them? I can't assign homework to one of you and not to the others. They wouldn't think that it was fair.

DAVID: Why can't you give homework to those who want it and leave it up to us? After all, those who don't want it, don't do it anyway.

TEACHER: Not always, David. Some do it anyway. I really don't know what to do. I hate to be unfair.

STEVE: Why don't we ask everyone how they feel about homework?

TEACHER: I really don't think that this is the way to settle this problem. I would consider cutting down on the amount of homework, if all of you agree to this.

HELEN: I think that this is fair.

JOAN: I am not going to do any sh——ty homework. It's fair that you should know this.

DAVID: There you go again. We all know how you feel, and nobody is going to stop you.

TEACHER: I would like to do something that has everyone's or almost everyone's approval, but I can't just make radical changes. I am not even allowed to. I am willing to try giving you less homework. How is that? Would you be willing to give this a try?

CANDY: It really makes no difference to me. I have no problems doing my homework.

ANN: How much is less?

TEACHER: I don't know. Maybe I will cut it down by a third. I have another suggestion. I can decide on the amount of homework according to how difficult the particular lesson will be. How do you feel about this?

DAVID: I suggest that we get no homework over the weekend so that we can really enjoy the weekend without having to worry about homework, and during the week you can cut it down by a third, as you said.

BILLY: Half.

TEACHER: We can stand here and argue about this all day. Let's see how many would agree to doing homework if I give you no work over the weekend.

PETER: And cut down by a third what you normally assign.

TEACHER: I would prefer to discuss each week what must be done before I commit myself to a third, unless you agree to doing homework over the weekend.

HELEN: That's fair.

TEACHER: How many would accept homework if I cut down the homework by a third whenever possible and gave no homework over the weekend, provided that we reevaluate this after we try it for a month? (Many hands go up.) I see that some of you did not commit yourselves. Does that mean that you want more homework or none?

SEVERAL: No homework.

TEACHER: This is very unrealistic. It is not entirely up to me to decide not to give you homework. I could cut down, but I really don't know how the principal, my supervisor, and your parents will react to this. I must give this some consideration.

I'll tell you what I would be willing to do. I will try what I just proposed. Let's see what happens. We can then discuss it again. This is all I can do. I would appreciate your understanding and your help in this matter. Our time is up. You have ample time to consider this and discuss it at our next group meeting. Until then, I will give you no work over the weekend and reduce the homework during the week.

In an earlier chapter on group discussions, it was mentioned that the teacher should get everyone to participate. In working with teenagers, it is important to confront the issues and to force adolescents to think about them. Not all issues are pertinent to all students. It is important to deal with crucial issues, even though all students are not aware of them.

Teenagers with their own values cannot be influenced individually. They need the group because it is a value forming agent. It is much easier to draw ten teenagers back to society than to work with just one of them.

The whole school system has to be built on discussion at every level: in the class, in a segment of the school, and among the teachers and the principals. The principal also should conduct group discussions with the teachers, since he should not decide alone what to do.

Each school, particularly junior high and high school, needs regular meetings in which students, teachers, and parents can get together to discuss their common problems. We can call these sessions "truce meetings." They should be on a level where participation for all is possible and where everybody can learn to understand each other and come to conclusions about solutions for their problems. Honest group discussion is the basis for a democratic school. Democracy itself is not possible without such meetings.

REFERENCE

Simons, Ida Harper. "A Guidance Program for Preadolescents," Dinkmeyer, Don C., editor. *Guidance and Counseling in the Elementary School*. New York: Holt, Rinehart and Winston, 1968.

SELECTED READINGS

Herbert, M. *Conduct Disorders of Childhood and Adolescence*. New York: Wiley, 1978.

Rogers, Carl R. *Freedom to Learn*. Columbus, Ohio: Merrill, 1969.

Chapter 24

Juvenile Delinquency

Juvenile delinquency has become one of the most serious problems of our society; it is especially noticeable now because of the rapid spread of drug abuse. No community or family is safe from the problem of delinquency and drug use. Most attempted solutions to the problem today are either punitive, which only deepen the warfare or permissiveness, which in turn only strengthen the adolescent's belief that he can do what he wants. Moralizing and reasoning are ineffective. Young people know when they do something wrong, and they know that it would be better if they did not do it, but this does not change their behavior or attitude.

When we talk to juvenile delinquents, we find that many of them suffer from a feeling of moral superiority; they look down upon society. They feel perfectly justified in punishing society for mistreating them, and they reveal their feelings of superiority by showing power and by defeating adults in authority whoever they are. They differ from normal teenagers in their degree of rebellion, for teenagers in general are critical of society and society's values.

Many delinquents are overambitious adolescents who set very high goals for themselves. They must be the best and they settle for nothing less than this. If they cannot be the best in socially acceptable behavior, they choose to be best in antisocial behavior. Being the worst is often a badge of honor for them.

We find that many delinquents have a pampered life-style, which makes them feel entitled to not be denied anything and to have their way. They resent the demands that life makes on them.

Reasons for Juvenile Delinquency

All sorts of reasons have been given for drug abuse. Some claim that drugs seem to offer adolescents an escape from a drab, depressing home life; some find that adolescents who come from affluent homes take drugs in order to escape boredom or to get even with demanding or autocratic parents; still others find that the majority of today's teenagers seek thrills and excitement, and drugs offer the greatest form of excitement. According to C. Murray (1976), adolescents seem to commit delinquent acts for three reasons:

1. the need to compensate for continued failure
2. economic needs brought on by the lack of marketable skills
3. too much idle time because of dropping out of school.

For Adlerians, causes do not exist in the sense that causes alone are responsible for people's actions. As we have already discussed, while all the above mentioned reasons for drug use are plausible, in the final analysis the individual decides how to react to his own experiences. There are many young people who come from impoverished areas or autocratic households and yet do not take drugs or become delinquents. We come back to explanations that were given already because we cannot stress enough the pitfalls of accepting causes for a person's behavior. The moment we do so, we set ourselves up for possible failure in helping young people to change.

Suggestions for Parents and Teachers in Dealing with Delinquents

There are a number of suggestions that we can offer to parents and teachers when they are dealing with delinquents. These techniques have proven to be effective whenever they have been applied.

The first step necessary when teachers and parents are dealing with delinquents is to give them the feeling that they are understood. Young people admire and appreciate any adult who communicates understanding of how they feel and of what they try to achieve through their behavior. Counseling a delinquent, therefore, involves a process of meaningful discussion—the kind that is bound to make the delinquent sit back and think. The counselor or the teacher must be a match for the delinquent and, in a sense, "trick" him if necessary, especially if he does not want any counseling.

COUNSELOR: Do you think that you will marry some day?
DELINQUENT: Probably.

COUNSELOR:	Do you think that you will have children?
DELINQUENT:	I don't know. Maybe.
COUNSELOR:	Would you like your child to be like you?
DELINQUENT:	My child won't be like me. (Frequent response)
COUNSELOR:	What makes you believe this?
DELINQUENT:	I just know it.
COUNSELOR:	Would you want your child to be like you?
DELINQUENT:	No. (Almost always)

Such a dialogue opens the way for the counselor to discuss mistaken goals and to help the delinquent understand himself. He receives no criticism or condemnation but rather insight into himself and to his actions.

Delinquents can be helped more effectively when they are counseled in a group, not because individual counseling has no value, but because delinquents are so peer conscious that group counseling and group discussions are more consequential. The teacher, because she teaches a group, has the potent means for facilitating the learning of positive values. The group can be influential in encouraging delinquents to change their behavior provided that the group creates a climate in which the individual student, no matter how he behaves, feels wanted and respected as a human being. This does not imply, however, that the class must accept his behavior. Group discussions were discussed in detail in Chapter 15.

At present, society shuts out the delinquents. The latter feel unwanted, not belonging and not respected. They feel no incentive to make any kind of positive contribution to a society that shuts them out. As a result, it is difficult for the educator or the counselor to motivate them to assume responsibilities toward others and be accountable for their behavior. Society would have to make it possible for them to feel needed, to feel that in spite of what they may have done in the past, they can still change and contribute to society. More than anything, we must provide opportunities for them to participate in decision-making. Unless they participate, they will feel no obligation to adhere to any decisions that others make for them. Unfortunately, parents and teachers often assume that they alone can decide what should be done, and they impose their decisions upon young people in general.

At a camp for juvenile delinquents the administration was successful in winning cooperation, until one day the principal arbitrarily decided to change the schedule from four study afternoons a week to two. The boys rioted and broke furniture in protest. This principal had violated the basic principal of participation in decision making, and it resulted in rebellion by the delinquents. When the principal realized his mistake, he asked the group to discuss the need for time allotted for afternoon studies, and he said that he would evaluate their decision and, hopefully, everyone would be satisfied. After several hours of debating the issue, the young people decided that two afternoons a week were all they wanted. It was exactly what the principal had decided, but before they felt that he had tried to force them into accepting a decision that he alone had made.

The riot was an overreaction to a dictate from an authority figure, but this is a typical example of what happens frequently when adults attempt to force delinquents into submission.

Solving problems can be done only on the basis of mutual respect. Young people have important contributions to make toward resolving problems. This is the essence of the democratic process, and this, in turn, opens means to changing society as a whole.

Other Suggestions for Dealing with Delinquents

Teachers can elicit help from former drug addicts and let them be discussion leaders. Rarely do former drug addicts advocate the use of drugs; on the contrary, they usually give an account of all the humiliations, the hardships, and often physical pain that they had to endure. In other words, these former delinquents can be a source of preventive education. They can act as "big brothers" or "sisters" who are caring and who are concerned about those in the process of becoming addicts themselves.

Teachers must distinguish between drug use and drug addiction and also determine if drugs are being used by young people because they are deeply discouraged and want to belong to a subgroup, which is better than not belonging, or because they want to show their power and to defy adults. This recognition will influence their treatment of the delinquents.

Counselors or teachers also must discuss the following things with the delinquent:

Could you possibly cut down on your use of drugs?
How much do you take now?
How much would you be willing to cut down?
Would you be willing to put yourself under a doctor's care?
Would you be willing not to smoke in school?

If the teenager agrees to any of the suggestions, the teacher must confront him with these two questions: "When will you start?" "Do we have an agreement?"

There are special formats for holding group discussions about drugs. Teachers and counselors can obtain these formats in any center that deals with drug prevention. But, the main emphasis of these discussions must always be on the *purpose* of behavior. For teachers who have students who take drugs, we suggest the following:

1. Set goals that are reachable and let the student experience the logical consequences of breaking an agreement. Such consequences should be discussed beforehand, and the student must agree to them. (See Chapter 13.)
2. Do not conduct group discussions when the student is high on drugs.
3. Show respect for the student so that he will respect you, in turn.
4. Accept the student in spite of his imperfections.
5. Encourage the student; do not defeat him.
6. Cooperate with the student; do not fight him.
7. Let the student feel useful and productive by enlisting his aid in solving problems, such as with his own drug addiction. Do not do it all for him in order to show him what a supercompetent adult you are.
8. Bring in experienced consultants.
9. Get together all teachers who have the same problem, and discuss and plan a preventive program together.
10. Since each class may have only one or two drug users, we suggest that all the students from the other classes who are on drugs should participate in the discussions and in finding solutions.
11. If possible, bring in the parents and guide them.

Parents are often very angry and ashamed when they find out that their child is on drugs, and often their methods of dealing with the problem only intensifies it.

A father came to a counselor for advice. He suspected that his son was taking drugs, but his son denied it. The father wanted to know what he could do to get the truth from his son. The counselor suggested that he tell his son that he and the boy's mother were concerned rather than angry, that they would like to help him if he were on drugs, and that they loved him and would do anything to help him.

A few days later, the boy came to see the counselor. He was very angry. He told the counselor that his father had induced him to tell "the truth" and that his father assured him that he wouldn't be angry or punish him. The boy then admitted to his father that he took drugs. It was true that his father did not scold or punish him; he just lifted his hands to heaven and cried out, "Oh, God, what have I done that you punish me so?"

This boy said that 100 lashes would not have been as painful to him as his father's reaction. He did not stop taking drugs. He only regretted having told his father.

Teachers should acquaint themselves with community referral centers and suggest to the student that he go there. At all times teachers should remember that they are not experts in such matters and that they should not feel discouraged if, in spite of everything they try, they have not been successful.

Frank Walton, a psychologist (1975), had excellent results when he used Adlerian principles with adolescents, many of whom had been serious delinquents. He has a program called "Project Win-Over." Walton addresses the students in the following manner: "Your ideas are very important to us. You are ___ (mentions number of students in the entire school), and there are only ___ number of teachers in the school. It would be a shame to waste so much brain power if we do not use you in solving our problems. If you don't talk, it will be most unfortunate because then the teachers will have to make all decisions themselves." He suggests the following:

1. Students and teachers should eat in the same dining room and should sit together at the tables.
2. There should be a common room for drinking coffee or soft drinks.
3. Students should be invited to propose amendments to school rules.
4. A policy should be implemented in which students could study and select a Student Council.
5. The Student Council should discuss problems with students.
6. Students, teachers, principals, secretaries, and janitors should all be present at the Student Council meetings.
7. The school should be referred to as "our school."
8. Students who are involved in vandalism should be invited to the meeting, and their help should be solicited.
9. Students who want power should be given responsible jobs so that they can experience success and feel accepted.
10. Students should have opportunities to negotiate contracts with regard to their work. A student may want to work at something that is different from what the rest of the class is doing.
11. Students should tutor other students.
12. Administrators should take time to mingle with students and talk to them.

Conclusions

Our objective is to help the delinquent to feel that he is capable of developing responsibility for and control over his own behavior. However, we cannot achieve this goal unless we help him first to experience our respect and our belief in him. Telling him that he must become responsible is something that he has heard before from his parents, judges, and other people. It falls on deaf ears. We must first befriend him before we can expect his cooperation. Acceptance by the class is of utmost importance. The peer group's encouragement carries more weight than all the lectures from adults. We must give him responsibilities that connote trust and respect—responsibilities they are bound to accept and enjoy. We must get them involved with school problems and listen to and try their suggestions, for only then will they believe that we respect their judgment and will they try to establish a relationship with us based on trust.

REFERENCES

Murray, C. *The Link Between Learning Disabilities and Juvenile Delinquency: Current Theory and Knowledge.* U.S. Department of Justice, Law Enforcement Administration, Washington D.C.: U.S. Government Printing Office, 1976.
Walton, Frank (Psychologist in private practice). "Project-Win-Over," from collection of private papers-1975, 660 Townes Road, Columbia, S.C. 29210.

SELECTED READINGS

Broder, P. K., Peters, G. W., and Zimmerman, J. *The Relationship between Self-Reported Juvenile Delinquency and Learning Disabilities: A Preliminary Look at the Data.* (National Criminal Justice Reference Service No. NCJ-50004, 1978.)
Maynard, R. *The Effects of Home Environment on School Performance.* Princeton, N.J., 1977 (ERIC Document Reproduction Service No. Ed 146 309).
Rutter, M. *Helping Troubled Children,* New York: Plenum Press, 1975.
West, D. J., and Farrington, D. P. *The Delinquent Way of Life.* New York: Crane Russak, 1977.

Chapter 25
Stealing

Stealing occurs frequently among children of all ages; among the poor, as well as the wealthy; among those who come from culturally well-to-do families, as well as from culturally impoverished ones.

Raymond Corsini and Genevieve Painter (1975) claim that overreacting to a child's misbehavior may actually reinforce that behavior because the child may enjoy the attention. Handling character problems is a touchy matter. We certainly do not want a child to think that morally unacceptable conduct is alright but, on the other hand, we do not want to frighten a child to such a degree that he is afraid to admit and discuss it. Let us illustrate this with the following example.

Bertha was the eldest of four children. She had to assume many responsibilities toward her younger siblings, especially after her mother died. Bertha was then 12 years old.

Bertha's father often was away from home, and she had to assume the role of both mother and father. When her father returned, he would give all of his attention to the younger children. Bertha felt very left out.

One day her father's pocketknife disappeared. After much searching, Bertha found it. Her father was so delighted that he hugged her and rewarded her with $1. Bertha had never experienced so much warmth and attention from her father. This experience gave her ideas: things started to disappear from the house, and usually it was Bertha who found them. Her father always rewarded her with a smile or a hug, until he caught on. Unfortunately, he punished her, and he withdrew his affection. This set Bertha in a real depression.

Corsini and Painter believe that

Angry lecturing and condemning are likely to do more harm than good. We should refrain from talking to the child like this: You are a thief and a liar! Not only did you steal but then, when I asked, you lied. People go to hell for lying and stealing! Such statements will probably make the child fearful and will certainly damage his self-respect.

Most children have stolen at one time or another. A child's attitude toward stealing depends on the culture in which he grows up, as well as on customs, traditions, religion, and training. In some groups stealing by children is not considered delinquent, especially in communities where people are poor. If a child steals food from the market and brings it home, he may be praised for the act. When a child steals in our society, we are shocked and frightened about his character development and may feel honor bound to return the stolen goods. We all know of a number of cases in which children have been severely punished, humiliated in front of others, or deprived of food or special privileges because they were caught stealing 5¢ out of a woman's purse or a candy bar from a store.

Respect for property is a product of social conventions that have existed for centuries. We are not born with the inherent sense that "what is mine does not belong to someone else" or the reverse. Respect for another person's property has to be learned. Children who have a great need to own property often find it difficult to respect the rights of others to own property. A child learns about what is "mine" when another child takes one of his toys. After a child learns "this is mine," he becomes aware of and can make the distinction between "mine" and "yours." Sometime after this distinction is made, the child recognizes that he cannot have everything he wants. Shortly after this, the child learns a lesson in elementary economics, which is, if you want something, you have to pay for it. He then knows what is fair, although he may act against his better judgment.

Owning property and enjoying property rights are two different things. Usually we give a child a toy, a record player, or some other object and then proceed to tell him what to do with it. How can we expect the child to respect the rights of others if we do not respect his rights?

At school children use equipment and other supplies as a class, and everyone in the room uses the record player, a game, balls, and the like. The manner in which they are used and the condition in which they are kept affect everyone, and the group might have something to say about how equipment is used.

One day Marie was marking on a new table in the classroom. Mike said, "Teacher, Marie is marking on your table." I replied, "My table? It's no more my table than it is your table or Marie's table. The table belongs to this school and, more particularly, to this classroom, so it is *our* table." A few minutes later, another child started marking on the table. At this point,

Marie turned to him and said, "Well, I'm not going to clean your old marks off this table." So they both cleaned off the table together.

The above example is a subtle lesson in respect for property and property rights. The more we let children assume responsibility for property, for property rights, and for their actions, the more they will respect property in general.

Learning to respect the belongings of others must be developed in the child, since it is an essential part of growing up. It must be taught through developing proper attitudes and appreciation for others and their rights, and through training in not only what is right and wrong but in willingness to do what is right.

Every teacher has had experiences with students who have taken possessions of others. In most cases, these students were reported to the principal and to the parents. A conference generally followed during which the child was faced with the facts and was told by the school authorities that if his behavior were repeated, he would face grave consequences. Often the mother cries and assures the principal and the teacher that this has never happened before, that she does not know from whom her child learned such bad behavior, and that he will suffer the consequences when she gets him home. Next, the teacher writes up the episode and places it in the child's folder as a constant reminder to future teachers to be on the alert.

When a person says, "My child steals," his statement tells us nothing. We know that people steal for a variety of reasons. Consequently, we need to look at the stealing from various angles. What prompts it? How is it reinforced? What are the consequences of the act? Is there a feeling of being poor and deprived? How does the child view himself? What is his background? How does he behave in school? How can we help him to find his place in the social order? We also need to know and recognize the difference between the first timer and the habitual thief. We need to look for a pattern in the child's theft.

A group of preadolescent boys developed a clever technique for smuggling books out of a public library. Their justification was that the library had enough money to replace the books. Superficially, it looked as if these boys did not know the difference between honesty and theft. Did they know the difference between the concept of "mine" and "yours"? Apparently not.

In looking for a reason for stealing, it is well to keep in mind that there are different types of stealing.

A mother came to school one afternoon to tell me about Tom. She burst into tears and told me that Tom had been picked up by the authorities for shoplifting. As she continued to sob, she also blurted out that her husband was in jail for stealing.

Here we have an example of a child who imitated the masculine pattern of his family. Children pattern themselves after impressive parental figures; learning takes place easily by watching others. It is impossible to say, "Do as I say, not as I do."

Miriam was a freshman in high school and came from a financially secure family. For several months, Miriam had been shoplifting from various stores. She never wore the articles but merely stuffed them in her dresser or closet. Her friends thought Miriam was the greatest, because she could snitch things without being caught.

Miriam had been dropping hints about her shoplifting for several weeks. She would say, "I saw the prettiest sweater. I thought about taking it, but I didn't." "Oh, Mother, they have the best smelling perfume at the store. Would you believe it, I just swiped a bottle of it?" After making these kinds of statements, she and her Mother would laugh the incident off as though it were a big joke. When this tactic did not work, Miriam left some of the stolen articles on the dining room table where her Mother could not miss them. At this point, they had a talk and came to me for help.

Here we find a girl who stole because she wanted attention from her family, peer recognition, and excitement. Now the parents pay more attention to Miriam. Before, both her parents were so busy working that neither of them took much time to enjoy their daughter.

Bernard was a second grader who stole money only from his mother. (Quite often his mother left change in her coat pocket.) Bernard would sneak nickels, dimes, and quarters. His mother noticed this and told him that he was a bad boy. She no longer left change in her coat, and he started taking money from her purse. Mother would chastise him by saying, "You bad boy, you have been in mother's purse again. How much did you take this time? Now you won't do that again, will you?" She would hide her purse in different places and tell him that he would not be able to find it, but he always did!

This is an example of a child who has learned to defeat his mother. His mother has reinforced Bernard's actions by constantly giving him opportunities to outsmart her.

These examples show different types of situations. It is impossible to put all these children into the same category and to treat them in the same manner. One child stole to follow a parental model; another stole to get attention; and another stole to defeat his mother.

The act of taking something should be examined in different ways, not just in terms of black or white, or good or bad. It can mean many things to a child. Stealing has strong consequences, and we need to substitute other behaviors for our customary reinforcement and to show the child alternatives for finding his place in life and for feeling important.

What other ways are there of getting peer recognition? What other ways are there to deal with family conflicts? What other ways are there of providing gratification? How can we reinforce different behavior patterns? In each of the preceding cases, the answers would be different, and dealing with each child should be different.

Briefly, the usual reason for stealing that children give is "for kicks," but other reasons include the need for peer recognition and status, irritation with a parent or other adult and the need, therefore, to defeat them, and the need to get what one wants regardless of the consequences. Stealing gratifies the desire for excitement, which is prevalent in our children and adolescents. However, stealing also may be a means of survival.

One of the most common motives for theft among children is bribery in order to win love and affection. The child wants to be the center of attention and has a strong urge to make himself noticed. Since to him it seems impossible to achieve his goal in positive or useful ways, he tries another.

Harold stole money in order to buy cigarettes for a group of somewhat older boys who would not accept him otherwise. When his father discovered this situation, he made Harold smoke an entire package of cigarettes, lighting one from the other, until the boy was so sick that he could not sit up. However, this experience did not cure him. His need to belong and to be accepted by the older boys was stronger than his fear of punishment, so he continued to steal for them.

Harold was only 10 years old, but he was tall and broad and looked like 14. He was embarrassed when he had to tell people that he was only in the third grade. He had failed twice and was still a poor student, despite his considerable intelligence. The children in his class ignored him, mostly because he kept away from them and acted aloof. He boasted about his friends, who were already in the seventh and eighth grades, and he often told them about their meetings and escapades.

Fortunately, this came to the teacher's attention only a few weeks after school started. The parents were cooperative. They soon realized that they had made some grave mistakes in dealing with the problem and changed their attitude and tactics. They were helped to understand that more than anything else, Harold needed to feel that he was somebody and that he had a place not only in school but at home as well. With the help of his parents and the class, Harold no longer felt the need for the friendship of the older boys. He became an integral member of his class, and he no longer had any need to steal.

In the next example we can see how a child's stealing and untruthfulness in general is an expression of her struggle for power over her mother. We can see also the child's desire to punish her mother for what she has done. When the child discovers the power she holds through stealing and lying, she uses these means to reduce her mother to helplessness and despair.

At the age of 10 Marsha was already a proficient thief. She stole mostly from 5-and-10-cent stores, taking candy, cosmetics, and knickknacks. She distributed the items, especially the candy among her friends. She hid the knickknacks in her bed, and she played with them and fondled them in the evening.

Eventually, Marsha was caught a few times, but in each case she was allowed to go free after getting a long lecture from the owner of the store or a salesperson. When the teacher learned about Marsha's escapades and when stealing was first discussed in class, Marsha not only laughed but called the other children "stupid" for not availing themselves of many commodities and goodies that were so easily accessible to them. "What are you afraid of?," she said, "Even if the police should catch you, they would never do anything to a child. They may punish your parents and hold them responsible, but they will let you go free. Besides, it's loads of fun to fool the salespeople, and when you pretend that you are sorry and you cry, they even let you keep the things you took."

Marsha was an only child of middle-aged parents. They adored and spoiled her. When she was 5 years old, her father died in a car accident, after which her mother clung to Marsha and gave into the child even more than before. When she was 8 years old, Marsha's mother fell in love with a man who did not take too well to Marsha. He was willing to marry the mother only if Marsha were to live away from home.

Thus, Marsha was placed in a boarding school. Here she became the despair of the staff, for she was not only aggressive, disobedient, and hostile but also extremely cunning and shrewd, evaded all problems, and induced the other children to do her dirty work, so that when they were discovered they seemed more guilty than she. Several times when her mother called for her during the weekend, Marsha hid and could not be found. A few times she ran away from her mother after they had left the boarding school, and her mother became desperate because she was unable to find her daughter, and she feared the worst.

Marsha was helped after some very trying months. She was helped mainly through group discussions, during which she began to understand the dynamics of her behavior, the goal she pursued, and the means she used to attain it. The members of the group, who understood her problem, reached out to her, and so did the teacher. As her attitude and her behavior improved, she was better accepted by her step-father. Marsha became much easier to live with and eventually was able to leave the boarding school.

It has been noted that acts of destructiveness quite often accompany the act of stealing. Destructiveness is usually a kind of hate or revenge in action. It also brings excitement. Many children who have suffered an injustice or feel slighted want to take revenge on others by being unfair.

A group of high-school girls from well-to-do families organized a social club outside of the school activities. The prerequisite to membership was shoplifting an expensive piece of clothing from one of the better stores. The girls went to the stores in twos or threes to make sure that the new recruit did not pay for the merchandise.

After initiation into the club, the requirement was that several articles were to be stolen each week and brought to a "bonfire party" every Saturday. At this time, all the articles were burned and plans were made for the following week. Under no circumstances were the articles to be worn, given away, or used in any manner.

These girls were brought up with little or no supervision from their parents. Usually, the only times they were really noticed was when they were in the way or when some social event was coming up; then their parents worried about whether their daughters would have escorts or they made arrangements so their daughters would be included.

Generally, the goal in stealing is to enrich oneself and to feel important by possessing more. There is also the feeling of being poor and deprived even if one is wealthy in a material sense.

There are children who steal because they are trained to do so by their parents. Yet neither of them is aware of the fact.

Ronnie was a fifth-grade boy who had been taking children's milk money. When the teacher mentioned this to Ronnie's mother during a conference, the mother became unreasonably upset. She insisted on punishing Ronnie in front of the entire class. She said that her husband would beat Ronnie with a stick. During all of this the mother was sobbing bitterly.

Later during a class discussion, Ronnie told the class how he stole tomatoes from a neighbor's garden. When the children asked him why he would do such a dishonest thing, he said that his mother always sent him to steal from the gardens when neighbors were away from home.

This is not unusual when we consider the number of parents who instruct their children to tell a peddler or a bill collector that they are not at home or to tell lies when someone calls on the telephone and they do not wish to talk. Parents do not realize how they teach children to regard a lie as an expedient thing if one does not want to get into trouble. Consider the parents who tell their children to lie about their age when they take public transportation or when they take them to any public places where children pay according to their age.

Most adults become upset if their children steal a nickle or a balloon. Yet how many adults cheat on their income tax or try to smuggle something through customs? Most adults, however, make a distinction between stealing from an individual and stealing from an organization. They are most hesitant to steal from an individual but think nothing of using the office stamps to mail their personal Christmas cards. Most children who steal do not make such a distinction; they steal when the opportunity offers itself.

One of the problems we face today is the attitude some store owners take toward petty thievery among children. In the example concerning Marsha, she confidently stated that "they won't do anything to a child." It is very difficult for parents and teachers to train children in morality when it is taken so lightly by people in the community. A child's sense of right and wrong comes from the attitudes of those with whom he is closely associated: first his immediate family and then the community.

Many teachers find themselves in a tough spot when some children in their class complain that something was stolen. Most are inclined to investigate. They feel obliged to find out the culprit. When they have some idea, they struggle to have the child admit the theft and to return what was stolen. Many teachers find it helpful to stay out of such struggles.

"Many children lie or steal in order to put something over." This makes them feel very superior to those who were not smart enough to find them out. If the child arranges the situation so that the teacher discovers his transgression, we can be sure that the purpose of it was to get attention. If, however, he tries to deny it, then we may be certain that he is trying to show his power. This child may feel that he has the right to get what he wants, regardless of the method.

> Fifteen-year-old Vernon was caught stealing a guitar from a music shop. When questioned, he said, "I wanted one, and I couldn't pay for it, so why not? It's not such a big loss for the store, and I wanted it." He could not accept that he did something wrong.

We must remember that the acts of lying or stealing are symptoms of a deeper underlying rebellion. A stolen article should be returned in almost all cases. We should, however, downgrade the seriousness and remain unimpressed. The child should be exposed to the logical consequences of his act: return the article or make restitutions. There should be no moral preaching. This may be very difficult for teachers who believe that they have the obligation to teach the child not to do such things. The child knows very well that he has transgressed, even when he argues the point. Scorn, criticism, and punishment, however, do not teach him *not* to lie or steal; on the contrary, they provide him with further ammunition and an increased desire to do wrong for the sake of power and to defeat adults. The child does not need any instruction; he knows very well that lying and stealing are wrong. Stealing reveals how little the child regards the clearest and most convincing moral principle. And, in spite of our indignation and our fear that the child may be on the road to crime, we can best influence the child by establishing a good relationship with him and by helping him see alternatives that will make him important in the eyes of others.

> Ed was caught stealing dictionaries from the school library. Although he was severely reprimanded and although he had to return the books, he continued stealing other people's belongings both in school and in his home.

When the counselor discussed with Ed the serious consequences that would follow his behavior, he said, "At least my father will have the satisfaction of being right in his predictions. He always tells me that I will end up in jail. He even cautioned my cousin not to associate with me because I am a criminal who is bound to be caught and punished sooner or later."

There is no surer means of driving a child into the arms of crime than to treat him like a felon and picture him as a future criminal. If we want to help him, we must first establish a relationship built on trust and respect. If we wait until the child deserves respect, we are adding to his defiance and to his conscious or subconscious wish to get even with us. This is especially true if the anger and the need to retaliate are directed toward parents. In such a case, our corrective efforts must include the counseling of the parents as well as of the youngster. Ed had to be helped to see how he was willing to "cut off his nose to spite his face" and was sacrificing his education, reputation, and future in order to get even with his father. He must be helped to see alternatives to his behavior to free himself from his overdependency on getting positive reinforcement from his parents, and to realize the power he gives to his father over his life. Both father and son need to be helped toward a better relationship and better communication. Some children need to be helped to understand how they lost the distinction between "mine" and "yours." This never occurs without deep-seated conflicts, but the incidental provocations to steal are various. One child steals because he wants to have immediately whatever his heart desires. He does not want to wait, and he does not care about the consequences. These are usually children who have received whatever they wanted when they were young and who cannot see why there should now be any deviations from this rule. Hence, sporadic thievery is common in uncontrolled children who have been indulged too much.

The child usually does not understand why he steals. When we ask the child why he has stolen, we get either a stubborn silence or a puzzled "I don't know." It is true; he does not know. It is up to the teacher, the counselor, or whoever works with the child to track down the deeper psychological motives behind his behavior of whether stealing served as an attention getting device or as a tool for power and revenge. The child, then, has to be confronted with his goal and helped to find a better solution to his problem.

Hannah was a well-behaved child of 8. She came from a well-established family in the community. She had everything she wanted, yet she often very skillfully stole from candy shops, stationery stores, and gift shops. Nobody could understand the reason for her acts. Hannah refused to tell them why she took things from stores or what she did with them. She was too frightened, not of punitive consequences from her parents, but of losing their love and respect.

One of the children in her class told the teacher that Hannah always brought sweets and gifts, which she distributed among the class. Why would this well-cared-for child resort to such behavior? Upon investigation, we learned that she was the youngest child in the family. In comparison with her older, very capable, and popular sister, Hannah felt insignificant. By handing out gifts to children, Hannah could impress them and distinguish herself. She was very successful, as most children wanted to play with her, sit next to her, and so on.

Hannah was helped to understand why she stole. She was encouraged to feel good about herself, and she was helped to realize that she could be liked for what she was, without having to impress the children through gift giving. Hannah's parents were helped to encourage the child and to give her a feeling of importance. They were told that they should never compare her with her sister or lecture or punish her because of her previous stealing. Hannah was greatly helped within a comparatively short time.

Quite different was the case of 15-year-old Robert. It was much more difficult to understand what moved this boy to take valuables and hide them at home. He neither sold them nor boasted of them. His situation, in brief, was the following:

His father was very strict, and Robert, the eldest of three children was particularly closely watched. He had a tendency to take life easy, and allowed himself liberties that his father could not condone. He took walks instead of studying, and failed to come home punctually. He smoked cigarettes quite early. All in all, he was in obvious revolt against his father. The middle brother, two years younger than Robert, was his opposite, As could be expected, this brother was notably careful and painstaking, and thus became the perfect example of his father's principles.

Robert, too, was unable to say why he stole. His earlier misdemeanors had been rather simple and harmless, but they all evinced his desire to triumph over order and his father. Everything he did was under cover. It was like a secret compensation: "You see, I do what I want, anyway!" Nor was it so senseless that he allowed his stealing to be discovered, for each revelation defied anew his father's ideas. These principles had proved themselves powerless. And herein, apparently, lay the boy's secret aim in life—to demonstrate the futility of the coercion exercised by the social order through his father" (Dreikurs, 1972, pp. 71–72)

This propensity to snap one's fingers at authority lies at the bottom of a great many defiant and even criminal acts. This tendency to get the better of someone explains many thefts by children. Only too often do we find that the root of the problem lies within the family—the child's position in the family constellation, and his perception of that position, and the parent's attitude toward the child as compared to their attitudes toward the other children. Teachers are not trained to investigate and are not knowledgeable of these factors. Therefore, they do not consider them when they deal with a student who steals. What they do mostly is dispose of such incidents with an excess of anger, punishment, threats, or demands that the parents handle the situation. In this way they often pour oil on the fire. The children may then determine to get even with both—the parents and the school. Of course, there are children who do a great deal of stealing that never comes to the attention of the family. Most of these children eventually give up this practice. We may say that often it is to the child's advantage if the parents do not know. Many readers may have been in this situation. There is hardly a child who did not take something at one time. This does not preclude that the child is or will turn out to be a thief. The child is bound to give up this practice if he is helped by an understanding teacher to develop social relationships in class, to experience success, and to feel valued.

Violence and Brutality

The stubborn resistance to order often assumes terrifying forms. Sometimes it is limited to fits of anger, in which case the child retains a certain goodwill and excuses his eruptions of brutality afterward. But when these outbursts occur frequently and without pretext of being involuntary, the last vestige of goodwill has vanished and the naked antagonism is revealed. This bold-faced brutality presupposes a mixture of weakness and violent oppression on the side of the parents. Intelligent children can develop the most efficient techniques for getting at their parents' vulnerable spots and thus may become a real menace.

Many of these children were very much indulged by their parents. When this indulgence is withdrawn, they try to force their parents to give in to them by making their parents fear what their child will do if he does not get his way. Many children are brutal because they were brought up with brutality. The cruelty shown to the child is often the source of the child's own brutality. The child reflects what he has experienced. Some have not actually been abused, but they feel that they have been and react against this feeling. Occasionally, brutality is merely a tool to experience the gratification of complete power over other human beings.

Excessive strictness, especially whipping, may stir up rebellion and arouse brutal behavior. This is especially true if one of the parents feels sorry for the child and makes up to him for the spouse's severity and gives in to the child's demands. Neglect may have the same effect. In both cases, the child feels justified in his desire to seek revenge. Before any improvement in the child's behavior can be achieved, the conflict must be ended, at least on the side of the parents. If a natural consequence cannot be easily and consistently applied, it is as well to do nothing at all. It may make a strong impression on the child if he suddenly recognizes that he no longer can intimidate and hurt.

What can the teacher do when she has a child in class who resorts to brutality? She cannot, in such a case, allow the child to abuse others. Still, she must be careful about when to interfere and when not to interfere. It is advisable for her to refer this child to the school psychologist or social worker. In most cases, the parents need counseling. The peer group can help this child realize that they do not appreciate his behavior and will not stand for it, but, at the same time, the peer group can be of greater influence on the child than the teacher. The class must not reject the child; on the contrary, the class must show interest, concern, and, at the same time, make it quite clear to this child that they do not admire his brutal behavior. They should watch for opportunities when the child does not resort to brutal behavior and show their appreciation. This is bound to encourage the child to reevaluate his usual behavior.

In some cases, especially if it concerns an adolescent, it may be advisable to remove the child from the parental home and place him either in a boarding school, with caring relatives, or in a foster home. Gradually, this child will learn to adapt himself to an orderly scheme of existence.

REFERENCES

Corsini, Raymond, and Painter, Genevieve. *The Practical Parent*. New York: Harper & Row, 1975.

Dreikurs, Rudolf. *Coping with Children's Misbehavior*. New York: Hawthorne Books, 1972.

Chapter 26
Lying and Swearing

Children pattern themselves after their parents or other important adults. They may learn to lie from their parents when they want to escape responsibility or punishment. Sometimes parents perpetuate a family lie in order to make their child appear to be a good boy or to preserve the family reputation. Children may lie for different purposes: to be left alone, to get attention, to impress or fool others, to get out of a situation, to hurt others, to respond to pressure, to fantasize, to excuse themselves, or to reduce their own anxiety. How does a child distinguish between legitimate and illegitimate lying?

Truth and Untruth

In most cases adults cannot tell what is true and what is not true. There are whole areas in which adults cannot be sure of whether a child is lying or telling the truth. They do not have control over reports, and they have no evidence if they do not observe the behavior. The consequences for lying are so uncertain. Sometimes adults punish children for telling the truth, and sometimes they reward them for lying. Sometimes, too, a parent's concept of a lie or the truth differs considerably from the child's concept.

Severe parents and teachers give children abundant reasons for lying. Untruth is then a simple method of escaping unreasonable punishment. A lie would have no meaning unless the truth were felt to be dangerous. Children who do not fear telling the truth, that is, who do not get punished by those who have power, rarely lie. Children will tell the truth if they feel sufficiently strong. Children lie out of fear or out of a need to appear superior in the eyes of others and to compensate for their own feelings of inadequacy or inferiority.

THE CASE OF JIMMY

Here is a detailed case description of a boy named Jimmy. One day, a boy entered my classroom and asked if I would allow him to "show and tell" something to my class. I granted permission, thinking that he had to make an announcement. To my surprise he pulled out a rock from his pocket and proceeded with a very interesting and competent lecture on gold mining. He said that he had visited several gold mines and that he had made a thorough study of the subject.

Our first impression of this boy would, no doubt, be that here is a child with a lot of guts and self-assurance who is interrupting a teacher in what she is doing. In spite of the interruption, we may be inclined to admire him for his competency and for sharing his knowledge with the entire class. However, the teacher, who has been trained to examine motivation of behavior and to analyze the goal and purpose that the child had set for himself, would immediately recognize that this child is taking the stage in order to be the center of attention.

There are two forms of attention that children seek. Some children, who do not yet believe in their ability to gain a place among their peers without the support of an adult, will seek the attention of the adult. Others are primarily concerned with getting attention from their peers. In this case we see that Jimmy wants attention from the group and that he has the ability to get it.

He thanked me for giving him permission to talk, adding that although he took much of my time it was not lost time, since the students learned something about gold mining.

This last remark makes us wonder if attention is all that the boy wants. In a very subtle way he has tried to place the teacher in a position in which she has to be thankful to him. There is an element of superiority in this remark, and it may indicate a need for power, although, at this point, it is limited to the intellectual level. His approach is well planned and well executed. There is no question in our minds about the intelligence of this boy.

He gave his name as Jimmy. He was a seventh-grade student. The boy aroused the teacher's curiosity, and she asked the seventh-grade teachers about him. None had him in class, and they did not know who he was.

LEARNING DIFFICULTIES CLASS

The following year, Jimmy's name appeared on the teacher's class list. She was surprised because she taught a class of children with learning difficulties, covering the subjects from first to fourth grade. At first she thought that perhaps Jimmy's name was put on her list by mistake, since supposedly he had been in the seventh grade the previous year. When she checked with his teacher she discovered that he had been only in the fourth grade the previous year, that he had repeated the second and third grades, and that he was classified as a nonreader.

The fact that Jimmy cannot read is our first important clue to Jimmy's problem. Why has this intelligent boy not learned how to read? We know that children who are not actually mentally defective can learn how to read. They may not, and usually do not, understand what they are reading, but they can learn to decipher the printed symbols and may actually read fluently. Children who do not learn how to read have excellent private reasons for not being willing to learn. We must investigate why Jimmy does not want to learn how to read. So far, we do not yet have enough information about Jimmy, but we can speculate and set up a tentative hypothesis. Is this boy an overindulged and dependent child? We know that there is a high correlation between dependency in children and their subconscious resistance to reading or to functioning independently.

We may also suspect that a younger brother or sister who is doing very well in school is a discouraging factor, but, so far we do not know.

The teacher also learned that he had accumulated a great deal of knowledge about various subjects and that he liked to show off his knowledge whenever he had a chance.

We can see that Jimmy is an ambitious boy. He seeks recognition and status. It would also appear that he is overcompensating for his feelings of inferiority since he is below grade level. He has succeeded in accumulating a great deal of knowledge beyond what the other children have, but where and how does he get it, since he cannot read?

On the first day of school, when the students introduced themselves, Jimmy made the following statement: "You are probably wondering how come a boy of my age happens to be in this class. All I can say is that I have had bad luck. I was sick most of my life, and I was in and out of hospitals most of the time. As you know, there are no schools in hospitals where one can learn how to read and how to spell. But there were many doctors in the hospital. They used to come and talk to me for hours, and from them I learned more about sickness and medicine and even operations than the nurses did."

When the children asked him what was wrong with him, he said that he had a rare disease, unknown to medicine before, and that his case will go down in history. When they asked what symptoms he had, he replied that this was still a secret and that he was not allowed to reveal anything about his illness, but that his case would soon be published and then everybody would be able to read about it.

There is no doubt in our minds that this is an overambitious child with a strong drive for superiority. He needs to be something special; being equal, and certainly being inferior to those around him, is unbearable for him. With such a belief he can never accept himself for what he is or gather enough power to move forward on his own. We may assume that he has been exposed to social humiliation over a long period of time. He may have been teased by his classmates and criticized by his family for his lack of progress in school. Perhaps he was also shamed by his teachers. Jimmy is trying to overcompensate for these humiliations by granting himself the kind of prestige that none of the others have. He must safeguard himself against further disgrace, even if he has to resort to cunning and lying.

There is something very pathetic in his defensive explanations about his illness and slowness in school. We sense his discouragement in spite of his exaggerated report of his importance.

If such a child is to regain his self-confidence, we must remove any pressure with regard to his learning. It is obvious that Jimmy was trying to get the admiration of the whole class. It is also obvious to the other children that he is telling lies. It is possible that Jimmy is aware of this also, but at this moment he has the center stage, which is very important to him.

The teacher asked the class if they could put Jimmy in charge of washing and bandaging minor cuts and bruises, since he knew so much about medicine. They thought that it was a good idea, because it would save the school nurse a lot of time.

The teacher is trying to induce the entire class to give Jimmy the experience of being needed and appreciated. This is her first opportunity to encourage him.

The following day, Jimmy came to class with a white band and a red cross over his arm. The teacher found him surrounded by children, explaining the meaning of the Red Cross and where and how it started. Again, he was well informed. When the teacher asked him where he gathered so much information, he replied that he had read about it, but he immediately corrected himself, saying that his uncle had told him about it. Evidently he suddenly remembered that only the previous day he had told the class that he could not read. The teacher complimented him, saying that some day he might become a great scientist.

We can see that on the one hand, Jimmy lacks self-confidence, but on the other hand, he is constantly seeking and finding ways to be the center of attention. We also notice in him the quality of leadership. It is no small success to have the entire class listen and pay attention to him.

It seems that the teacher succeeded in giving Jimmy a feeling of being welcome. She ignored his deficiencies and in this way opened the door to his feeling of belonging to the class. Her success was a result of her determination to use every opportunity to show respect for and a belief in him, something he may have never experienced before.

JIMMY'S FAMILY CONSTELLATION
Jimmy was the oldest of three children and the only boy. His grandparents had emigrated from Greece when his father was a young man.

This is additional important information about Jimmy that will hopefully lead to a better understanding of Jimmy's problem. We know that the position a child holds in the family constellation is a great factor in his personality development. Jimmy is a firstborn child and a male. This is an important consideration, especially the fact that his father and grandparents came from a patriarchal society, where the man is the boss of the house and where a male child automatically inherits certain birth rights not granted to girls. Much is expected of this boy.

Our next piece of important information is that he is dethroned by a girl. Unfortunately, we do not know for how long Jimmy was an only child. However, we may assume that as the firstborn he may have been pampered and indulged. Before the first girl was born, he may have been treated like a prince by the entire family.

Jimmy's father became a very successful businessman. He married an American girl who was a school teacher. In addition to the immediate family, there lived in the house Jimmy's mother's brother, a chemist, and his paternal grandparent.

Jimmy may have been the center of attention of many adults. In a sense, he had more than one set of parents. There is a strong possibility that he was exposed to different influences and values because his grandparents and his father came from a different cultural background than his mother and his uncle.

Jimmy's mother was a very sick woman who spent a great deal of time in the hospital. His two sisters were very close, and they left Jimmy out of their relationship and activities. Both of them were good students. The sister closest in age to him was a grade higher in school than he was.

Our first assumption seems to be confirmed. Jimmy was defeated by a younger sister who not only dethroned him but also surpassed him in school. This is very threatening to any firstborn, especially to a boy of Jimmy's cultural background.

His grandparents favored the girls, who were affectionate, helpful in the house, and smart. They considered Jimmy to be stupid, a liar, and lazy.

Most children find support in their grandparents. Usually, grandparents are indulgent and gentle with their grandchildren, no matter what the children may do. In this case, even the grandparents have failed Jimmy.

Jimmy's father was very disappointed in his son. He made no secrets about his feelings. He told Jimmy that he would never amount to anything, and he threatened that he would not leave his business to a "good-for-nothing son."

Here is an abundance of significant data from a psychological point of view. We notice a very definite struggle with his father. Both of them are discouraged. The father seems to have given up all hopes of making a *man* out of Jimmy—a man with self-confidence and with a sense of responsibility toward the family and toward the future.

Jimmy may be as overambitious as his father is, and therefore afraid that he will not be able to live up to his standards. He may not feel that he is a man: he is a male, but he does not compare with his father. This increases his feelings of inadequacy. He is a first child, however, and he must maintain his position at all costs. We see that Jimmy cannot compete with his sisters, so he gives up. But he had to find something that would bring attention from his father, and so he became a problem child, thus keeping his father continuously busy with him. We now see that he is acting intelligently but for the wrong purpose.

We also see that Jimmy is creative and resourceful. He operates with a wide range of purposes. At times he is seeking attention, and at times he is in a subtle power contest. Surely, he could change his behavior at home and at school if, subconsciously, he would not resist pressure. We may also suspect an element of revenge, especially against his father. From his point of view, opposing his father has brought him success.

During a conference with Jimmy's father, the teacher learned that Jimmy's father blamed Jimmy's difficulties partly on heredity (from his wife's family) and partly on his wife, who, he felt, "pampered and spoiled the boy." The teacher also found out that Jimmy had a close relationship with his mother, that he spent much time with her, amusing her with funny stories, and that he always cried when she left for the hospital.

This warrants further speculation. We notice an unusual alliance, namely, between mother and son. This probably is an alliance against the father. We may assume that the father is also disappointed in his wife who is sick so often and that he neglects her. Although we have no details about the home situation, we may assume that Jimmy is siding with her against his father. We do not know to what extent his mother may plead with her husband not to be so strict with Jimmy, thus protecting him. Since she is a sick woman, he may yield to her but not without resentment against both of them.

It is interesting to note the extent to which Jimmy has been a focal point of opposing forces within the family: grandparents, father, and sisters against Jimmy and his mother. We still do not know the role that the uncle plays in the family, but we can assume that he, too, is on Jimmy's side.

Jimmy cries when his mother goes to the hospital. This is our first indication that he tries to get attention by obtaining pity for himself. But knowing his father's values and attitudes toward the male sex, we can only assume that his father feels more contemptuous over such displays of weakness.

The teacher learned that Jimmy was always a healthy boy. He had never been in a hospital.

It is possible that Jimmy obtained his information about hospitals from his mother. His school records showed that he had been a show-off since kindergarten and that he was frequently absent from school. Jimmy probably felt that he had no status in class.

JIMMY'S POSITION IN CLASS
Jimmy was the oldest student in class. At first, he was very conscious of this fact. He used every opportunity to remind the class that he was in the class only because of the years he had spent in the hospital.

Being much older than the other children in his class is an unfortunate strike against Jimmy. His discouragement is twofold: he doubts that he can do the work as well as the other, younger children, but at the same time he feels that he must show them that he is superior to them.

Once, after he had again brought up the subject of the years he had spent in hospitals, the teacher asked the class why Jimmy gave this matter so much thought and why he used every opportunity to remind them of it. This developed into an animated discussion. Some children said that Jimmy must feel very ashamed to be so far behind in school, and this was how he justified it. Some said that Jimmy thought that by telling them about the hospital they would feel sorry for him and would not be so critical of him. Others said that he wanted to be noticed and admired. Jimmy denied that he wanted any of these things. The teacher asked the class if, in their opinion, Jimmy got anything out of this kind of behavior. Some felt that it served as an excuse for not doing any work, but the majority of the children felt that Jimmy was so afraid that nobody would notice him that he demanded their attention by telling stories in which he was something special.

Here the teacher is taking the first step in soliciting the help of the group by discussing Jimmy's behavior, not from a critical point of view but to help Jimmy and all the children in class to look for purposes in behavior. It is interesting to notice how well the children understood that Jimmy was safeguarding himself by telling them that he could not read because he was in the hospital, thereby hoping that his failure would be excused without having to assume any responsibility for it.

The teacher asked the group if Jimmy could get attention in any other way, and if so, if they could tell him in what way. The children said that they admired him very much for his knowledge in science and for his ability in sports.

Jimmy's ability in sports is surprising. We would have expected that such realistic achievement that puts him ahead of his class would suffice to flatter his ego and that it would be this area that he would exploit in order to have status with his peers. For this very ambitious child, being good in just one area is, evidently, not sufficient. He does not think that he is good enough unless he is exceptional. There were other children in class who were also good in sports, but Jimmy could stand no competition.

Jimmy, who was sulking until then, looked up and smiled for just an instant. He quickly resumed his angry expression.

At this point, Jimmy is determined to show them that they are wrong. Perhaps he is continuing in the classroom the power contest he has with his father. He tries to defeat both by his display of obstinacy. Smiling openly would to him be an admission that they were correct in their evaluation.

The teacher asked him if he knew that the children admired him, and he shook his head. When she asked for a show of hands of those who admired and liked him, most of the children raised their hands. The teacher asked Jimmy to look up and count his friends, but he refused. He was angry for the rest of the day.

This supports the above supposition. He does not give in easily. However, it is possible that this experience had encouraging effects. Probably Jimmy never before experienced an open display of acceptance by his peer group.

The teacher had decided to encourage Jimmy in sports since this required no reading.

The teacher was careful not to choose a subject or an activity in which Jimmy might possibly fail or do poorly. She was trying to build on his strength.

The teacher discussed this with the students one day when Jimmy was not in school. They all thought that this was a good idea.

Some may argue that this was not a spontaneous and natural reaction on the part of the class and that the teacher plotted, using the class in her endeavor. This is absolutely true. However, it does not diminish its effectiveness. If any, it demonstrates that, basically, children are good and eager to be of help to others provided that we lead and motivate them in this direction.

The next time that the group met for a regular class discussion one of the students suggested that the class form a baseball league with Jimmy as its leader. They also suggested that they invite another class to join them. Jimmy liked this idea very much, and he went to work immediately. He went into the other classroom to talk to the teacher about the suggestion. When he returned, he looked radiant. He had managed to organize the first match. The children showed open amazement and admiration.

Jimmy soon became the leader of both groups. He practiced with them after school, and he reported daily to the children in class.

The significance of this maneuver lies in the fact that the teacher spotted Jimmy's one advantage—his ability in sports—and acted upon it. She moved him from a negative to a positive position, for he is moving into active participation.

From that day on Jimmy participated in all activities that did not require reading. No one made any point of the fact. When the children read, Jimmy either listened or he occupied himself with something without disturbing the class.

When the teacher suggested to him that he could be helped by any student he might like to work with, he refused such help. He did, however, agree to let the teacher work with him for 15 minutes each day.

This is the first breakthrough that will lead in the right direction. Discouragement has been counteracted by initial success, but this is only a start that may or may not develop further. We hope that this will be a turning point for this child. The teacher has succeeded by now in winning Jimmy's cooperation, but this does not indicate that she has also succeeded in changing his outlook or his goal.

Every now and then the children would ask Jimmy to join any reading group he would like. They assured him that this would make them happy, that they would like to help him, and that they could help him if he would let them, but he still refused.

This situation confirms our feeling of Jimmy's obstinacy. A child who feels that life is worth living only if he is superior to others will stay away from activities that do not provide him with the opportunity to prove his superiority. Such a child lacks the courage to be imperfect.

One day the teacher told the children a story about a boy who wanted very much to know how to swim but who refused to go into the water until he knew how to swim. At this, Jimmy burst out in uncontrollable laughter. He said that this boy must be very stupid to think that he could learn how to swim without going into the water. The teacher agreed with him that this boy would never learn how to swim in this manner but that she did not think that this boy was necessarily stupid. She then asked the class to think of a reason this boy might have for not going into the water. Most children felt that he was afraid that he would never learn how to swim and did not want other people to know this. By saying that he would first have to learn how to swim before he would go into the water, this boy thought that he could protect himself from showing his real reason. The children emphasized that what this boy felt and what he did was not smart but that this was no indication that he was dumb otherwise.

The teacher then asked Jimmy if he knew anyone who behaved in a similar way to this boy. He did not reply to the question.

It is interesting to see how a child who does not understand the behavior of another person therefore assumes that the person is stupid but never associates his own behavior with such an interpretation. Although children are quick to understand the purpose of other people's behavior when they personally are not involved, this does not hold true when it concerns their own behavior. Such children must be helped to understand the fictitious goal that they have set for themselves.

At the end of the day, after the class was dismissed, Jimmy stopped at the teacher's desk and told her that he realized that she had meant him when she asked him that question. She agreed with him and asked if he intended "to go into the water." Jimmy cried for the first time. He said that he was ashamed that the children would laugh if they heard his halting reading.

Did Jimmy cry in order to get the teacher's sympathy or was this a first admission that he might be wrong? We are inclined to believe the latter. If so, this would indicate his first courageous step.

In a mirror technique, the teacher succeeded in showing him how silly his actions were, without shaming him in the process. (In the mirror technique another person takes on the role of the identified person and talks and behaves exactly like this person does. This gives the identified person an opportunity to learn how he comes across to others.) She told him that she did not think that the children would laugh at him if he read aloud but that he would have to find this out for himself. He said that he wanted to wait a little longer.

So far Jimmy has consistently declined all friendly invitations to try to read. Although he wants to wait a little longer, he is not actually refusing. This is hopeful. It is important to notice that the teacher has made no promises to Jimmy, not only because she is in no position to make any, but more so because it is important for Jimmy to learn to take chances. It is his fear of failure that paralyzes him; therefore, he must concentrate on removing such fears, even at the risk of failure.

As the students progressed in their reading and as they started to give book reports, Jimmy's mood changed. He appeared gloomy and absentminded. He also started to cut classes.

What might be the reason for this change? There is definitely a sign of new discouragement. Possibly the fact that the other children are successful and receive attention, especially when they give book reports, is discouraging to Jimmy. Too little attention might be being paid to him. This kind of reversal or regression is not rare in overambitious children when they think that they are losing ground.

One day he announced that the club to which he belonged (which he had never mentioned before) was sending him to New York City to play in a baseball tournament and that he would be absent for three days. Everyone was very curious about this trip, and they asked many questions. Jimmy was once more in his element. He did not show up for three days. When he returned, he gave a full report of the events and of the places he visited: Times Square, Radio City, and others. Again, he was well informed and could answer most of the questions posed by the curious students.

We see how ingenious this boy is, and how well he lays plans and executes them.

Suddenly it occurred to the teacher that she had not asked Jimmy to bring a statement from his parents regarding his trip and that this might have been another tall tale. She called his home and learned that he had never been away from home; that every morning he left as usual, but he did not return until the time he normally returned.

This should not surprise us. He was driven by his need to be special.

During the next discussion meeting, the teacher asked the class if they could figure out why children tell tall tales. She did not mention what she had learned about Jimmy. Most children felt that tall tales were told by people who did not believe that they could find admiration from others in any other way. They also brought out that these people never gave themselves a chance to find out if they were right and that they often operated on false assumptions. Jimmy did not participate in the discussion. The teacher asked him if he would like to comment, but he shook his head and remained silent.

It may sound as if the teacher is demanding too much of the children. Many teachers may question the advisability of involving the class in the problems of an individual child. This indicates that the teacher lacks confidence in the children's ability and eagerness to understand behavior, and especially to be helpful to others. Children want to solve their problems, and school is the best, if not the only place, where such training is possible. We must be careful not to extend our adult anxieties and inadequacies to children and thereby teach them to avoid facing problems and finding solutions to them. At all times, we must refrain from fault-finding and from becoming punitive.

We notice that in this example the teacher did not make any fuss, nor did she confront Jimmy directly with his lie. She did not even mention Jimmy's name during the discussion. In a way, the teacher was put on the spot, having transgressed a school regulation, which requires children to bring notes from home whenever they want to take off from school. The average teacher probably would have reported the incident to the principal. How different this situation might have turned out had she done so. All that was gained would have been destroyed, and she would have lost the friendly relationship that she had established with the child.

The following morning Jimmy came to school somewhat earlier than usual. He came straight to the teacher's desk and told her that he had heard that she had called his father. He demanded to know why she had done it. He appeared very angry.

It is not uncommon for children who operate out of a need for power to consider anything that may indicate disapproval by others as unfair. Perhaps Jimmy was trying to get the teacher involved in an argument.

The teacher told him that she had violated a school regulation by not asking for a note from his parents and that for her own protection as well as his she needed confirmation from his parents that they gave their approval for his absence. The teacher also added that she liked him and that she wanted to do all she could to help him, but in order for her to know what to do, she had to know the facts. She also pointed out that the children in class felt the same as she did and that he must surely have noticed it. The teacher reminded him of the discussion that the group had had the previous day, regarding discouraged people. The teacher told him that she felt that he was such a person, afraid of failure to such a degree that he would not risk the chance of trying and finding out if he was right or wrong. She asked him, "Could it be that you feel worthless unless you occupy a special position by being different and superior to others?" Jimmy's mouth began to twitch and his eyes filled with tears. The teacher told him, further, that he was waiting for a miracle from heaven with regard to his reading and with regard to feeling accepted for what he was. She said, "Jimmy, haven't you noticed that all of us like and respect you for what you are? For us you needn't be anything else."

This may sound like a lecture. In a way it is. However, there are times when private counseling is necessary. The teacher actually has indicated that she understands and even sympathizes with him because he avoids reading. She has appealed to his ambition, but at the same time she has pointed out how unimportant it is to be exceptional because he is liked for what he is. She has put no cloak of moral indignation over his lying to her; in fact, the lie is not even discussed.

Jimmy answered that he realized that he was only fooling himself and not the others. He said that he felt this a number of times, but the fear of being laughed at kept him from joining a reading group. Again he asked her to promise him that nobody would laugh if he read. The teacher told him that she could not give him such a promise and that it would take courage to find out for himself and to face such a possibility. She added, "I am sure of one thing, though. The children will have more respect and admire you more for having the courage to try, no matter how poorly you perform, than they will if you continue being different. This is a decision that must come from you alone." He said that he would think about it and would tell her in the morning.

The next day Jimmy pulled up his chair and joined a reading group. All the children smiled; some waved at him. The boy next to him put his arm around him. When Jimmy's turn came to read, he blushed, hesitated for a moment, and then started pronouncing the words he could read. The teacher jumped in quickly whenever she anticipated a word that he might not know. When he had finished, he blew out and in a boisterous way said, "Well, I did better than I thought. In fact, I think that I did rather well."

The teacher did not get into a power contest with Jimmy. She did not argue, nor did she make promises. But she proved to be his friend. As a consequence, he cooperated with her, and he mustered up his courage. She had succeeded in restoring Jimmy's confidence in himself and in others.

We notice that in Jimmy's remark there is more of a humorous bravado than sincere belief in what he is saying. His old pattern is still visible, but it is not so deeply entrenched as before.

Conclusion

Frustrated overambition is often the main reason for giving up. Jimmy had to learn to believe in himself and to respect himself as he was before anyone could help him. The teacher and the group gave Jimmy the incentive to overcome his disbelief in his own ability and to have the courage to accept the fact that in some areas others would be superior to him without feeling humiliated or rejected because of this. The teacher went to great lengths to provide him with proof of the fallacy of his original thinking. However, without the help of the group, she might not have succeeded. We see in this example that the group was being used, not only to influence the child to want to learn and to exercise self-discipline, but also to exercise a corrective influence over the child's attitudes and behavior. At all times we must remember that when the teacher or the group can convince the child of the futility of his goal and can show him alternatives, he is likely to consider and change it. He then will turn to constructive direction.

Appendix: Years Later

It may be of interest to the reader that Jimmy now is a TV actor and is frequently performing. His basic life-style has not changed. He still tries to be the center of attention, and the spotlights are on him. However, he is using constructive, socially acceptable means to achieve his goal. Interestingly, he has chosen a profession that requires constant reading.

Why Children Lie

Sometimes children lie when their imagination runs away with them. Sometimes they confuse fantasy with reality. It we accuse these children of deliberately lying, we run the risk of making real liars out of them.

> Herman, a fourth grader, was always telling the class about his dog Timber. He told the class about the tricks that Timber could perform, what a wonderful watchdog he was, and how Timber would protect him. Each week he would come to school and tell about the wonders of Timber.

As it turned out, Herman did not own a dog, and none of his relatives or close friends had such a dog.

Would you say that Herman was lying, that he had a very active imagination, or that he did not know the difference between truth and fiction? These questions are sometimes quite difficult to answer. In Herman's case, this was probably a truthful account of what was going on in his imagination.

What is a flagrant lie? How do we distinguish this kind of lie from another kind? How do we know it is a lie?

Hank was a third grader who had a consistent pattern of telling lies. The teacher might make a simple request, such as, "Hank, please clean the apple cores out of your desk." A few minutes later Hank would say, "I cleaned my desk and put the apple cores in the wastebasket." When the teacher would check the desk, she would find that the apple cores were still there.

Another time the teacher might say, "Hank, your coat is on the floor; please hang it up." A few minutes later Hank would say that he had hung up his coat. When the teacher would check, the coat would still be on the floor.

In this example there was never an excuse of any kind given. The teacher would be checking to see if an actual lie had been told. Is this child's goal to be deceptive? If the teacher thinks so, then she should label it lying. Many children lie just in order to put something over on adults.

Some children lie because they are curious to see what will happen when they do lie. Usually, this is of short duration if little attention is paid to those lies or jokes are made about them. Unfortunately, most adults make a big fuss and thus show the child that his method works.

There are times when a lie may put a teacher into a situation in which she does not know what to do. Doing the opposite of what the child thinks or expects can be very effective. The teacher can say to the child, "People can always fool me. I guess I'm a sucker for lies." This takes the enjoyment out of feeling superior, and the child often feels foolish. Sometimes children even apologize when the teacher without anger or provocation admits her weakness.

One day a teacher was called to the door of her classroom, and while she was talking with the principal there was some confusion in the room. Somehow the pencil sharpener had been emptied and its contents strewn on the floor.

Since the teacher did not know who had spilled the shavings, she mentioned that the mess would have to be swept and picked up. The children volunteered the information that Randy had made the mess. Randy immediately stated in no uncertain terms that he had not spilled the shavings. The teacher then asked for a volunteer to sweep up the shavings, and Tom immediately started to clean up the floor.

At this point Randy looked up and gruffly said, "Leave that stuff alone, Tom. That's my mess, and I'll clean it up."

In this particular case, the teacher did not ask who made the mess, nor did she respond when several children volunteered the information. Had the teacher confronted Randy, he would have denied the act, as this was his pattern. Since he was not challenged and did not get the response he expected, he was able to come forth with his statement.

We would like the child who is lying to think that there is something good about any acceptance of him if he does not lie. We are making the assumption that the truth has some good in it. Is it possible for the child to recognize this?

There are two major ways to fight lying successfully. The first is to make the lie ineffectual in some way by undercutting the desired results. A cardinal rule: "Don't challenge a lie." It does not do any good. There are several ways to cut down the child's desired consequences. Do not pay attention to fantastic stories; do not respond or give recognition to something you do not think is correct; and do not ask for the rest of a fantastic story.

Children learn to do what is expected of them in their everyday contacts with adults. Again, we need to realize that we cannot teach children by telling them or talking to them; we can teach them only by showing them through our actions and deeds. Sometimes at home a mother can undercut the child's lies by inviting the children to make a game of lying, of which he soon will tire.

We should not be afraid that the child who lies is on the road to delinquency. Lying, like any other behavior pattern, needs to be understood in relation to the entire personality of the child, and measures to improve the situation must be taken accordingly.

Swearing

When a child swears or uses a bad word, he is looking for its shock value. If we respond as he wishes and are shocked or make an issue of the matter, we encourage his further use of these words. We can take the wind out of his sails by playing dumb: "What is it you said? I don't understand that word. What does it mean?" The child then is likely to abandon this tactic.

Several times throughout this book we have suggested that teachers have a discussion with their students about their mutual problems. Much of this depends upon their ability to respect the child, even when they disagree with him. Mostly, they hammer away at the child's transgressions and try to impress him with what they think. They want to mold his character, his mind, and his personality as if he were a bit of soft clay. This does not mean that we should not or cannot influence him and guide him; it merely means we cannot force him into our mold.

Each child has his own creativity; each child responds to what he encounters in his life, each child has his own individual hand in the shaping of his personality.

Chapter 27

Fighting

Fighting among children is a familiar problem to all teachers. Teachers feel a deep concern about the endless fighting that goes on in class or on the playground. It is not only disruptive and takes up much of the teacher's time, but to many teachers it becames worrisome because they associate fighting with possible criminal behavior.

Problems with Relationships

Most teachers have tried every known procedure to stop fights, and still fighting continues. Fighting among children has become accepted as a normal form of child behavior. We do not believe, however, that it is normal just because it occurs so regularly. Children do not have to fight. When they fight, there is something wrong in their relationships. If children continue to fight, they obviously are gaining some satisfaction. This evaluation presupposes that we recognize behavior as purposive. A great deal of the teacher's energy goes into settling fights and trying to teach children to get along together.

We cannot be satisfied with the usual explanations for fighting: that it is caused by an aggressive nature or drive, or by heredity, and so on. From our point of view, we feel that we need to understand a child's behavior in terms of the field in which it occurs and the purpose that it serves.

Whatever the reason behind the child's fighting, the teacher only makes it worse when she interferes, tries to solve the quarrel, or separates the children. Whenever a teacher interferes in a fight she is depriving the children of the opportunity of learning how to resolve their own conflicts. It is extremely difficult for teachers to see why fights between children are none of their business. They consider it their duty to teach children not to fight. We do not dispute that this is necessary. Unfortunately, however, interference and arbitration does not bring such a result. Although it may stop the children from fighting momentarily, it fails to teach them how to avoid future fights or how to settle conflicts in other ways.

When the teacher protects one child, the child who is defeated will get even with his more successful peer. Thus, as soon as this fight seems to be settled, another is brewing.

Whenever the teacher takes sides, one child becomes the victor and the other, the vanquished. In most cases, the victor (the one who manages to convince the teacher of his innocence) started the fight in the first place, not always in a physical manner but possibly in a way that provokes the other child.

Establishing Guilt

In a fight it is difficult to establish who is guilty. It is not the result of the misbehavior of just one child. The good one may egg on the bad one by daring him, by pushing him, or by provoking transgressions in hundreds of ways.

The most effective approach is to let the children settle their differences and find solutions by themselves. We should always first try to let them settle their own problems before we jump in, but letting the child settle his own problems is not entirely a solution. It is only a momentary solution. The teacher must help the child to understand why he fights and what he hopes to achieve through fighting. There are children who will fight even though they know that they will lose and end up with a bloody nose. Still, they feel honor bound to fight.

In most cases, teachers and principals admonish and punish the child that supposedly started the fight, disregarding the children who stood by and encouraged the fighting. Often these children even applaud the winner and hold him in high esteem because they feel that he can beat up anyone. The children who encourage others to fight often are the real culprits, yet they get away with it. Many a fight would not have taken place if the fighters had fought without an audience paying attention to them, because this would have taken the fun out of fighting. Teachers should help the class understand what is going on. All those who are involved in the fight—the fighters as well as those who encourage the fighting—are guilty, and all should be dealt with.

Many children fight because this is the only area in which they experience success and receive attention.

A bully is always a child who, as a result of initial discouragement, has assumed that a person has prestige only when he can show his power.

This child is discouraged; he is not always naughty or mean. We must recognize behavior as a mistaken approach brought about through discouragement.

The Teacher's Role

The teacher should avoid all discouraging remarks if she wants to help the child. Although she grants him the right to settle his own disputes and assume responsibility for, as well as consequences of his behavior, she should refrain from adding insult to injury through scolding, shaming, or threats, because this teaches the child nothing.

It is our own sense of superiority over our children that makes us think that they are too little to solve problems or to take frustration in their stride. This false impression must be acknowledged and replaced with trust and confidence in the child's ability and with a desire to provide guidance. Certainly we should not abandon a child to fate, nor should we let him experience the full impact of life all at once, but we should be constantly on the alert for opportunities to step back and allow the child to experience his own strength. We should stand ready to step in at such a point at which the problem becomes too much for the child to handle. If the teacher has to step in, she should be careful not to pass judgment and antagonize one of the children involved in the fight. The teacher may do one of the following:

1. She may ask the children to stop fighting and to discuss the problem with her or with the class.
2. She may ask them to stop fighting temporarily and to continue with a referee.
3. She may ask them to stop and let a "court" consisting of students settle the dispute.

The teacher should not preach or threaten. She may, however, tell the students that they have a choice: to stop the fight immediately or to settle it in any of the above mentioned ways or she would be forced to call the school authorities. She should let the children know that she would prefer that the class handle this situation. In most cases, this meets with good results. It rarely happens that the fight continues to a point at which force has to be used.

Many teachers get themselves hopelessly entangled with children who are in conflict, especially with younger children. Hardly a day goes by without a child complaining to the teacher that someone hit him, pushed him, or started a fight. Teachers who use role playing will lose very little time over such fights. At no time should a teacher permit herself to become the referee in such quarrels. During the weekly group discussions, the teacher and the class should discuss the purpose of fighting and what to do with children who fight. One solution may be to ask the fighters to leave the room and not return until they have settled their fight. Often the quarrel ends before the children reach the door, especially when they realize that the teacher has no intention of getting involved. Young children take little pleasure in staying out of class when they are sent out by the teacher.

In general, teachers hesitate to let children go on fighting. They are afraid that one of the children may get hurt, especially when a weaker child is beaten by a bully. Furthermore, they feel that it is expected of them to stop fights and prevent children from getting hurt. This is a question that deserves careful scrutiny. For one thing, children can get hurt regardless of the teacher's vigilance; the moment the teacher turns her head, the children often resume their fight. Our experience shows that the chances of the children getting hurt are reduced when the children learn to settle their own fights, if for no other reason than that they understand the purpose of their fighting. They also learn to solve their differences in other ways.

There are children who become involved in fights that are fought by others. When questioned, such a child may reply, "I pounded Harry because I saw him hit Mike." Or, "He was hitting Susan, and it is not right to hit girls. They can't defend themselves, so I let him have it." The child feels not only justified in what he did but expects to be praised for his gallant behavior. Should we discourage children from helping others who are in distress? Should the child receive no recognition for having stuck out his neck in order to help somebody else? This would depend on the situation and on the child's goal for getting involved in this fight (see Chapter 4). Each child and each situation is unique and should be evaluated in its own light. If we do not recognize the quest for power when the child plays the role of the gallant rescuer, we may only encourage his mistaken goal by approval and encouragement. How can we help him understand the real purpose for his gallant behavior? This must be done during class discussions, and it ought to be done very carefully and sensitively, as we can see in the following example.

"Larry has been in three fights this week. In each case, he got involved in a fight that did not concern him personally. Larry claims that in each case he had to get into the fight in order to help one of the kids who was fighting. I would appreciate if the class took a few minutes to consider what happened and to give us your views on this matter."

Through a process of leading questions, the group suddenly recognized Larry's goal, which was to be in a revered position, one in which he received admiration from everyone for being a great hero. The teacher pointed out to Larry that these are the only times when he wanted to do something for others. For instance, the other day, Larry bought three taffy apples for himself when the high school girls came around to sell them. Yet Sam, for whom he had risked himself in a fight, could not afford to buy one. Larry never thought of sharing his apples with Sam. The group also reminded Larry of the time that he had twisted Sam's wrist until Sam cried, which showed how little he really liked Sam.

Let us consider Larry's situation and some possible consequences. If the fighting usually occurs after school, then the logical thing is for Larry to stay about ten minutes after the other children have been dismissed. They would be home already or would have such a head start that Larry would not come in contact with them. On the other hand, if the fighting occurs mostly during recess time, then perhaps Larry should remain in his classroom at that time. Another solution would be for Larry to remain by the teacher's side during recess for several days.

Boys Cannot Touch Girls

A common and frequent type of quarreling occurs between boys and girls, in which the girls usually insist that they have been picked on. Of course, in such a case, as in the previous one, no one takes the blame. It is always the other who started the fight. Upon careful observation, we may find that the girls, having been brought up to believe that their sex protects them from being hit by boys, frequently provoke them to a point at which even an angel would lash out. The girls abuse and dare the boys in every possible way, yet the minute a boy retaliates, the girls go screaming and crying to the teacher and demand that the teacher consider "their rights as women," namely, protection and revenge.

Juliana was a typical example. Hardly a day passed when she did not complain to the teacher that a boy had hit or pushed her for no reason. When the boy accused her of having provoked the fight, she denied it vehemently and always demanded that the teacher punish the boy. When the group discussed this problem during their discussion period, she carried on and demanded, "Won't you punish him? He is not supposed to touch a girl." References to "girls shouldn't be touched by boys" made the teacher suspicious. She decided to observe Juliana more carefully when the children were out on the playground. Not long after the class had gone out for recess, an incident took place.

As soon as the class reached the playground, Juliana gathered a few girls around her and instructed them on the positions and the strategy that they should take. Next, she placed herself close to a boy who was playing ball with the others, snatched his cap, ran off with it, and threw it to one of her accomplices who in turn threw the cap to the next girl in line. When the cap reached the last girl, she threw it over the fence. All this time, the boy was frantically trying to retrieve his cap. Juliana was hysterical with laughter. When the cap was thrown into the street, the boy demanded that Juliana go and get it. She told him to get it himself and kicked him in the shins. In the meantime, the other boys had gathered around the two children. They too demanded that Juliana get the cap. One of the boys took her by her arm and tried to lead her toward the gate. She, in turn, pushed him so hard that he fell. During this time she continued laughing and telling the boy that he could do nothing to her. When the boy picked himself up, he knocked Juliana down. This was the signal for which she had been waiting. She went running to the teacher, sobbing, showing her dirty dress, and insisting that she had been unfairly attacked by the boys. When the teacher told Juliana that she had watched the incident from beginning to end, and that she had seen how Juliana went about organizing her group of girls and how she had provoked the boys, Juliana replied, "Anyway, they are not supposed to touch me. My mother told me so, and I will tell my mother how they beat me up."

In Juliana's personal folder the teacher found evidence that she had been in similar fights before. However, none of her teachers had recognized Juliana's real problem. One of her teachers wrote, "Juliana is a sweet girl and is generally liked by the girls. She is not accepted by the boys. They often hurt her." Another teacher had written, "Juliana's social adjustment is generally good. She gets along better with girls. The boys like to tease her because she is a pretty girl."

Juliana's is not an isolated case. Many girls tease and provoke boys, hoping that the boys will not retaliate because boys are not supposed to touch girls. If they get away with it, it gives them the feeling of being superior and of having special rights and privileges. If the boys retaliate, the girls capitalize on getting the sympathy of those who share their belief, be they children, parents, or teachers. Frequently, a teacher will tell a boy that a gentleman never touches a woman, no matter what she does.

This situation can be changed only if the children are helped to understand the meaning of democratic living and of what is and is not fair. During class discussions, Juliana began to understand the reasons for her behavior.

When the teacher asked the class how many of them thought that it was right and fair that a boy should never strike a girl no matter what she does, none of the boys raised their hands, and out of 17 girls, only two raised theirs. In further questions, such as, "Why isn't it fair?" the class began to consider and to talk about democratic living: equal rights, fairness, respect for others, and so on (see Chapter 9). Juliana participated little in the discussion, but when she was asked what she thought of giving everybody equal rights and of the unfairness of hurting others, she admitted that she, too, thought hurting others was wrong. When the teacher asked the class why they thought Juliana took such great pleasure in making the boys angry, most children understood Juliana's goal. Some said, "She wants to make herself important and show the boys that she has more power than they do." Others said, "She gets a lot of attention from everybody—the whole class and the teacher." A boy added, "And from her mother, because she will go home and complain that we are after her for no reason, and then her mother will think she is right." Juliana's best girl friend said, "Juliana wants people to feel sorry for her so that everybody will be nice to her."

Juliana, it may be interesting to know, was very small for her age; many people thought she was in first grade although she was really in third grade. She was also the second of five children, all girls. She told the teacher that every time her mother was pregnant her parents hoped it would be a boy and each time they were disappointed. Since having a boy was so important to her parents and since her wish to be a boy was so strong, she intended to show everybody that she could be better than any boy by raising her status to "untouchable," someone the boys could not fight with. She felt, indeed, very sorry for herself.

Hypersensitivity Expressed as Hostility

A fight is not necessarily of a physical nature. Some children express their hostility through a display of hypersensitivity to any situation in which they feel slighted, criticized, or dominated. This hostility expresses itself in continuous silent withdrawal, crying, clamming up to a point at which a teacher cannot get one word out of the child, a hurt look, feigning illness, as well as other manifestations that would make the teacher feel guilty for what she has done to the child. In all these manifestations the child may show unbelievable endurance and stubborness until the teacher makes up to him.

Claudette is a good example of the child who tries to manipulate the teacher and other children to give into her out of pity. She will cry with bitter tears for hours, whimpering like a hurt dog, until the teacher tells her, "Alright, Claudette, stop crying. All is forgiven." Usually, children go over to her to comfort her. In the end, she manages to make everybody fell guilty for having put her in such a miserable situation.

Lizzie behaved similarly when the teacher reprimanded her for some misdeed or poor work. After crying for a while without getting the desired sympathy from the teacher, she slipped a note on the teacher's desk that usually read as follows: "I know you don't love me. You love the others but not me. I love you very much. Answer immediately if you love me or not. I get a headache when I cry." Or she would say, "I loved you yesterday, but today I don't. You are mean to me."

Michael retaliates by sulking and throwing angry looks at the teacher. He refuses to talk and actually holds his hands over his mouth to make sure that no word will escape him. Neither the teacher nor his classmates can get a sound out of him. He can easily keep this up for several days. Yet, during all this time, he may be doing his work, even finish in time, something that he normally does not do. However, he refuses to let the teacher check his work. He also refuses to join in the oral reading.

What can a teacher do to help such children? In the first place, the teacher must recognize that all of them are fighting and trying to punish her by their method of nonparticipation and by their silent accusation of being rejected. The worst thing a teacher can do is to get into a power contest with these children and insist that the child do as he is told or else. If any action is to be taken, then it must be one of leaving the child alone; not scolding and not punishing him. The child, however, must be helped to understand the reason for his behavior and what he is trying to achieve by it. In most cases such children use their hypersensitivity in order to control others through their passivity. If they have been successful in making their parents submit to them by applying this method, they will try the same trick at school. The group can be of greater help to such children than the teacher.

The teacher may ask the class if anyone could tell why Michael or Lizzie was crying and refused to talk. The following dialogue might take place.

CHILD: Because he is angry.

TEACHER: But why is he angry?

CHILD: He is angry because he had to do over his spelling.

ANOTHER CHILD: He is angry because you don't pay attention to him.

TEACHER: Do you really believe that doing over his spelling would bother him so much? Could there be another reason?

CHILD: Maybe he thinks that if he cries long enough, he won't have to do it over again.

TEACHER: You mean because there's won't be any time then?

CHILD: No, because you will feel sorry for him and you will tell him to stop crying and not to do the work if it makes him so unhappy.

TEACHER: How does he try to make me feel?

SOME CHILDREN: Bad.

TEACHER: Would you say that he tries to make me feel guilty, as though I did something wrong?

CHILD: That's right.

TEACHER: How does he try to make all of you feel?

CHILD: He wants us to feel sorry for him.

TEACHER: What else is he trying to get out of this, besides not doing the work? What did Lucy do several times when she went over to Michael?

ANOTHER CHILD: She spent a lot of time with him trying to cheer him up. He probably wants this from you, and he wants to get attention.

TEACHER: But why would a child do this?

CHILD: Because he wants the others to feel bad and make up to him.

TEACHER: Make up how?

CHILD: Make up by letting him do what he wants.

Sooner or later somebody will hit on the real motive behind this kind of behavior. When the teacher asks Michael if it could be true that he wants to have his way all the time, he may deny it, but his facial expression usually will betray him. If the conversation is conducted in a friendly manner, Michael, or any child, will usually admit that this is the true reason.

The teacher may then speak directly to Michael and say, "You see, Michael, you don't know why you behave this way, and I don't blame you. However, I would like to show you how unfair you are and how much you hurt yourself and others. I treated you like I do everybody else. If I didn't, then you could justly think that I don't care about you. I do care very much. By not letting me help you, you sort of push me away from you. I know you don't mean to do this, but if you think about it, you'll realize that this is what happens. Would you rather I not bother with you and allow you to make all the mistakes?"

It is very seldom that a young child will accept such a proposition. He may want to have the cake and eat it too. This must be pointed out to him in a friendly manner. He must see the impossibility of this. If the child continues to sulk, however, the teacher may tell him to take a day or two and think about the discussion. There should be no further discussion or attention given to the child's crying until he, of his own accord, changes his behavior. At this point, such a child should receive praise from the teacher. This is the time to give him the desired attention.

Jealousy

Jealousy is closely related to the need to excel. The jealous child feels inferior to others, especially to those who get recognition and attention because of their good academic performance. He compares himself with others, never feeling that he can measure up to them. This may be the cause of fighting and punishing those he considers superior.

Cecil was such a child. Every time he performed poorly, regardless of whether it was in a subject matter, sports, or games, he retaliated by beating up the child who was ahead of him. The children were aware of this—all but Cecil, that is. He argued that during the game the others had cheated or made fun of him. He could never admit that he was at fault. Finally, the group appointed a student to record Cecil's performance in class. Thus, they could show him that in each case he punished the child who had been a little more successful in an area on that particular day. When confronted with these facts, Cecil had no argument. He claimed that he did not realize that this was what he always did. He was right—he did not realize it until that moment. Gradually his fighting subsided.

Not every case brings results as quickly and comparatively smoothly as that of Cecil. Some children require longer and more intense work. In almost all cases, the child will change his method of obtaining his goal as soon as his behavior is shown to him. As we succeed in convincing the child that we are interested in him personally and that we accept him for what he is and for what he is trying to be, he may change his negative approach to a positive one, namely that of trust, cooperation, and enjoyment of being a member of a group with equal rights.

This does not mean that we should discourage children from wanting and from trying to better themselves. On the contrary, children need constant encouragement and recognition for every step they take, but they must be helped to enjoy going forward for its own sake and not as a means of controlling or surpassing others.

The Need to Be First

The need to be first is another form of subtle fighting that is seldom recognized by adults. One child is good in order to show others how bad they are in comparison. Another child is jealous and ambitious in order to be first. A child never allows himself to use his own judgment and act on it, if he thinks that it might displease the teacher. We may expect that sooner or later such a child will stumble into situations that cannot be controlled by him. Then his hostilities may come to the fore. The course of aggression will depend on the child's goals and the amount of success he has had with similar behavior patterns at other times, when things did not go according to his expectations.

The following example may serve to illustrate such behavior.

Mary was an excellent student from the very first day she entered school. She was known to all of the teachers as an exceptionally bright girl. She was the envy of many children who openly admitted that they would like to be like her. At home she was placed on a pedestal; nothing was ever denied her because of the honor she brought to the family. Mary was always friendly. She never refused to help another child, but she made no special effort to make close friends. During recess she preferred to stay in class and to read or to do some other work. She did not refuse to go out when the teacher asked her to, but each day she requested to be allowed to stay in and work.

She had few friends outside of school. Her mother insisted that she join the Brownies, so she did. However, she never talked about her experiences as the other girls did. The children expected and accepted that Mary's work was always perfect. They talked about her to their parents, and it was not unusual that some parent would ask the teacher to point out Mary as the wonderful child to them.

One can imagine the shock every one experienced when one day Mary threw a tantrum when she missed three works in a spelling test. There were two other students who had perfect scores. First, Mary tore up her paper. Then she proceeded to tear up the spelling book, throwing the pages at the other two students. She screamed that the others cheated, that she was always the best, and that she always would be. It was impossible to quiet her down. Since she was always so good and cooperative, this was a unique situation for the teacher, who felt self-conscious for having to insist that Mary leave the room until she calmed down.

Mary did not understand any more than did her schoolmates what had happened to her and why. This was a situation in which a teacher who lacked the understanding of children's goals might have said, "The child must have been ill; she was certainly not herself."

Mary needed an understanding attitude from her teacher. She needed to be helped to understand that she was concerned with the attention she received from being first and that if she did not get attention this way, she would get it through a tantrum. Apparently, she felt secure only as long as she occupied this position, and she felt entitled to it. She had to be helped to understand that a person does not need to be on top in order to have a place. She also had to see the terrible strain she had put on herself by having to be ahead at all times and at all costs.

Later, when this was discussed in the group, not just as Mary's problem but as one that is found in many children and adults, the class could actually observe the relief on Mary's face. During the discussion, the teacher helped the children to see and to understand that strong competition is really a form of pushing others down, because the person wants always to be in a superior position.

TEACHER: You have been so wonderful in understanding the reasons for our behavior that I thought that it might be a good idea to talk over why people who are always very good in everything suddenly show anger and sometimes even meanness.

FIRST CHILD: Well, if somebody is always good in everything but one day he isn't, then he thinks it's unfair to him.

TEACHER: What is unfair?

CHILD: It is unfair that he should not do well if he always does well.

TEACHER: Do you all agree with this?

SECOND CHILD: I think that if a child is always good in everything, he thinks that he will always be good in everything, and then if he isn't, he gets mad.

TEACHER: At whom does he get mad?

CHILD: I guess he gets mad at those who did better.

TEACHER: Could he be mad at somebody else also?

THIRD CHILD: He might be mad at himself because he didn't do better.

FIRST CHILD: He might be mad at the teacher because she marked him wrong.

TEACHER: Do you think a good child would be satisfied if the teacher marked him right even though he was wrong?

THIRD CHILD: Maybe not, but he is probably mad mostly at himself because he made mistakes.

TEACHER: Do you think that a person must be good at everything at all times and that he must never make a mistake?

MANY CHILDREN: No.

TEACHER: Let us think for a moment. Why would somebody always want to be the best in everything?

ONE CHILD: Because everybody likes him better and his mother sometimes buys him something if he is the best. My mother gave me $1 when I got a good report card.

ANOTHER CHILD: If someone is the best in everything, he thinks that he is smarter than everybody else and that nobody can do better than he can.

TEACHER: And if somebody does do better, how do you think such a person might feel? I mean, in addition to being angry.

ONE CHILD: He might feel scared that now he is not good anymore.

ANOTHER CHILD: He might feel that now people won't like him as much.

TEACHER: Yes, I think that this could be true—that anyone who is used to being first all the time might feel that making a mistake is a threat to him. Can anyone explain why this would be threatening?

CHILD: Well, it is as if you were to threaten somebody, and if he didn't do what he was supposed to do, he would be punished.

TEACHER: That is right. Such a person is afraid that people might not look up to him as much as before and might not admire him as much. Can you tell me how this might affect him at home? Let's think of how most parents behave when their child is always the best and how they might react if their child is not the best anymore.

ONE CHILD: The parents are proud of him, but when he is not the best any-more they are not proud of him.

ANOTHER CHILD: I don't think that this is true, because if he is not the best this doesn't mean that he is bad. Besides, he may not be the best one day, but he may be the best the next day.

TEACHER: I'm so glad that you brought this up, Gloria. Nobody can be the best always, and nobody should be, because then no one else would have a chance to be best once also. But do we really have to be best? Let's see, if we want to be best, then how do we want others to be?

ONE CHILD: Bad.

TEACHER: Perhaps, not bad, but something else.

ANOTHER CHILD: We want others to be less good than we are.

TEACHER: Yes, we want others to be worse. We don't feel happy as long as somebody else does better than we do. Isn't this foolish, especially when we do quite well? If we just give ourselves a chance to do the best we can, we will see that we won't mind if somebody else does better than we do once in a while. At home, too, we will be happier if we don't always have to show how bad our brother or our sister is. Why don't we try it and see for ourselves?

The discussion may be resumed after a few days. The teacher may ask the children if they have thought any further about the discussion they had the previous day. If any children raise their hands, she may ask them to state their conclusions. She may even casually ask Mary what her opinion was of the discussion.

A teacher may ask a show of hands of those children who threaten their parents that they will drop in their schoolwork if their parents do not give in to some of their demands. Hands always go up. The teacher may ask these children to tell the class how they have threatened their parents and how it has paid off. This gives the teacher the opportunity to show how they use punishment in an unfair manner. It also gives her a chance to talk about the merits of learning for its own sake. A teacher can ask, "For whom do you study, Jim?" Invariably, he will answer, "For myself." The teacher can then ask, "Do you really? Just think, if you fall behind in your work because your parents won't let you watch television, whom do you punish?" It is seldom that a child does not see the point.

It helps if the teacher can work with the parents to help them to understand the importance of changing their attitude toward the child's schoolwork and toward curbing their own ambitions, for behind every overambitious child we will find overambitious parents or one parent whose attitude toward being first has instilled in the child distorted values about achievement. It becomes a question of helping the parents as well as the child to change this attitude.

The teacher may ask the class if they can think of other ways children sometimes punish others, without mentioning specific names or situations. Together, they may point out that sometimes children punish others who do better in tests or in general work, and that sometimes they punish other children because these other children have toys or other things that they themselves do not have. The child to whom this applies takes in the conversation. The teacher may notice a pensive look on his face, even though nobody is talking about him specifically. At another time, when a child is guilty of such a misdeed, the teacher may ask him, "Do you remember the discussion the class had about why we sometimes punish others? Could it be that you lashed out at Susan because she had a higher score than you did in arithmetic?"

Again, we must remember to show the child that he is not being evaluated by the score he makes on tests but by what he is as a person. We must encourage him to do well in his work, especially if we know that he is capable. However, we must discourage the kind of competition that leads to the goal of needing to be better than others or else learning is not worthwhile.

Conflict Solving Techniques

Teachers can no longer resolve conflicts by fighting or giving in. Fighting or imposing one's values violates respect for the child, and giving in, or permissiveness, violates respect for the adult. In a democratic setting, conflicts have to be resolved by following four basic steps. They are:

1. Establish mutual respect.
2. Pinpoint the issue.
3. Explore alternatives.
4. Come to a new agreement by shared decision making.

   1. *Establish mutual respect.* We cannot influence another person unless we have a good relationship with that person. A good relationship rests on mutual respect. Unless the child feels respected, it will be difficult for the teacher to motivate him and to change his behavior.
   2. *Pinpoint the issue.* Pinpointing the issue of the conflict helps the child to realize the private logic of his behavior, for instance:

Jacque attacks children whenever they perform well. The teacher asks for a reason, but he claims that he is only trying to be amusing or funny.

TEACHER: Jacque, do you know that you always attack people when they do well?

JACQUE: (No answer)

TEACHER: Do you know why you do this?

JACQUE: I told you; I'm only joking.

TEACHER: Are you aware that you never joke when children perform poorly?

JACQUE: No.

TEACHER: Could it be that you think that you can't do as well?

JACQUE: Maybe.

TEACHER: Could it be that you are angry at yourself because of this?

JACQUE: Maybe.

TEACHER: Could it be that you are also angry at these children?

JACQUE: (No answer)

The teacher has pinpointed the true reasons for Jacque's "joking."

3. *Exploring alternatives.* In any transgression the teacher and the student should explore all possibilities for dealing with the problem effectively.

TEACHER: I understand how you feel, Jacque. Could you handle your feelings differently?

JACQUE: I don't know.

TEACHER: May I make a suggestion?

JACQUE: Sure.

TEACHER: Would you be willing to say or do nothing?

JACQUE: I could say something nice.

TEACHER: Only if you feel like it. But would you be willing to say nothing? Would you be willing to accept help from me and the students in the areas in which you would like to improve?

JACQUE: I don't know.

4. *Come to a new agreement by shared decision making.* The students and the teacher reach a decision and come to an agreement.

TEACHER: Would you know if you had a little more time?

JACQUE: I think so.

TEACHER: Could you give me your answer tomorrow?

JACQUE: Yes.

TEACHER: Is this an agreement?

JACQUE: Yes.

The first and the last step in resolving a conflict have already been discussed as part of the establishment of democratic procedures in the classroom. Steps two and three require a clear understanding of how to deal with the four goals. In evaluating a teacher's efforts to cope with a conflict situation, the points made above can serve as a yardstick. They indicate effective approaches and explain failures due to violation of the basic principles of conflict solving.

Part 5
Parental Involvement

Chapter 28

Parent-Teacher Conferences

In former times children were sent to school for only one purpose, namely, to learn subjects and skills. Character formation, citizenship, values, and attitudes were the responsibility of the parents. A teacher's job was to teach, to impart knowledge, and to discipline those who did not learn and those who strayed from accepted rules and regulations. Those who made progress according to the requirements were promoted, whereas those who did not were flunked. This was accepted as just and proper. Parents rarely went to the teacher to discuss their child's progress or problems. The teacher was always right, at least, this is what the parents told their children.

By and large, this procedure worked, but times have changed. Today we seek the cooperation of the parents in order to help the child in school. This is frowned on by some teachers; others reject it entirely. It was much simpler for teachers when their sole responsibility was to teach and to grade.

It has become imperative that the school assume responsibility in character building. What has brought about this change? The impact of the democratic spirit, now prevailing in our society, affects child-parent relationships, and as a result, the parents lose control of their children. Today the educator has the obligation to help parents and children as well. The work of home and school can greatly benefit from the cooperation between teachers and parents. They should be partners, helping each other, but care must be taken so that the cooperation of the parents does not become a collusion against the child. Actually, it is a three-way enterprise. Parents and teachers have the responsibility to prepare a child for life, and they must pool their resources in order to build fruitful relationships.

Some people will reject this educational philosophy because they believe that school problems and home problems should be kept apart, the former being the sole responsibility of the educator, and the latter, of the parents. Their rejection is based on the belief that teachers should not be counselors, that working together with parents demands too much of the teacher's time, that parents may start to dictate school policy and procedure, that nothing good will come of it, and last, that this is not what teachers are being paid for.

Such opposition usually comes from those who are not familiar with modern trends in education.

What Purpose Can Parent-Teacher Interviews Serve?

Parent-teacher conferences serve a number of purposes. Knowing the home situation, the family's values, the way the child is treated, what the parents expect of their child, the position the child holds in the family, the child's relationship with his siblings and friends, and other pertinent information, enables the teacher to plan long-term procedures for the individual child more successfully. By understanding the home situation, she is better prepared to help parents in their difficulties with their children. This also proves to the child that both the parents and the teacher are really interested in him and in his welfare, which, in many cases, has the effect of encouragement.

Having the teacher and the parents talk together serves to unite the two areas of the child's life—his home and his school—and enables both to plan more effectively for the child than when the teacher and parents do not know whether they differ in their methods of treating the child. The more the two understand each other, the less the child will play school against home, and vice versa. Here is an example.

James, a third-grade student who got into frequent fights with the other children in class, insisted that his father had told him to sock anyone who called him a nasty name. He conveniently interpreted the slightest offense as a just provocation to sock the child. When the class discussed this with him, he felt that he was being attacked and criticized for doing something that his father had told him to do.

When the teacher spoke to his father, he admitted having advised his son to do so but only in extreme cases. When he learned that James considered every situation as extreme and was involved in frequent fights, he was displeased. Nevertheless, he felt that this could not hurt James in his general development and that fighting was a healthy boyish outlet for excess energy.

In the light of James' general behavior, we may assume that he knew all along how he should behave but that he chose to use his father's advice to defy the school rules. James' father, on the other hand, had no idea that his advice gave sanction to his son's behavior. He needed to realize that James had no friends because of his aggressiveness and that such behavior does not develop good human relationships. Only after this was pointed out did the father realize that he had given his son wrong advice. The father then told James that he had given him wrong advice. This created confusion in James' mind. For one thing, he could not easily accept the fact that his father had made a serious error in judgment, and furthermore, the new perspective demanded a change in his behavior that he did not like. He told the teacher, "Look what a mess my dad got me into. Now I can do nothing when the children call me nasty names." This was later discussed in class, and James was helped to understand that he would not be in a "mess" unless he made one and that there were other means of feeling important. Here is another example:

Frances, 9 years old, was a child whom we call teacher-deaf. She never heard what was said to her, never knew what the teacher expected of her in class, and consequently, never did any work. This went on for some time. When the teacher discussed this behavior with Frances' mother, she replied, "She doesn't know what to do because you never tell her." When asked on what basis she was making this accusation, she said, "I know, because Frances always tells me that the reason she doesn't do her work is that she doesn't know what to do and that you never tell her what to do." The teacher asked her if Frances had ever mentioned that the other children in class knew what to do. To this the mother replied, "I know what you are driving at, but, you see, unless you tell Frances what you want her to do, she doesn't understand you." The teacher asked, "Do you mean that I should tell Frances separately what the assignment is?" The mother replied, "I am afraid you have to, otherwise she won't know what is expected of her." The teacher learned that at home the parents had to tell Frances many times what they wanted her to do, and even then she insisted that she did not understand or that she forgot what they had told her. Therefore, she felt that she had the right to demand special service.

This example illustrates the different approach of home and school. Not only does Frances expect and demand that the teacher give directions for schoolwork to Frances personally, but the mother does also. This is not a unique example. On the contrary, many parents accept and support the kind of behavior that Frances displayed, and in this manner fortify the child's fallacious concept of how she must act in order to receive special attention. It becomes a matter of helping parents to understand children's goals in their behavior.

In talking with parents, many opportunities arise in which they give, indirectly, valuable information to the teacher about general family attitudes, their view of discipline, whether the child has any responsibilities at home, and if so, whether he carries them out voluntarily or whether he has to be forced or coaxed. If the latter is the case, how do the parents do it and how much success do they have?

The parents, too, can gain much information about their child from the teacher. They learn about his behavior at school and the teacher's evaluation of him. They learn about the hopes and expectations she has for him. They acquaint themselves with the various rules and regulations of the school, as well as those made by the teacher or by the children in class. Finally, the parents have a chance to learn something about the general program of the class in which their child spends so many hours each day. Too many parents have no idea what their children do in school.

How to Invite Parents

The success of a parent-teacher conference may well depend on the way the teacher invites a parent to come to school. This is especially true of parents who have come to school many times before because their child is a behavior problem, has difficulties in learning, or both. These parents have been confronted with similar problems so many times without receiving any constructive suggestions that they consider another visit to the teacher a waste of their time, and they resent such a request. They often feel accused. Often they feel bitter toward the teacher and toward the school in general, because they think that the school has let them down. It is not uncommon for a teacher to hear some parents say, "When I received your note, I began to tremble before I even read it." Or, "What has he done this time?" Or, "Billy came home crying. He was so afraid to give me your note. I have told him that I'll skin him alive if I ever get another note from school."

In such an instance the parents' anger may be the cause for a bad start. First, even the most skilled teacher may have difficulty reassuring the parents that there is no cause for alarm, especially if they, too, have had a problem with the child. Second, the parents' anger may arouse angry feelings in the teacher that she may not be able to conceal. Her reaction might antagonize the parents further.

It is advisable to tell the child that the note contains nothing bad and that there is no cause for alarm. This puts the child at ease. Often, if the child knows that his parents may become upset, he will relieve his parents' anxiety by saying, "The teacher said that there is nothing bad in the note."

Sometimes, when a teacher senses that a child is afraid to have his parents come to school, she can discuss this with him before sending the invitation. He can be assured that his parents are not invited in order to accuse him but to plan what they can do to help him and to make him happier. The teacher can then ask, "What do you say? Shall we invite them?" It is seldom that the child still refuses to have his parents come. Usually, asking for his advice and consent makes him feel important and removes any fear and resentment.

If the child objects to having his parents come to school, the teacher can tell him that she will wait a while. After a week or ten days, she can then confront him with the same situation. This time she can tell him that she cannot wait any longer and that she would feel better if they agreed on inviting his parents. She can both assure him that her main concern is to help him and that she, the teacher, cannot do so by herself. Should he still refuse, she can use the group to help him understand why he refuses and the purpose this serves (see Chapter 14). This rarely happens, however.

The conference should be made by appointment, and sufficient time should be allowed for parents and teacher to discuss their interests and problems. Casual conferences, such as telephone calls and quick informal talks when parents drop in unexpectedly, especially during school hours, are of less value, but they should not be minimized or avoided.

Conferences in the home of the child help the teacher to see the child in his environment, which may shed considerable light on his general behavior. A home visit may be indicated if for some reason the parents cannot come to school. Advisedly, the teacher should notify the parents of her intention to visit the home and ask for a convenient time. Unexpected home visits, although very enlightening, may put the parents in an embarrassing situation.

A teacher recalls the time when the parents of Sarah, a very hostile and aggressive child, ignored her invitations to come to school for a conference. After receiving no answer to several of her letters, she decided to pay them a surprise visit. When she arrived, she found the home in terrible disorder, and the mother was in her housecoat and had curlers in her hair. When the teacher told her who she was, the mother literally snarled at her, "What do you want? I have no time to see you." And she didn't see her, in spite of the teacher's protest. It certainly did not help the teacher's relationship with Sarah, who witnessed the disrespect her mother showed for the teacher.

Although the teacher had also experienced pleasant unannounced visits, the experience with Sarah's mother made her more cautious. Such a visit may only add to the parents' antagonism toward school and toward the teacher, which in turn may hurt the child.

Sometimes a teacher invites a child to participate in a conference with his parents. This is a tremendous help in the case of a child who tells untrue stories at home about school. Caution should be taken so that this child will not be placed in a position where he might be shamed or scolded by the parents in front of the teacher. Usually, the teacher gets in touch with the parents and prepares them for such a conference, asking them to listen to the facts without getting angry. To cite an incident, here is the case of Peter.

Peter had told his mother that the teacher scratched his neck, and the mother was rightfully angry. When she came to school, the following conversation took place.

TEACHER: I am terribly sorry that I had to ask you to come immediately, and I appreciate your coming. You seemed so angry on the telephone. Now, would you be so kind as to tell me in Peter's presence the reason for your anger?

MOTHER: He came home crying, showing me the scratch on his neck, saying that you did it. Peter, why don't you show your teacher the scratch on your neck.

PETER: It doesn't hurt me anymore.

TEACHER: Peter, when did I scratch you and for what reason?

PETER: Well, when you put your hand on my neck this morning, it hurt.

TEACHER: I can't recall putting my hand on your neck. Could you help me remember under what circumstances I put my hand on your neck?

PETER: When you bent over to look at my work, you touched me here and it hurt me.

MOTHER: Show her the scratch.

TEACHER: I'm sorry if I hurt you. I did not know, because you said nothing. But how could I have scratched you?

PETER: I couldn't sleep last night because my neck hurt me so.

MOTHER: What do you mean by "last night?" You said that the teacher scratched you this morning.

PETER: She hurt me when she touched me there. I think that I scratched myself at night.

The teacher could see that the mother was forgetting their agreement and was about to explode, but a wink from the teacher helped the mother to control herself. The teacher told Peter that this was an unfortunate misunderstanding and that he should be more careful about how he told a story in the future.

The point is that without the presence of the child, this incident might have assumed serious complications and impaired the relationship with the parent.

The presence of the parents is often very helpful to the discouraged child who is made to feel worthless by his parents. To such a child, it means a great deal to hear his teacher praise him in the presence of his parents. This may be very encouraging to both parents and child.

Letters to parents should impart a feeling of warmth, friendliness, and welcome. They should immediately convey an interest in the child. A letter may read:

Dear Mrs. Cooper,

I have not yet had the pleasure of meeting you. Laura often mentions you to me. She is a very likable little girl, and I enjoy having her in my class.

I should like to discuss her progress with you, as well as plan with you some possible steps we may both take in order to make school a happy place for her.

Could you come to see me any day next week, after the children are dismissed from class? This would make talking more pleasant, as we won't be interrupted. Please let me know when I may expect you.

Sincerely yours,

In contrast, letters conveying anger or anxiety on the part of the teacher may increase or fortify the same feelings within the parents. As a consequence, more pressure is brought to bear on the child, and it may increase the antagonism that some parents harbor against teachers and school.

To illustrate this point, let us examine the following letter:

Dear Mrs. Cooper,

I have written three letters to you concerning Laura's behavior at school, which you have ignored. Her behavior has become increasingly worse, and it has reached a point where I refuse to cope with it unless you assume your responsibility. Your indifference toward this situation is, in my opinion, an important factor in Laura's misbehavior.

I expect you Thursday at 3:30 p.m.

Sincerely yours,

What purpose does such a letter serve? Such letters are usually written when teachers are at their wit's end and do not know what to do with the child. This example is a very clear demonstration of how the teacher's reaction to the child's misbehavior reflects the same goals that we encounter in the child.

In this particular situation, we can see a teacher who feels threatened and angered by the lack of response both from the parent and the child. We can also see a completely discouraged teacher who is throwing her hands up in despair.

The mother is just as helpless as the teacher. We must assume that this child has had difficulty in school all along and that the mother has been called to school many times about the bad things her child has done. The mother has never received any insight into how she continues to fortify the child's wrong attitudes by her response, nor has she been helped with practical suggestions in dealing with the child at home. Very often this is why parents do not respond to the teacher's request for conferences.

In this situation the teacher will grab at any means to exonerate herself. Consequently, she blames the parents. This is not necessarily done on a conscious level. The general trend is to pass the buck and put the blame on the parents. Although we fully recognize that the problems children have at school often start before they enter school and that the home is the source of the child's discouragement, we cannot and must not put the blame on the parents who, in their ignorance, do what they think is best for their children.

If teachers were better trained in child behavior, they could have helped such a child in kindergarten and eliminated the problem. In this respect the school has failed the parent rather than that the parent has failed the school.

The Interview

Before meeting with the parents, it may be helpful for the teacher to jot down a tentative list of topics she may want to discuss. She may prepare a few samples of the child's work, including pictures, stories, or a workbook. It is important that some of these samples deserve praise. If the child has produced absolutely nothing that merits praise, the teacher may tell of some clever or funny remarks of the child that were appreciated by the class. She may tell of an incident in which the child was helpful to her or another child. In talking about the child's work, it is important for the teacher to begin with a positive report, pointing out a child's strengths before mentioning his weaknesses. (The teacher must keep in mind that parents usually need encouragement.) For instance, the teacher may say, "Mike has a firm, clear handwriting. It is so easy to check his work." Or, "Mike has an unusually rich vocabulary." Most children have some positive qualities or have done something worth praising, either in a subject matter or in human relationships.

A good place to begin may also be in telling the parents about something in which the child has shown particular interest, like working puzzles, watering the plants, running errands, music, dancing, telling jokes, checking papers, or helping other children.

An interview may have a good start if the teacher asks the parents how they feel about the child's progress at school. If the parents say that the child does not seem happy in school, it is wise for the teacher not to show surprise or hurt feelings. If the child is really not happy, she would know it. She may say, "Yes, this is also my feeling, and this is one of the reasons I was so anxious to talk with you. I feel that we must find the root of his unhappiness and make some specific plans for school and for home that might help him." The parents may insist that their child is quite happy at home but unhappy in school. Although this may be questionable, the teacher has a better chance of winning the parents over by not expressing her doubts. She may ask the mother how she came to this conclusion. Inevitably, the teacher may be able to show the parents that the child's unhappiness at school stems from his inability to accept a situation in which he cannot have his way, from his wanting to stay at home with her, or from his feelings of inadequacy or inferiority to others.

The main purpose of the first conference is to establish a relationship with the parents based on confidence and the realization that both teacher and parents have a common goal. Such realization will, in most cases, lead to cooperation and a better understanding. Most parents participate actively in a conference if they are made to feel at ease and respected. The following conference took place between a teacher and the mother of a 9-year-old boy who performed poorly academically.

MOTHER: I am Mrs. Thomas, David's mother.

TEACHER: How do you do, Mrs. Thomas. I am so glad to meet you, and I'm very happy that you could come. David told me this morning that he wasn't sure if you would be able to come. In fact, he told me not to expect you.

MOTHER: I wonder why he said that? I did not tell him that I might not come.

TEACHER: It doesn't matter as long as you are here.

MOTHER: I must speak to him and find out why he told you such a lie.

TEACHER: Why don't we get acquainted first, and then we'll see if it's necessary to mention this to David. Perhaps he thought that you were exceptionally busy today. He is very observant. He notices many things that most children do not see.

MOTHER: Yes, he observes many things. Too many, if you ask me.

TEACHER: He is a very smart little fellow with a great deal of imagination. Would you care to see the story he wrote last week? He read it to the class, and we all enjoyed it tremendously.

MOTHER: Oh, yes, he told me about it.

TEACHER: Did he? What did he say?

MOTHER: Oh, he came home bragging about the wonderful story he wrote and how everyone applauded.

TEACHER: What did you say to him?

MOTHER: I don't like when he comes home bragging, especially since he is not doing so well in school.

TEACHER: Did he tell you that?

MOTHER: Not exactly, but I got it out of him. First he told me that all is going well, but when I asked specific questions, he had to admit that things weren't so well. I always find out.

TEACHER: Would you mind telling me what specific questions you asked him?

MOTHER: I asked him if he finishes his work on time, and he said that he finishes sometimes. Well, "sometimes" is not good enough for me, and I hope, not enough for you. I told him that if he didn't finish every day he'd be in big trouble with me and that I would go to school to find out.

TEACHER: Do you think that he might have been worried about your coming to school today?

MOTHER: I'm sure he was. I think that may be the reason he told you that I wouldn't come. He probably thought that you wouldn't wait for me then.

TEACHER: Why is he so afraid, assuming that you did find out that he doesn't do his work?

MOTHER: He knows that he would be punished.

TEACHER: How do you punish him? What do you do?

MOTHER: He gets it with the strap.

TEACHER: Do you usually use a strap on him?

MOTHER: Sometimes I do, and sometimes his father does. But we don't always use the strap. Sometimes we send him to his room, and sometimes we take away television privileges or other privileges. But mostly we have to spank him.

TEACHER: Does he mind you then?

MOTHER: For a while he does.

TEACHER: This means that you have to punish him often.

MOTHER: Oh, yes, very often.

TEACHER: For how long have you been punishing him for not doing his schoolwork?

MOTHER: Oh, almost for as long as he has been going to school. He would have done nothing if we hadn't laid down the law.

TEACHER: Have you ever tried any other method?

MOTHER: We have tried everything. We have given him money and toys for good behavior, and it didn't work. We locked him in his room, and it did not help. We tried almost everything. Only a good spanking will make him work.

TEACHER: It may make him work for a while, as you yourself said. By forcing him to do reading and homework, he cannot develop a proper attitude toward it. Also, there is the danger that, although he does not enjoy the actual work you force him to do, he may enjoy the attention you give him.

MOTHER: I can see by your talking that he isn't doing well in school.

TEACHER: He is doing well in the things he enjoys and for which he receives recognition.

MOTHER: What things? Does he read well? Does he finish his work every day? Are you pleased with his work?

TEACHER: There are certain things he does quite well and which please me. He likes to write, and he enjoys working with clay. He wrote several very good original stories. Would you care to read them?

MOTHER: Can he spell? I don't understand how he can write stories when he can't spell.

TEACHER: He is not a good speller, but if I were to make an issue of it, he would give up writing his stories, and that would be a pity. He may, in time, if we encourage him to write, take more interest in spelling. We must build on the positive, and thereby encourage him to attempt to learn the things that seem to him too difficult now. If we criticize him all the time, we only discourage him further. Can you see what I mean?

MOTHER: I think I understand what you mean. But what can I do to help him?

TEACHER: Mrs. Thomas, would you mind trying a different approach for a few weeks? If it doesn't work, you can always go back to your old methods.

MOTHER: What do you suggest we do?

TEACHER: Would you try not to question him about school and not make him do any schoolwork?

MOTHER: You mean I should do nothing?

TEACHER: Not nothing. Do things with him that he will like, like playing games, singing, talking, maybe cooking or baking—anything that he will enjoy doing with you. In addition, you may start training him to accept responsibilities at home. Does he have any responsibilities at home?

MOTHER: He is supposed to take out the garbage, but he forgets most of the time. We go through so much aggravation making him do it that I decided to do it myself.

TEACHER: Did David choose to take out the garbage, or did you decide that?

MOTHER: I thought that this would be the easiest thing for him to do.

TEACHER: Why don't you let him choose to do something that he would want to do? Talk it over with him. Asking him for his consent or advice will make him feel important. Most children will assume responsibilities but do not like to be pressured. You see, if he chooses his job, he assumes a responsibility, which is different from forcing him to accept one. In class, he usually carries out the responsibilities that he himself has assumed.

MOTHER: And what if he doesn't remember?

TEACHER: This could be discussed with him also. Decide on a logical consequence, something with a direct bearing on what he is doing, and then apply it. He won't resent it because he has already helped you to decide on what the consequence should be.

MOTHER: I'll talk it over with my husband and tell him what you suggested.

TEACHER: Please do. I hope that he will be willing to try my suggestions. Please, let me know what you have decided to do, and if I can help you in any way, don't hesitate to call on me.

MOTHER: I'll call you soon.

This is one example of an interview with a parent. The general approach and topics to be discussed will depend on the child's difficulties and on the attitude of the parents. In all situations, however, we try to win the parents, just as we try to win the child.

In this particular incident, the mother followed the suggestions, was consistent about her new approach, and had good results.

The parents' satisfaction with David at home had a direct influence on his attitude toward school. David found out that he could get attention through useful means.

If a child has difficulty in school, the parents should know about it once he has reached third or fourth grade. Difficulties do not start all of a sudden. Often parents do not know how to help their child. They are completely unaware of how their own behavior toward their child contributes or may even be the source of his difficulties. Mrs. Thomas was unaware that her negative attention, scolding, nagging, and punishing intensified David's problem. Frances' mother did not realize that she was encouraging her daughter to be a bad listener by repeating her requests so often.

There are the parents who have definite ideas about how their child must be treated at school and at home and who come to the conference in order to tell them to the teacher. This holds especially true of parents who believe in strict discipline and who challenge the teacher and her methods. They may be critical because she does not use enough discipline; other parents may think she is too strict. The former almost always are parents who have used corporal punishment for years without any results, yet expect the teacher to use the same method and get results. It is easier to convince the strict parents that their methods are useless than it is to convince those who complain that the teacher is too strict. Because they are convinced that allowing their child free and unrestricted rights gives the child the feeling of being loved and of having security, parents allow their children to rule and control them. Consequently, they resent any restrictions that the teacher puts on the child and demand that the child be given the same freedom in class that he enjoys at home.

The following example illustrates this kind of parent. It concerns the mother of Frank, a 9-year-old boy who was in the third grade.

Frank was a year behind in school because his mother had been reluctant to send him to kindergarten when he was 5. She felt he was too young to be away from home and might pick up all kinds of diseases from other children. At 6 he went to first grade but had to be put back into kindergarten because of his inability to adjust. In spite of this, he was no more ready for first grade than he was the year before, but because of his age, he was promoted from one grade to the next. Frank made no progress in school. In addition, he was a behavior problem in class, paying no attention to the teacher, disregarding school rules and regulations, and staying home frequently, either the entire day or half the day.

When he was scolded or reproached for his behavior, he would start to cry. His crying would gradually increase to sobbing. He could keep this up for hours, until the children regretted having reprimanded him and asked him for forgiveness. This would happen even after the class discussed his behavior and the purpose of his crying. They kept falling for his trap. He always succeeded in making others feel guilty if they did not act according to his wishes.

Frank was the youngest of five children, all of whom were either married or living away from home.

From his mother the teacher learned that not only did the parents make a toy out of him, granting him every whim, but his siblings did so as well. The mother said that they all loved him so and that, in addition, it was hard to refuse him anything since he was so sensitive and easily hurt. His father was especially afraid to upset Frank. He bought him many toys, went to bed with him at night, and waited for him to fall asleep. Frank would not go to bed unless his father went also. Before leaving the house in the morning, Frank would tell his mother what he wanted for lunch and for dinner. If she did not comply with his wishes, his father would take him to a restaurant.

Frank's parents were completely unaware of how their treatment of Frank at home encouraged his uncooperative behavior at school. It took some time before his mother could understand that they had made a little tyrant out of their son and that he now controlled their lives. It was even more difficult to convince the father that he was doing his son harm and depriving him of a normal development. However, after several conferences with both parents, the parents agreed to put some restrictions on Frank and to refrain from letting him dictate to them. In time, Frank's behavior changed both at home and in school. It was a slow, gradual process, but it went steadily uphill. This would not have happened had the teacher held the belief that the home situation was none of her business.

The teacher must be a good listener. She must be constantly alert, picking up clues and follow up on them. For example, if a parent says, "My child is very shy," the teacher may ask, "Could you tell me how this is expressed and what you do?" In this way, she might learn that the parent felt sorry for him and came to his aid. The teacher may succeed in pointing this out to them. If a mother says that she does not let her child do a sloppy job, she may want perfection from the child. This mother may set too high goals and discourage him in this way. She does not realize that a child needs recognition for merely trying to be useful. He may lose all desire to be of help again if his performance did not live up to his parents' expectations, if he should get scolded, or if his efforts were belittled. These parents need to be helped to understand that their own ambitions are hindering the child from developing pleasure and pride in the things that he can do according to his ability.

If a mother refers to her youngest child as "my baby," even though he is already 9 or 10 years old, we may assume that the child is being held back in his development. The teacher must, in a gentle way, point out to the mother what she is doing. Such children often fear growing up because they are afraid to lose the position of being the "baby" and pampered.

If a mother tells of another of her children who is always good and who never causes any trouble, it may give the teacher a clue to the difficulties the child has both at school and at home. In the competition with this good sibling, her student probably gave up and tried to have a place at home by receiving attention in a destructive way.

Many parents are impressed with the "yes" child—the one who gets satisfaction from the ready compliance that has always brought approval. Often these children fear to express any disagreement or anger because they depend so much on approval and on being liked. They frequently lack initiative and live in constant fear of displeasing others. The parents are usually not aware of this. Their satisfaction with this kind of behavior encourages the child in his fallacious convictions. He never develops the important courage to be imperfect.

If a parent comes to an interview angry about some incident or because she is convinced that coming to school is a waste of time, the teacher would do well to listen until this parent has told her story and blown off some steam. By listening attentively she may gather some information that may help her in understanding the child's present problems. Anger often fades away when it is met with a genuine wish to understand. Usually, the parent calms down as soon as she realizes that the teacher is concerned and sympathetic to her feelings. Then the parent becomes more approachable and will listen to what the teacher has to say.

In certain situations, however, a teacher may disarm an angry parent, as the following example will illustrate.

Mr. Koda arrived ten minutes late for his interview. He stopped at the door and said, "I am a busy man, so don't keep me more than a few minutes. What is it you wanted to talk to me about?"

TEACHER: I am sorry to have bothered you, Mr. Koda. I did not know you were so busy. Besides, it wouldn't be fair to Jim if I were to take only a few minutes to talk to his father. Under the circumstances it would be better if we postponed this conference. Thank you for coming. Goodbye.

MR. KODA: Well, I'm here already. If it takes a little longer, I'll stay a little longer, just don't keep me more than is necessary. I have a business, you know, and can't stay away all day.

TEACHER: Yes, I know, Mr. Koda. But since a conference would be of help to Jim and to me only if we could talk without having to watch the clock, I really believe that it would be better if you came some other day when you could spare the time. I will always be glad to see you. I am very fond of your son.

MR. KODA: I'd rather stay, if you don't mind, and talk as long as it is necessary. Jimmy often mentions your name. He is very fond of you, too.

TEACHER: I'm glad you're staying. You have a very interesting boy, Mr. Koda.

MR. KODA: Maybe so, but I have no luck with him. I don't know what makes him so lazy.

TEACHER: I wouldn't say that Jimmy is lazy. He may appear that way because he is not working in school, but this is not due to laziness.

MR. KODA: Then what is it due to?

TEACHER: I believe that he is overambitious and very discouraged. He doesn't believe that he can succeed, and so he doesn't even try.

MR. KODA: Jimmy ambitious? I'd give anything if he had any ambition. I keep on telling him that. Why should he be discouraged? Who discourages him? Believe me, no kid ever gets more from parents than he does.

TEACHER: You mean that you give him material things?

MR. KODA: Yes, and we give him love, too.

It was a slow process for the teacher to try to explain to this father that giving material things without giving a child a sense of accomplishment, of respect, and of parental approval is of little value, and may do harm to the child's self-concept and to his general development. We discussed Jim's position in the family, the father's open disappointment in his son, the scolding and humiliation to which he exposed him, and how this undermined Jim's self-respect and sense of worth. Equally, spoiling him, whether by his father or by his mother, had deprived Jim of developing his own strength and added to his sense of being a failure. At this point, Jim did not believe that he was good enough as he was, nor did he believe that doing average work would gain him the prestige he desired. He felt that he had to be something special, far superior to the other children, and since he did not believe that he could attain such a position, he gave up trying. This expressed itself especially in areas in which he feared failure, such as reading and spelling. He concentrated on sports because he was sure he would be successful. In addition, he manufactured deeds and achievements in order to gain status with the class.

Mr. Koda became very much interested in our discussion. He came to a number of conferences, and we discussed possible steps that would encourage Jim both at home and at school and that would bring him recognition with realistic achievement.

If we review what happened in this interview, we see that in the first place, the teacher did not let the father throw or intimidate her with anger. She remained courteous, expressed her belief in his son, and also her regret that the father had no time to help her with his boy. Had the teacher responded emotionally, expressed her disappointment or shown anger, she would have spoiled her chances for Mr. Koda's cooperation. The teacher did not become defensive but directed the father's attention to an objective observation of his child's potential and the means he used to obtain recognition. She did not argue with the father, because she did not want to build a wall between the father and herself, which, in turn, would have hurt Jimmy.

The feelings with which the parents come to an interview differ widely. Some come with definite ideas about what they want for their child. Some have definite ideas about the kind of discipline they want and openly criticize the teacher for being too lenient or too strict: "I want you to keep him in during lunch until he finishes his work," or, "I don't want you to keep him in during recess or any other time when the other children go out, regardless of whether he does his work or not." Some parents will say, "I don't want you to discuss him in front of the group." Others will demand, "Shame him and embarrass him in front of the class. This may make an impression on him."

Some parents are inclined to jump to the defense of their child regardless of the incident. They cannot admit that their child has done any wrong, either out of a belief that such admission may do harm to the child or out of a fear that it may put them in a bad light as parents.

Parents who believe that the teacher is blaming them for the child's difficulties in school must be reassured and put at ease as quickly as possible. The teacher could say the following to such a parent:

> "I am sorry to have given you the impression that you are to blame. I am sure that you did the best you could, and I hope that you feel the same way about me. Both of us are concerned about Helen, and, of course, we both want to do everything possible to help her. It is for this reason that I asked you to come to school. As we talk, we may realize where either one of us has made mistakes and how they can be rectified."

During the discussion that follows, the teacher may learn about a class situation of which she was completely unaware. For instance, the parent may tell the teacher that his child feels that the teacher does not like him. This needs to be investigated. The child may have gotten this erroneous concept because of some remark or action on the teacher's part. She may learn that this child does not like to sit next to his neighbor. This may happen in spite of the sociogram the teacher administered. She could then seat him next to the classmate of his choice.

In discussing this frankly with the parents, without being on the defensive, the teacher can help them to realize her genuine concern and her willingness to change her methods, if need be. This makes it easier for parents to accept suggestions from the teacher.

Some parents come to complain about other children who pick on their child and demand that the teacher do something about it. This may be a clue to their child's feelings about other children, his dependency on parental protection, his need for their sympathy, or his use of this as a means to keep the parents busy with him.

The teacher should listen without brushing off accusations. She should listen to the parents' account of how their child behaved in other classes, with children in the neighborhood, and with his siblings. As the teacher listens, she should be able to sense the feeling of the parent, which should help her to understand the present difficulties this child has in social relationships. Often the parent describes the home situation as a battleground in which both parents become involved in their children's fights and feel that they must protect Irving at home from being hurt by his sisters and brothers. The teacher may explain that such protection only weakens the child and that many children get into fights deliberately in order to involve the parents. This may be a means of conveying to the parents "how bad the others are and how good I am," or, "I am small and weak and must be protected," which is not necessarily true. If these children were left to fight their own battles, they would probably learn how to take care of themselves or (which is more likely) not to get into fights. The teacher must explain this to the parents and suggest that they stay out of their child's quarrels. The teacher may tell the parents of similar cases that were solved in the proposed manner. She may offer comments and information about children in general, leading to more insight into children's behavior.

The teacher's interest in whatever the parents have to say and her desire to learn from them, will put the parents at ease so that they will talk freely and willingly. The teacher should try to be objective and sympathetic when she attempts to see how each parent views his child.

Communication with the parent is not necessarily on a verbal level. The teacher may easily betray her feelings of anger, discouragement, contempt for the parents by severity in her voice, a critical look, a movement indicating impatience, or other signs indicating antagonism. The teacher must be aware of such possibilities. This does not imply that she must necessarily agree with what the parents are doing or share their point of view. Listening attentively is, in itself, a means of giving encouragement.

Conferences Regarding Homework, Grades, and Subject Matter

Parents need a reeducation with regard to homework and the responsibility they have in this matter. This should be conveyed by the teacher as soon as the child enters school. Most parents are made to believe that they are responsible for the homework of their children. Also, they are sincerely convinced that they help the child academically when the force him to do the homework and offer their assistance with it.

The fallacy of their thinking is manifold. By taking over the responsibility of the child's homework, the child is deprived of developing a sense of responsibility, of becoming independent, and of learning from his faulty attitude.

A parent who takes over this responsibility for the child may never be free from this servitude. In time, the parents will begin to resent this bondage and will demand independent behavior from the child, something for which he has never been trained. This will inevitably lead to conflict.

Homework may become a strong weapon in the child's hands, something that he can use effectively to extort privileges or to exploit and punish ambitious parents. Therefore, parents must be helped not only to place homework in the hands of the child, but to be less concerned, even when they do not talk about it. The value of homework is primarily a way of training the child to work on his own and to accept responsibilities.

Helping the child may also reinforce an incorrect evaluation of his capacities and of how he must act to be successful. If he has little self-confidence, it will only strengthen this concept. If he seeks constant attention, his helplessness brings him the desired satisfaction and reinforces his belief that this is how he must act.

If the teacher finds it necessary to give homework, she must first win the cooperation of her students. Enforced homework has little educational value. In many cases, the time spent on imposed homework is wasted. The child does not learn from repetition unless he has first grasped the meaning of what he is doing. Mere mechanical repetition without understanding is futile. In too many cases the children see no value in the assignment and consider their task busy work. Very often, it is exactly that. All the child learns is to hate school and the teacher. At any rate, the parents should stay out of it.

Parents can help the child by explaining to him why they will not give him much help. They must provide a place where the child can work undisturbed. An important aspect is the time for doing homework. Children will accept the responsibility more readily if they are given a chance to go out and play or watch a favorite TV program after a long day in school.

Often parents ask in complete dismay. "Do you mean to say that I should do nothing to help my child?" This becomes a ticklish situation requiring judgment on the part of the teacher so that she neither antagonizes the parents nor harms the child. The teacher could usually answer in the following manner:

> "Of course you are concerned and want to help, and I am sure that you will be able to help your child, but not until we have helped him change his attitude toward learning, that is, not until he enjoys it and asks for help. Right now, he resents it, and being forced into it makes him fight you and dislike studies. Making him do homework does not provide a learning situation. If it were, you would not have to force him to do it each day for so many months. By now, he should be able and willing to do his work on his own if he has profited from your pressure. I would suggest that you withdraw from this struggle and not force him to do any work. Discuss this with your child first. Tell him that he is old enough and smart enough to take care of his school obligations himself. It will be up to him whether he does or does not do his homework. However, if he should ask you to explain something to him, by all means, do so, but after he understands what he must do, leave him alone. When he wants to read to you, tell him that you will be glad to listen to him and that it will give you pleasure. Won't you, please, try this method for a few weeks and then come to see me again? If it doesn't work, we may have to try something else."

As we have already pointed out, homework only has a value if it is done by the child out of a sense of responsibility and a desire to make progress. Parents may discuss homework policies with their child, help him decide the time he should work, and allow him sufficient time to do the work. They should not interrupt the child with requests and questions while he is working. Neither should they peek in every few minutes to see how much he has done. If the child chooses to do nothing during the allotted time, then we must look for deeper causes and eliminate them before we can expect the child to do his work well and profit from it.

One should never deprive children of play because of homework. Children who spend two-thirds of the day in school, where all of their activities are organized and supervised, need time when they can play or talk with whomever they please, or engage in some activity all by themselves. They look forward to coming home where their lives are different, just as much as they look forward to going back to school in the morning.

Report Cards

The conventional method of reporting pupil status and progress to parents has been a controversial issue for many years. There are those who demand the report card as a way of summarizing the child's progress and success in his academic achievement and social adjustment. Others claim that it is an inadequate evaluation and interpretation of his progress, that it is misleading to the parents, and that it may do harm to the child because poor grades may discourage him, whereas high grades may develop wrong values. Furthermore, it may cause friction between parents and teachers, confuse them, and cause tension and worry. Finally, it can never convey what the child really knows or is capable of doing.

Reporting pupil progress to parents has been and still is one of the most frustrating and most unsatisfactory aspects of a teacher's job. Educators have tried for years to devise a new and more accurate form of reporting pupil progress, without much success. So far, no report card has conveyed to parents what the teacher wants them to know.

The parent-teacher conference is the only possible means of realistically reporting a student's progress, both academic and social, to his parents. Much more can be said by the teacher than can be written. Parents can ask questions about what they do not understand.

Reading

Reading is one of the subjects about which parents are most anxious, and where they put the most pressure on the child. Usually parental anxiety does not develop until the child is in the third or fourth grade and has not made progress. Their anxiety and pressure only increases the child's negative attitude toward reading and his feeling of inadequacy. The child dreads the time when he must read to his parents, for they shame and discourage him in the process of teaching.

Some children utilize their lack of academic achievement to keep their parents busy with them. For the child this may become a means of taking his parents away from the other members of the family or of keeping mother or father all to himself.

Parents do not realize, and often cannot understand, why the child would enjoy such negative attention. "How can he possibly want this, knowing how angry he makes me and that I may even punish him?" they ask. These parents need help in understanding the child's private logic, his goal of power, and the means by which he tries, usually with success, to achieve it. What can parents do to help strengthen the child's reading? There are a number of things they can do.

Probably, the most important step in developing a child's liking for reading is for the parents to read themselves. It is not uncommon to find that the parents who put much emphasis on reading rarely read a book themselves. They claim that they have no time. This does not stop them from telling their child how important it is to read and how much pleasure they derive from it. Logically, a child asks himself, "If it is so important and so pleasant, how come my mother and father never read anything except newspapers? It can't be as important as all that." Children may pattern themselves after their parents and take on their values.

Every family should have a set reading time. If the child is still too young to read by himself, the parents can read to him, choosing a variety of reading materials and discussing the material with him in a stimulating way. Preaching, explaining, and forcing the child to read does not stimulate him but, rather, results in boredom and a hatred for the subject.

When a child begins to read by himself and wants to read to his parents, they should show interest and enjoyment as they listen to him. It is absolutely necessary for them to avoid any criticism when he makes mistakes, for them never to shame him. Parents should follow along as the child reads and quickly, but casually, pronounce any word that might cause the child difficulty. This prevents embarrassment. If the child does not understand a word, they may look it up in a dictionary together. Parents can take the child to the library and allow him to choose his own books. With careful guidance, the child will learn to choose critically and wisely.

Parents can buy interesting books for their child and encourage him to build his own library. Parents should not insist that their child read only in his own room but instead should make every room in the house available to him for the purpose of reading.

It is a mistake to compare children in achievement or to hold up a sibling as an example. This may only drive the discouraged learner to withdraw further, since he fears that he cannot compete with his smarter brother or sister.

How Parents Can Help a Child Who Has Difficulties in Arithmetic

In general, if the child has difficulty with arithmetic or any other subject besides reading, the problems tend to be similar. There are ways in which parents can help their child without actually teaching him. The first and most important step is to plan situations in which the child can use numbers in an enjoyable manner. They can play simple games requiring counting, matching numbers, comparing, measuring quantity, and so forth. In helping mother set the table, the child may count the silverware, plates, and glasses. Together, mother and child may count the steps from the kitchen to the table, to the door, and so forth. They can play games, such as horseshoes and parcheesi, in which the child does the scoring. Children may help to make the grocery or laundry list; they should be encouraged to buy something at the store and bring home the change. This may then be recounted with the parent. Playing ball or jumping and counting is another way to teach the meaning of numbers. In each case, the parent must avoid pressuring the child. Such activities are accepted by the child only if the child enjoys them as he does playing games.

Older children who have problems with numbers are usually already discouraged and afraid of the subject. Their difficulties may well express their general inability to solve other problems in life. Helping these children with the mechanical aspect of arithmetic is of little value. Parents need to understand their part in what caused these difficulties, as well as the extent to which they have and are still contributing to the present state by trying to solve the child's problems for him instead of by guiding him to find the solutions by himself. After the child has been helped to trust his own judgment, a good tutor may help him catch up with the subject.

When and Why Some Parents Become Alarmed

The majority of parents become more alarmed when their children develop disturbing behavior than when they fail academically. Teachers, as a rule, find it more difficult to approach and to help parents whose children are behavior problems. Why is this so?

There are numerous reasons for this panic. When the child has difficulty learning a subject matter, the parents may assume that this is the school's or the teacher's fault, or they may blame it on hereditary deficiencies. Next, they may believe that with special help at home, either by them or by a tutor, the problem may be eased, if not entirely alleviated. They may consider transferring the child to another school, especially to a private school, which, they hope, will take care of the problem. In other words, they can find a number of ways to put the blame on everyone except themselves. Behavioral transgressions, however, reflect directly on them as parents.

They regard them as indictments against themselves and feel personally deficient and powerless. They see themselves as failures, embarrassed and humiliated. Some challenge the teacher to remedy the situation by disciplining the child, while others refuse to discuss the matter.

It is often extremely difficult to reach any understanding with such parents, because they do not listen to what the teacher has to say.

Let's consider another case:

Rachel's mother became indignant when she was told that her daughter did not make friends at school because she called other children ugly names and used vulgar speech. At first, Rachel's mother insisted that this was not true, that the children deliberately manufactured these tales in order to get Rachel into trouble. Next, she maintained that if it were true, Rachel must have picked up such language in school, for at home nobody ever used foul language. When she was assured that using such language was only a symptom of a more serious problem, she became even angrier and shouted, "How dare you make such an accusation?" The teacher's concern was for Rachel's loneliness and how she could help her. However, it was impossible to convey this to Rachel's mother who had only one thing in mind, namely to divert the blame from herself, even though she was not being blamed.

Some parents panic because they have heard so much about juvenile delinquency and fear that their child is heading in that direction. Their immediate reaction is, "I must take him to a psychiatrist before he gets into serious trouble." Every now and then, they actually do so, in spite of the teacher's advice to try, if only for a while, to change their way of treating the child at home. They find it difficult, however, to associate their method of bringing up their child with his behavior.

The teacher should be able to explain to the parents why their child misbehaves and what they can do to correct the situation. They can teach the child self-control through the application of logical consequences, which does not mean demanding blind obedience. Such obedience is superficial and does not last. There is little value in making children obey. Rigid discipline may develop overdependence and fearfulness of new situations if there is no one around to tell the child what to do.

The teacher should take the opportunity to tell the parents about the class council (see Chapter 15) and how this self-government helps the children to develop self-discipline and to understand their own problems, as well as those of other children. In this way, they learn how to help and encourage one another, how to evaluate a situation, and then how to make their own decisions. This gives the teacher an opportunity to explain to the parents how they can train their children and achieve greater cooperation and harmony at home through the use of the family council see (Chapter 29).

Other Suggestions for Parents

Most parents who have been counseled are very grateful for the experience. Few have another place where they can take their problems or where someone will be interested in helping them (see Chapter 23).

Teachers can and must help troubled parents. Many suggestions have been outlined in this chapter. Teachers must, however, he careful not to swamp parents with too many suggestions at one time, for they may become frightened and discouraged.

We should like to mention that almost every teacher, at one time or another, has an unsuccessful interview with a parent. Even the best and most skilled teacher may say the wrong thing. The wrong gesture or the wrong tone of voice may spoil the interview and prevent the desired results.

Teachers must be careful of how they word their suggestions. We have found that it is most acceptable to parents when we invite them to try our suggestions for a while and find out for themselves. We must be careful to point out that there is no assurance that the child will respond favorably immediately, but he may. However, we may point out that other parents with similar problems have had good results when they tried a new approach.

Frequent Arguments Given by Parents

"I'm afraid that he takes after me. I never could stop talking in class. Don't you think that he might have inherited this trait from me? As a matter of fact, my mother told me that she had the same trouble herself."

"I must admit, I never was much of a reader myself. I hardly ever read anything but a newspaper or a magazine. My husband isn't much of a reader either, but I insist that my children read every day."

"School is nothing but a playground these days. In my day there was no nonsense. We had to study, and we did. I don't know if it's because of the new system that children play so much in school or because the teachers just like to make it easier for themselves."

"If you ask me, you are using too much psychology. I don't believe in all this nonsense. Why should my child feel insecure? He gets everything he wants. He has a good home."

"What do you mean, 'He is insecure?' You should see him jump off the diving board and ride his bike without holding on. He is not afraid of anything."

"I can't understand why parents are called to school so often these days. School problems are your problems. I have my own problems, and I don't bother you with them."

"If you have problems with my child, it is your business to know what to do.

That's what you are trained for and what you are getting paid for. I don't see why we parents have to help the teacher."

"John is a sensitive child. You can't treat him like you treat any other child. I don't mean that he should get special treatment, but you know what I mean. He is different."

"My child isn't used to frustrations. At home we allow him to do what he wants to do. Why shouldn't he have all the freedom he wants in his own home? Then at school he is required to do certain things at a certain time. He is restricted, and he becomes disturbed. He is used to being his own boss."

"I'm sorry to hear that my Jimmy causes so much trouble. Maybe we ought to put him in a private school."

"I think that you just don't like my daughter. I must speak to the principal about it immediately. I want her out of your class."

"Jimmy never had any trouble in school until he came to you."

"The children in this neighborhood are a bad influence on Charles. You know this neighborhood isn't what it used to be. Some very undesirable people have moved in. We try to keep Charles away from the other children, but he has learned a lot of bad things from them anyway."

"Maybe if you moved his seat away from Tommy things would be better. We never did like this boy, and we're sure that he is a bad influence on our boy."

"Do you think that his thinness may have something to do with his listlessness? He is such a bad eater. He hardly eats at all. How can he have the energy to concentrate on his work?"

"Why don't you shame him in front of the entire class? Embarrass him in front of everybody, and this may teach him a lesson."

"Why don't you use the good old paddle? It never hurt me any, and it will do my boy some good. Believe me, we couldn't stand it if we didn't paddle him when he deserved it."

"I'm a very busy man, and I can stay only for a few minutes. Now, what can I do for you? Well, I leave the upbringing of the children to their mother. This is a mother's job. Why don't you get in touch with my wife and have her come to see you?"

"I spoke to our doctor about Jimmy's trouble in school. He told me not to worry—that Jimmy will outgrow this stage. Frankly, I was a devil myself at his age, and I came out alright."

"Teachers try to take out their frustration on the kids. This is nothing new. Any little thing they do becomes a big problem. John is a normal boy— the way I like a boy to be. A good fight now and then is good for him. It makes no difference who is at fault or who started it. Let him have his fight."

"I had no idea that Sally was so bad in school. This is the first time that I've heard of it. If the records say that she was a problem in the other classes, I knew nothing about it."

"I tried everything. I promised to give him $1 for every good grade on his report card. We bought him a special bike in return for his promise that he would be a good boy. He promises everything, but he never keeps his promises. We don't know what to do any more."

"I wish I had a dime for every time I was called to school. When John brings a note from school, I get so upset that I start shaking."

"I hate to say this about my own child, but I'm afraid he is no good. I am not one of those mothers who tries to fool themselves and who shut their eyes to the truth. My husband and I have tried everything. We have tried giving him much love, and it hasn't done any good. We have tried punishing him, spanking him, and locking him up in his room, but nothing has helped."

"Don't you believe that some children are born with a bad streak in them? I honestly think that my John was bad from the day he was born. We had no trouble with the other children, but we always had trouble with him."

"John is lazy. He is the laziest thing at home. I can talk myself hoarse and he won't do a thing. I know what you are up against."

"I thought that when he gets to you, you would straighten him out. Guess I was wrong about that."

"I know exactly when his troubles started. In second grade, he had a very bad teacher. He had no trouble until he had her."

"I can't understand why he has trouble with reading and spelling in school when he does so well at home. He reads for me, and I give him spelling words, and he has no trouble at all."

"Wait until I get home. I'll skin him alive. No child of mine is going to behave that way."

"I can't understand why Anne should have so much trouble in school. None of my other children had any trouble. After all, they were brought up exactly in the same way and in the same family."

"He is not a bad boy at home. My only trouble with him is that he follows me around like a shadow. He wants to sit on my lap, and he even wants me to carry him to bed. He is getting so heavy that I can hardly lift him."

"I am afraid I cannot help you. His mother pampers him to death. She makes a real sissy out of him. If I say, "No," he runs to her crying, and she lets him have his way."

"He is very much like his father. He inherited his father's stubbornness and other traits, which are not especially praiseworthy."

Chapter 29
The Family Council

Teachers can help parents by showing them how the training children receive at home is reflected in their behavior in school and in the community. They train children either to conform to or defy the rules of society. Parents should prepare the child for socialized living, but they often do not know how to do it. They no longer have the power to make children behave and study or to stop them from being destructive, but they can and often want to learn what to do. The first step is often to set up a family council.

What Is a Family Council?

Teachers can help parents to establish democratic practices in their homes by having scheduled family meetings, or councils. A family council is a cooperative discussion of topics of common interest, a meeting in which all family members sit together, encourage each other in their endeavors, and reach decisions concerning family matters.

The family council is the best way to resolve the everyday problems of all family members. Regular family meetings encourage and promote responsibility, initiative, and cooperation. They stimulate sensitivity to the needs of others in the family. Family meetings give every member of the family a chance to express himself freely and the opportunity to listen to others and participate in the responsibilities of the family.

The family council is based on the same principles of mutual respect, trust, equality, and cooperation that we have discussed in previous chapters dealing with the class council and the democratic classroom. Nobody has the right to dictate, and no one has the obligation to submit to dictates.

Consideration for other family members replaces satisfaction of personal desires. The family council has much more significance than as the place where the family decides who will do the various household tasks.

Every member of the family who is old enough to express an opinion should be included. Children can help and should be able to voice an opinion in family affairs. This makes family life more enjoyable and helps to prepare youngsters for responsibility.

The family council, more than anything else, provides each member with a sense of equal status, both in regard to rights and in regard to obligations; in this sense it facilitates the application of democratic principles to family life.

If the sessions are used by the parents to explain, preach, scold, or impose their will on their children, then the council is not democratic and will fail in its purpose. Each parent, like any other member of the family, can merely submit his point of view to the group. The first objective of the sessions should be the willingness of all to listen sincerely to what each has to stay. Before any satisfactory solutions can be found, the new routine of listening to each other and understanding what the other means has to be firmly established (Dreikurs, 1948).

The family meeting should not be a gripe session but a source of working out solutions to problems. Each person who expresses a complaint is expected to present his suggested solution.

It is important that children learn to do their part around the home. Along with the rights children have go certain responsibilities. Children need to have choices in the jobs that they do, and they should be allowed to decide when to do them, assuming that the decision does not interfere with the rest of the family members. A list of jobs could be made, such as emptying wastebaskets, taking out garbage, cleaning the basin, setting and clearing the table, washing the dishes, and the like. If the children do not follow through, this should be discussed during the next family meeting. The family must then decide on ways to deal with them.

In a well-functioning household, no one person should have to shoulder the full responsibility. If parents and the other family members are willing to accept the family meeting as the medium for working out problems, they do not need to feel discouraged if things do not always go as they should. It is more important for the children and parents to follow through with their assignments than to have things go smoothly all the time. Sometimes one family member may be reluctant to carry out his job. This requires patience. Although the daily routine may be disrupted, there is no need for discouragement or hostility. If the parents are consistent in what they are doing and let things take care of themselves, many things will eventually straighten themselves out, particularly if these problems are dealt with in the family council.

In the beginning the family meetings can involve such things as planning family fun, evening snacktimes, parties, and holiday fun, what is to be served, household chores, privacy within the family, use of the bathroom, use of the telephone, respect for property, important problems between family members, and so forth.

At times it may be impossible to reach agreement on a particular problem, and it may be necessary to postpone the decision until the next meeting. Meanwhile, family members can sort out their feelings and ideas. A delayed decision can be an effective cooling off technique.

Most urgent decisions are not as urgent as the parents or the child may be inclined to believe. All members of the family need to acquire the patience to function under circumstances that are not to their liking. Most parents find it difficult to stand by quietly when something goes wrong or when the child misbehaves. What they can do and usually are doing may not correct the situation. However, anything seems preferable to a "wait-and-see" attitude. In the absence of a decision by the family council, everyone has the right to do what he considers best, but no decision about what others should do has validity, unless it is approved by the council. One of the first decisions may be what to do in case of real danger. Then, on an agreed signal, any discussion should be omitted and immediate compliance guaranteed. In most other conflict situations, it is sufficient for the parent to withdraw and leave the children to their own resources, without an audience.

Once a decision has been made, any alteration has to wait for the next session. In the interim, no one has the right to impose his decision on others. On the other hand, if a decision for certain actions or functions is neglected by the children, the parents are not bound by it either. For instance, if the mother accepts the responsibility of shopping and cooking, while the children assume the task of washing the dishes, it is not up to the mother to insist that they do their part, but, naturally, she cannot cook if the kitchen has not been cleared. In such a case, both parents should dine out.

For most parents, particularly for the mothers, this is a difficult lesson to learn. A mother is impressed with her sense of obligation and responsibility, and she feels negligent if she does not take care of the needs of all. As a consequence, the children have no chance to take on responsibilities themselves. If mother is willing to accept the family council as supreme authority, she does not have to feel guilty if things do not always go as they should.

Giving children a real part in the family pays off in many ways. It gives them the feeling that "this is my family," and makes them more willing to take part in it. It gives them the feeling that their parents are considering them as individuals. The family meeting gives the children valuable experience in learning to make decisions, in taking responsibility, and in learning to handle family finances. It also gives them experience in the democratic way of life (Poffenberger, 1953).

Children need training and guidance in decision making. If the child errs in his decisions, he needs to be able to follow through on his idea to discover his error for himself rather than to have his idea vetoed by his parents or to be faced with the "I-told-you-so" attitude.

One child of 9 decided on a money making venture: he would grow tomatoes. The area he chose was barren of good soil, and it was rock laden and quite small. The immediate response from the family might well have been, "Nonsense." However, they refrained from speaking their first impulse. The youngster's idea was treated to a dignified consideration, and it was agreed that he should go ahead. He and his dad hauled rock, dug, and seeded the area. The garden turned into a paradise for tomato bugs, and the entire crop was lost.

Parents have to be able to let their children accept the responsibility for their decisions and actions. Children learn quickly, and in no time at all, they will begin to make sound decisions. Children learn to sort out their ideas and thoughts in a logical and orderly fashion through practice in expressing themselves in the family group. Children also learn to evaluate the thoughts and ideas of others and give consideration to the thoughts and decisions of the group.

Steps to follow in decision making are:

1. Recognize that there is a problem.
2. Present facts.
3. Analyze the facts. See the problems from the other person's point of view.
4. Think out the possible solution.
5. Agree on a solution.
6. Evaluate the decision at next family council.
   a. Was the decision carried through?
   b. Did it help "relieve" the problem?
   c. Should it continue; should it be changed?

How to Organize and Conduct the Family Meeting

Parents should discuss the concept of family meetings with all and explore the following:

1. *The structure.* How to structure the sessions of family meetings:
   a. What type of topics can be comfortably discussed in the family? Examples: planning family fun, household chores, mealtime problems, and so forth.
   b. What topics need to be reserved for parental consideration? Examples: financial problems, health problems, and so forth.

   c. How will the family handle touchy problems such as sex, marital relationships, and so forth?

     How much freedom can the children be given in decision making, such as buying a house, buying a car, selecting paint for the living room, and so forth?

2. *Ways of starting.* There are several ways of introducing the concept of the family council to the family.

   a. Directive—Informing the children that from now on they will try to solve their problems by sitting as a family group, discussing the problem, and arriving at a workable solution.

   b. Nondirective—Wait until a problem arises for the parent to solve. At this point the parents inform the children that they will discuss this problem when all members of the family are present. When all are assembled, and without going into detail, the family can go about finding the answers and solutions to the problems. Parents should use the family meeting structure and procedures during the meeting. At the end of the meeting, the family evaluates as a group what has happened. It is during this time that the concept of the family meeting is explained. For example, the parent might say:

     "The idea of having family meetings is to be able to sit together as a family and to share our joys and sorrows, as well as to work out our problems together. Talking things over as a family gives us more ideas on how to handle our problems and on different ways of doing things. We need your ideas and want to know how you feel about things. We know that sometimes you have better solutions than we do. We think we can have a much happier family. Family meetings would be held weekly and everyone would get to share their ideas. What do you all think?"

3. *Setting the stage.* Choose a table where each member of the family can pull up a chair. Let even a toddler join the group, for he will soon learn not to disrupt if he is removed as soon as he disturbs the group.

   a. Encourage every member who lives in the home to join the group.

   b. Have a notebook and a pen handy to keep a permanent record of the decisions reached.

   c. Have the family take their places at the table, and keep these places for all future meetings.

   d. Rotate the official duties around the family circle. One way to do this would be according to age. The oldest child would preside at the second meeting, and the person on his right would be the secretary, and so forth, until all members of the family who can read and write have officiated, and then the circle begins over again. When two children take the official roles, the parents become participating members and must abide by the general rules. The chairperson has to stop the procedures as soon as the voices and the tempers rise, because otherwise nobody would be willing to listen.

4. *The first family meeting.* Mother and father should act as chairperson

and secretary. If mother is one who always keeps track of things, let father be the secretary. If father usually keeps the peace and order, let mother be the chairperson.

a. The first meeting should last no longer than 15–20 minutes, as this is as long as order can be easily kept in a family that is not used to acting jointly.

b. When the family has had some experience in holding meetings, ideas will come readily, but at first it is best for the parents to be prepared.

c. Call the very first meeting for the specific purpose of planning family fun. Let each have their say in what the fun will be. Mother and father can offer suggestions but should not force their own ideas.

   The reason for limiting the first family meeting to planning family fun is because it will encourage more members to participate, and because it is less threatening to all. The family will have a better chance of having a successful meeting.

   Sometimes a family member does not wish to participate in the family meeting. The meeting should be held without him. The absence of a member can be used to reach a decision he may not like. If he wants to change it, he will have to come to the next meeting.

5. *Suggested procedures for family council meetings.* Procedures should be outlined by the parents and presented to the family group for approval, disapproval, or revision.

a. A chairperson and secretary should preside at each meeting.

b. The officers should rotate so that each member experiences this privilege and responsibility.

c. A definite day should be set for the council to meet each week.

d. When a person wishes to speak, he must raise his hand and be given the floor by the chairperson. No one can interrupt or speak until he has been recognized by the chairperson. The person recognized must speak about the problem or issue at hand.

e. All members of the family are invited to participate.

f. Once a decision has been made, any alteration in that decision has to wait until the next session. In the interim, no one has the right to decide on a different course of action or to impose his decision on others.

g. Suggested order of business for family meetings would be:

   1. Call the meeting to order.
   2. Read the decisions reached from previous meetings (starting with the second meeting).
   3. Announce activities for the coming week: P.T.A. meeting, school dance, ball game, and so on.
   4. Discuss unfinished business, problems still unsolved, and decisions that need to be made.
   5. Present new business, new problems, and new decisions to be reached.
   6. Discuss future plans.

Difficulties in Maintaining a Family Council

Instituting the family council requires the realization that a fundamentally new and untried course of action has begun. It requires time and effort to get all members of the family used to such procedures. Parents and children alike are not prepared for it. They do not trust each other; consequently, they do not have much faith in any project that requires cooperation. Children are afraid that this is merely another trick to make them behave and do the things they do not want to do. Parents fear that demands and decisions by their children are out of place. For this reason, the council sessions are often a burden to all. Sometimes it may be difficult to start them, in other cases, the first enthusiasm shortly may wane. Making the council effective may impose hardships on the parents for the time being. If the difficult period can be tolerated without discontinuance of council sessions, its effects should be highly beneficial to all concerned.

After setting the stage for a family council, there may be resistance from one or more members of the family. The father may refuse to participate because of a fear of losing his authority and importance in the family. He may also resist because of the manner in which his wife has approached him. As an example, many times we see parents who are involved in a power struggle with one another. The husband would consider accepting the wife's suggestions as a sign of submission. In some cases refusal to participate in a family council can be a retaliatory weapon by one parent against the other.

The reasons for a child's refusal to join a family council are the same as for the child's misbehavior. It might be to receive attention by being different or to show the family that he will do only what he wants to do. In either case, the family council should function with those present. If, for instance, the family decides to go to the park on Sunday, and the family member who was absent from the meeting objects to the choice, it can then be pointed out to him that had he participated, he could have influenced the decision.

Without confidence in and respect for the other members of the family, there is no way to discuss mutual difficulties and conflicts, and no opportunity to find solutions.

Difficulty in establishing and maintaining a democratic relationship is often responsible for the discontinuation of the family council. Parents may start off with good intentions and a high degree of enthusiasm, but before long, either they or the children violate the basic premises of a democratic procedure, and the council loses its meaning and function. Maintaining a family council requires considerable persistence, a willingness to see one's own mistakes, and the ability to change one's attitude and to respect that of others. One needs courage to explore and to chart new courses without fear and distrust and the conviction that the others also want to live in harmony and peace, but they may not know how to achieve this goal.

Students Can Initiate the Family Council

Since not all teachers come in contact with all parents, the teacher can suggest that the students present the idea of the family council to their parents. If the teacher has been having regular class council meetings each week, the children will understand the premise and the method.

The following reports are examples of some experiences from students who started family councils at the suggestion of their teacher.

In our home there were three teenagers who constantly bickered over the use of the telephone. There were many other areas of strife, but the use of the phone was an everyday occurrence. I introduced the idea of the family council to my family. My parents jumped at the idea. We were able to solve the phone problem by limiting the length of the calls and by each of us having a specific time to use the phone.

Since my parents work, my sister and I were given several jobs to do. We both felt our parents were unfair. We used to shirk our duties and it seemed like everyone was mad all the time. One day in class council I was telling how unfair I was being treated. The teacher suggested a family meeting. I talked my sister into it, and then we got our parents to go along with it. Imagine our surprise when we discovered that my sister and I were really the ones who were unfair. Our parents didn't say this. It came out in our discussion when we listed all the jobs that needed to be done at home. How could we have forgotten that mom cooked our meals; mended, washed, and ironed our clothes; shopped for groceries; cleaned house; and so forth. Dad did his share with household maintenance; taking care of our two cars; helping mom with shopping; keeping the basement, garage, and porch straightened; and keeping the yard, flowers, and hedges in shape. They did all these things in addition to working full time.

We are now a much happier and contented family and have our meetings regularly. As a result, each family member alternates cooking the evening meal. We plan our menus for the week, and my sister and I are learning to shop. Dad is teaching me how to take care of the cars. We share many things together and even have time for fun.

At our house we were given an allowance, but if we didn't do our jobs around the house, our parents would deduct 10 cents here and 10 cents there. Sometimes we would end up with nothing. I got our parents to sit down and talk with my brother and me about this problem. We didn't get too far, but everyone thought talking together was a good idea—at least mom and dad didn't get mad. We would have a meeting when some issue came up. After a few months, we decided to have weekly meetings, and my parents talked to the teacher and got some pointers. Since then, our meetings have been real good, and somehow our family seems closer and more cooperative. Also, we finally got the issue of allowances straightened out. Everyone in our family has an allowance that belongs to him to use as he wishes. No one can take it away. If my brother and I need extra money, we earn it by doing other jobs.

When I was in the sixth grade and my sister was in the third grade, we really wanted a set of encyclopedias. My teacher had suggested the idea of family meetings, which my parents thought was O.K. At our regular family council, we discussed the pros and cons and decided we could get a set if we all helped to pay for it. My sister and I agreed to pay $1 a month from our allowance until the books were paid for. When I look back on it now, I know that the $12 we each paid was very small in relation to the total bill. However, I know that it was the cooperation of the entire family and the feeling that my sister and I could share in the experience of such a venture that was really valuable.

Let us briefly repeat the basic principles in conducting a family council meeting.

1. The goal of a family council is the establishment of a democratic family, in which every member shares the responsibility for the solution of every problem. It is directed toward the improvement of relationships, the recognition of each member as an equal, giving each the opportunity to deal with all others on the basis of mutual respect without fighting or giving in. Thus, the family council is the laboratory for the development of skills needed in a democratic society.

2. The first task of the family council meeting is to listen to each other without arguing or attempting to change each other, even without considering the solutions of problems, until full cooperation of all is achieved. No problem needs to be solved immediately by parents who often feel that they cannot tolerate what is going on. They often can change the situation by merely doing what can be done without telling anyone else what he should do.

3. Only after a friendly, cooperative atmosphere is established can the family begin to solve problems. Such a friendly atmosphere can, at times, be quickly established, so that the discussion will not have to wait too long. No discussion should be continued if it leads to hostility.

4. Every problem is a problem for all. Every member of the family should be invited but not forced to state his own interpretation of the problem and his suggestions for a solution. Some problems will be easy to solve, but others may have to be tabled until full agreement is reached by all.

5. The family council does not provide means for better manipulation of children, nor does it mean abdication of parental guidance and influence. The parents have to learn how to be democratic leaders.

6. Children have to learn how to function in a democratic setting. Therefore, the chair of the family council should rotate. If a child is unwilling or unable to exert his influence in keeping the sessions going harmoniously, then an effective approach may have to wait until the next meeting. Thus, all unresolved problems have to be delayed (see point 2).

7. Every member of the family has the right not to participate. The only

pressure that can be exerted is a decision that the absent member, be it parent or child, may not like. In order to rescind it, the child will have to wait for the next meeting. It is essential that a decision not humiliate or hurt the absentee.

8. If a child does not behave or disturbs the session, the discussion has to stop until the child is quiet. The power of silence is stronger than any comment, criticism, or forceful action.

9. It is not advisable to hold emergency sessions. Any problem can wait for the next session. In the meantime, the parents are not only free but obliged to act the way they see fit, and thereby to exert their nonverbal influence.

10. During the session, and only then, can parents help the children to recognize their mistaken goals. Such disclosure should not be thrown at a child. His goals should be merely suggested as a possibility. If a disclosure implies attack or humiliation, it loses its value. The children can, however, learn to understand each other and themselves, but verbal expression of such understanding should not be a family routine, rather, it should be restricted to the weekly sessions. If the children use them in the interim, then such misuse has to be considered as a special form of fighting between them. The parents should treat the fight in the usual form of disinvolvement but bring it up for discussion at the next family meeting.

REFERENCES

Dreikurs, Rudolf. *The Challenge of Parenthood*. New York: Hawthorne Press, 1948.

Poffenberger, Thomas. *The Family Council—Kids Can Confer*. Extension Bulletin 739, Corvallis, Oreg.: Oregon State College, July 1953.

RECOMMENDED READINGS

Corsini, Raymond, and Painter, Genevieve. *The Practical Parent*. New York: Harper & Row, 1975.

Dreikurs, Rudolf, Gould, Shirley, and Corsini, Raymond. *Family Council*. Chicago. Ill.: Henry Regnery Company, 1974.

Dreikurs, Rudolf, Grunwald, Bernice Bronia, and Pepper, Floy C. *Maintaining Sanity in the Classroom*. New York: Harper & Row, 1971.

Dreikurs, Rudolf. *The Challenge of Parenthood*. New York: Hawthorne Press, 1948.

Poffenberger, Thomas. *The Family Council—Kids Can Confer*. Extension Bulletin 739, Corvallis, Oreg.: Oregon State College, July 1953.

Chapter 30
Parent Education

It seems to be well within the scope of this book to concern ourselves with the problem of parents. Among all the professional groups, the teachers are in a better position to educate parents than any other group, perhaps with the exception of the pediatrician. To fulfill this task, they must acquaint themselves with the problems of parents and with methods of solving them. For this reason, effective approaches to parent education must be part of the teacher training.

Let us face the facts. Many parents are ill prepared to raise children. It seems that they have lost a knowledge that others possess, that is, how to raise their young. The simplest routines of family living become perplexing problems. Many parents find it difficult to get the children up in the morning and to school on time, or to bed at night, without scolding and fighting. Many families begin each day with a fight. Many young children seem to lose the natural tendency to eat. They have to be coddled and coaxed, and reminded and threatened, thus making each mealtime a torture. How to get children to keep their rooms clean or to put their toys and clothes away is a major puzzle to which many parents still seek an answer. We take it for granted that brothers and sisters will fight for every advantage and forget that the term "brotherly love" once implied the height of consideration and devotion. Little of this is found in our families. The slightest contribution to the welfare of the family, such as daily chores, is fraught with conflict and frustration. The child's responsibility to study, to practice, or to apply himself is often the source of endless friction.

The strongest evidence of a universal parental failure is our concern with parent education. If parents knew what to do with their children, they would not need books, lectures, study groups, or classes.

The reason for this predicament is the democratic evolution. Raising children was always based on tradition. With the change from an autocratic to a democratic society, the traditional methods of influencing children became obsolete. Pressure, especially through punishment, is no longer effective. It was necessary and adequate in an autocratic society, but it fails in our present era. In the course of the democratic evolution, adults have lost their power over children. They can no longer control them by force or make them behave or perform. The eternal smoldering conflict between the generations, which in the past was contained by the power of the adult, has burst into the open with the waning of adult authority. Parents and children are at war, which is the basis of the generation gap. At times, the struggle may take on subtle forms; at other times, it exhibits the full brutality of warfare. Misunderstanding is rampant, and distrust reigns. Children feel misunderstood and abused; adults feel discarded and defeated. We need a new tradition for raising children, a tradition based on recognition of social equality between parents and children and one that embodies mutual respect.

More is needed than a recommendation of a general attitude of love and tolerance. Parents need to know what they can do and what they should not do in dealing with their children, particularly in moments of conflict and of disrupted order. They need practical information, both about effective methods and about the motivation of children. In bygone times, children posed few problems. They could be forced to do what they were supposed to do. Pressure insured compliance with demands and regulations. Today parents need to know how to stimulate the child's cooperation, respect for order, and willingness to share the responsibility for all members of the family.

Most of the methods that parents can learn to use are identical with those that teachers have to know. They have been described in this book in great detail. For this reason, parents may benefit equally from studying a book written for teachers, as teachers may profit from books written for parents. They are all in the same boat, but each group has certain advantages and disadvantages. The teacher can work with the whole class group in influencing the concepts and values of her students, whereas the parents are limited to working with the family group to exert its influence on each child, and often the children in the family council side with each other against the parents. This then requires more democratic leadership to withstand the pressure and to move toward a solution of conflicts. The conflicts within the family are often much more intense than in the school. On the other hand, the parents, in the sequence of so many transactions between them and the children, have many more opportunities to apply logical consequences. They need more careful study of this method to replace the authority of the adult with the pressure of reality (Dreikurs and Grey, 1970).

One of the greatest drawbacks to parent education is the difficulty entailed in stopping parents, particularly mothers, from talking incessantly.

As a rule, children do not listen, since a great deal of this talk is not used for communication but as ammunition. Why is it so difficult for a mother to stop talking? Because she does not know what else to do in a conflict situation. Unlike the teacher, she is burdened with tremendous responsibility of raising children without really knowing how to do it. This deep sense of responsibility, which most mothers have, leads to constant frustration if she cannot get her child to behave as he should. This personal involvement, this nagging fear of not being a good mother, is the reason many teachers can get along with their students so much better than with their own children. Unlike the mothers, the teachers are not involved with every deficiency of the child, and many fathers behave like mothers, although fathers usually do not talk as much and, therefore, the children listen to them.

The need for encouragement is, naturally, as great in the family as in school. However, the constant fear of being defeated prevents mothers from exerting an encouraging influence. Most of the methods used in raising children present them with a sequence of discouraging experiences. Either through indulgence, by doing for the children what they could do for themselves, or by the humiliating effects of scolding, coaxing, threatening, and punishing, the mothers prevent the children from experiencing their own strength. Teachers have many more opportunities to exert an encouraging influence on the child, particularly if they can win the cooperation of his peers.

We, as a society, have the tremendous responsibility of helping parents do their almost superhuman job. The schools can contribute more than any other group to the training of parents. This training should begin during adolescence. On the junior high or high school level, students can be exposed to instruction about how to influence young children. What is needed for this purpose is to make kindergarten or nursery school experiences available to them, provided that the kindergarten teacher is fully equipped to use effective methods with the children in her classes.

As previously mentioned, one of the ways to educate parents is to offer courses that prepare children for parenthood. Parent education should start before an individual becomes a parent. The following reports describe how a large metropolitan school district incorporated this type of training into its curriculum.

The home economics curriculum in our school district offered relationships and child development as a sequence of courses from the seventh through the twelfth grades. In the seventh, eighth, and ninth grades, much time was devoted to the basic principles in dealing with children. In the tenth, eleventh, and twelfth grades, the impact of the family and its relationship to the setting of values, concepts, and beliefs was stressed. The students became aware of the interrelationships among the family members and the family constellation, the use of logical consequences as a method of discipline, and the four goals of misbehavior as a method of understanding a child's actions.

A coed course was offered to senior boys and girls as an elective. In discussing the content of this course with the students, it was noted that many wanted to learn how to improve their interpersonal relationships, how to solve family problems, how to avoid family arguments, how to prepare themselves for the business of parenthood, how to take care of simple household mechanics, how to select a house or an apartment, how to furnish a home artistically, how to feed a family nutritionally, and how to mend clothing. They wanted a course in depth and not just a course on how to select their mates or what to expect of a date.

The backbone of the course dealt with preparation for parenthood and life. In order to give the students background material, they were assigned outside readings and discussed the basic psychological needs of people. From this material and information, they developed their own concepts of basic needs and combined them with the developmental tasks of children, teenagers, young adults, parents, and the aged.

One of the requirements of the course was to observe children in various situations: on the playground, at home during different hours of the day and evening, in nursery school, at the store, and so forth. Those who were able, attended the Family Education Center on Saturdays. Students who could not attend the counseling sessions asked that tapes be made so that they could listen to them. They listened to the tapes on their independent study time and used them as a basis for discussions in their small groups. Many of the students influenced their parents to attend the Family Education Center.

Three research papers were required during the year. The first one was a rather soul-searching paper: "Who Am I and/or What Sort of Person Am I?" The second: "The Qualities of a Good Mother or a Good Father," whichever the case may be (not a good parent, however). The third paper was: "Essential Elements in a Good Marriage Relationship."

Many of the students learned to communicate with their parents and how they react and interact with their families. They also learned that if they changed their behavior, the other person had no alternative but to change his. They gained insight into their own reactions and could accept responsibility for their own actions. Their questions were deep and searching and dealt with values.

In our Parent Education Centers the whole family—parents and children —is interviewed in front of teachers, other parents, and interested people in the community. The purpose of this kind of counseling is not primarily to help any one family with their problems but to acquaint other parents with effective methods of child rearing. There are no two mothers alike in personality, background, experience, and yet, it is hard to believe to what extent all mothers make the same mistakes. They talk too much; they do not share responsibility with their cihldren; they get themselves involved in power conflicts; and so on. In many cases parents learn much more from an interview with other parents than from personal counseling. As observers they are not involved and are not defensive and, therefore, are more ready to grasp the new approaches.

Such centers should be established throughout the communities, preferably within school systems. Every school should have a Parent Education Center to which the teachers cannot only refer their difficult students but also participate in the counseling with the parent. Teachers' training institutions are beginning to include such centers for the training of teachers. In this way, student teachers learn to understand the development of children and the particular problems of the parents. Through such training, teachers become capable of helping the parents of the students.

Here is a description of a community Parent-Teacher Education Center (Lowe and Christenson, 1966).

The purpose of this venture is to facilitate parents, teachers, and children learning to work cooperatively and effectively in the many activities which bring them together.

The function of the community Parent-Teacher Education Center is education in character. A community advisory board from the cooperating P.T.A. serves to interpret the program for the community and provides some financial assistance. A professional advisory board serves to assure the highest level of professional service possible. The center's contribution is on a community service basis.

The setting for a community Parent-Teacher Education Center grows out of a group approach to solving problems of adult-child relationships. Parents, teachers, and other interested persons, under the leadership of the counselor, share in the solutions to problems of human relationships in a given family. The group counseling sessions are open to professional and lay persons alike. The assumption here is that all attending are interested in learning more about how they might improve their own interrelationships; thus, many may profit from the deliberations of a few.

Any family experiencing difficulty in interpersonal relationships, which has as its primary focal point one or more preschool or elementary school children, is eligible for counseling. Families learn of the center from various sources. There is no planned program of announcements, public or private. Families come to the center with various motives, all of which relate to seeking some kind of assistance.

Parent Study Groups

Among the many ways by which we help parents in their difficult task of raising children, we have found parent study groups to be the most effective. There is a difference between when a mother reads a book alone and when she reads it together with a group of other mothers who discuss it.

It may be interesting to know how our study groups have developed. A mother who had attended regularly the weekly sessions of a family education center had moved to another city. She missed the weekly sessions that supported her in a surrounding of other mothers who objected to her methods. Thus, she invited a few friends to study one of our books together.

Soon there were several mother's study groups in her community. They objected to professional supervision. They wanted to help each other, and this became the tradition for the study groups. They are different from courses for parents, which come to an end and leave parents to shift for themselves. At the present time, our suggested methods of dealing with the problems of the child are still controversial and find professional and lay objections. Therefore, the parents came to the conclusion that they have to help themselves and continue to do so. Many who have finished with one group, become the leader of another.

The book usually used by the study groups is *Children: The Challenge* (Dreikurs and Soltz, 1964). We also have a *Study Group Leader's Manual* (Soltz, 1967), so that any parent can start a group of his or her own without any previous knowledge of the material.

Sometimes parents in a larger community form an organization with coordinators to help each group if it runs into difficulty. In some states, statewide coordination has been established. If the use of one book has been exhausted, other books are available, such as *The Challenge of Parenthood* (Dreikurs, 1948) or *A Parent's Guide to Child Discipline* (Dreikurs and Grey, 1970).

In many cases, study groups of parents are inaugurated by the principal of a school or by individual teachers who may start a group themselves, because they, too, are parents. Similarly, teachers may get together with their friends to study this book.

This is one of the many examples of how people are beginning to help themselves and each other. Self-help groups are becoming a strong force in our society.

REFERENCES

Dreikurs, R. *The Challenge of Parenthood.* New York: Hawthorne Press, 1948.

Dreikurs, R., and Grey, L. *A Parent's Guide to Child Discipline.* New York: Hawthorne Press, 1970.

Dreikurs, R., and Soltz, V. *Children: The Challenge.* New York: Hawthorne Press, 1964.

Lowe, R. N., and Christenson, O. C. *Guide to Enrollees.* Community Parent-Teacher Education Centers, School of Education. Eugene, Oreg.: University of Oregon, 1966.

Soltz, V. *Study Group Leader's Manual.* Chicago: Alfred Adler Institute, 1967.

Epilogue

We consider the teacher to be a vital influence in the development of the child. Not only can she influence the child in his development, but she can also change society through her students. This is crucial in these days of violent upheaval.

At present our children are exposed to all the injustices, antagonisms, and hostilities that presently characterize our whole world. As every well-trained teacher may succeed in undoing the damages that parents and the community have done to the child, so can she contribute to new forms of relationships and transactions and to the acceptance of more adequate social values.

It is unfortunate that teachers often put up resistance to new approaches to classroom management and to changes in their relationships with students. They maintain that their tasks are already difficult enough and that they cannot be burdened with the learning of new techniques and with new responsibilities. They demand that the students must change their behavior and attitudes without realizing that this is possible only if they, the teachers, change their own attitudes and responses to their students' provocations. Teachers who have applied our methods can attest to the fact that their jobs have become easier and that they enjoy their work more, since they are successful in uniting the class and in getting the students involved in finding solutions to classroom problems.

The suggestions offered in this book can lighten the task of teachers only if they are well understood, applied consistently, and applied with confidence. We must remember that children vary in their responses: whereas some children respond almost immediately, others may be stubborn for a while and challenge the teacher in order to achieve their mistaken goals.

Teachers who are aware of this will not become discouraged or give up if they do not see immediate results in all their students.

We must recognize that this book deals not merely with effective techniques that bring cooperation and harmony between teacher and students but with a philosophy of education and human relationships.

The qualities that a teacher needs most are courage and confidence in herself and in her worth as she is, a human being, bound to make mistakes but endowed with an unbelievable strength and ability to change life around her.

Index